React Cookbook

Create dynamic web apps with React using Redux, Webpack, Node.js, and GraphQL

Carlos Santana Roldan

Packt

BIRMINGHAM - MUMBAI

React Cookbook

Commissioning Editor: Kunal Chaudhari
Acquisition Editor: Larissa Pinto
Content Development Editor: Francis Carneiro
Technical Editor: Diksha Wakode
Copy Editor: Safis Editing
Project Coordinator: Alinka Dias
Proofreader: Safis Editing
Indexer: Pratik Shirodkar
Graphics: Jason Monteiro
Production Coordinator: Arvindkumar Gupta

First published: August 2018

Production reference: 1290818

Published by Packt Publishing Ltd.
Livery Place
35 Livery Street
Birmingham
B3 2PB, UK.

ISBN 978-1-78398-072-7

www.packtpub.com

Contributors

About the author

Carlos Santana Roldan is a senior web developer with more than 11 years of experience. Currently, he is working as a React Technical Lead in Disney ABC Television Group. He is the founder of Codejobs.com, one of the most popular developer communities in Latin America, training people in web technologies such as React, Node.js, and JavaScript.

I would like to express my deepest appreciation and special gratitude to all those from the Packt Editorial team who helped me complete this book, especially Francis Savio Carneiro, Larissa Pinto, and Diksha Wakode.

I'd also like to thank Adrian Aguirre and Tony Guerrero for all the help in the book. Finally, my deepest thanks to my wife, Cristina Rojas, for the support; my parents, Francisco Santana and Thelma Roldan, who have supported me in my professional growth; and my friends and family who helped manifest the book.

About the reviewer

Mayur Tanna is a senior IT consultant working with CIGNEX Datamatics. He has worked on various high-value projects with international clients such as World Bank and the United Nations and played a key role in creating the architecture of those projects using the latest technologies, including React, Angular, Node.js, MongoDB, Spring Boot, Firebase, Amazon Web Services, and Google Cloud Platform. Mayur is the co-author of the book *Serverless Web Applications with React and Firebase*. He holds a master's degree in Computer Applications and has trained lot of engineering students through tech workshops. In his free time, he plays table tennis and cricket.

I want to thank my wife, Dr. Purna, my parents, Mr. Ratilal and Mrs. Nirmala, my li'l child, Dhyey, and the rest of my family, who have supported and encouraged me in spite of all the time it took me away from them. Without their support, the review of this book would not have been possible. I would also like to thank the Packt team for giving me the opportunity to review this book.

Packt is searching for authors like you

If you're interested in becoming an author for Packt, please visit `authors.packtpub.com` and apply today. We have worked with thousands of developers and tech professionals, just like you, to help them share their insight with the global tech community. You can make a general application, apply for a specific hot topic that we are recruiting an author for, or submit your own idea.

To the memory of my two grandmothers, Maria Concepción Carrillo, and Ana María Ochoa, to my mother, Thelma C. Roldán, and my father Francisco Santana, for their sacrifices and for exemplifying the power of determination and dedication.

– Carlos Santana Roldán

Table of Contents

Preface

Nowadays exists tons of JavaScript libraries, frameworks, and tools for Web development. However, we should evaluate each technology to see if it fits for our project requirements. That's why I want to introduce to you React, one of the most powerful libraries to create dynamic UIs. Right now is the most popular library (not a framework) made by Facebook. I have worked with others JS frameworks such as AngularJS (also the new versions Angular 2, 4, 5), Backbone.js, Ember, and Vue.js in different projects but I can tell you that using React I enjoy more to developing new Web applications.

React has changed the way of doing Web applications and combined with Redux, we get a powerful frontend architecture that makes sense not only to experienced developers but also to those who're just starting their frontend journey.

The book introduces all the tools and best practices of React in simple recipes easy to follow, all of the recipes in this book are 100% practical and each one has the necessary code to understand all the important things.

Welcome to a better future and have fun reading and learning from this book.

Who this book is for

The book can be used by any developer who has a basic knowledge of building web applications. Mainly for JavaScript developers but not limited to any other type of devs.

What this book covers

`Chapter 1`, *Working with React*, React is a JavaScript library (MIT License) made by Facebook to create interactive UIs. It's used to create dynamic and reusable components. The most powerful thing about React is that can be used in the client, server, mobile applications and even VR applications.

`Chapter 2`, *Conquering Components and JSX* , this chapter contains recipes related to how to create components in React. We are going to learn how to create React components (class components, pure components, and functional components) and organize our project structure.

`Chapter 3`, *Handling Events, Binding and Useful React Packages,* this chapter contains recipes related to handling events, binding methods in React and we will implement some of the most useful React packages.

`Chapter 4`, *Adding Routes to Our Application with React Router,* in this chapter, we are going to learn how to add dynamic routes in our project using React Router v4.

`Chapter 5`, *Mastering Redux,* Redux is a predictable state container for JavaScript apps. That means Redux can be used with vanilla JavaScript or frameworks/libraries such as Angular and jQuery. Redux is mainly a library responsible for issuing state updates and responses to actions.

`Chapter 6`, *Creating Forms with Redux Form,* Forms are a fundamental part of any web application, and in the following recipes, we are going to learn how to use forms with and without Redux Form.

`Chapter 7`, *Animations with React,* Animations are very common in any web application. Since CSS3, animations have become widespread and easy to implement. The most common use of animations are transitions, where you can change CSS properties and define the duration or delay.

`Chapter 8`, *Creating an API with Node.js Using MongoDB and MySQL,* Node.js is widely used as a backend for web applications because it is easy to create an API and its performance is better than technologies such as Java, PHP, and Ruby. Usually, the most popular way to use Node.js is by using a framework called Express.

`Chapter 9`, *Apollo and GraphQL,* GraphQL is an Application Layer Query Language which can be used with any database, also is an open source (MIT license) created by Facebook. The main difference with REST is that GraphQL does not use endpoints but queries instead and is supported by most of the server languages such as JavaScript (Node.js), Go, Ruby, PHP, Java, Python, and so on.

`Chapter 10`, *Mastering Webpack 4.x,* Webpack 4 does not need a configuration file by default. Before in the oldest versions, you must have a configuration file, but of course, if you need to customize Webpack 4 to your project needs, you can still create a configuration file which will be way easier to configure.

`Chapter 11`, *Implementing Server-Side Rendering,* Probably you don't need to worry about Server Side Rendering (SSR) if you don't care too much about SEO. Currently, the Googlebot supports Client Side Rendering (CSR), and it can index our site in Google, but if you care about SEO and you are worried about improving the SEO on others Search Engines like Yahoo, Bing or DuckDuckGo then using Server Side Rendering (SSR) is the way to go.

`Chapter 12`, *Testing and Debugging,* testing and debugging are very important for any project that wants to have the best quality. Unfortunately, many developers do not care about testing (unit tests) because they think that will reduce the speed of the development and some of them leave it until the end of the project. In my personal experience, I can say that testing since the beginning of the project will save you time because at the end you will have fewer bugs to fix.

`Chapter 13`, *Deploying to Production,* now is time to deploy our application to production and show it to the world. In this chapter, you will learn how to deploy our React Application using one of the best cloud services: Digital Ocean.

`Chapter 14`, *Working with React Native,* React Native is a framework for building mobile apps using JavaScript and React. Many people think that with React Native you make some "mobile web app" or a "hybrid app" (like Ionic, PhoneGap or Sencha) but you build a native app because React Native converts your React code to Java for Android and Objective-C for iOS apps.

To get the most out of this book

To master React, you need to have a fundamental knowledge of JavaScript and Node.js. The book mostly targets Web developers, and at the time of writing, the following assumptions were made for the reader:

- The reader knows how to install the latest version of Node.js.
- An intermediate developer who can understand JavaScript ES6 syntax.
- Little experience with CLI tools and Node.js syntax.

The book also has a little for Mobile developers (iOS and Android) using React Native, if you are a beginner you should learn how to install Android SDK or the iOS simulator with Xcode.

Download the example code files

You can download the example code files for this book from your account at `www.packtpub.com`. If you purchased this book elsewhere, you can visit `www.packtpub.com/support` and register to have the files emailed directly to you.

You can download the code files by following these steps:

1. Log in or register at `www.packtpub.com`.
2. Select the **SUPPORT** tab.
3. Click on **Code Downloads & Errata**.
4. Enter the name of the book in the **Search** box and follow the onscreen instructions.

Once the file is downloaded, please make sure that you unzip or extract the folder using the latest version of:

- WinRAR/7-Zip for Windows
- Zipeg/iZip/UnRarX for Mac
- 7-Zip/PeaZip for Linux

The code bundle for the book is also hosted on GitHub at `https://github.com/PacktPublishing/React-Cookbook`. If there's an update to the code, it will be updated on the existing GitHub repository.

We also have other code bundles from our rich catalog of books and videos available at `https://github.com/PacktPublishing/`. Check them out!

Warnings or important notes appear like this.

Tips and tricks appear like this.

Get in touch

Feedback from our readers is always welcome.

General feedback: Email `feedback@packtpub.com` and mention the book title in the subject of your message. If you have questions about any aspect of this book, please email us at `questions@packtpub.com`.

Errata: Although we have taken every care to ensure the accuracy of our content, mistakes do happen. If you have found a mistake in this book, we would be grateful if you would report this to us. Please visit `www.packtpub.com/submit-errata`, selecting your book, clicking on the Errata Submission Form link, and entering the details.

Piracy: If you come across any illegal copies of our works in any form on the Internet, we would be grateful if you would provide us with the location address or website name. Please contact us at `copyright@packtpub.com` with a link to the material.

If you are interested in becoming an author: If there is a topic that you have expertise in and you are interested in either writing or contributing to a book, please visit `authors.packtpub.com`.

Reviews

Please leave a review. Once you have read and used this book, why not leave a review on the site that you purchased it from? Potential readers can then see and use your unbiased opinion to make purchase decisions, we at Packt can understand what you think about our products, and our authors can see your feedback on their book. Thank you!

For more information about Packt, please visit `packtpub.com`.

1
Working with React

In this chapter, the following recipes will be covered:

- Introduction
- Working with the latest JS features in React
- What's new in React?
- Using React on Windows

Introduction

React is a JavaScript library (MIT License) made by Facebook to create interactive UIs. It's used to create dynamic and reusable components. The most powerful thing about React is that can be used in the client, server, mobile applications, and even VR applications.

In the modern web, we need to manipulate the DOM constantly; the problem is that doing this a lot may affect the performance of our application seriously. React uses a Virtual DOM, which means that all updates occur in memory (this is faster than manipulating the real DOM directly). The learning curve of React is short in comparison with other JavaScript frameworks such as Angular, Vue, or Backbone, mainly because the React code is mostly written with modern JavaScript (classes, arrow functions, string templates, and so on) and does not have too many patterns used to write code, like Dependency Injection, or a template system, like in Angular.

Companies such as Airbnb, Microsoft, Netflix, Disney, Dropbox, Twitter, PayPal, Salesforce, Tesla, and Uber are extensively using React in their projects. In this book, you will learn how to develop your React applications in the way they do, using best practices.

Working with the latest JS features in React

As I said in the introduction, React is mainly written with modern JavaScript (ES6, ES7, and ES8). If you want to take advantage of React, there are some modern JS features that you should master to get the best results for your React applications. In this first recipe, we are going to cover the essential JS features so you are ready and can start working on your first React application.

How to do it...

In this section, we will see how to use the most important JS features in React:

1. `let` and `const`: The new way to declare variables in JavaScript is by using `let` or `const`. You can use `let` to declare variables that can change their value but in block scope. The difference between `let` and `var` is that `let` is a block scoped variable that cannot be global, and with `var`, you can declare a global variable, for example:

```
var name = 'Carlos Santana';
let age = 30;

console.log(window.name); // Carlos Santana
console.log(window.age);  // undefined
```

2. The best way to understand "block scope" is by declaring a `for` loop with `var` and `let`. First, let's use `var` and see its behavior:

```
for (var i = 1 ; i <= 10; i++) {
  console.log(i); // 1, 2, 3, 4... 10
}

console.log(i); // Will print the last value of i: 10
```

3. If we write the same code, but with `let`, this will happen:

```
for (let i = 1 ; i <= 10; i++) {
  console.log(i); // 1, 2, 3, 4... 10
}

console.log(i); // Uncaught ReferenceError: i is not defined
```

4. With `const`, we can declare constants, which means the value can't be changed (except for arrays and objects):

```
const pi = 3.1416;
pi = 5; // Uncaught TypeError: Assignment to constant variable.
```

5. If we declare an array with `const`, we can manipulate the array elements (add, remove, or modify elements):

```
const cryptoCurrencies = ['BTC', 'ETH', 'XRP'];

// Adding ERT: ['BTC', 'ETH', 'XRP', 'ERT'];
cryptoCurrencies.push('ERT');

// Will remove the first element: ['ETH', 'XRP', 'ERT'];
cryptoCurrencies.shift();
// Modifying an element
cryptoCurrencies[1] = 'LTC'; // ['ETH', 'LTC', 'ERT'];
```

6. Also, using objects, we can add, remove, or modify the nodes:

```
const person = {
  name: 'Carlos Santana',
  age: 30,
  email: 'carlos@milkzoft.com'
};
// Adding a new node...
person.website = 'https://www.codejobs.com';

// Removing a node...
delete person.email;

// Updating a node...
person.age = 29;
```

7. **Spread operator**: The spread operator (...) splits an iterable object into individual values. In React, it can be used to push values into another array, for example when we want to add a new item to a Todo list by utilizing `setState` (this will be explained in the next chapter):

```
this.setState({
  items: [
    ...this.state.items, // Here we are spreading the current items
    {
  task: 'My new task', // This will be a new task in our Todo list.
    }
  ]
});
```

8. Also, the Spread operator can be used in React to spread attributes (props) in JSX:

```
render() {
  const props = {};

  props.name = 'Carlos Santana';
  props.age = 30;
  props.email = 'carlos@milkzoft.com';
  return <Person {...props} />;
}
```

9. **Rest parameter:** The `rest` parameter is also represented by `...`. The last parameter in a function prefixed with `...` is called the rest parameter. The rest parameter is an array that will contain the rest of the parameters of a function when the number of arguments exceeds the number of named parameters:

```
function setNumbers(param1, param2, ...args) {
  // param1 = 1
  // param2 = 2
  // args = [3, 4, 5, 6];
  console.log(param1, param2, ...args); // Log: 1, 2, 3, 4, 5, 6
}
setNumbers(1, 2, 3, 4, 5, 6);
```

10. **Destructuring**: The destructuring assignment feature is the most used in React. It is an expression that allows us to assign the values or properties of an iterable object to variables. Generally, with this we can convert our component props into variables (or constants):

```
// Imagine we are on our <Person> component and we are
// receiving the props (in this.props): name, age and email.
render() {
  // Our props are:
  // { name: 'Carlos Santana', age: 30, email:
   'carlos@milkzoft.com' }
  console.log(this.props);
  const { name, age, email } = this.props;
  // Now we can use the nodes as constants...
  console.log(name, age, email);

  return (
    <ul>
      <li>Name: {name}</li>
      <li>Age: {age}</li>
      <li>Email: {email}</li>
    </ul>
  );
}

// Also the destructuring can be used on function parameters
const Person = ({ name, age, email }) => (
  <ul>
    <li>Name: {name}</li>
    <li>Age: {age}</li>
    <li>Email: {email}</li>
  </ul>
);
```

11. **Arrow functions**: ES6 provides a new way to create functions using the => operator. These functions are called arrow functions. This new method has a shorter syntax, and the arrow functions are anonymous functions. In React, arrow functions are used as a way to bind the `this` object in our methods instead of binding it in the constructor:

```
class Person extends Component {
  showProps = () => {
    console.log(this.props); // { name, age, email... }
  }

  render() {
    return (
```

```
        <div>
          Consoling props: {this.showProps()}
        </div>
      );
    }
  }
```

12. **Template literals**: The template literal is a new way to create a string using backticks (\` \`) instead of single quotes (' ') or double quotes (" "). React use template literals to concatenate class names or to render a string using a ternary operator:

```
render() {
  const { theme } = this.props;

  return (
    <div
      className={`base ${theme === 'dark' ? 'darkMode' :
    'lightMode'}`}
    >
      Some content here...
    </div>
  );
}
```

13. **Map**: The `map()` method returns a new array with the results of calling a provided function on each element in the calling array. Map use is widespread in React, and is mainly used to render multiple elements inside a React component; for example, it can be used to render a list of tasks:

```
render() {
  const tasks = [
    { task: 'Task 1' },
    { task: 'Task 2' },
    { task: 'Task 3' }
  ];

  return (
    <ul>
      {tasks.map((item, key) => <li key={key}>{item.task}</li>}
    </ul>
  );
}
```

14. **Object.assign()**: The `Object.assign()` method is used to copy the values of all enumerable own properties from one or more source objects to a target object. It will return the target object. This method is used mainly with Redux to create immutable objects and return a new state to the reducers (Redux will be covered in `Chapter 5`, *Mastering Redux*):

```
export default function coinsReducer(state = initialState, action) {
  switch (action.type) {
    case FETCH_COINS_SUCCESS: {
      const { payload: coins } = action;

      return Object.assign({}, state, {
        coins
      });
    }

    default:
     return state;
  }
};
```

15. **Classes**: JavaScript classes, introduced in ES6, are mainly a new syntax for the existing prototype-based inheritance. Classes are functions and are not hoisted. React uses classes to create class *Components*:

```
import React, { Component } from 'react';

class Home extends Component {
  render() {
    return <h1>I'm Home Component</h1>;
  }
}

export default Home;
```

16. **Static methods**: Static methods are not called on instances of the class. Instead, they're called on the class itself. These are often utility functions, such as functions to create or clone objects. In React, they can be used to define the `PropTypes` in a component:

```
import React, { Component } from 'react';
import PropTypes from 'prop-types';
import logo from '../../images/logo.svg';

class Header extends Component {
  static propTypes = {
    title: PropTypes.string.isRequired,
```

```
      url: PropTypes.string
    };

    render() {
      const {
        title = 'Welcome to React',
        url = 'http://localhost:3000'
      } = this.props;

      return (
        <header className="App-header">
          <a href={url}>
            <img src={logo} className="App-logo" alt="logo" />
          </a>
          <h1 className="App-title">{title}</h1>
        </header>
      );
    }
  }

  export default Header;
```

17. **Promises**: The `Promise` object represents the eventual completion (or failure) of an asynchronous operation and its resulting value. We will use promises in React to handle requests by using axios or fetch; also, we are going to use Promises to implement the server-side rendering (this will be covered in `Chapter 11`, *Implementing Server-Side Rendering*).
18. **async/await**: The async function declaration defines an asynchronous function, which returns an `AsyncFunction` object. This also can be used to perform a server request, for example using axios:

```
Index.getInitialProps = async () => {
  const url = 'https://api.coinmarketcap.com/v1/ticker/';
  const res = await axios.get(url);

  return {
    coins: res.data
  };
};
```

What's new in React?

This paragraph was written on August 14, 2018, and the latest version of React was 16.4.2. The React 16 version has a new core architecture named Fiber.

In this recipe, we will see the most important updates in this version that you should be aware of to get the most out of React.

How to do it...

Let's see the new updates:

1. **Components can now return arrays and strings from render**: Before, React forced you to return an element wrapped with a <div> or any other tag; now it is possible to return an array or string directly:

```
// Example 1: Returning an array of elements.
render() {
  // Now you don't need to wrap list items in an extra element
  return [
    <li key="1">First item</li>,
    <li key="2">Second item</li>,
    <li key="3">Third item</li>,
  ];
}

// Example 2: Returning a string
render() {
  return 'Hello World!';
}
```

2. Also, React now has a new feature called **Fragment**, which also works as a special wrapper for elements. It can be specified with empty tags (<></>) or directly using `React.Fragment`:

```
// Example 1: Using empty tags <></>
render() {
  return (
    <>
      <ComponentA />
      <ComponentB />
      <ComponentC />
    </>
  );
}
```

```
// Example 2: Using React.Fragment
render() {
  return (
    <React.Fragment>
      <h1>An h1 heading</h1>
      Some text here.
      <h2>An h2 heading</h2>
      More text here.
      Even more text here.
    </React.Fragment>
  );
}

// Example 3: Importing Fragment
import React, { Fragment } from 'react';
...
render() {
  return (
    <Fragment>
      <h1>An h1 heading</h1>
      Some text here.
      <h2>An h2 heading</h2>
      More text here.
      Even more text here.
    </Fragment>
  );
}
```

3. **Error boundaries** with from the official website:

A JavaScript error in a part of the UI shouldn't break the whole app. To solve this problem for React users, React 16 introduces a new concept of an "error boundary". Error boundaries are React components that catch JavaScript errors anywhere in their child component tree, log those errors, and display a fallback UI instead of the component tree that crashed. Error boundaries catch errors during rendering, in lifecycle methods, and in constructors of the whole tree below them. A class component becomes an error boundary if it defines a new lifecycle method called componentDidCatch(error, info).

```
class ErrorBoundary extends React.Component {
  constructor(props) {
    super(props);
    this.state = {
      hasError: false
    };
  }
```

```
  componentDidCatch(error, info) {
    // Display fallback UI
    this.setState({
      hasError: true
    });
    // You can also log the error to an error reporting service
    logErrorToMyService(error, info);
  }

  render() {
    if (this.state.hasError) {
      // You can render any custom fallback UI
      return <h1>Something went wrong.</h1>;
    }
    return this.props.children;
  }
}

// Then you can use it as a regular component:
render() {
  <ErrorBoundary>
    <MyComponent />
  </ErrorBoundary>
}
```

4. **Better server-side rendering** with from the official site:

   React 16 includes a completely rewritten server renderer. It's really fast. It supports streaming, so you can start sending bytes to the client faster. And thanks to a new packaging strategy that compiles away process.env checks (Believe it or not, reading process.env in Node is really slow!), you no longer need to bundle React to get good server-rendering performance.

5. **Reduced file size** with from the official site: "Despite all these additions, React 16 is actually smaller compared to 15.6.1.
   - react is 5.3 kb (2.2 kb gzipped), down from 20.7 kb (6.9 kb gzipped)
   - react-dom is 103.7 kb (32.6 kb gzipped), down from 141 kb (42.9 kb gzipped)
   - react + react-dom is 109 kb (34.8 kb gzipped), down from 161.7 kb (49.8 kb gzipped)

   That amounts to a combined 32% size decrease compared to the previous version (30% post-gzip)."

TIP: If you want to check the latest updates on React, you can visit the official React blog: `https://reactjs.org/blog`.

Using React on Windows

I'm not a big fan of Windows for development since it's kind of problematic to configure sometimes. I will always prefer Linux or Mac, but I'm aware that a lot of people who are reading this book will use Windows. In this recipe, I'll show you the most common problems you may have when you try to follow the recipes in this book using Windows.

How to do it...

We'll now see the most common problems using Windows for development:

1. **Terminal**: The first problem you will face is to use the Windows terminal (CMD) because it does not support Unix commands (like Linux or Mac). The solution is to install a Unix Terminal; the most highly recommended is to use the **Git Bash** Terminal, which is included with **Git** when you install it (`https://git-scm.com`), and the second option is to install **Cygwin**, which is a Linux Terminal in Windows (`https://www.cygwin.com`).
2. **Environment variables**: Another common problem using Windows is to set environment variables. Generally, when we write npm scripts, we set environment variables such as `NODE_ENV=production` or `BABEL_ENV=development`, but to set those variables in Windows, you use the `SET` command, which means you need to do `SET NODE_ENV=production` or `SET BABEL_ENV=development`. The problem with this is that if you are working with other people that use Linux or Mac, they will have problems with the `SET` command, and probably you will need to ignore this file and modify it only for your local environment. This can be tedious. The solution to this problem is to use a package called cross-env; you can install it by doing `npm install cross-env`, and this will work in Windows, Mac, and Linux:

```
"scripts": {
  "start": "cross-env NODE_ENV=development webpack-dev-server --
   mode development --open",
  "start-production": "cross-env NODE_ENV=production webpack-dev-
   server --mode production"
}
```

3. **Case-sensitive files or directories**: In reality, this also happens on Linux, but sometimes it is very difficult to identify this problem, for example, if you create a component in the `components/home/Home.jsx` directory but in your code you're trying to import the component like this:

```
import Home from './components/Home/Home';
```

Normally, this won't cause any problems on Mac but can generate an error on Linux or Windows because we are trying to import a file with a different name (because it's case-sensitive) into the directory.

4. **Paths**: Windows uses a backslash (\) to define a path, while in Mac or Linux they use a forward slash (/). This is problematic because sometimes we need to define a path (in Node.js mostly) and we need to do something like this:

```
// In Mac or Linux
app.use(
  stylus.middleware({
    src: __dirname + '/stylus',
    dest: __dirname + '/public/css',
    compile: (str, path) => {
      return stylus(str)
        .set('filename', path)
        .set('compress', true);
    }
  })
);

// In Windows
app.use(
  stylus.middleware({
    src: __dirname + '\stylus',
    dest: __dirname + '\public\css',
    compile: (str, path) => {
      return stylus(str)
        .set('filename', path)
        .set('compress', true);
    }
  })
);

// This can be fixed by using path
import path from 'path';
// path.join will generate a valid path for Windows or Linux and Mac
app.use(
  stylus.middleware({
```

```
    src: path.join(__dirname, 'stylus'),
    dest: path.join(__dirname, 'public', 'css'),
    compile: (str, path) => {
      return stylus(str)
        .set('filename', path)
        .set('compress', config().html.css.compress);
    }
  })
);
```

2
Conquering Components and JSX

In this chapter, the following recipes will be covered:

- Creating our first React component
- Organizing our React application
- Styling a component with CSS classes and inline styles
- Passing props to a component and validating them with PropTypes
- Using local state in a component
- Making a functional or stateless component
- Understanding React lifecycle methods
- Understanding React Pure Components
- Preventing XSS vulnerabilities in React

Introduction

This chapter contains recipes related to how to create components in React. We are going to learn how to create React components (class components, pure components, and functional components) and organize our project structure. We'll also learn how to use React local state, implement all the React lifecycle methods, and finally, we'll see how to prevent XSS vulnerabilities.

Creating our first React component

The component is the essential part of React. With React you can build interactive and reusable components. In this recipe, you will create your first React component.

Getting ready

First, we need to create our React application using `create-react-app`. Once that is done, you can proceed to create your first React component.

Before you install `create-react-app`, remember that you need to download and install Node from `www.nodejs.org`. You can install it for Mac, Linux, and Windows.

Install `create-react-app` globally by typing this command in your Terminal:

```
npm install -g create-react-app
```

Or you can use a shortcut:

```
npm i -g create-react-app
```

How to do it...

Let's build our first React application by following these steps:

1. Create our React application with the following command:

    ```
    create-react-app my-first-react-app
    ```

2. Go to the new application with `cd my-first-react-app` and start it with `npm start`.
3. The application should now be running at `http://localhost:3000`.
4. Create a new file called `Home.js` inside your `src` folder:

    ```
    import React, { Component } from 'react';

    class Home extends Component {
      render() {
        return <h1>I'm Home Component</h1>;
      }
    }

    export default Home;
    ```

    File: src/Home.js

5. You may have noticed that we are exporting our class component at the end of the file, but it's fine to export it directly on the class declaration, like this:

```
import React, { Component } from 'react';
export default class Home extends Component {
  render() {
    return <h1>I'm Home Component</h1>;
  }
}
```

File: src/Home.js

TIP: I prefer to export it at the end of the file, but some people like to do it in this way, so it depends on your preferences.

6. Now that we have created the first component, we need to render it. So we need to open the `App.js` file, import the `Home` component, and then add it to the render method of the `App` component. If we are opening this file for the first time, we will probably see a code like this:

```
import React, { Component } from 'react';
import logo from './logo.svg';
import './App.css';
class App extends Component {
  render() {
    return (
      <div className="App">
        <header className="App-header">
          <img src={logo} className="App-logo" alt="logo" />
          <h1 className="App-title">Welcome to React</h1>
        </header>
        <p className="App-intro">
          To get started, edit <code>src/App.js</code>
          and save to reload.
        </p>
      </div>
    );
  }
}

export default App;
```

File: src/App.js

7. Let's change this code a little bit. As I said before, we need to import our `Home` component and then add it to the JSX. We also need to replace the `<p>` element with our component, like this:

```
import React, { Component } from 'react';
import logo from './logo.svg';

// We import our Home component here...
import Home from './Home';
import './App.css';

class App extends Component {
  render() {
    return (
      <div className="App">
        <header className="App-header">
          <img src={logo} className="App-logo" alt="logo" />
          <h1 className="App-title">Welcome to React</h1>
        </header>
        {/* Here we add our Home component to be render it */}
        <Home />
      </div>
    );
  }
}

export default App;
```

File: src/App.js

How it works...

As you can see, we imported `React` and `Component` from the React library. You probably noticed that we are not using the `React` object directly. To write code in JSX, you need to import `React`. JSX is similar to HTML, but with a few differences. In the following recipes, you will learn more about JSX.

This component is called a `class` component (`React.Component`), and there are different types: pure components (`React.PureComponent`) and functional components, also known as stateless components, which we will cover in the following recipes.

If you run the application, you should see something like this:

There's more...

In our example, we created the `Home.js` file, and our component's name is `Home`.

> All React component names should start with the first letter capitalized in both the file and the class name. To begin with, it might feel uncomfortable for you to see this, but this is the best practice in React.

Some of the main differences between JSX and HTML are the attributes names. You may have noticed that we are using `className` instead of `class`. This is the only special attribute name. Others that are two words separated by a dash need to be converted to camelCase, for example, `onClick`, `srcSet`, and `tabIndex`. The `aria-*` and `data-*` attributes still uses the same nomenclature (`data-something` and `aria-label`).

Organizing our React application

In this recipe, we will learn how to structure our project in a better way.

How to do it...

We can create React components with the default structure that `create-react-app` provides, but in this recipe, I'll show you a better way to organize the project so that we are ready when for when the application grows.

1. We need to create a new React app (check the last recipe if you haven't created a React app yet)

2. Currently, our React application directory tree looks like this:

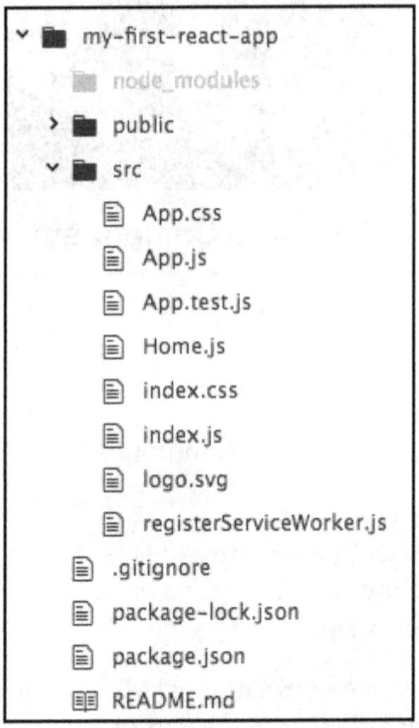

3. We need to create `src/components` and `src/shared` directories
4. After this, we need to create the `src/components/Home` directory for our component and move `Home.js` into this folder
5. The `App.js` file stays at the `src/components` level
6. Also, `App.css` and `App.test.js` will stay at `src/components` level
7. Move the `logo.svg` file to `src/shared/images`
8. Our `index.js` will stay at the `src/` level
9. Now your directory tree should look like this:

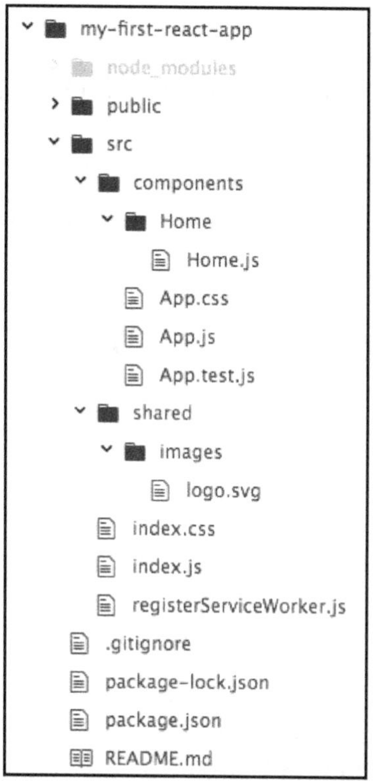

> **TIP:** I highly recommend that you create another directory for shared components, `src/shared/components`. I'll explain more about this in the next recipes.

10. In the `App.js` file, change the `logo` and `Home` imports:

```
import logo from '../shared/images/logo.svg';
import Home from './Home/Home';
```

File: src/components/App.js

11. After you changed that, we need to open the `index.js` and fix the import path for the `App` component:

```
import App from './components/App';
```

File: src/index.js

How it works...

This new structure will give us more flexibility to group our React components smartly. With this new structure, we are going to be able to create sub-components, if we need them, and that is very important when developing complex applications with React.

In the next recipes, we will see how to share components in our application.

Styling a component with CSS classes and inline styles

In the last recipe, we learned how to create a class component. Now let's add some CSS to our `Home` component.

In React, one of the best practices is to have the style file in the same directory as the component. If you have worked with PHP, Node, or any other server language, you probably write your styles in a `style.css` file, and you include it using a `link` tag in your template. React uses Webpack, which is the most popular module bundler at the moment. With Webpack, we can configure the way that we want to handle our styles (using CSS directly or by using a CSS preprocessor such as Sass, Stylus, or Less CSS), and with Webpack we can implement CSS modules. This is a powerful way to avoid the three main issues of CSS:

- No more conflicts (unintentional CSS overwrites)
- Explicit dependencies (styles per component)
- No global scope

In `Chapter 10`, *Mastering Webpack 4.x*, we will cover Webpack, and we'll be able to implement CSS modules using Sass or Stylus in our project.

How to do it...

We will now go about adding CSS to our `Home` component:

1. Create a new application, or use the previous one (`my-first-react-app`).

2. Then create a new CSS file for our `Home` component. Let's reuse the `Home` component we created in the last recipe. Now you need to create a `Home.css` file at the same level as your `Home.js` file (inside the `components` folder). Before you create this file, let's modify our `Home` component a little bit:

```
import React, { Component } from 'react';

// We import our Home.css file here
import './Home.css';

class Home extends Component {
  render() {
    return (
      <div className="Home">
        <h1>Welcome to Codejobs</h1>

        <p>
          In this recipe you will learn how to add styles to
          components. If you want to learn more you can visit
          our Youtube Channel at
          <a href="http://youtube.com/codejobs">Codejobs</a>.
        </p>
      </div>
    );
  }
}

export default Home;
```

File: src/components/Home/Home.js

3. We'll now add styles to our `Home.css`. Basically, we wrapped our component into a `div` with a `className` of Home, and inside we have an `<h1>` tag with the text `Welcome to Codejobs`, and then a `<p>` tag with a message. We need to import our `Home.css` file directly, and then our CSS file will look like this:

```
.Home {
    margin: 0 auto;
    width: 960px;
}

.Home h1 {
    font-size: 32px;
    color: #333;
}
```

```
.Home p {
    color: #333;
    text-align: center;
}

.Home a {
    color: #56D5FA;
    text-decoration: none;
}

.Home a:hover {
    color: #333;
}
```

File: src/components/Home/Home.css

4. Now let's suppose you need to add an inline style. We do this with the style property, and the CSS properties need to be written in camelCase and between `{{ }}`, like this:

```
import React, { Component } from 'react';

// We import our Home.css file here
import './Home.css';

class Home extends Component {
  render() {
    return (
      <div className="Home">
        <h1>Welcome to Codejobs</h1>
        <p>
          In this recipe you will learn how to add styles to
          components. If you want to learn more you can visit
          our Youtube Channel at
          <a href="http://youtube.com/codejobs">Codejobs</a>.
        </p>

        <p>
          <button
            style={{
              backgroundColor: 'gray',
              border: '1px solid black'
            }}
          >
            Click me!
          </button>
        </p>
      </div>
```

```
    );
  }
}

export default Home;
```

File: src/components/Home/Home.js

5. You also can pass an object to the `style` property like this:

```
import React, { Component } from 'react';

// We import our Home.css file here
import './Home.css';

class Home extends Component {
  render() {
    // Style object...
    const buttonStyle = {
      backgroundColor: 'gray',
      border: '1px solid black'
    };

    return (
      <div className="Home">
        <h1>Welcome to Codejobs</h1>
        <p>
          In this recipe you will learn how to add styles to
          components. If you want to learn more you can visit
          our Youtube Channel at
          <a href="http://youtube.com/codejobs">Codejobs</a>.
        </p>
        <p>
          <button style={buttonStyle}>Click me!</button>
        </p>
      </div>
    );
  }
}

export default Home;
```

File: src/components/Home/Home.js

How it works...

As you can see, it is straightforward to connect a CSS file to our component, and if you followed all the steps correctly, your site should look like this:

There's more...

You're probably curious about how the CSS code is added to the browser since we haven't imported a CSS file to our project directly (by using a `<link>` tag, for example). Well, you will be surprised to see that the CSS code is being injected into our `<head>` tag using the `<style>` tag for each imported stylesheet. If you inspect your project with Chrome DevTools you will see something like this:

```
<title>React App</title>
<style type="text/css">body {
  margin: 0;
  padding: 0;
  font-family: sans-serif;
}
</style>
▼<style type="text/css">
  .Home {
    margin: 0 auto;
    width: 960px;
  }

  .Home h1 {
    font-size: 32px;
    color: #333;
  }

  .Home p {
    color: #333;
    text-align: center;
  }

  .Home a {
    color: #56D5FA;
    text-decoration: none;
  }

  .Home a:hover {
    color: #333;
  }
</style>
```

This behavior is because the `style-loader` is a Webpack loader that is being used by default in our application when we create it with `create-react-app`:

```
▼<style type="text/css">
  .App {
    text-align: center;
  }

  .App-logo {
    -webkit-animation: App-logo-spin infinite 20s linear;
            animation: App-logo-spin infinite 20s linear;
    height: 80px;
  }

  .App-header {
    background-color: #222;
    height: 150px;
    padding: 20px;
    color: white;
  }

  .App-title {
    font-size: 1.5em;
  }

  .App-intro {
    font-size: large;
  }

  @-webkit-keyframes App-logo-spin {
    from { -webkit-transform: rotate(0deg); transform: rotate(0deg); }
    to { -webkit-transform: rotate(360deg); transform: rotate(360deg); }
  }

  @keyframes App-logo-spin {
    from { -webkit-transform: rotate(0deg); transform: rotate(0deg); }
    to { -webkit-transform: rotate(360deg); transform: rotate(360deg); }
  }
</style>
```

There is no way to modify the Webpack configuration directly when we use `create-react-app` because it is using a package called `react-scripts`, but in `Chapter 10`, *Mastering Webpack,* we will see how to configure our Webpack without using a starting kit such as `create-react-app`.

There are more Webpack loaders that do different things, such as `css-loader` for CSS modules, `sass-loader` to implement Sass, `stylus-loader` to implement Stylus, and `extract-text-plugin` to move the CSS code to a `.css` file instead of injecting it to the DOM (usually, this is only used in production).

Passing props to a component and validating them with PropTypes

So far, you are getting familiar with React components, but there is more to it than rendering static HTML. Like any application, we need to be able to send information (via props) to different elements. In this recipe, we are going to create new components: `Header`, `Content`, and `Footer` (we will group these components into a folder called `layout`), and we will send some props (as attributes and as children) and validate them with `PropTypes`.

How to do it...

Taking the same of the React application we created before, let's create first our `Header` component.

1. At this point, our current header is placed on `App.js`:

```
import React, { Component } from 'react';
import logo from '../shared/images/logo.svg';
import Home from './Home/Home';
import './App.css';

class App extends Component {
  render() {
    return (
      <div className="App">
        <header className="App-header">
          <img src={logo} className="App-logo" alt="logo" />
          <h1 className="App-title">Welcome to React</h1>
        </header>

        <Home />
      </div>
    );
  }
}

export default App;
```

File: src/components/App.js

2. Let's move that header to our new `Header` component and then import it into the `App` component. Because the layout components are global or shared, we need to create a layout directory in our shared components directory (`src/shared/components/layout`).
3. Before you continue, you must install a package called `prop-types` to use the `PropTypes` validation:

```
npm install prop-types
```

4. `PropTypes` was initially released as part of the React core module and is commonly used with React components. `PropTypes` is used to document the intended types of properties passed to components. React will check the props passed to your components against those definitions, and it will send a warning in development if they don't match:

```
import React, { Component } from 'react';
import PropTypes from 'prop-types';
import logo from '../../images/logo.svg';

class Header extends Component {
  // Here you can define your PropTypes.
  static propTypes = {
    title: PropTypes.string.isRequired,
    url: PropTypes.string
  };

  render() {
    const {
      title = 'Welcome to React',
      url = 'http://localhost:3000'
    } = this.props;

    return (
      <header className="App-header">
        <a href={url}>
          <img src={logo} className="App-logo" alt="logo" />
        </a>
        <h1 className="App-title">{title}</h1>
      </header>
    );
  }
}

export default Header;
```

File: src/shared/components/layout/Header.js

5. The `static` PropTypes property is basically an object where you need to define the types of prop you will pass. `array`, `bool`, `func`, `number`, `object`, `string`, and `symbol` are primitive types, but there are also particular types, such as `node`, `element`, `instanceOf`, `oneOf`, `oneOfType`, `arrayOf`, `objectOf`, `shape and any`. There is an optional property called `isRequired` that can be added to any type if the prop must be required and will produce a React warning if is not defined.
6. Import and render our `Header` component:

```
import React, { Component } from 'react';
import Home from './Home/Home';
import Header from '../shared/components/layout/Header';
import './App.css';

class App extends Component {
  render() {
    return (
      <div className="App">
        <Header title="Welcome to Codejobs" />
        <Home />
      </div>
    );
  }
}

export default App;
```

File: src/components/App.js

TIP: Don't get confused with the `<Header/>` component, it is not the same as the `<header>` tag from HTML5, that's why in React is recommended to use capital letters in the class names.

7. All the properties passed to our components are contained in this props. You may have noticed that we are only sending the `title` prop because it is the only one that is required. The `url` prop is optional and also has a default value in the destructuring (`http://localhost:3000`). If we don't pass the title prop, even if we have a default value **Welcome to React** in the destructuring we are going to get a warning like this:

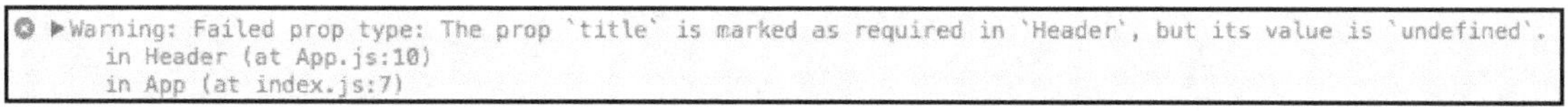

Warning: Failed prop type: The prop `title` is marked as required in `Header`, but its value is `undefined`.
in Header (at App.js:10)
in App (at index.js:7)

8. Create our `Footer` component:

```
import React, { Component } from 'react';

class Footer extends Component {
  render() {
    return (
   <footer>&copy; Codejobs {(new Date()).getFullYear()}</footer>
    );
  }
}

export default Footer;
```

File: src/shared/components/layout/Footer.js

9. So far, we only have passed props as attributes (with self-closed components `<Component />`), but there is another way to pass props as children (`<Component>Children Content</Component>`). Let's create a `Content` component and send our `Home` component as a child of content:

```
import React, { Component } from 'react';
import PropTypes from 'prop-types';

class Content extends Component {
  static propTypes = {
    children: PropTypes.element.isRequired
  };

  render() {
    const { children } = this.props;

    return (
      <main>
        {children}
      </main>
    );
  }
}

export default Content;
```

File: src/shared/components/layout/Content.js

10. With those changes, our `App.js` file should now look like this:

```
import React, { Component } from 'react';
import Home from './Home/Home';

// Layout Components
import Header from '../shared/components/layout/Header';
import Content from '../shared/components/layout/Content';
import Footer from '../shared/components/layout/Footer';

import './App.css';

class App extends Component {
  render() {
    return (
      <div className="App">
        <Header title="Welcome to Codejobs" />

        <Content>
          <Home />
        </Content>
        <Footer />
      </div>
    );
  }
}

export default App;
```

File: src/components/App.js

How it works...

PropTypes validations are very important for developers because they force us to define which type of prop we are going to receive in our components and validate whether some of them are required or not.

If you followed all the steps correctly, you should see something like this:

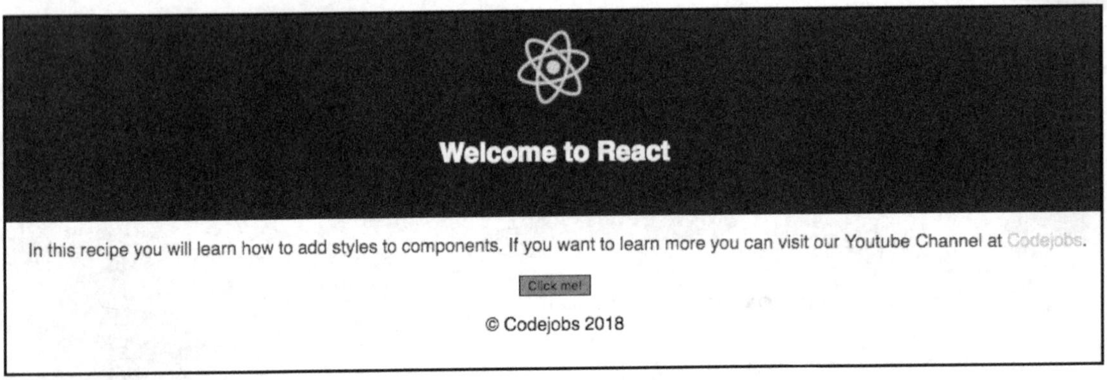

There's more...

As you can see, there are many ways to send props to components. There are more ways to receive props, such as using Redux (through a container) or React Router, but those are topics that we are going to cover in the next chapters.

Using local state in a component

The local state is a fundamental feature of React for creating dynamic components. Local state is only available on class components, and each component manages its state. You can define the initial value of the state on the component's constructor, and when you update the value of the state, the component will be re-render itself.

Local state is helpful with toggles, for handling forms, and is used to manage information within the same component. It is not recommended to use local state if we need to share data between different components. In that scenario, we need to implement Redux state, which we will cover in `Chapter 5`, *Mastering Redux*.

How to do it...

Let's define our initial state. Let's see how it works the component's `render` method when the local state is updated:

1. Using our `Home` component, we are going to add a constructor and define our initial state:

```
import React, { Component } from 'react';
import './Home.css';

class Home extends Component {
  constructor() {
    // We need to define super() at the beginning of the
    // constructor to have access to 'this'
    super();
    // Here we initialize our local state as an object
    this.state = {
      name: 'Carlos'
    };
  }

  render() {
    return (
      <div className="Home">
        {/* Here we render our state name */}
        <p>Hi my name is {this.state.name}</p>
      </div>
    );
  }
}

export default Home;
```

File: src/components/Home/Home.js

2. In this example, we are defining our local state in the constructor as an object, and in the render, we are printing the value directly. We are using `super()` at the beginning of the constructor. This is used to call the parent constructor, `(React.Component)`. If we don't include it, we will get an error like this:

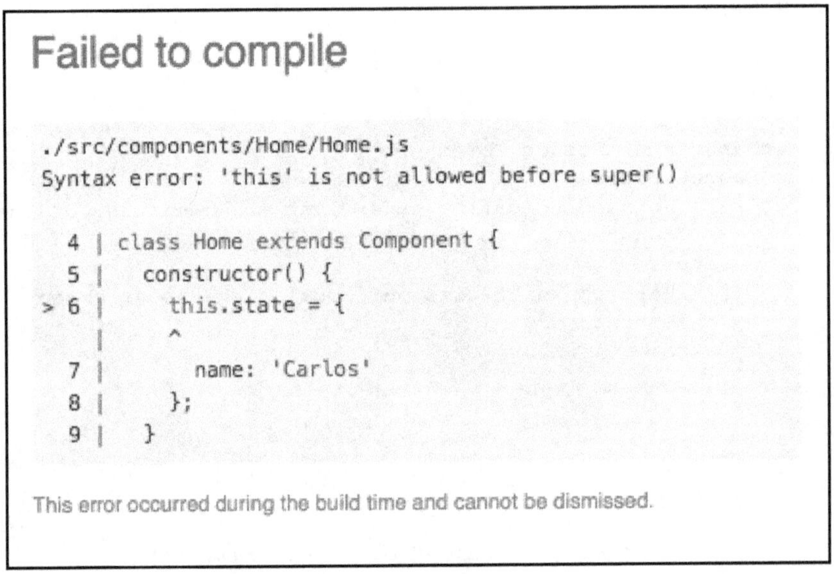

Failed to compile
./src/components/Home/Home.js
Syntax error: 'this' is not allowed before super()
4 | class Home extends Component {
5 | constructor() {
> 6 | this.state = {
| ^
7 | name: 'Carlos'
8 | };
9 | }
This error occurred during the build time and cannot be dismissed.

3. After we added `super()`, we need to define our initial state as a regular object:

```
this.state = {
  name: 'Carlos'
};
```

4. **Updating our local state with** `this.setState()`: Right now, this is just a state that is not being updated. That means that the component will never re-render again. To update the state, we need to use the `this.setState()` method and pass the new value of the state. We can add a `setTimeout` to update the name state after 1 second (1,000 milliseconds), so we need to modify our `render` method like this:

```
render() {
  setTimeout(() => {
    this.setState({
      name: 'Cristina' // Here we update the value of the state
    });
  }, 1000);
```

```
      console.log('Name:', this.state.name);

      return (
        <div className="Home">
          <p>Hi my name is {this.state.name}</p>
        </div>
      );
    }
```

5. If you run this in your browser, you will see the first value of the state is **Carlos**, and 1 second after this it will change to **Cristina**. I have added a `console.log` to log the value of the state name. If you open your browser console, you will see this:

```
Name: Carlos
Name: Cristina
Name: Cristina
Name: Cristina
Name: Cristina
Name: Cristina
Name: Cristina
Name: Cristina
Name: Cristina
Name: Cristina
Name: Cristina
Name: Cristina
Name: Cristina
Name: Cristina
Name: Cristina
Name: Cristina
Name: Cristina
Name: Cristina
Name: Cristina
```

6. **Updating our local state in the** `componentDidMount` **lifecycle method**: You're probably wondering why is repeated so many times. It is simple; this is the way React works. Every time we update a state the method render is fired, and in this code, we added a `setTimeout` which updates the state after a second. That means that the `render` method is being called every second, causing an infinitive loop. This will affect the performance of our application, and that's why you need to be careful when you update a state. As you can see updating it in the render method is not a good idea. So, where should I update the state? Well, it depends on your application, but for now, I'll show you a method that is part of the React lifecycle called `componentDidMount()`:

```
import React, { Component } from 'react';
import './Home.css';

class Home extends Component {
  constructor() {
    super();

    this.state = {
      name: 'Carlos'
    };
  }

  componentDidMount() {
    setTimeout(() => {
      this.setState({
        name: 'Cristina'
      });
    }, 1000);
  }

  render() {
    console.log('Name:', this.state.name);

    return (
      <div className="Home">
        <p>Hi my name is {this.state.name}</p>
      </div>
    );
  }
}

export default Home;
```

File: src/components/Home/Home.js

7. If you run this code and you see the console, now you will see this:

```
Name: Carlos
Name: Cristina
```

How it works...

With `componentDidMount`, we avoided the infinite loop. The reason why this is a better approach is that `componentDidMount` is being executed just once when the component is already mounted, and in that method, we are executing our `setTimeout` and updating the name state only once. In the following recipes, we are going to learn more about React lifecycle methods.

There's more...

Local state is also used to handle forms, but we will cover forms in `Chapter 6`, *Creating Forms with Redux Form.*

Making a functional or stateless component

So far, we have only learned how to create *class components* in React. These components are useful when you need to handle local state, but in some cases, we will need to render static markup. For static components, we need to use functional components, also known as stateless components. This will improve the performance of our application.

In the *Passing props to a component and validating them with PropTypes* recipe, we created some layout components (`Header`, `Content`, and `Footer`). These components, as you may imagine, are frequently not dynamic (unless you want to have a toggle menu or some user information in the header), so in this case, we can convert them into functional components.

How to do it...

It's now time to convert our `Header` component to a functional component:

1. First, let's see what the current `Header` component looks like:

```
import React, { Component } from 'react';
import PropTypes from 'prop-types';
import logo from '../../images/logo.svg';

class Header extends Component {
  static propTypes = {
    title: PropTypes.string.isRequired,
    url: PropTypes.string
  };

  render() {
    const {
      title = 'Welcome to React',
      url = 'http://localhost:3000'
    } = this.props;

    return (
      <header className="App-header">
        <a href={url}>
          <img src={logo} className="App-logo" alt="logo" />
        </a>
        <h1 className="App-title">{title}</h1>
      </header>
    );
  }
}

export default Header;
```

File: src/shared/components/layout/Header.js

2. The first thing to do is to convert our class component into an arrow function, and with this change, we don't need to import `React.Component` anymore. The second part of the migration is to pass the props as parameter in the function instead of getting them from `this.props`, and the last step is to move our static `propTypes` as a node of the function. After those changes, our code should look like this:

```
import React from 'react';
import PropTypes from 'prop-types';
```

```
import logo from '../../images/logo.svg';

// We created a component with a simple arrow function.
const Header = props => {
  const {
    title = 'Welcome to React',
    url = 'http://localhost:3000'
  } = props;

  return (
    <header className="App-header">
      <a href={url}>
        <img src={logo} className="App-logo" alt="logo" />
      </a>
      <h1 className="App-title">{title}</h1>
    </header>
  );
};

// Even with Functional Components we are able to validate our
// PropTypes.
Header.propTypes = {
  title: PropTypes.string.isRequired,
  url: PropTypes.string
};

export default Header;
```

File: src/shared/components/layout/Header.js

> **TIP:** A functional component is an equivalent to just having the render method. That's why we only need to return the JSX directly.

3. After we migrated our `Header` component, we will migrate the `Footer` component; this is easier because it does not have props. First, let's see what our `Footer` component looks like:

```
import React, { Component } from 'react';

class Footer extends Component {
  render() {
    return (
      <footer>
        &copy; Codejobs {(new Date()).getFullYear()}
      </footer>
```

```
    );
  }
}

export default Footer;
```

File: src/shared/components/layout/Footer.js

4. Now, as a functional component, it should look like this:

```
import React from 'react';

// Since we don't have props, we can directly return our JSX.
const Footer = () => (
  <footer>&copy; Codejobs {(new Date()).getFullYear()}</footer>
);

export default Footer;
```

File: src/shared/components/layout/Footer.js

> In this case, as you can see, we need to create an arrow function without parameters (because we don't have any props) and directly return the JSX we need to render.

5. Converting the `Content` component to a functional component:

```
import React, { Component } from 'react';
import PropTypes from 'prop-types';

class Content extends Component {
  static propTypes = {
    children: PropTypes.element.isRequired
  };

  render() {
    const { children } = this.props;

    return (
      <main>
        {children}
      </main>
    );
  }
}
```

```
export default Content;
```

File: src/shared/components/layout/Content.js

6. This component is similar to our `Header` component. We need to pass the props as parameters and keep our `propTypes`:

```
import React from 'react';
import PropTypes from 'prop-types';

const Content = props => {
  const { children } = props;

  return (
    <main>
      {children}
    </main>
  );
};

Content.propTypes = {
  children: PropTypes.element.isRequired
};

export default Content;
```

File: src/shared/components/layout/Content.js

How it works...

Even with functional components, we can validate our `PropTypes`. Remember, if you don't need any dynamic data or local state then you should consider using a stateless component. This will improve the performance of your application.

There's more...

A functional component not only does not have a state but also does not have the React lifecycle methods either.

Understanding React lifecycle methods

React provides methods to handle the data during the lifecycle of a component. This is very useful when we need to update our application at particular times.

How to do it...

In this section, we are going to explain each example independently.

Todo list – implementing ComponentWillMount

In this recipe, you will learn about the lifecycle methods in React. We will see how the information flows through the methods since the component is pre-mounted, mounted, and unmounted. The Todo list that we will develop in this recipe will look like this:

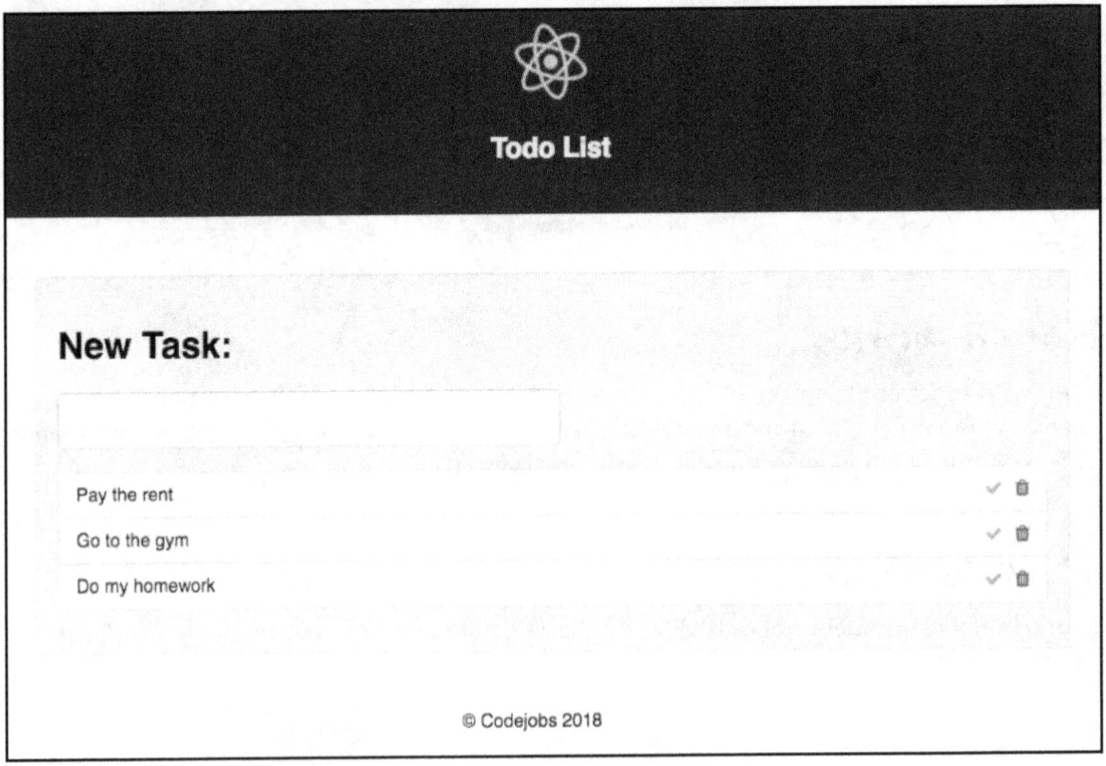

1. For this Todo list, we need to create a new folder called `Todo` into our `components` directory, and you also need to create files called `Todo.js` and `Todo.css`. This is the skeleton of the `Todo` component:

```
import React, { Component } from 'react';
import './Todo.css';

class Todo extends Component {
  constructor() {
    super();
  }

  componentWillMount() {

  }

  render() {
    return (
      <div className="Todo">
        <h1>New Task:</h1>
      </div>
    );
  }
}

export default Todo;
```

File: src/components/Todo/Todo.js

2. **Constructor:** A constructor is a unique method that is executed before the object is initialized. A constructor can use the `super` keyword to call the constructor of the super class (parent class). This method is used to initialize our local state or to bind our methods. For the Todo list, we need to initialize the local state in the constructor with some values in the task and `items` array:

```
constructor() {
  super();

  // Initial state...
  this.state = {
    task: '',
    items: []
  };
}
```

3. The `componentWillMount` method is executed once before the component is mounted. In this case, before our component is mounted we need to update our `items` state with the default tasks:

```
componentWillMount() {
  // Setting default tasks...
  this.setState({
    items: [
      {
        id: uuidv4(),
        task: 'Pay the rent',
        completed: false
      },
      {
        id: uuidv4(),
        task: 'Go to the gym',
        completed: false
      },
      {
        id: uuidv4(),
        task: 'Do my homework',
        completed: false
      }
    ]
  });
}
```

4. We are using `uuidv4` to generate random IDs. To install this package, you need to run the following command:

```
npm install uuid
```

5. And then you need to import it like this:

```
import uuidv4 from 'uuid/v4';
```

6. After we defined our default tasks, let's see how we need to render the Todo list:

```
render() {
  return (
    <div className="Todo">
      <h1>New Task:</h1>

      <form onSubmit={this.handleOnSubmit}>
        <input
          value={this.state.task}
          onChange={this.handleOnChange}
        />
```

```
        </form>

        <List
          items={this.state.items}
          markAsCompleted={this.markAsCompleted}
          removeTask={this.removeTask}
        />
      </div>
    );
  }
```

7. Our JSX is divided into two parts. The first one is a form with an input that is connected to our local state (`this.state.task`), and we will save the task when the user submits the form (`onSubmit`). The second part is the component list where we are going to display our Todo list (or tasks list), passing the items array and the `markAsCompleted` (to mark a task as a completed) and `removeTask` (to remove the task from the list) functions.
8. The `handleOnChange` method is for connecting our input value with our state task:

```
  handleOnChange = e => {
    const { target: { value } } = e;

    // Updating our task state with the input value...
    this.setState({
      task: value
    });
  }
```

9. The `handleOnSubmit` method is for updating the `items` state and pushing the new task to the array:

```
  handleOnSubmit = e => {
    // Prevent default to avoid the actual form submit...
    e.preventDefault();

    // Once is submited we reset the task value and we push
    // the new task to the items array.
    if (this.state.task.trim() !== '') {
      this.setState({
        task: '',
        items: [
          ...this.state.items,
          {
            id: uuidv4(),
            task: this.state.task,
```

```
            complete: false
          }
        ]
      });
    }
  }
```

10. The `markAsCompleted` function is going to be called from our `List` component and needs to receive the `id` of the task we want to mark as completed. With this, we can find the specific task in our items array, modify the node as completed, and then update the local state:

```
markAsCompleted = id => {
  // Finding the task by id...
  const foundTask = this.state.items.find(
    task => task.id === id
  );

  // Updating the completed status...
  foundTask.completed = true;

  // Updating the state with the new updated task...
  this.setState({
    items: [
      ...this.state.items,
      ...foundTask
    ]
  });
}
```

11. The `removeTask` function is also being called from the `List` component, and like `markAsCompleted`, we need to receive the `id` to remove the specific task:

```
removeTask = id => {
  // Filtering the tasks by removing the specific task id...
  const filteredTasks = this.state.items.filter(
    task => task.id !== id
  );

  // Updating items state...
  this.setState({
    items: filteredTasks
  });
}
```

12. Let's put all the pieces together. Our `Todo` component should look like this:

```
import React, { Component } from 'react';
import uuidv4 from 'uuid/v4';
import List from './List';
import './Todo.css';

class Todo extends Component {
  constructor() {
    super();

    // Initial state...
    this.state = {
      task: '',
      items: []
    };
  }

  componentWillMount() {
    // Setting default tasks...
    this.setState({
      items: [
        {
          id: uuidv4(),
          task: 'Pay the rent',
          completed: false
        },
        {
          id: uuidv4(),
          task: 'Go to the gym',
          completed: false
        },
        {
          id: uuidv4(),
          task: 'Do my homework',
          completed: false
        }
      ]
    });
  }

  handleOnChange = e => {
    const { target: { value } } = e;

    // Updating our task state with the input value...
    this.setState({
      task: value
    });
```

```
}

handleOnSubmit = e => {
  // Prevent default to avoid the actual form submit...
  e.preventDefault();

  // Once is submitted we reset the task value and
  // we push the new task to the items array.
  if (this.state.task.trim() !== '') {
    this.setState({
      task: '',
      items: [
        ...this.state.items,
        {
          id: uuidv4(),
          task: this.state.task,
          complete: false
        }
      ]
    });
  }
}

markAsCompleted = id => {
  // Finding the task by id...
  const foundTask = this.state.items.find(
    task => task.id === id
  );

  // Updating the completed status...
  foundTask.completed = true;

  // Updating the state with the new updated task...
  this.setState({
    items: [
      ...this.state.items,
      ...foundTask
    ]
  });
}

removeTask = id => {
  // Filtering the tasks by removing the specific task id...
  const filteredTasks=this.state.items.filter(
    task => task.id !== id
  );

  // Updating items state...
```

```
    this.setState({
      items: filteredTasks
    });
  }

  render() {
    return (
      <div className="Todo">
        <h1>New Task:</h1>

        <form onSubmit={this.handleOnSubmit}>
          <input
            value={this.state.task}
            onChange={this.handleOnChange}
          />
        </form>

        <List
          items={this.state.items}
          markAsCompleted={this.markAsCompleted}
          removeTask={this.removeTask}
        />
      </div>
    );
  }
}

export default Todo;
```

File: src/components/Todo/Todo.js

13. Now that we have completed our `Todo` component, let's see what our `List` component looks like:

```
import React from 'react';

const List = props => (
  <ul>
    {props.items.map((item, key) => (
      <li
        key={key}
        className={`${item.completed ? 'completed' : 'pending'}`}
      >
        {/*
          * If the task is completed we assign the
          * .completed class otherwise .pending
          */}
        {item.task}
```

```
            <div className="actions">
              {/*
                * Using a callback on the onClick we call our
                * markAsCompleted function
                */}
              <span
                className={item.completed ? 'hide' : 'done'}
                onClick={ () => props.markAsCompleted(item.id) }
              >
                <i className="fa fa-check"></i>
              </span>

              {/*
                * Using a callback on the onClick we call
                * our removeTask function
                */}
              <span
                className="trash"
                onClick={ () => props.removeTask(item.id) }
              >
                <i className="fa fa-trash"></i>
              </span>
            </div>
          </li>
        ))}
      </ul>
    );

    export default List;
```

File: src/components/Todo/List.js

14. Every time we use a `.map` function to render multiple React elements from an array, we must add the key prop to each item we created. Otherwise, we will get a React warning like this:

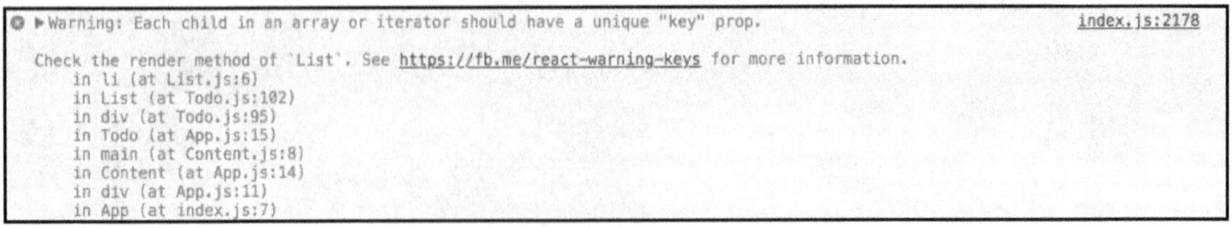

▶Warning: Each child in an array or iterator should have a unique "key" prop.
index.js:2178
Check the render method of `List`. See https://fb.me/react-warning-keys for more information.
in li (at List.js:6)
in List (at Todo.js:102)
in div (at Todo.js:95)
in Todo (at App.js:15)
in main (at Content.js:8)
in Content (at App.js:14)
in div (at App.js:11)
in App (at index.js:7)

15. You have probably noticed that we also included some Font Awesome icons, and to make it work we need to add the Font Awesome CDN into the main `index.html` file:

```
<head>
  <title>React App</title>
  <link
href="https://maxcdn.bootstrapcdn.com/font-awesome/4.7.0/css/font-a
wesome.min.css"
    rel="stylesheet"
  />
</head>
```

File: public/index.html

16. The last part is the CSS for the Todo list (you're free to change the styles if you prefer):

```
.Todo {
    background-color: #f5f5f5;
    border-radius: 4px;
    border: 1px solid #e3e3e3;
    box-shadow: inset 0 1px 1px rgba(0,0,0,.05);
    margin: 50px auto;
    min-height: 20px;
    padding: 20px;
    text-align: left;
    width: 70%;
}

.Todo ul {
    margin: 20px 0px;
    padding: 0;
    list-style: none;
}

.Todo ul li {
    background-color: #fff;
    border: 1px solid #ddd;
    display: flex;
    justify-content: space-between;
    margin-bottom: -1px;
    padding: 10px 15px;
}

.Todo ul li .hide {
    visibility: hidden;
```

```
}

.Todo ul li.completed {
    background-color: #dff0d8;
}

.Todo ul li .actions {
    display: flex;
    justify-content: space-between;
    width: 40px;
}

.Todo ul li span {
    cursor: pointer;
}

.Todo ul li .done {
    color: #79c41d;
    display: block;
}

.Todo ul li .trash {
    color: #c41d1d;
    display: block;
}

.Todo form input {
    background-color: #fff;
    border-radius: 4px;
    border: 1px solid #ccc;
    box-shadow: inset 0 1px 1px rgba(0,0,0,.075);
    color: #555;
    font-size: 14px;
    height: 34px;
    line-height: 34px;
    padding: 6px 12px;
    width: 40%;
}
```

File: src/components/Todo/Todo.css

17. Don't forget to import the `Todo` component into your `App` component. Otherwise, the component won't render:

```
import React, { Component } from 'react';
import Todo from './Todo/Todo';
import Header from '../shared/components/layout/Header';
import Content from '../shared/components/layout/Content';
import Footer from '../shared/components/layout/Footer';
import './App.css';

class App extends Component {
  render() {
    return (
      <div className="App">
        <Header title="Todo List" />

        <Content>
          <Todo />
        </Content>

        <Footer />
      </div>
    );
  }
}

export default App;
```

File: src/components/App.js

18. If you followed all the instructions correctly you should see the Todo List like this:

- The initial state with default tasks:

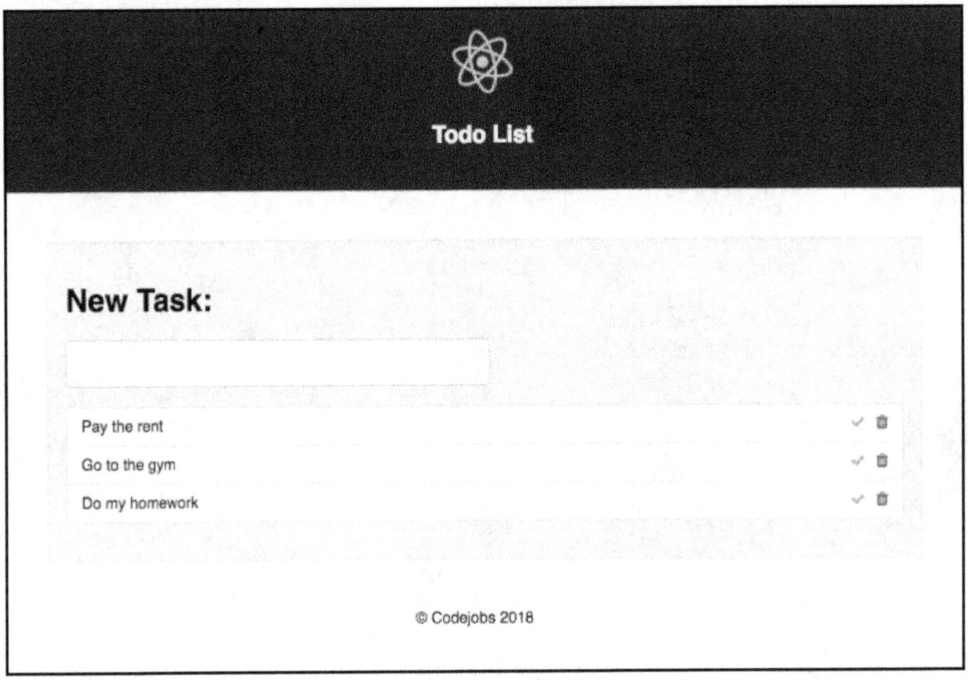

- Adding a new task:

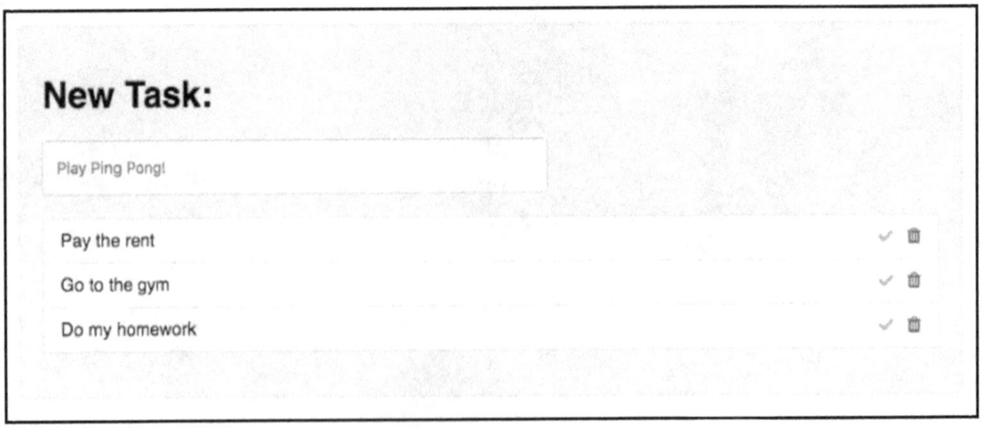

- Write the task title and then press *Enter*:

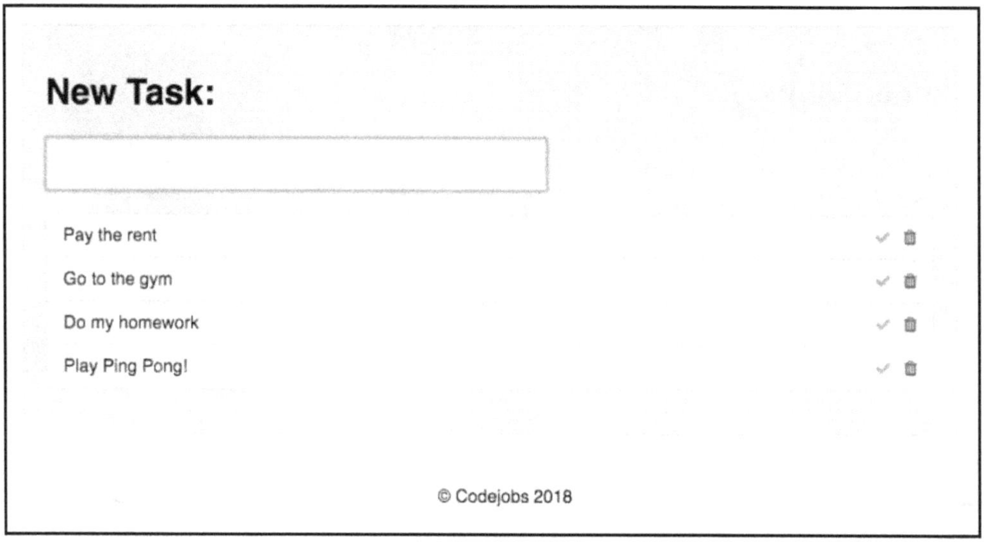

- Mark a task as complete:

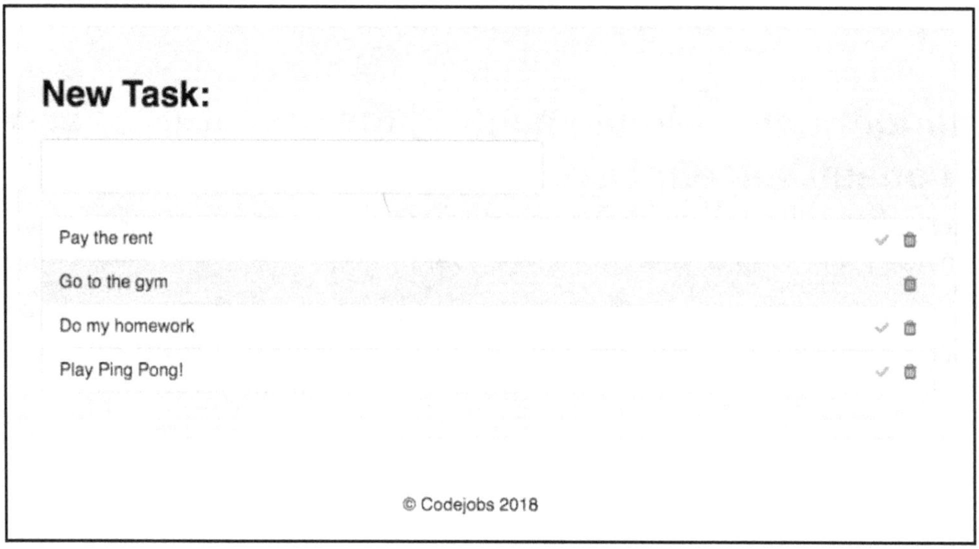

- Removing a task:

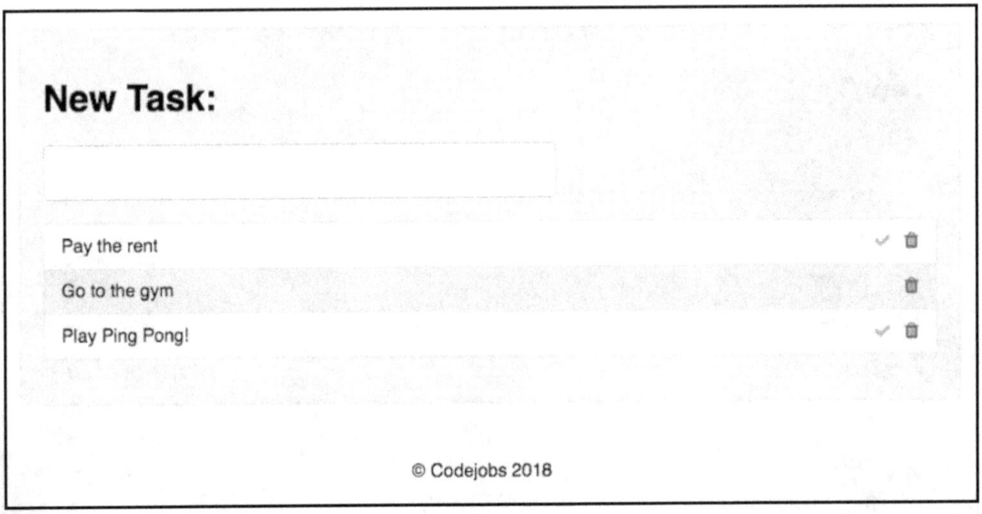

I challenge you to save the tasks using `localStorage` instead of defining the default tasks with `componentWillMount`.

Pomodoro timer – implementing the constructor and componentDidMount

To understand `componentDidMount`, we are going to create a Pomodoro Timer (if you don't know what it is you can read this: `https://en.wikipedia.org/wiki/Pomodoro_Technique`).

Our Pomodoro timer will look like this:

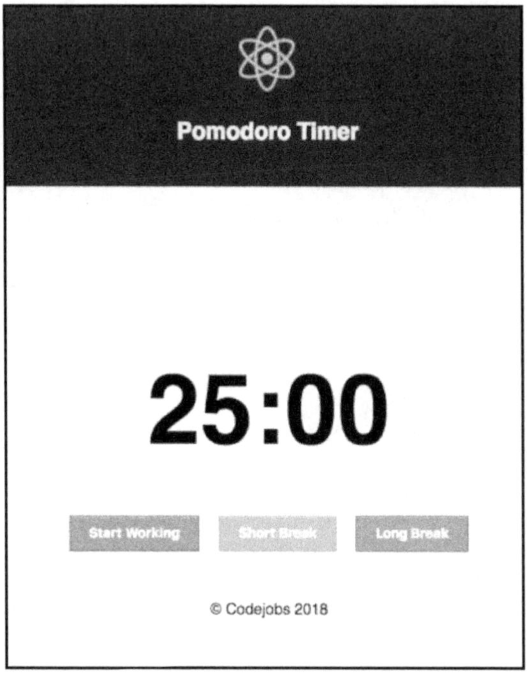

Creating our Pomodoro Timer:

1. The first thing we need to do is to create a new folder called `Pomodoro` in our `components` directory, as well as a file called `Timer.js` and the CSS file, `Timer.css`. This is the skeleton of the class component we will use for this component:

```
import React, { Component } from 'react';
import './Timer.css';

class Timer extends Component {
  constructor() {
    super();
  }

  componentDidMount() {

  }

  render() {
    return (
      <div className="Pomodoro">
```

```
      </div>
    );
  }
}

export default Timer;
```

File: src/components/Pomodoro/Timer.js

2. For our Pomodoro timer, we need to initialize our local state in the constructor with some values for the time and for the alert (when the time is over):

```
constructor() {
  super();

  // Initial State
  this.state = {
    alert: {
      type: '',
      message: ''
    },
    time: 0
  };

  // Defined times for work, short break and long break...
  this.times = {
    defaultTime: 1500, // 25 min
    shortBreak: 300, // 5 min
    longBreak: 900 // 15 min
  };
}
```

3. The `componentDidMount` method is called once the component is mounted and is executed just once. In this case, once our component is mounted we need to update our time state with the default time (25 min), and to do this, we need to create a new method called `setDefaultTime` and then execute it in our `componentDidMount` method:

```
componentDidMount() {
  // Set default time when the component mounts
  this.setDefaultTime();
}

setDefaultTime = () => {
  // Default time is 25 min
  this.setState({
```

```
      time: this.times.defaultTime
    });
  }
```

4. After we defined our default time to our time state, let's see how we need to render the Pomodoro Timer. Our `render` method should look like this:

```
render() {
  const { alert: { message, type }, time } = this.state;

  return (
    <div className="Pomodoro">
      <div className={`alert ${type}`}>
        {message}
      </div>

      <div className="timer">
        {this.displayTimer(time)}
      </div>

      <div className="types">
        <button
          className="start"
          onClick={this.setTimeForWork}
        >
          Start Working
        </button>
        <button
          className="short"
          onClick={this.setTimeForShortBreak}
        >
          Short Break
        </button>
        <button
          className="long"
          onClick={this.setTimeForLongBreak}
        >
          Long Break
        </button>
      </div>
    </div>
  );
}
```

5. In this case, our JSX is very simple. We are getting the values from the local state (`message`, `type`, and `time`) and displaying a div to show our alert when the user receives an alert message. We have another div to show our timer, and here we are passing our current time (expressed in seconds) to the `displayTimer` method, which will convert those seconds into `mm:ss` format. The last piece of the layout are the buttons to select the type of timer (start working for 25 min, short break for 5 min, or long break for 15 min), and you may have noticed that we are executing different methods on the `onClick` event for each type of timer.
6. `setTimeForWork`, `setTimeForShortBreak`, and `setTimeForLongBreak`: The purpose of these three functions is to update the alert message depending on the type of the timer and then call a common function called `setTime`, passing as a parameter the specific time for each option. Let's first see what these three functions should look like:

```
setTimeForWork = () => {
  this.setState({
    alert: {
      type: 'work',
      message: 'Working!'
    }
  });

  return this.setTime(this.times.defaultTime);
}

setTimeForShortBreak = () => {
  this.setState({
    alert: {
      type: 'shortBreak',
      message: 'Taking a Short Break!'
    }
  });

  return this.setTime(this.times.shortBreak);
}

setTimeForLongBreak = () => {
  this.setState({
    alert: {
      type: 'longBreak',
      message: 'Taking a Long Break!'
    }
  });
```

```
    return this.setTime(this.times.longBreak);
  }
```

7. As we learned in the previous recipes when we specify our methods with arrow functions in our class they are automatically bound (they have access to the "this" object). That means we don't need to bind them on the constructor. Now let's create our setTime method:

```
setTime = newTime => {
  this.restartInterval();

  this.setState({
    time: newTime
  });
}
```

8. As you can see, we executed a new method called restartInterval(), and we updated our local state with the newTime variable, which we passed as a parameter (it can be 1,500 seconds = 25 min, 300 seconds = 5 min or 900 seconds = 15 min). You probably noticed, from the name of the function, that we are going to use a setInterval function, which is used to call a function every X milliseconds. Our restartInterval function should be like this:

```
restartInterval = () => {
  // Clearing the interval
  clearInterval(this.interval);

  // Execute countDown function every second
  this.interval = setInterval(this.countDown, 1000);
}
```

9. In this case, we first cleared our interval with clearInterval(this.interval). This is because the user can switch between the different types of the timer, so we need to clear the interval each time we set a new timer. After we cleared the interval, then we call the countDown function every second using setInterval. The countDown function is as follows:

```
countDown = () => {
  // If the time reach 0 then we display Buzzzz! alert.
  if (this.state.time === 0) {
    this.setState({
      alert: {
        type: 'buz',
        message: 'Buzzzzzzzz!'
      }
```

```
      });
    } else {
      // We decrease the time second by second
      this.setState({
        time: this.state.time - 1
      });
    }
  }
```

10. The last piece of this puzzle is the `displayTimer` function, which will convert the time into an `mm:ss` format and display it in our component:

```
  displayTimer(seconds) {
    // Formatting the time into mm:ss
    const m = Math.floor(seconds % 3600 / 60);
    const s = Math.floor(seconds % 3600 % 60);
    return `${m < 10 ? '0' : ''}${m}:${s < 10 ? '0' : ''}${s}`;
  }
```

11. Let's put it all together:

```
  import React, { Component } from 'react';
  import './Timer.css';

  class Timer extends Component {
    constructor() {
      super();

      // Initial State
      this.state = {
        alert: {
          type: '',
          message: ''
        },
        time: 0
      };

      // Defined times for work, short break and long break...
      this.times = {
        defaultTime: 1500, // 25 min
        shortBreak: 300, // 5 min
        longBreak: 900 // 15 min
      };
    }

    componentDidMount() {
      // Set default time when the component mounts
      this.setDefaultTime();
```

```
}

setDefaultTime = () => {
  // Default time is 25 min
  this.setState({
    time: this.times.defaultTime
  });
}

setTime = newTime => {
  this.restartInterval();

  this.setState({
    time: newTime
  });
}

restartInterval = () => {
  // Clearing the interval
  clearInterval(this.interval);

  // Execute countDown every second
  this.interval = setInterval(this.countDown, 1000);
}

countDown = () => {
  // If the time reach 0 then we display Buzzzz! alert.
  if (this.state.time === 0) {
    this.setState({
      alert: {
        type: 'buz',
        message: 'Buzzzzzzzz!'
      }
    });
  } else {
    // We decrease the time second by second
    this.setState({
      time: this.state.time - 1
    });
  }
}

setTimeForWork = () => {
  this.setState({
    alert: {
      type: 'work',
      message: 'Working!'
    }
```

```
    });

    return this.setTime(this.times.defaultTime);
  }

  setTimeForShortBreak = () => {
    this.setState({
      alert: {
        type: 'shortBreak',
        message: 'Taking a Short Break!'
      }
    });

    return this.setTime(this.times.shortBreak);
  }

  setTimeForLongBreak = () => {
    this.setState({
      alert: {
        type: 'longBreak',
        message: 'Taking a Long Break!'
      }
    });

    return this.setTime(this.times.longBreak);
  }

  displayTimer(seconds) {
    // Formatting the time into mm:ss
    const m = Math.floor(seconds % 3600 / 60);
    const s = Math.floor(seconds % 3600 % 60);

    return `${m < 10 ? '0' : ''}${m}:${s < 10 ? '0' : ''}${s}`;
  }

  render() {
    const { alert: { message, type }, time } = this.state;

    return (
      <div className="Pomodoro">
        <div className={`alert ${type}`}>
          {message}
        </div>

        <div className="timer">
          {this.displayTimer(time)}
        </div>
```

```
            <div className="types">
              <button
                className="start"
                onClick={this.setTimeForWork}
              >
                Start Working
              </button>
              <button
                className="short"
                onClick={this.setTimeForShortBreak}
              >
                Short Break
              </button>
              <button
                className="long"
                onClick={this.setTimeForLongBreak}
              >
                Long Break
              </button>
            </div>
          </div>
        );
      }
    }

    export default Timer;
```

File: src/components/Pomodoro/Timer.js

12. After we have completed our component, the last step is to add our styles. This is the CSS used for the Pomodoro timer. Of course, you can change it if you prefer:

```
.Pomodoro {
    padding: 50px;
}

.Pomodoro .timer {
    font-size: 100px;
    font-weight: bold;
}

.Pomodoro .alert {
    font-size: 20px;
    padding: 50px;
    margin-bottom: 20px;
}

.Pomodoro .alert.work {
```

```
    background: #5da423;
}

.Pomodoro .alert.shortBreak {
    background: #f4ad42;
}

.Pomodoro .alert.longBreak {
    background: #2ba6cb;
}

.Pomodoro .alert.buz {
    background: #c60f13;
}

.Pomodoro button {
    background: #2ba6cb;
    border: 1px solid #1e728c;
    box-shadow: 0 1px 0 rgba(255, 255, 255, 0.5) inset;
    color: white;
    cursor: pointer;
    display: inline-block;
    font-size: 14px;
    font-weight: bold;
    line-height: 1;
    margin: 50px 10px 0px 10px;
    padding: 10px 20px 11px;
    position: relative;
    text-align: center;
    text-decoration: none;
}

.Pomodoro button.start {
    background-color: #5da423;
    border: 1px solid #396516;
}

.Pomodoro button.short {
    background-color: #f4ad42;
    border: 1px solid #dd962a;
}
```

File: src/components/Pomodoro/Timer.css

Don't forget to import the `<Timer />` component into `App.js`. If you follow everything correctly, you should see the Pomodoro timer working like this:

- Working:

- Taking a short break:

- Taking a long break:

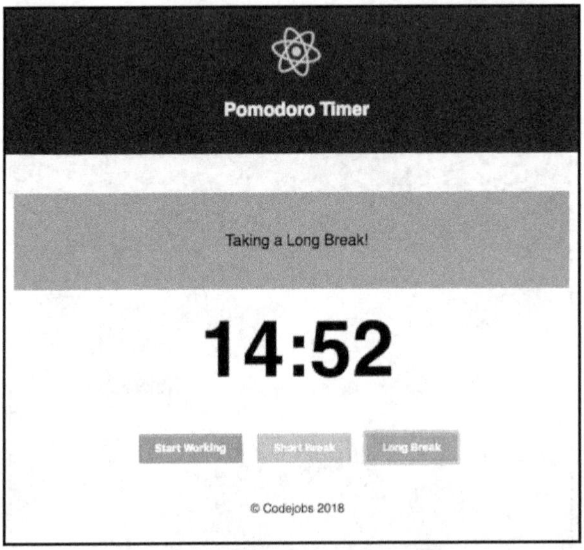

- Buzzzz - time over!:

I challenge you to add a Play, Pause, and Reset buttons to control the timer.

Crypto coins exchanger – implementing shouldComponentUpdate

Today, everyone is talking about Bitcoin, Ethereum, Ripple, and other cryptocurrencies. Let's create our own Crypto Coins Exchanger to learn how `shouldComponentUpdate` works.

Our exchanger will look like this:

1. We'll sell entire coins. That means we won't trade with decimals; everything should be an integer, and each currency costs $10 dollars. Our code is simple, so let's take a look:

```
import React, { Component } from 'react';
import './Coins.css';

class Coins extends Component {
  constructor() {
    super();

    // Initial state...
    this.state = {
      dollars: 0
    };
  }

  shouldComponentUpdate(props, state) {
    // We only update if the dollars are multiples of 10
    return state.dollars % 10 === 0;
  }

  handleOnChange = e => {
    this.setState({
      dollars: Number(e.target.value || 0)
    });
  }

  render() {
    return (
      <div className="Coins">
        <h1>Buy Crypto Coins!</h1>

        <div className="question">
          <p>How much dollars do you have?</p>

          <p>
            <input
              placeholder="0"
              onChange={this.handleOnChange}
              type="text"
            />
          </p>
        </div>

        <div className="answer">
          <p>Crypto Coin price: $10</p>
          <p>
```

```
            You can buy <strong>{this.state.dollars / 10}</strong>
            coins.
          </p>
        </div>
      </div>
    );
  }
}

export default Coins;
```

File: src/components/Coins/Coins.js

2. We are updating our dollars state every time the user writes something in the input and converting the value to a number, but if you run this code, you will probably notice that when you put in a number under 10, the message **You can buy 0 coins** doesn't change until you write 10, 20, 30, 40, and so on.
3. `shouldComponentUpdate`: This method is one of the most important methods that improve the performance of our application. It receives two parameters (props, state) every time we update a local state, and when a prop is updated this method is executed. The returned value must be boolean, which means that if you intentionally write the following, your component will never update because this method will block it from updating:

```
shouldComponentUpdate(props, state) {
  return false;
}
```

4. But, on the other hand, if you return true or even if you don't define this method at all, the default behavior of React is always to update the component, which in some cases can cause a performance issue when we are rendering vast views and handling a lot of data that changes regularly.

5. In our example, we are returning true only when the number of dollars that the user enters is a multiple of 10. That's why you only see the component updating in this case:

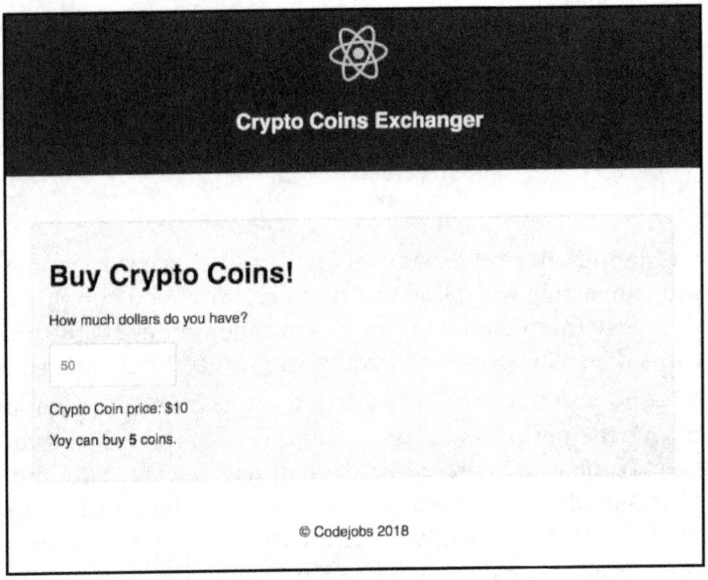

6. But it is not going to work for numbers that are not multiples of 10:

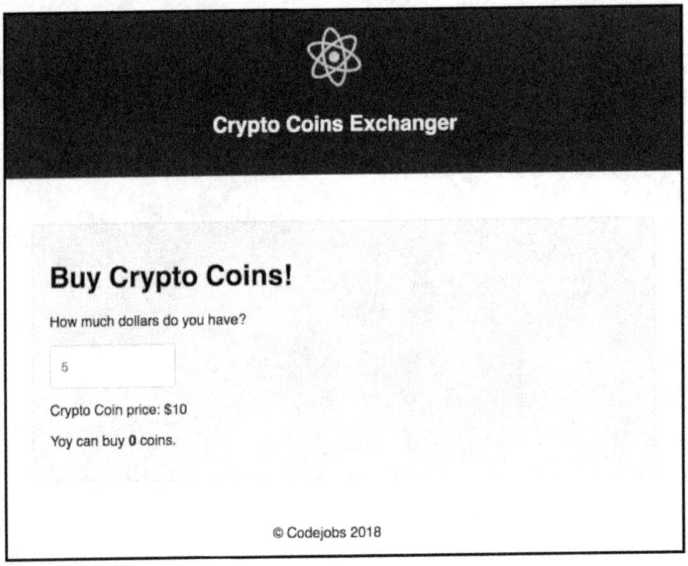

7. Now, if we remove the `shouldComponentUpdate` method from our component or we directly return a `true` value, the component will update every time we write a number, and this will be the result:

8. As you can see, with `shouldComponentUpdate`, we can control the updates of our component, and this improves the performance of the application significantly. The last piece of our example is the CSS:

```
.Coins {
  background-color: #f5f5f5;
  border-radius: 4px;
  border: 1px solid #e3e3e3;
  box-shadow: inset 0 1px 1px rgba(0,0,0,.05);
  margin-bottom: 20px;
  margin: 50px auto;
  min-height: 20px;
  padding: 19px;
  text-align: left;
  width: 70%;
}

.Coins input {
  background-color: #fff;
  border-radius: 4px;
  border: 1px solid #ccc;
```

```
    box-shadow: inset 0 1px 1px rgba(0,0,0,.075);
    color: #555;
    font-size: 14px;
    height: 34px;
    line-height: 34px;
    padding: 6px 12px;
    width: 120px;
}
```

File: src/components/Coins/Coins.css

Notes – implementing componentWillReceiveProps and componentWillUnmount

In this example, we are going to create a simple list of notes where, every 10 seconds, we will simulate that we receive an update from the service with new data, and with `componentWillReceiveProps`, we will register the last time we got an update from the server:

1. The `componentWillReceiveProps` method is called right before rendering. Like `shouldComponentUpdate`, it is called whenever new props are passed to the component, or the state has changed. In this example, we need to create fake data, but data normally needs to come from an actual service:

```
export const notes1 = [
  {
    title: 'Note 1',
    content: 'Content for Note 1'
  },
  {
    title: 'Note 2',
    content: 'Content for Note 2'
  },
  {
    title: 'Note 3',
    content: 'Content for Note 3'
  }
];

export const notes2 = [
  {
    title: 'Note 4',
    content: 'Content for Note 4'
  },
  {
```

```
    title: 'Note 5',
    content: 'Content for Note 5'
  },
  {
    title: 'Note 6',
    content: 'Content for Note 6'
  }
];
```

File: src/components/Notes/data.js

2. After we've created our fake data, let's create our component:

```
import React, { Component } from 'react';
import moment from 'moment';
import './Notes.css';
const formatTime = 'YYYY-MM-DD HH:mm:ss';

class Notes extends Component {
  constructor() {
    super();

    // We save the first date when the data is
    // rendered at the beginning
    this.state = {
      lastUpdate: moment().format(formatTime).toString()
    }
  }

  componentWillReceiveProps(nextProps) {
    // If the prop notes has changed...
    if (nextProps.notes !== this.props.notes) {
      this.setState({
        lastUpdate: moment().format(formatTime).toString()
      });
    }
  }
  render() {
    const { notes } = this.props;

    return (
      <div className="Notes">
        <h1>Notes:</h1>

        <ul>
          {notes.map((note, key) => (
            <li key={key}>{note.title} - {note.content}</li>
          ))}
```

```
          </ul>

          <p>Last Update: <strong>{this.state.lastUpdate}</strong>
          </p>
        </div>
      );
    }
  }

  export default Notes;
```

File: src/components/Notes/Notes.js

3. In this example, we are using the `moment.js` library. To install it, you need to run the following command:

```
npm install moment
```

4. Now, in our `App.js` file, we are going to simulate that after 10 seconds of the first render, we will receive a new update from the service and render the new notes:

```
import React, { Component } from 'react';
import Notes from './Notes/Notes';
import Header from '../shared/components/layout/Header';
import Content from '../shared/components/layout/Content';
import Footer from '../shared/components/layout/Footer';

// This is our fake data...
import { notes1, notes2 } from './Notes/data';
import './App.css';

class App extends Component {
  constructor() {
    super();

    // The first time we load the notes1...
    this.state = {
      notes: notes1
    };
  }

  componentDidMount() {
    // After 10 seconds (10000 milliseconds) we concatenate our
    // data with notes2...
    setTimeout(() => {
      this.setState({
```

```
          notes: [...this.state.notes, ...notes2]
        });
      }, 10000);
    }

    render() {
      return (
        <div className="App">
          <Header title="Notes" />

          <Content>
            <Notes notes={this.state.notes} />
          </Content>

          <Footer />
        </div>
      );
    }
  }

  export default App;
```

File: src/components/App.js

5. The last part is the CSS file:

```
.Notes {
  background-color: #f5f5f5;
  border-radius: 4px;
  border: 1px solid #e3e3e3;
  box-shadow: inset 0 1px 1px rgba(0,0,0,.05);
  margin-bottom: 20px;
  margin: 50px auto;
  min-height: 20px;
  padding: 19px;
  text-align: left;
  width: 70%;
}

.Notes ul {
  margin: 20px 0px;
  padding: 0;
  list-style: none;
}

.Notes ul li {
  background-color: #fff;
  border: 1px solid #ddd;
```

```
    display: flex;
    justify-content: space-between;
    margin-bottom: -1px;
    padding: 10px 15px;
    position: relative;
  }
```

File: src/components/Notes/Notes.css

6. If you run the application, you will see something like this:

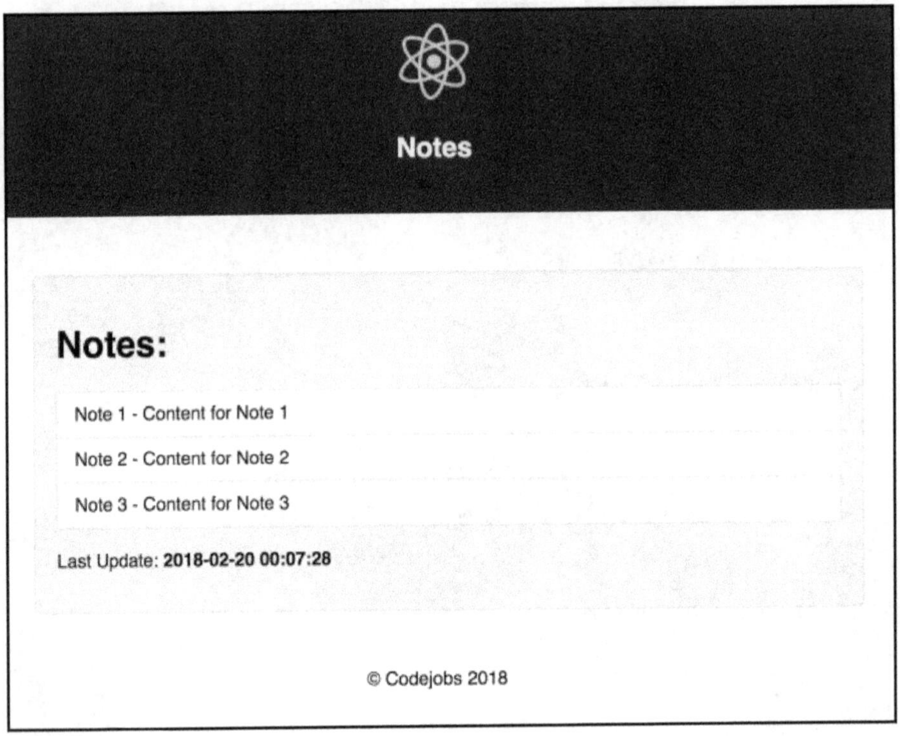

7. After 10 seconds you will see this:

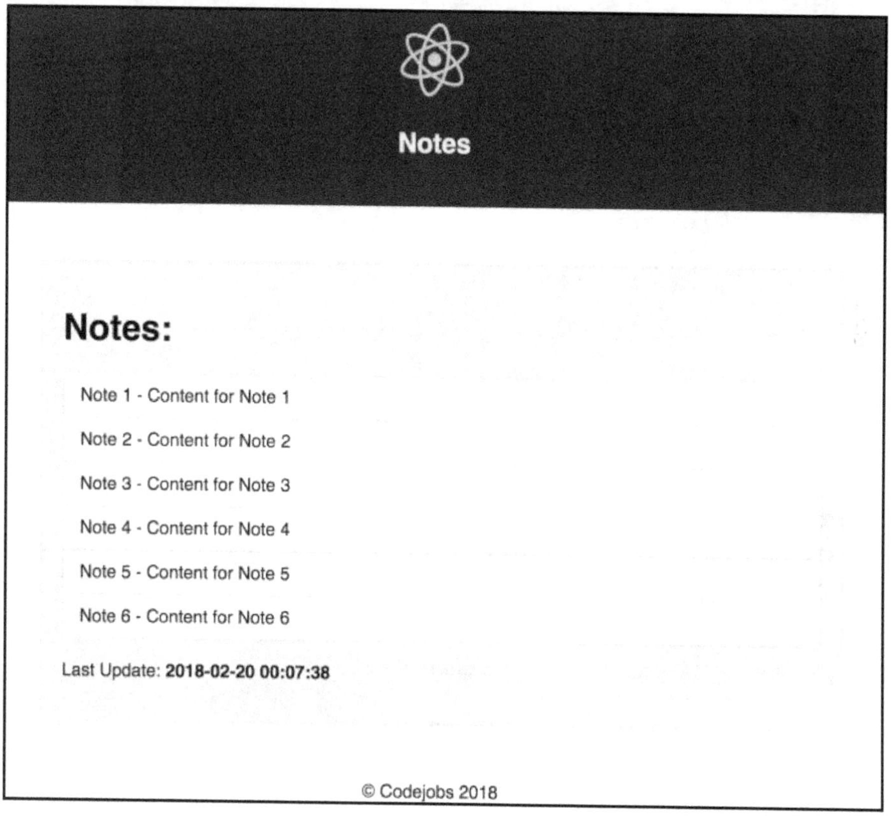

8. As you can see, the Last Update date has changed from **2018-02-20 00:07:28** to **2018-02-20 00:07:38** (10 seconds later).
9. `componentWillUnmount`: This is the last method to be called immediately before the component is removed from the DOM. Generally, is used to perform a clean-up for any DOM elements or timers created by the `componentWillMount` method. Let's modify our code a little bit to be able to call this method. In our `Notes` component, you can add this code after the `render` method:

```
    componentWillUnmount() {
      console.log('Hasta la vista baby!');
      document.body.style = 'background: black;';
      document.getElementById('unmountMessage').style.color =
'white';
    }
```

10. We need to modify our `index.html` file to manually include a button that won't be part of React:

```
<body>
  <div id="root"></div>

  <div id="unmountMessage">There is no mounted component!</div>

  <button
    id="unmount"
    style="margin:0
auto;display:block;background:red;color:white;"
  >
    Unmount
  </button>
</body>
```

File: public/index.html

11. And then, in our `index.js` file, where we are rendering our `<App />` component, let's add some extra code (we need actually to remove the element from the DOM):

```
import React from 'react';
import ReactDOM from 'react-dom';
import './index.css';
import App from './components/App';
import registerServiceWorker from './registerServiceWorker';

const unmountButton = document.getElementById('unmount');

// Is not very common to remove a Component from the DOM,
// but this will be just to understand how
// componentWillUnmount works.
function unmount() {
  ReactDOM.unmountComponentAtNode(
    document.getElementById('root')
  );
  document.getElementById('unmountMessage')
    .style.display = 'block';
  unmountButton.remove();
}

unmountButton.addEventListener('click', unmount);

document.getElementById('unmountMessage')
  .style.display = 'none';
```

```
ReactDOM.render(<App />, document.getElementById('root'));
registerServiceWorker();
```

File: src/index.js

12. With this, we will have a hideous red button at the bottom of our page, and when we click it, we are going to unmount our component. The background will go black, and we will display the text "**There is no mounted component!**", and the console will display **Hasta la vista baby!**:

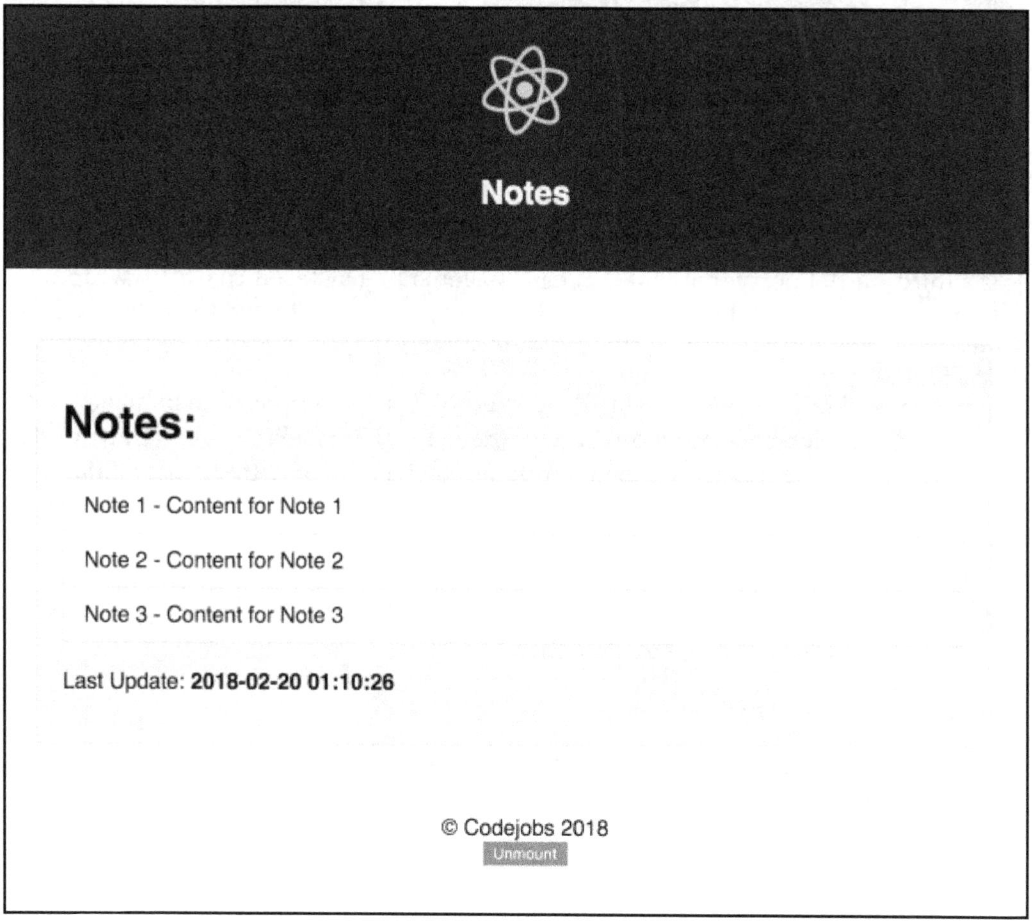

13. After you click the button, you will see this:

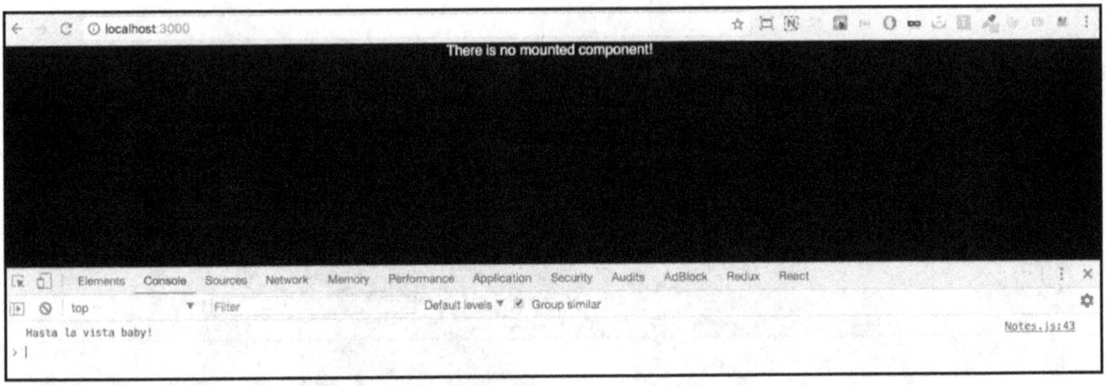

C3.js chart – implementing componentDidUpdate

C3.js is a third-party library that makes it easy to generate D3-based charts by wrapping the code required to construct the entire chart. That means you don't need to write any D3 code anymore:

1. `componentDidUpdate`: This React method is normally used to manage third-party UI elements and interact with the native UI. When we use a third-party library such as C3.js, we need to update the UI library with the new data. Install C3.js with npm:

```
npm install c3
```

2. After we install C3.js, we need to add the C3 CSS file to our `index.html`. For now, we can use the CDN they provide:

```
<!-- Add this on the <head> tag -->
<link
href="https://cdnjs.cloudflare.com/ajax/libs/c3/0.4.10/c3.min.css"
rel="stylesheet" />
```

File: public/index.html

3. Now we can create our `Chart` component:

```
import React, { Component } from 'react';
import c3 from 'c3';
import './Chart.css';

class Chart extends Component {
  componentDidMount() {
    // When the component mounts the first time we update
    // the chart.
    this.updateChart();
  }

  componentDidUpdate() {
    // When we receive a new prop then we update the chart again.
    this.updateChart();
  }

  updateChart() {
    c3.generate({
      bindto: '#chart',
      data: {
        columns: this.props.columns,
        type: this.props.chartType
      }
    });
  }

  render() {
    return <div id="chart" />;
  }
}

export default Chart;
```

File: src/components/Chart/Chart.js

4. As you can see, we are executing the `updateChart` method on `componentDidUpdate`, which is executed every time the user receives a new prop from `App.js`. Let's add some logic that we need in our `App.js` file:

```
import React, { Component } from 'react';
import Chart from './Chart/Chart';
import Header from '../shared/components/layout/Header';
import Content from '../shared/components/layout/Content';
import Footer from '../shared/components/layout/Footer';
import './App.css';

class App extends Component {
  constructor(props) {
    super(props);

    this.state = {
      chartType: 'line'
    };

    this.columns = [
      ['BTC', 3000, 6000, 10000, 15000, 13000, 11000],
      ['ETH', 2000, 3000, 5000, 4000, 3000, 940],
      ['XRP', 100, 200, 300, 500, 400, 300],
    ];
  }

  setBarChart = () => {
    this.setState({
      chartType: 'bar'
    });
  }

  setLineChart = () => {
    this.setState({
      chartType: 'line'
    });
  }

  render() {
    return (
      <div className="App">
        <Header title="Charts" />

        <Content>
          <Chart
            columns={this.columns}
```

```
            chartType={this.state.chartType}
          />

          <p>
            Chart Type
            <button onClick={this.setBarChart}>Bar</button>
            <button onClick={this.setLineChart}>Line</button>
          </p>
        </Content>

        <Footer />
      </div>
    );
  }
}

export default App;
```

File: src/components/App.js

5. Now let's add some basic styles to our `Chart` component:

```
p {
  text-align: center;
}

button {
  background: #159fff;
  border: none;
  color: white;
  margin-left: 1em;
  padding: 0.5em 2em;
  text-transform: uppercase;
  &:hover {
    background: darken(#159fff, 5%);
  }
}

#chart {
  background: #fff;
  width: 90%;
  margin: 1em auto;
}
```

File: src/components/Chart.css

6. In this case, we are creating some charts to display information about the most important cryptocurrencies today (BTC - Bitcoin, ETH - Ethereum and XRP - Ripple). This is how it should look:

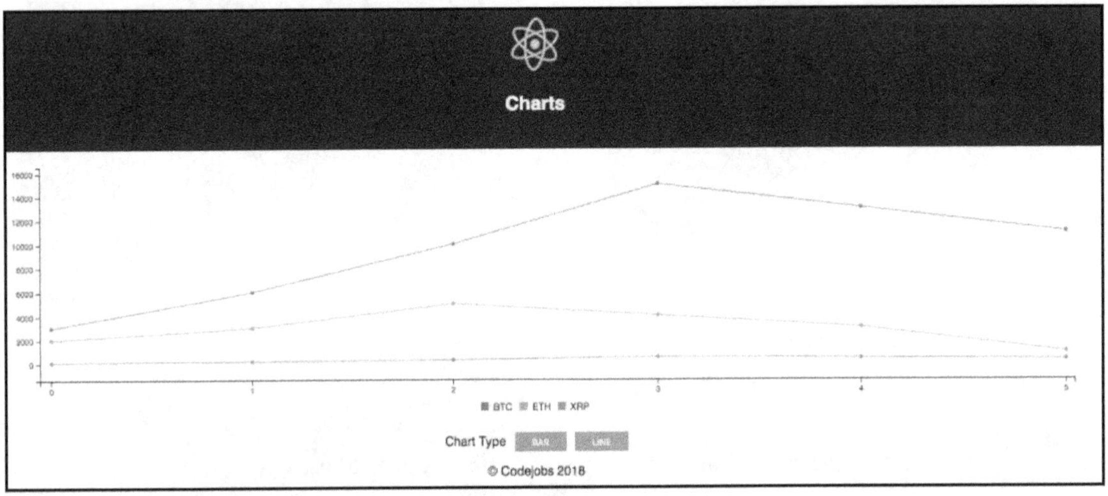

This image gives you an idea of how the line charts look like

7. We have two buttons to switch between chart types (bar or line). If we click on BAR, we should see this chart:

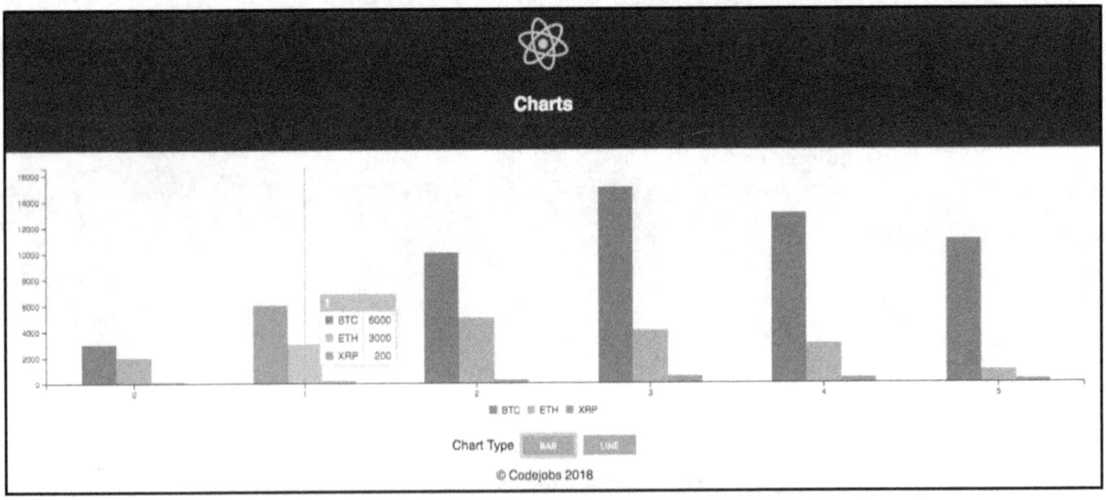

This image gives you an idea of how the bar charts look like.

8. If you remove the `componentDidUpdate` method from the `Chart` component, then when you press the buttons the chart is not going to update. This is because every time we need to refresh the data, we need to call the `c3.generate` method, and in this case, React's `componentDidUpdate` method is very useful.

Basic animation – implementing componentWillUpdate

In this example, we are going to learn how to use `componentWillUpdate`:

1. `componentWillUpdate` allows you to manipulate a component just before it receives new props or a new state. It is typically used for animations. Let's create a basic animation (fade in/fade out) to see how to use it:

```
import React, { Component } from 'react';
import './Animation.css';

class Animation extends Component {
  constructor() {
    super();

    this.state = {
      show: false
    };
  }

  componentWillUpdate(newProps, newState) {
    if (!newState.show) {
      document.getElementById('fade').style = 'opacity: 1;';
    } else {
      document.getElementById('fade').style = 'opacity: 0;';
    }
  }

  toggleCollapse = () => {
    this.setState({
      show: !this.state.show
    });
  }

  render() {
    return (
      <div className="Animation">
        <button onClick={this.toggleCollapse}>
          {this.state.show ? 'Collapse' : 'Expand'}
```

```
          </button>

          <div
            id="fade"
            className={
              this.state.show ? 'transition show' : 'transition'
            }
          >
            This text will disappear
          </div>
        </div>
      );
    }
  }

  export default Animation;
```

File: src/components/Animation/Animation.js

2. As you can see, we are validating the show state with `newState` and observe that it is true. Then we add `opacity 0`, and if it is false, we add `opacity 1`. An important thing I want to mention about `componentWillUpdate` is that you can't update the state (which means you are not able to use `this.setState`) in this method because it will cause another call to the same method, creating an infinite loop. Let's add some styles:

```
.Animation {
background: red;
 }
.Animation .transition {
transition: all 3s ease 0s;
color: white;
padding-bottom: 10px;
}
.Animation .transition.show {
padding-bottom: 300px;
background: red;
}
```

File: src/components/Animation/Animation.css

3. If you run the application, you will see this view:

4. After you click on the button, you will see an animation with the text fading out, and the red div will be expanded, giving you this result:

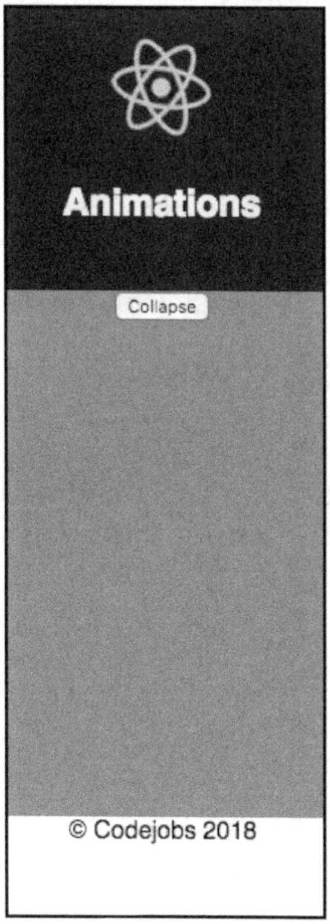

How it works...

As you can see with all those examples, React lifecycle methods are used to handle different scenarios in our application. In `Chapter 5`, *Mastering Redux*, we are going to see how to implement Redux and how the lifecycle methods can work with Redux states.

Understanding React Pure Components

Many people get confused by the difference between a Functional Component and a Pure Component. Most of them think they are the same, but this is not true. When we use a Pure Component, we need to import `PureComponent` from React:

```
import React, { PureComponent } from 'react';
```

If your React component's render method is "pure" (that means it renders the same result, given the same props and state), you can use this function to improve the performance of your application. A Pure Component performs a shallow comparison for the props and nextProps objects as well as the state and nextState objects. Pure components do not include the `shouldComponentUpdate(nextProps, nextState)` method, and if we try to add it, we will get a warning from React.

```
▸Warning: Home has a method called shouldComponentUpdate(). shouldComponentUpdate should not be used when
 extending React.PureComponent. Please extend React.Component if shouldComponentUpdate is used.
```

In this recipe, we will create a basic example to understand how Pure Components works.

Getting ready

For this recipe, we need to install the Chrome extension React Developer Tools to do a simple debug in our application. In `Chapter 12`, Testing and Debugging, we will delve into this topic.

You can download React Developer Tools from `https://chrome.google.com/webstore/detail/react-developer-tools/fmkadmapgofadopljbjfkapdkoienihi`.

How to do it...

We will create a component where we will sum all the numbers entered in an input. We can take some of the last recipes to start from there:

1. The first thing we will do is to modify our `App.js` and include the Numbers component:

```
import React, { Component } from 'react';
import Numbers from './Numbers/Numbers';

import Header from '../shared/components/layout/Header';
import Content from '../shared/components/layout/Content';
import Footer from '../shared/components/layout/Footer';
import './App.css';

class App extends Component {
  render() {
    return (
      <div className="App">
        <Header title="Understanding Pure Components" />

        <Content>
          <Numbers />
        </Content>

        <Footer />
      </div>
    );
  }
}

export default App;
```

File: src/components/App.js

2. Now we will create the Numbers component:

```
// Dependencies
import React, { Component } from 'react';

// Components
import Result from './Result';

// Styles
import './Numbers.css';
```

```
class Numbers extends Component {
  state = {
    numbers: '', // Here we will save the input value
    results: []  // In this state we will save the results of the sums
  };

  handleNumberChange = e => {
    const { target: { value } } = e;

    // Converting the string value to array
    // "12345" => ["1", "2", "3", "4", "5"]
    const numbers = Array.from(value);

    // Summing all numbers from the array
    // ["1", "2", "3", "4", "5"] => 15
    const result = numbers.reduce((a, b) => Number(a) + Number(b), 0);

    // Updating the local state
    this.setState({
      numbers: value,
      results: [...this.state.results, result]
    });
  }

  render() {
    return (
      <div className="Numbers">
        <input
          type="number"
          value={this.state.numbers}
          onChange={this.handleNumberChange}
        />

        {/* Rendering the results array */}
        <ul>
          {this.state.results.map((result, i) => (
            <Result key={i} result={result} />
          ))}
        </ul>
      </div>
    )
  }
}

export default Numbers;
```

File: src/components/Numbers/Numbers.js

3. Then, let's create the Result component (as a Class Component):

```
import React, { Component } from 'react';

class Result extends Component {
  render() {
    return <li>{this.props.result}</li>;
  }
}

export default Result;
```

File: src/components/Numbers/Result.js

4. Finally, the styles:

```
.Numbers {
  padding: 30px;
}

.Numbers input[type=number]::-webkit-inner-spin-button,
.Numbers input[type=number]::-webkit-outer-spin-button {
  -webkit-appearance: none;
  margin: 0;
}

.Numbers input {
  width: 500px;
  height: 60px;
  font-size: 20px;
  outline: none;
  border: 1px solid #ccc;
  padding: 10px;
}

.Numbers ul {
  margin: 0 auto;
  padding: 0;
  list-style: none;
  width: 522px;
}

.Numbers ul li {
  border-top: 1px solid #ccc;
  border-left: 1px solid #ccc;
  border-right: 1px solid #ccc;
  padding: 10px;
}
```

```
.Numbers ul li:first-child {
  border-top: none;
}

.Numbers ul li:last-child {
  border-bottom: 1px solid #ccc;
}
```

File: src/components/Numbers/Numbers.css

How it works...

If you run the application, you will see this:

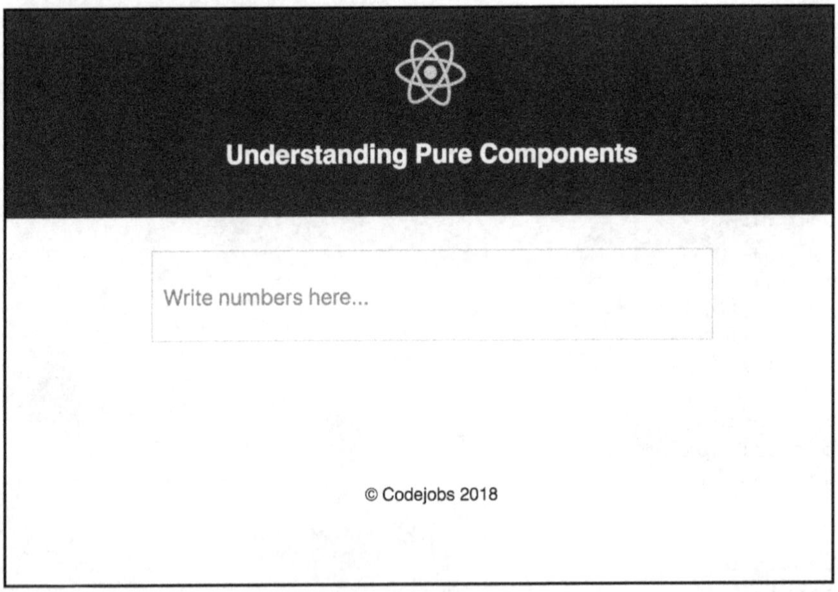

As you can see, we are using an input with type number, which means we will only accept numbers if you start writing numbers (1, then 2, then 3, and such), you will see the results of the sum on each row (0 + 1 = **1**, 1 + 2 = **3**, 3 + 3 = **6**).

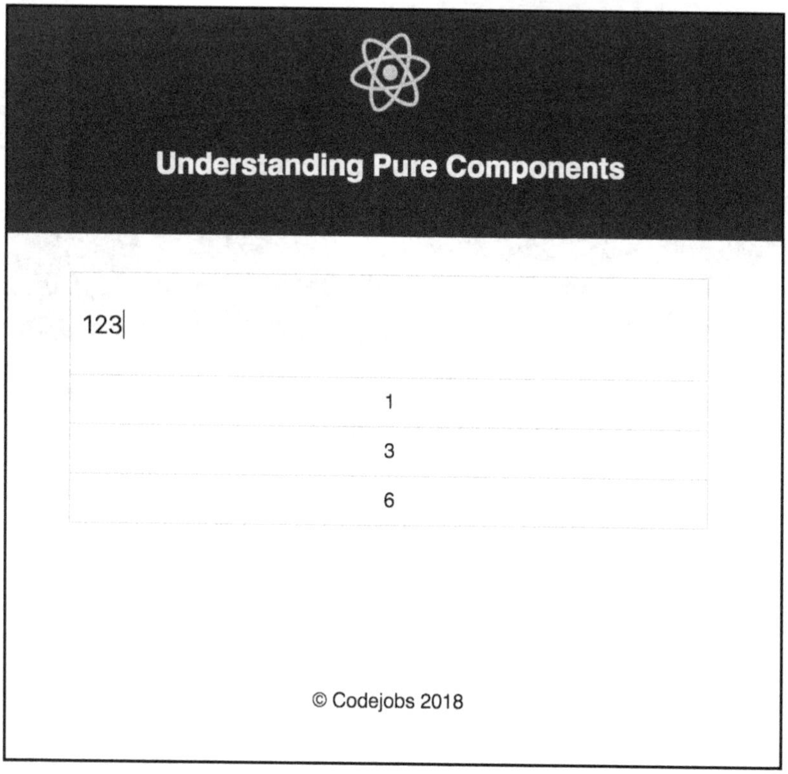

Probably this looks very simple to you, but if let's inspect the application using React Developer Tools, we need to enable the Highlight Updates option.

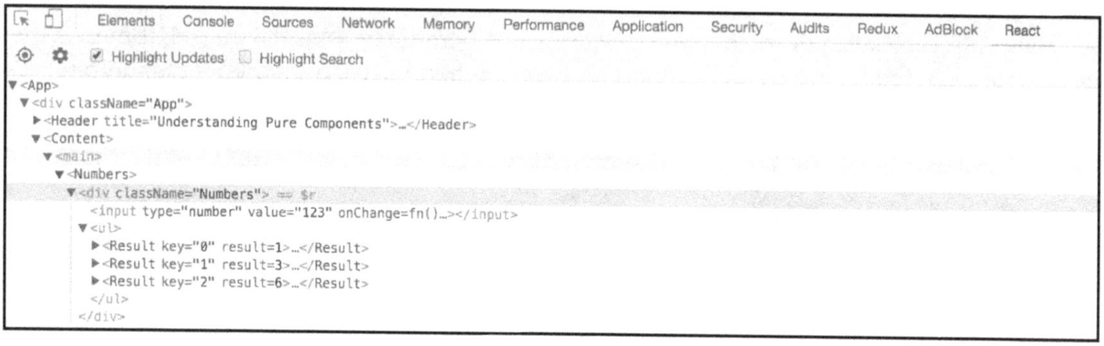

After this, start writing multiple numbers in the input (quickly), and you will see all the renders that React is performing.

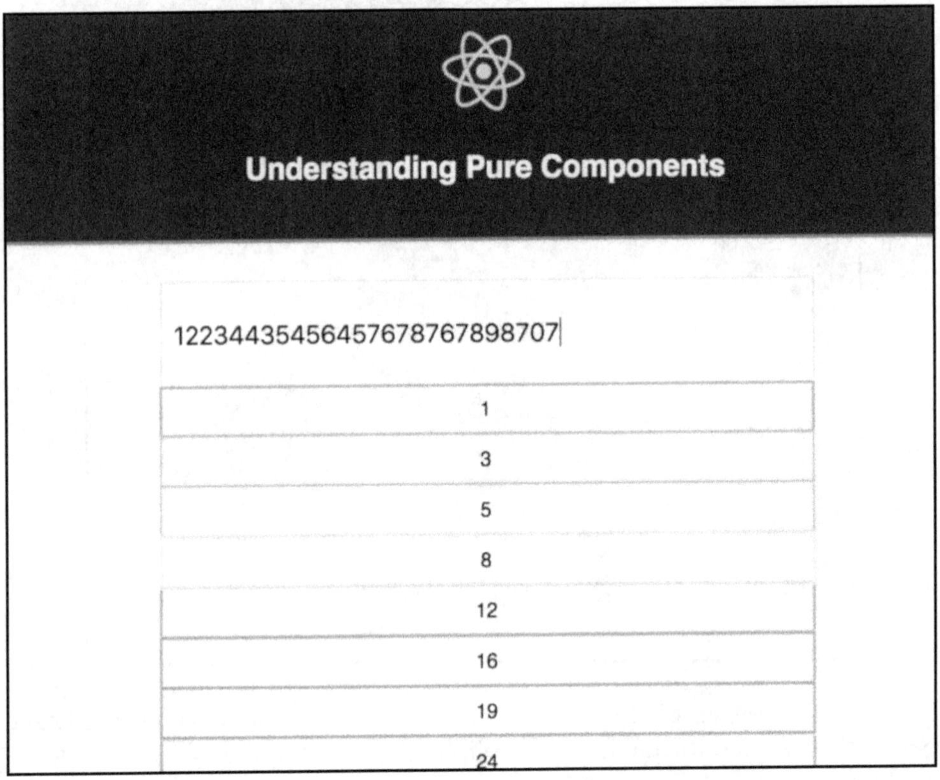

As you can see, React is doing a lot of renderings. When the highlights are red, it means the performance of that component is not good. Here's when Pure Components will help us; let's migrate our Result component to be a Pure Component:

```
import React, { PureComponent } from 'react';

class Result extends PureComponent {
  render() {
    return <li>{this.props.result}</li>;
  }
}

export default Result;
```

File: src/components/Numbers/Result.js

Now if we try to do the same with the numbers, let's see the difference.

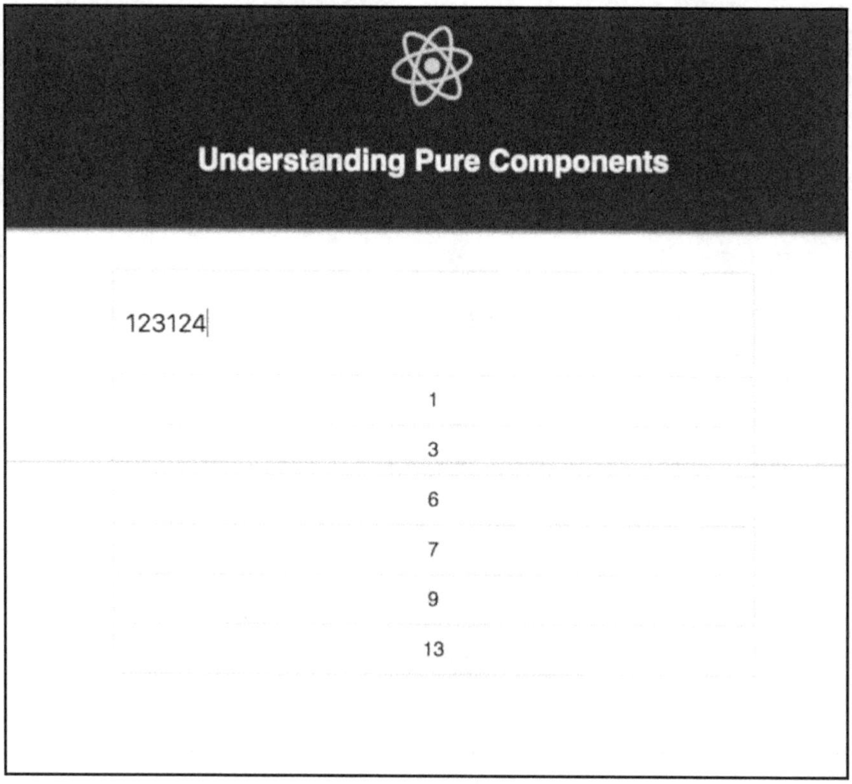

As you can see, with the Pure Component React, do less renders in comparison to a Class Component. Probably now you think that if we use a Stateless component instead of a Pure Component, the result will be the same. Unfortunately, this won't happen; if you want to verify this, let's change the Result component again and convert it into a Functional Component.:

```
import React from 'react';

const Result = props => <li>{props.result}</li>;

export default Result;
```

File: src/components/Numbers/Result.js

Even the code is less, but let's see what happen with the renders.

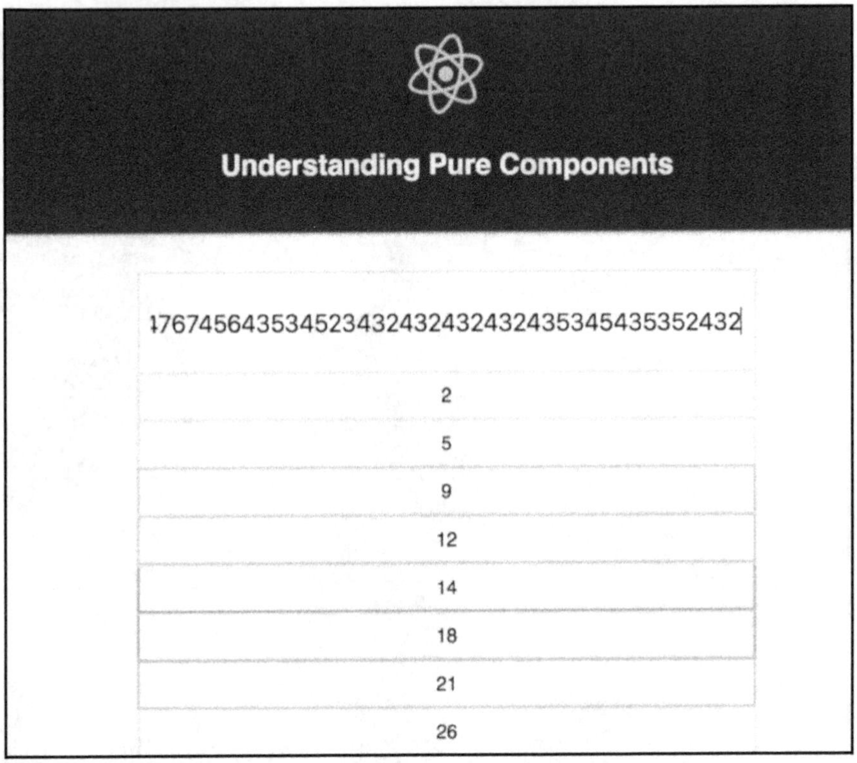

As you can see, the result is the same as the Class Component, which means not all the time using a Stateless component necessary will help us improve the performance of our application. If you have components that you consider are pure, consider converting them into Pure components.

Preventing XSS vulnerabilities in React

In this recipe, we are going to learn about cross-site scripting (XSS) vulnerabilities in React. XSS attacks are widespread in web applications, and some developers are still not aware of this. XSS attacks are malicious scripts that are injected into the DOM of unprotected web applications. The risks can vary with each application. It could just be an innocent alert script injection or, worse, someone can get access to your cookies and steal your private credentials (passwords), for example.

Let's create an XSS component to start playing around a little bit with some XSS attacks. We are going to have a response variable that is simulating a response from a real server, and we will simulate that we are using Redux's initial state (we are going to see Redux in `Chapter 5`, *Mastering Redux*).

How to do it...

We will now see how to create our XSS component:

1. Create an XSS component:

```
import React, { Component } from 'react';

// Let's suppose this response is coming from a service and have
// some XSS attacks in the content...
const response = [
  {
    id: 1,
    title: 'My blog post 1...',
    content: '<p>This is <strong>HTML</strong> code</p>'
  },
  {
    id: 2,
    title: 'My blog post 2...',
    content: `<p>Alert: <script>alert(1);</script></p>`
  },
  {
    id: 3,
    title: 'My blog post 3...',
    content: `
      <p>
     <img onmouseover="alert('This site is not secure');"
     src="attack.jpg" />
      </p>
    `
```

```
  }
];

// Let's suppose this is our initialState of Redux
// which is injected to the DOM...
const initialState = JSON.stringify(response);

class Xss extends Component {
  render() {
    // Parsing the JSON string to an actual object...
    const posts = JSON.parse(initialState);
    // Rendering our posts...
    return (
      <div className="Xss">
        {posts.map((post, key) => (
          <div key={key}>
            <h2>{post.title}</h2>

            <p>{post.content}</p>
          </div>
        ))}
      </div>
    );
  }
}

export default Xss;
```

File: src/components/Xss/Xss.js

2. If you render this component, you will see something like this:

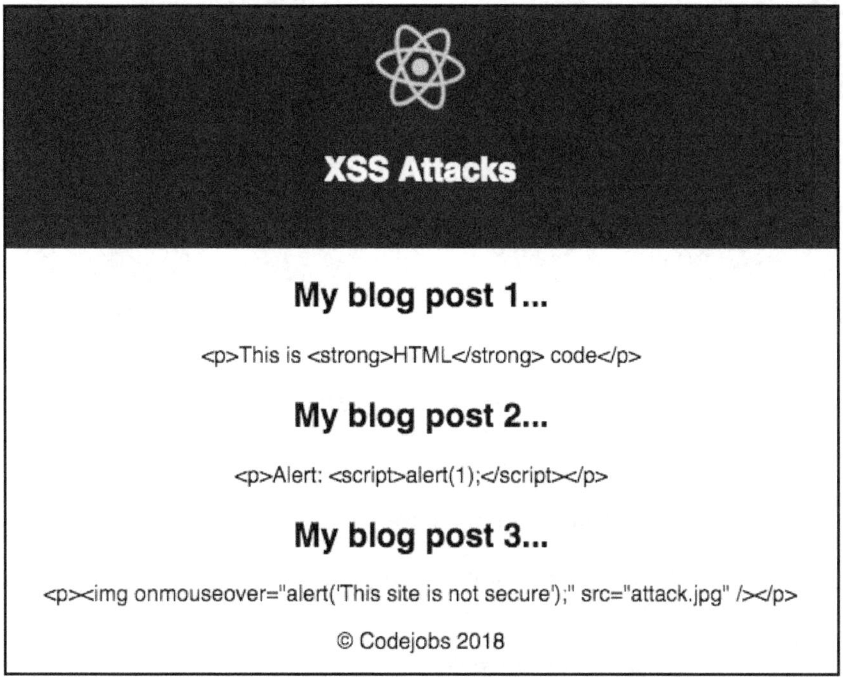

XSS Attacks
My blog post 1...
<p>This is <strong>HTML</strong> code</p>
My blog post 2...
<p>Alert: <script>alert(1);</script></p>
My blog post 3...
<p><img onmouseover="alert('This site is not secure');" src="attack.jpg" /></p>
© Codejobs 2018

3. As you can see, by default, React prevents us from injecting HTML code directly into our components. It is rendering the HTML as a string. This is good, but sometimes we need to insert HTML code in our components.
4. Implementing `dangerouslySetInnerHTML`: This prop probably scares you a little bit (maybe because it explicitly says the word danger!). I'm going to show you that this prop is not too bad if we know how to use it securely. Let's modify our previous code, and we are going to add this prop to see how the HTML is rendering it now:

```
import React, { Component } from 'react';
  // Let's suppose this response is coming from a service and have
  // some XSS attacks in the content...
  const response = [
    {
      id: 1,
      title: 'My blog post 1...',
      content: '<p>This is <strong>HTML</strong> code</p>'
    },
    {
```

```
      id: 2,
      title: 'My blog post 2...',
      content: `<p>Alert: <script>alert(1);</script></p>`
    },
    {
      id: 3,
      title: 'My blog post 3...',
      content: `
        <p>
          <img onmouseover="alert('This site is not secure');"
          src="attack.jpg" />
        </p>
      `
    }
];

// Let's suppose this is our initialState of Redux
// which is injected to the DOM...
const initialState = JSON.stringify(response);

class Xss extends Component {
  render() {
    // Parsing the JSON string to an actual object...
    const posts = JSON.parse(initialState);

    // Rendering our posts...
    return (
      <div className="Xss">
        {posts.map((post, key) => (
          <div key={key}>
            <h2>{post.title}</h2>
            <p><strong>Secure Code:</strong></p>
            <p>{post.content}</p>
            <p><strong>Insecure Code:</strong></p>
            <p
              dangerouslySetInnerHTML={{ __html: post.content }}
            />
          </div>
        ))}
      </div>
    );
  }
}

export default Xss;
```

File: src/components/Xss/Xss.js

5. Our site should now look like this:

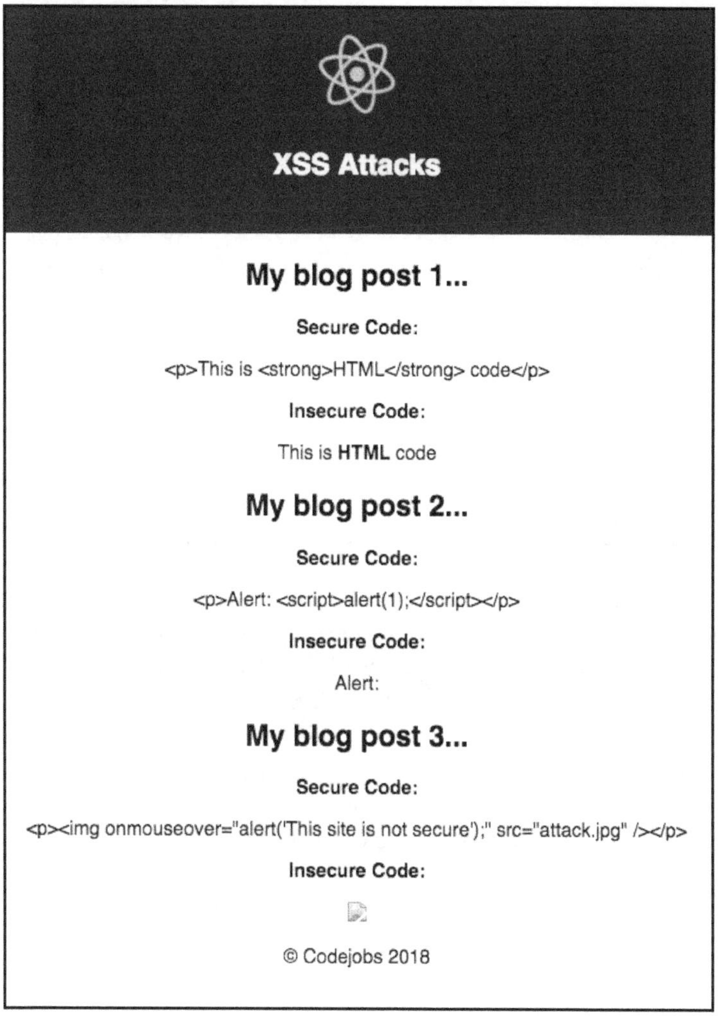

6. It is interesting, probably you thought that the content of "My blog post 2" will fire an alert in the browser but does not. If we inspect the code the alert script is there.

```
▼<div class="Xss">
  ▶<div>…</div>
  ▼<div>
     <h2>My blog post 2...</h2>
    ▶<p>…</p>
     <p><p>Alert: <script>alert(1);</script></p></p>
    ▶<p>…</p>
    ▼<p>
      ▼<p>
          "Alert: "
          <script>alert(1);</script>
        </p>
     </p>
  </div>
  ▶<div>…</div>
 </div>
```

7. Even if we use `dangerouslySetInnerHTML`, React protects us from malicious scripts injections, but it is not secure enough for us to relax on the security aspect of our site. Now let's see the issue with **My blog post 3** content. The code `<img onmouseover="alert('This site is not secure');" src="attack.jpg" />` is not directly using a `<script>` tag to inject a malicious code, but is using an `img` tag with an event (`onmouseover`). So, if you were happy about React's protection, we can see that this XSS attack will be executed if we move the mouse over the image:

localhost:3000 Says
This site is not secure
OK
My blog post 1...
Secure Code:
<p>This is <strong>HTML</strong> code</p>
Insecure Code:
This is HTML code
My blog post 2...
Secure Code:
<p>Alert: <script>alert(1);</script></p>
Insecure Code:
Alert:
My blog post 3...
Secure Code:
<p><img onmouseover="alert('This site is not secure');" src="attack.jpg" /></p>
Insecure Code:
© Codejobs 2018

8. **Removing XSS attacks**: This is kind of scary, right? But as I said at the beginning of this recipe, there is a secure way to use dangerouslySetInnerHTML and, yes, as you may be thinking right now, we need to clean our code of malicious scripts before we render it with dangerouslySetInnerHTML. The next script will take care of removing `<script>` tags and events from tags, but of course, you can modify this depending on the security level you want to have:

```
import React, { Component } from 'react';

// Let's suppose this response is coming from a service and have
// some XSS attacks in the content...
const response = [
  {
    id: 1,
    title: 'My blog post 1...',
    content: '<p>This is <strong>HTML</strong> code</p>'
  },
  {
    id: 2,
    title: 'My blog post 2...',
    content: `<p>Alert: <script>alert(1);</script></p>`
  },
  {
    id: 3,
    title: 'My blog post 3...',
    content: `
      <p>
        <img onmouseover="alert('This site is not secure');"
        src="attack.jpg" />
      </p>
    `
  }
];

// Let's suppose this is our initialState of Redux
// which is injected to the DOM...
const initialState = JSON.stringify(response);

const removeXSSAttacks = html => {
  const SCRIPT_REGEX =
/<script\b[^<]*(?:(?!<\/script>)<[^<]*)*<\/script>/gi;

  // Removing the <script> tags
  while (SCRIPT_REGEX.test(html)) {
    html = html.replace(SCRIPT_REGEX, '');
  }
```

```
  // Removing all events from tags...
  html = html.replace(/ on\w+="[^"]*"/g, '');

  return {
    __html: html
  }
};

class Xss extends Component {
  render() {
    // Parsing the JSON string to an actual object...
    const posts = JSON.parse(initialState);

    // Rendering our posts...
    return (
      <div className="Xss">
        {posts.map((post, key) => (
          <div key={key}>
            <h2>{post.title}</h2>
            <p><strong>Secure Code:</strong></p>
            <p>{post.content}</p>
            <p><strong>Insecure Code:</strong></p>
            <p
              dangerouslySetInnerHTML=
            {removeXSSAttacks(post.content)}
            />
          </div>
        ))}
      </div>
    );
  }
}

export default Xss;
```

File: src/components/Xss/Xss.js

9. If we look at the code now, we will see that now our render is more secure:

```
    <h2>My blog post 2...</h2>
  ▶<p>…</p>
    <p><p>Alert: <script>alert(1);</script></p></p>
  ▶<p>…</p>
  ▼<p>
      <p>Alert: </p>
    </p>
  </div>
▼<div>
    <h2>My blog post 3...</h2>
  ▶<p>…</p>
    <p><p><img onmouseover="alert('This site is not secure');" src="attack.jpg" /></p></p>
  ▶<p>…</p>
  ▼<p>
    ▼<p>
        <img src="attack.jpg">
      </p>
    </p>
```

10. **The problem with JSON.stringify**: So far, we have learned how to inject HTML code into a React component with `dangerouslySetInnerHTML`, but there is another potential security issue using JSON.stringify. If we have an XSS attack (`<script>` tag inside the content) in our response and then we use JSON.stringify to convert the object to a string, the HTML tags are not encoded. That means that if we inject the string into our HTML (like Redux does with the initial state), we will have a potential security issue. The output of `JSON.stringify(response)` is this:

```
    [
        {"id":1,"title":"My blog post 1...","content":"<p>This is
<strong>HTML</strong> code</p>"},
        {"id":2,"title":"My blog post 2...","content":"<p>Alert:
<script>alert(1);</script></p>"},
        {"id":3,"title":"My blog post 3...","content":"<p><img
onmouseover=\"alert('This site is not secure');\"
src=\"attack.jpg\" /></p>"}
    ]
```

11. As you can see, all the HTML is exposed without any encoding characters, and that is a problem. But how we can fix this? We need to install a package called `serialize-javascript`:

```
npm install serialize-javascript
```

12. Instead of using `JSON.stringify`, we need to serialize the code like this:

```
import serialize from 'serialize-javascript';

// Let's suppose this response is coming from a service and have
// some XSS attacks in the content...
const response = [
  {
    id: 1,
    title: 'My blog post 1...',
    content: '<p>This is <strong>HTML</strong> code</p>'
  },
  {
    id: 2,
    title: 'My blog post 2...',
    content: `<p>Alert: <script>alert(1);</script></p>`
  },
  {
    id: 3,
    title: 'My blog post 3...',
    content: `<p><img onmouseover="alert('This site is not
    secure');" src="attack.jpg" /></p>`
  }
];

// Let's suppose this is our initialState of Redux which is
// injected to the DOM...
const initialState = serialize(response);
console.log(initialState);
```

13. The output of the console is as follows:

```
   [
      {"id":1,"title":"My blog post
1...","content":"\u003Cp\u003EThis is
\u003Cstrong\u003EHTML\u003C\u002Fstrong\u003E
code\u003C\u002Fp\u003E"},
      {"id":2,"title":"My blog post
2...","content":"\u003Cp\u003EAlert:
\u003Cscript\u003Ealert(1);\u003C\u002Fscript\u003E\u003C\u002Fp\u0
03E"},
      {"id":3,"title":"My blog post
3...","content":"\u003Cp\u003E\u003Cimg onmouseover=\"alert('This
site is not secure');\" src=\"attack.jpg\"
\u002F\u003E\u003C\u002Fp\u003E"}
   ]
```

14. Now that we have our code with HTML entities (encoded) instead of directly having HTML tags, and the good news is that we can use `JSON.parse` to convert this string again into our original object. Our component should look like this:

```
import React, { Component } from 'react';
import serialize from 'serialize-javascript';

// Let's suppose this response is coming from a service and have
// some XSS attacks in the content...
const response = [
  {
    id: 1,
    title: 'My blog post 1...',
    content: '<p>This is <strong>HTML</strong> code</p>'
  },
  {
    id: 2,
    title: 'My blog post 2...',
    content: `<p>Alert: <script>alert(1);</script></p>`
  },
  {
    id: 3,
    title: 'My blog post 3...',
    content: `<p><img onmouseover="alert('This site is not
secure');"
    src="attack.jpg" /></p>`
  }
];

// Let's suppose this is our initialState of Redux which is
// injected to the DOM...
const secureInitialState = serialize(response);
// const insecureInitialState = JSON.stringify(response);

console.log(secureInitialState);

const removeXSSAttacks = html => {
  const SCRIPT_REGEX =
/<script\b[^<]*(?:(?!<\/script>)<[^<]*)*<\/script>/gi;

  // Removing the <script> tags
  while (SCRIPT_REGEX.test(html)) {
    html = html.replace(SCRIPT_REGEX, '');
  }

  // Removing all events from tags...
  html = html.replace(/ on\w+="[^"]*"/g, '');
```

```
    return {
      __html: html
    }
  };

  class Xss extends Component {
    render() {
      // Parsing the JSON string to an actual object...
      const posts = JSON.parse(secureInitialState);

      // Rendering our posts...
      return (
        <div className="Xss">
          {posts.map((post, key) => (
            <div key={key}>
              <h2>{post.title}</h2>
              <p><strong>Secure Code:</strong></p>
              <p>{post.content}</p>
              <p><strong>Insecure Code:</strong></p>
              <p>
dangerouslySetInnerHTML={removeXSSAttacks(post.content)}
              />
            </div>
          ))}
        </div>
      );
    }
  }

  export default Xss;
```

File: src/components/Xss/Xss.js

How it works...

As you can see, XSS attacks are widespread, and many websites suffer from this problem without knowing it. There are other injections attacks, such as SQL injections, that could happen in an API if we don't take minimal security precautions.

There's more...

Here are some security recommendations:

- Always sanitize users' content that comes from forms.
- Always use `serialize` instead of `JSON.stringify`.
- Use `dangerouslySetInnerHTML` only when absolutely necessary.
- Do unit tests for your components, and try to cover all the possible XSS attacks (we are going to see unit tests in `Chapter 12`, *Testing and Debugging*).
- Always encrypt passwords with `sha1` and `md5`, and do not forget to add a salt value (for example, if the password is `abc123`, then your salt can be encrypted like this: `sha1(md5('$41tT3xt_abc123'))`.
- If you use cookies to store sensitive information (personal information and passwords mainly), you can save the cookie with Base64 to obfuscate the data.
- Add some protection to your API (security tokens) unless you need to be public. There is a recipe about security tokens in `Chapter 8`, *Creating an API with Node.js Using MongoDB and MySQL*.

3
Handling Events, Binding and Useful React Packages

In this chapter, the following recipes will be covered:

- Binding methods using the constructor versus using arrow functions
- Creating form elements with events
- Displaying information in a modal with react-popup
- Implementing Airbnb React/JSX Style Guide
- Updating our title and meta tags with React Helmet

Introduction

This chapter contains recipes related to handling events, binding methods in React and we will implement some of the most useful React packages.

Binding methods using the constructor versus using arrow functions

In this recipe, we are going to learn the two ways of binding methods in React: using the constructor and using arrow functions.

How to do it...

This recipe is straightforward, and the goal is to bind a method using the class constructor and using arrow functions:

1. Let's create a new component called `Calculator`. We will create a basic calculator with two inputs and one button. The skeleton of our component is as follows:

```
import React, { Component } from 'react';
import './Calculator.css';

class Calculator extends Component {
  constructor() {
    super();

    this.state = {
      number1: 0,
      number2: 0,
      result: 0
    };
  }

  render() {
    return (
      <div className="Calculator">
        <input
          name="number1"
          type="text"
          value={this.state.number1}
        />
        {' + '}
        <input
          name="number2"
          type="text"
          value={this.state.number2}
        />
        <p><button>=</button></p>
        <p className="result">{this.state.result}</p>
      </div>
    );
  }
}

export default Calculator;
```

File: src/components/Calculator/Calculator.js

2. Now we are going to add two new methods, one to handle the inputs (`onChange` event) and one to manage the result button (`onClick`). We can use the same `handleOnChange` method for both inputs. Since we have the names of the fields (which are the same as the state) we can dynamically update each state, and in the `handleResult` method, we just sum both numbers:

```
handleOnChange(e) {
  const { target: { value, name } } = e;

  this.setState({
    [name]: Number(value)
  });
}

handleResult(e) {
  this.setState({
    result: this.state.number1 + this.state.number2
  });
}
```

3. Now in our `render` method, we need to add the events to the inputs and the button:

```
render() {
  return (
    <div className="Calculator">
      <input
        onChange={this.handleOnChange}
        name="number1"
        type="text"
        value={this.state.number1}
      />
      {' + '}
      <input
        onChange={this.handleOnChange}
        name="number2"
        type="text"
        value={this.state.number2}
      />
      <p>
        <button onClick={this.handleResult}>=</button>
      </p>
      <p className="result">{this.state.result}</p>
    </div>
  );
}
```

4. Our CSS code for this is as follows:

```
.Calculator {
  margin: 0 auto;
  padding: 50px;
}

.Calculator input {
  border: 1px solid #eee;
  font-size: 16px;
  text-align: center;
  height: 50px;
  width: 100px;
}

.Calculator button {
  background: #0072ff;
  border: none;
  color: #fff;
  font-size: 16px;
  height: 54px;
  width: 150px;
}

.Calculator .result {
  border: 10px solid red;
  background: #eee;
  margin: 0 auto;
  font-size: 24px;
  line-height: 100px;
  height: 100px;
  width: 100px;
}
```

File: src/components/Calculator/Calculator.css

5. If you run the application right now, you will see that if you try to write something in the inputs or you click on the button, you will get an error such as this:

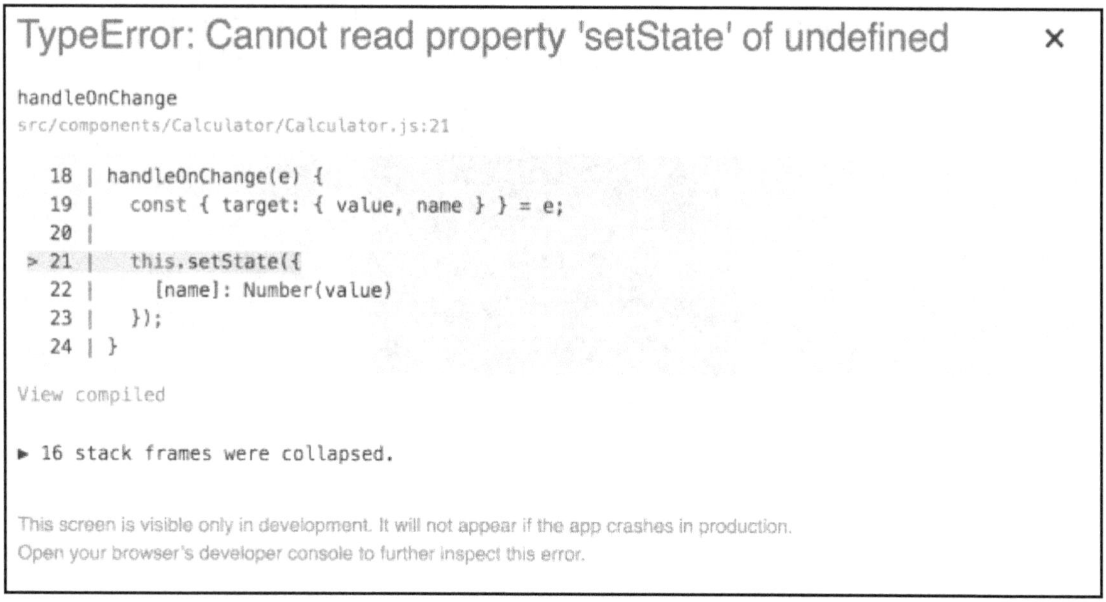

TypeError: Cannot read property 'setState' of undefined
handleOnChange
src/components/Calculator/Calculator.js:21
18 | handleOnChange(e) {
19 | const { target: { value, name } } = e;
20 |
> 21 | this.setState({
22 | [name]: Number(value)
23 | });
24 | }
View compiled
▶ 16 stack frames were collapsed.
This screen is visible only in development. It will not appear if the app crashes in production.
Open your browser's developer console to further inspect this error.

6. The reason is that we need to bind those methods to the class to have access to it. Let's bind our methods first using our constructor:

```
constructor() {
  super();

  this.state = {
    number1: 0,
    number2: 0,
    result: 0
  };

  // Binding methods
  this.handleOnChange = this.handleOnChange.bind(this);
  this.handleResult = this.handleResult.bind(this);
}
```

7. Using the constructor to bind the methods is good if you want to list all of them on the top of the component. If you look at the `Calculator` component, it should look like this:

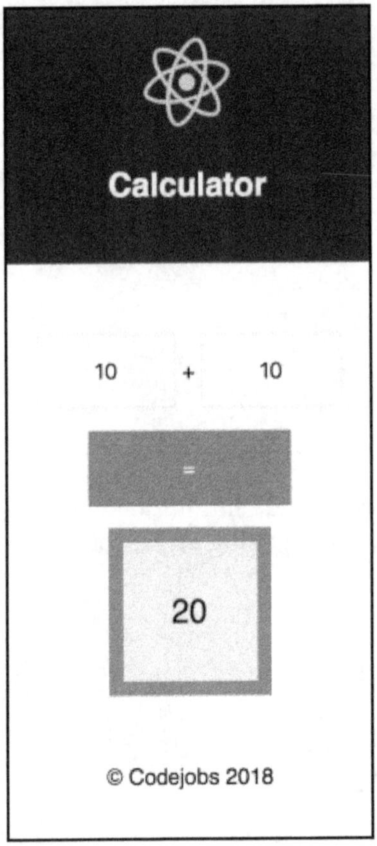

8. Now let's use arrow functions to automatically bind our methods instead of doing it on the constructor. For this you need to remove your bindings methods in the constructor and change the `handleOnChange` and `handleResult` methods to arrow functions:

```
constructor() {
  super();

  this.state = {
    number1: 0,
    number2: 0,
    result: 0
```

```
    };
  }
  // Changing this method to be an arrow function
  handleOnChange = e => {
    const { target: { value, name } } = e;

    this.setState({
      [name]: Number(value)
    });
  }
  // Changing this method to be an arrow function
  handleResult = e => {
    this.setState({
      result: this.state.number1 + this.state.number2
    });
  }
```

9. You will get the same result. I prefer arrow functions to bind methods because you use less code and you don't need to add the methods to the constructor manually.

How it works...

As you can see, you have two options to bind methods in your React components. The constructor option is most commonly used at the moment, but the arrow functions are getting more popular. You decide which binding option you like the most.

Creating form elements with events

You may have noticed in the previous chapter that we used some simple forms with events, but in this recipe, we will see this topic in more depth. In `Chapter 6`, *Creating Forms with Redux Form*, we are going to learn how to handle forms with Redux Form.

How to do it...

Let's create a new component called `Person`:

1. The skeleton we are going to use for this component is as follows:

```
import React, { Component } from 'react';
import './Person.css';

class Person extends Component {
  constructor() {
    super();

    this.state = {
      firstName: '',
      lastName: '',
      email: '',
      phone: ''
    };
  }

  render() {
    return (
      <div className="Person">

      </div>
    );
  }
}

export default Person;
```

File: src/components/Person/Person.js

2. Let's add the `firstName`, `lastName`, `email`, and `phone` fields to our form. The `render` method should look like this:

```
render() {
  return (
    <div className="Person">
      <form>
        <div>
          <p><strong>First Name:</strong></p>
          <p><input name="firstName" type="text" /></p>
        </div>

        <div>
```

```
            <p><strong>Last Name:</strong></p>
            <p><input name="lastName" type="text" /></p>
          </div>

          <div>
            <p><strong>Email:</strong></p>
            <p><input name="email" type="email" /></p>
          </div>

          <div>
            <p><strong>Phone:</strong></p>
            <p><input name="phone" type="tel" /></p>
          </div>

          <p>
            <button>Save Information</button>
          </p>
        </form>
      </div>
    );
  }
```

3. Let's use these CSS styles for our form:

```
  .Person {
    margin: 0 auto;
  }

  .Person form input {
    font-size: 16px;
    height: 50px;
    width: 300px;
  }

  .Person form button {
    background: #0072ff;
    border: none;
    color: #fff;
    font-size: 16px;
    height: 50px;
    width: 300px;
  }
```

File: src/components/Person/Person.css

4. If you run your application, you should see this view:

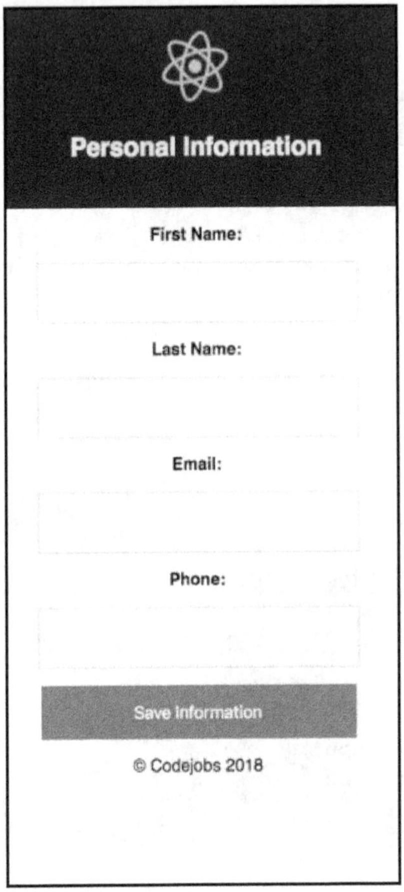

5. Let's use our local state in the inputs. The only way we can retrieve the values from the inputs in React is by connecting the value of each field to a specific local state like this:

```
render() {
  return (
    <div className="Person">
      <form>
        <div>
          <p><strong>First Name:</strong></p>
          <p>
            <input
              name="firstName"
```

```
                type="text"
                value={this.state.firstName}
              />
            </p>
          </div>

          <div>
            <p><strong>Last Name:</strong></p>
            <p>
              <input
                name="lastName"
                type="text"
                value={this.state.lastName}
              />
            </p>
          </div>

          <div>
            <p><strong>Email:</strong></p>
            <p>
              <input
                name="email"
                type="email"
                value={this.state.email}
              />
            </p>
          </div>

          <div>
            <p><strong>Phone:</strong></p>
            <p>
              <input
                name="phone"
                type="tel"
                value={this.state.phone}
              />
            </p>
          </div>

          <p>
            <button>Save Information</button>
          </p>
        </form>
      </div>
    );
  }
```

> **TIP:** If you try to type something, you will notice that you are not allowed to write anything, and this is because all the inputs are connected to the local state, and the only way we can re-render the typed text is by updating the local state.

6. As you can imagine, the only way we can update our local state is by detecting a change in our inputs, and that will happen when the user inputs something. Let's add a method for the `onChange` event:

```
handleOnChange = e => {
  const { target: { value } } = e;

  this.setState({
    firstName: value
  });
}
```

> Like I mentioned in the last recipe when we use an arrow function in our methods we are automatically binding the class to the method. Otherwise, you will need to bind the method in the constructor. In our `firstName` input, we need to call this method on the `onChange` method:

```
<input
  name="firstName"
  type="text"
  value={this.state.firstName}
  onChange={this.handleOnChange}
/>
```

7. But here we have a problem. If we have four fields, then you will probably think you need to create four different methods (one for each state), but there is a better way to solve this: to get the value of the input name within the `e` (`e.target.name`) object. In this way, we can update all the states with the same method. Our `handleOnChange` method should now look like this:

```
handleOnChange = e => {
  const { target: { value, name } } = e;

  this.setState({
    [name]: value
  });
}
```

8. With this `([name])` syntax in the object, we can update all the states we have in our forms dynamically. Now we need to add this method to the `onChange` of all the inputs. After this, you will be able to write into the inputs:

```
render() {
  return (
    <div className="Person">
      <form>
        <div>
          <p><strong>First Name:</strong></p>
          <p>
            <input
              name="firstName"
              type="text"
              value={this.state.firstName}
              onChange={this.handleOnChange}
            />
          </p>
        </div>

        <div>
          <p><strong>Last Name:</strong></p>
          <p>
            <input
              name="lastName"
              type="text"
              value={this.state.lastName}
              onChange={this.handleOnChange}
            />
          </p>
        </div>

        <div>
          <p><strong>Email:</strong></p>
          <p>
            <input
              name="email"
              type="email"
              value={this.state.email}
              onChange={this.handleOnChange}
            />
          </p>
        </div>

        <div>
          <p><strong>Phone:</strong></p>
          <p>
            <input
```

```
                name="phone"
                type="tel"
                value={this.state.phone}
                onChange={this.handleOnChange}
              />
            </p>
          </div>

          <p>
            <button>Save Information</button>
          </p>
        </form>
      </div>
    );
  }
```

9. All forms need to submit the information they have collected from the user. We need to use the `onSubmit` event of our form and call a `handleOnSubmit` method to retrieve all the input values through the local state:

```
handleOnSubmit = e => {
  // The e.preventDefault() method cancels the event if it is
  // cancelable, meaning that the default action that belongs to
  // the event won't occur.
  e.preventDefault();

  const { firstName, lastName, email, phone } = this.state;
  const data = {
    firstName,
    lastName,
    email,
    phone
  };
  // Once we have the data collected we can call a Redux Action
  // or process the data as we need it.
  console.log('Data:', data);
}
```

10. After we created this method we need to call it on the `onSubmit` event of the `form` tag:

```
<form onSubmit={this.handleOnSubmit}>
```

11. Now you can test this. Open your browser console, and when you write some values in the inputs you will be able to see the data:

```
Data:                                                                                    Person.js:37
▼{firstName: "Carlos", lastName: "Santana", email: "carlos@milkzoft.com", phone: "(222)-333-4444"}
   email: "carlos@milkzoft.com"
   firstName: "Carlos"
   lastName: "Santana"
   phone: "(222)-333-4444"
```

12. We need to validate the required fields. Let's suppose that the `firstName` and `lastName` fields are mandatory. If a user doesn't write a value in the fields, we want to add an error class to display a red border around the input. The first thing you need to do is to add a new local state for errors:

```
this.state = {
  firstName: '',
  lastName: '',
  email: '',
  phone: '',
  errors: {
    firstName: false,
    lastName: false
  }
};
```

13. You can add any fields you want to validate here, and the value is Boolean (`true` means there is an error, `false` means it is okay). Then, in the `handleOnSubmit` method, we need to update the state if we have an error:

```
handleOnSubmit = e => {
 // The e.preventDefault() method cancels the event if it is
 // cancelable, meaning that the default action that belongs to
 // event won't occur.
e.preventDefault();

  const { firstName, lastName, email, phone } = this.state;

  // If firstName or lastName is missing then we update the
  // local state with true
  this.setState({
    errors: {
      firstName: firstName === '',
      lastName: lastName === ''
    }
  });

  const data = {
    firstName,
    lastName,
    email,
```

```
    phone
  };

  // Once we have the data collected we can call a Redux Action
  // or process the data as we need it.
  console.log('Data:', data);
}
```

14. Now, in your `render` method you need to add a ternary validation in the `className` prop of the `firstName` and `lastName` fields, and if you want to be fancy you can also add an error message below the inputs:

```
render() {
  return (
    <div className="Person">
      <form onSubmit={this.handleOnSubmit}>
        <div>
          <p><strong>First Name:</strong></p>
          <p>
            <input
              name="firstName"
              type="text"
              value={this.state.firstName}
              onChange={this.handleOnChange}
              className={
                this.state.errors.firstName ? 'error' : ''
              }
            />
            {this.state.errors.firstName
              && (<div className="errorMessage">Required
            field</div>)}
          </p>
        </div>

        <div>
          <p><strong>Last Name:</strong></p>
          <p>
            <input
              name="lastName"
              type="text"
              value={this.state.lastName}
              onChange={this.handleOnChange}
              className={
                this.state.errors.lastName ? 'error' : ''
              }
            />
            {this.state.errors.lastName
              && <div className="errorMessage">Required
```

```
            field</div>}
          </p>
        </div>

        <div>
          <p><strong>Email:</strong></p>
          <p>
            <input
              name="email"
              type="email"
              value={this.state.email}
              onChange={this.handleOnChange}
            />
          </p>
        </div>

        <div>
          <p><strong>Phone:</strong></p>
          <p>
            <input name="phone" type="tel" value=
            {this.state.phone}
             onChange={this.handleOnChange} />
          </p>
        </div>

        <p>
          <button>Save Information</button>
        </p>
      </form>
    </div>
  );
}
```

15. The last step is to add the error classes, `.error` and `.errorMessage`:

```
.Person .error {
  border: 1px solid red;
}

.Person .errorMessage {
  color: red;
  font-size: 10px;
}
```

16. If you submit your form without `firstName` or `lastName` now, you will get this view:

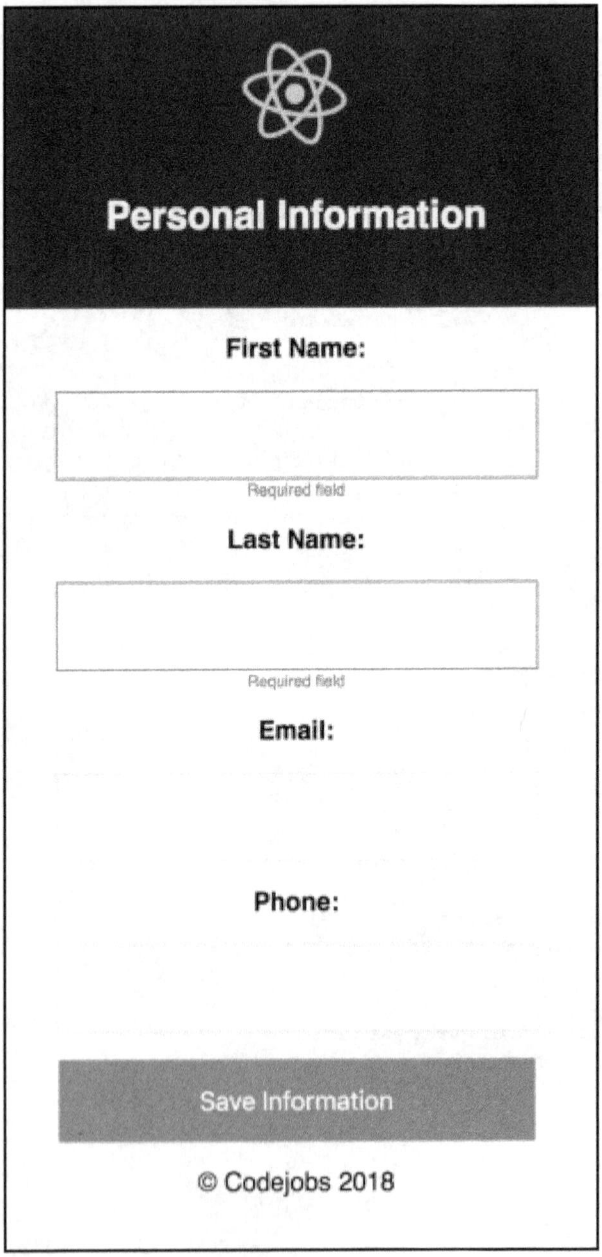

17. The full `Person` component should be like this:

```
import React, { Component } from 'react';
import './Person.css';

class Person extends Component {
  constructor() {
    super();

    this.state = {
      firstName: '',
      lastName: '',
      email: '',
      phone: '',
      errors: {
        firstName: false,
        lastName: false
      }
    };
  }

  handleOnChange = e => {
    const { target: { value, name } } = e;

    this.setState({
      [name]: value
    });
  }

  handleOnSubmit = e => {
    // The e.preventDefault() method cancels the event if it is
    // cancelable, meaning that the default action that belongs
    // to the event won't occur.
    e.preventDefault();

    const { firstName, lastName, email, phone } = this.state;

    // If firstName or lastName is missing we add an error class
    this.setState({
      errors: {
        firstName: firstName === '',
        lastName: lastName === ''
      }
    });

    const data = {
      firstName,
      lastName,
```

```
      email,
      phone
    };

    // Once we have the data collected we can call a Redux Action
    // or process the data as we need it.
    console.log('Data:', data);
  }

  render() {
    return (
      <div className="Person">
        <form onSubmit={this.handleOnSubmit}>
          <div>
            <p><strong>First Name:</strong></p>
            <p>
              <input
                name="firstName"
                type="text"
                value={this.state.firstName}
                onChange={this.handleOnChange}
                className={
                  this.state.errors.firstName ? 'error' : ''
                }
              />
              {this.state.errors.firstName
                && <div className="errorMessage">Required
              field</div>}
            </p>
          </div>

          <div>
            <p><strong>Last Name:</strong></p>
            <p>
              <input
                name="lastName"
                type="text"
                value={this.state.lastName}
                onChange={this.handleOnChange}
                className={
                  this.state.errors.lastName ? 'error' : ''
                }
              />
              {this.state.errors.lastName
                && <div className="errorMessage">Required
              field</div>}
            </p>
          </div>
```

```
              <div>
                <p><strong>Email:</strong></p>
                <p>
                  <input
                    name="email"
                    type="email"
                    value={this.state.email}
                    onChange={this.handleOnChange}
                  />
                </p>
              </div>

              <div>
                <p><strong>Phone:</strong></p>
                <p>
                  <input
                    name="phone"
                    type="tel"
                    value={this.state.phone}
                    onChange={this.handleOnChange}
                  />
                </p>
              </div>

              <p>
                <button>Save Information</button>
              </p>
            </form>
          </div>
        );
      }
    }

    export default Person;
```

File: src/components/Person/Person.js

How it works...

Forms are essential for any web application, and handling them with React is easy using local state, but it is not the only way to manage them. If your forms are complex, with multiple steps (are typically used on user registration), you probably need to keep the values throughout the entire process. In this scenario, it is painless to handle forms using Redux Form, which we are going to learn about in `Chapter 6`, *Creating Forms with Redux Form*.

There's more...

There are more events you can use in React:

Keyboard events:

- `onKeyDown` is executed when a key is depressed
- `onKeyPress` is executed after the key is released, but before `onKeyUp` is triggered
- `onKeyUp` is executed last after the key is pressed

Focus events:

- `onFocus` is executed when a control receives focus
- `onBlur` is executed when a control loses focus

Forms events:

- `onChange` is executed when the user changes the value in a form control
- `onSubmit` is a particular prop for `<form>` that is called when a button is pressed, or when the user hits the `return` key within a field

Mouse events:

- `onClick` is when the mouse button is pressed and released
- `onContextMenu` is when the right button is pressed
- `onDoubleClick` is when the user performs a double-click
- `onMouseDown` is when the mouse button is depressed
- `onMouseEnter` is when the mouse moves over an element or its children
- `onMouseLeave` is when the mouse leaves an element
- `onMouseMove` is when the mouse moves
- `onMouseOut` is when the mouse moves off an element or over one of its children
- `onMouseOver` is when the mouse moves over an element
- `onMouseUp` is when a mouse button is released

Drag and drop events:

- `onDrag`
- `onDragEnd`
- `onDragEnter`
- `onDragExit`
- `onDragLeave`
- `onDragOver`
- `onDragStart`
- `onDrop`

For drag and drop, events I recommend using the `react-dnd` (`https://github.com/react-dnd/react-dnd`) library.

Displaying information in a modal with react-popup

A modal is a dialog box/popup that is displayed over the current window, is suitable for almost all projects. In this recipe, we will learn how to implement a basic modal using the `react-popup` package.

Getting ready

For this recipe, you need to install `react-popup`. Let's do it with this command:

```
npm install react-popup
```

How to do it...

Using the last recipe's code, we are going to add a basic popup to display information about the person that we registered in the form:

1. Open your `App.jsx` file and import the `Popup` object from `react-popup`. For now, we are going to import `Popup.css` (the code is too large to put it in here, but you can copy and paste the CSS demo code from the code repository for this project: `Chapter03/Recipe3/popup/src/components/Popup.css`). Then, after `<Footer />` add the `<Popup />` component:

```
import React from 'react';
import Popup from 'react-popup';
import Person from './Person/Person';
import Header from '../shared/components/layout/Header';
import Content from '../shared/components/layout/Content';
import Footer from '../shared/components/layout/Footer';
import './App.css';
import './Popup.css';

const App = () => (
  <div className="App">
    <Header title="Personal Information" />

    <Content>
      <Person />
    </Content>

    <Footer />

    <Popup />
  </div>
);

export default App;
```

File: src/components/App.js

2. Now, in our `Person.js` file, we need to include the popup as well:

```
import React, { Component } from 'react';
import Popup from 'react-popup';
import './Person.css';
```

3. Let's modify our `handleOnSubmit` method to implement the popup. First, we need to validate that we are receiving at least the `firstName`, `lastName`, and `email` (phone will be optional). If we get all the necessary information, then we will create a popup and display the user's information. One of the things I like about `react-popup` is that it allows us to use JSX code in its content:

```
handleOnSubmit = e => {
  e.preventDefault();

  const {
    firstName,
    lastName,
    email,
    phone
  } = this.state;

  // If firstName or lastName is missing we add an error class
  this.setState({
    errors: {
      firstName: firstName === '',
      lastName: lastName === ''
    }
  });
  // We will display the popup just if the data is received...
  if (firstName !== '' && lastName !== '' && email !== '') {
    Popup.create({
      title: 'Person Information',
      content: (
        <div>
          <p><strong>Name:</strong> {firstName} {lastName}</p>
          <p><strong>Email:</strong> {email}</p>
          {phone && <p><strong>Phone:</strong> {phone}</p>}
        </div>
      ),
      buttons: {
        right: [{
          text: 'Close',
           action: popup => popup.close() // Closes the popup
        }],
      },
    });
  }
}
```

How it works...

If you did everything correctly, you should be able to see the popup like this:

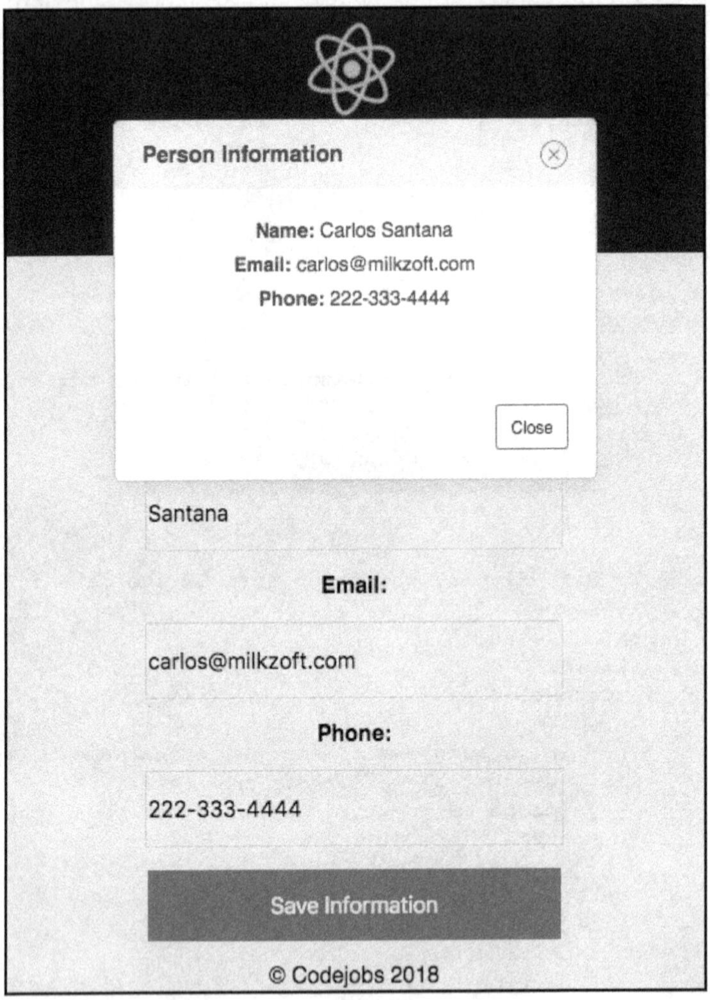

As you can see in the code, the phone is optional, so if we don't include it we won't render it:

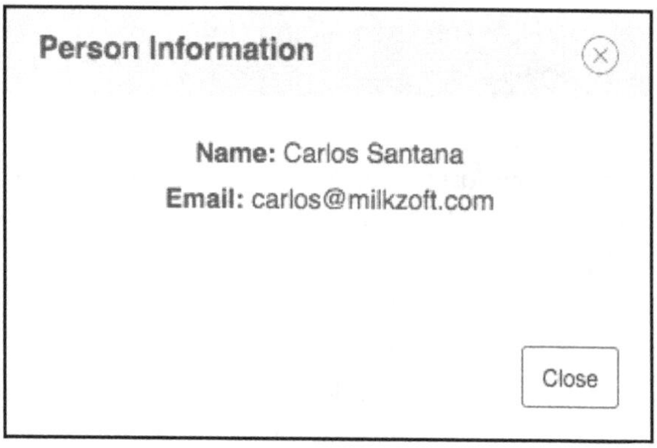

There's more...

`react-popup` provides configuration to execute an action. In our example, we used that action to close the popup when the user presses the `Close` button, but we can pass Redux actions to do other things, such as send some information or even add forms inside our popup.

Implementing Airbnb React/JSX Style Guide

Airbnb React/JSX Style Guide is the most popular style guide for coding in React. In this recipe, we are going to implement the ESLint with the Airbnb React/JSX Style Guide rules.

Getting ready

To implement the Airbnb React/JSX Style Guide, we need to install some packages, such as `eslint`, `eslint-config-airbnb`, `eslint-plugin-babel`, and `eslint-plugin-react`.

I don't like to force anyone to use a specific IDE, but I would like to recommend some of the best editors to work with React.

- **Atom** - `https://atom.io`
    - In my personal opinion, Atom is the best IDE for working with React. For this recipe, we are going to use Atom.
    - **Pros**:
        - MIT License (open source)
        - Easy to install and configure
        - Has a lot of plugins and themes
        - Works perfectly with React
        - Support for Mac, Linux, and Windows
        - You can use Nuclide to React Native (https://nuclide.io)
    - **Cons**:
        - It's slow compared with other IDEs (if you have 8 GB of RAM you should be fine)
- **Visual Studio Code** (VSC) - `https://code.visualstudio.com`
    - VSC is another good IDE for working with React.
    - **Pros**:
        - MIT License (open source)
        - Easy to install
        - It has a lot of plugins and themes.
        - Works perfectly with React
        - Support for Mac, Linux, and Windows
    - **Cons**:
        - Microsoft (I'm not a big fan of Microsoft)
        - Configuration can be confusing at the beginning
- **Sublime Text** - `https://www.sublimetext.com`
    - Sublime Text was my first love, but I have to accept that Atom has taken its place.
    - **Pros**:
        - Easy to install
        - Has a lot of plugins and themes
        - Support for Mac, Linux, and Windows

- **Cons**:
    - Is not free ($80 USD per license).
    - Is still not mature enough to work with React.
    - Some plugins are hard to configure.

Installing all the necessary packages:

```
npm install eslint eslint-config-airbnb eslint-plugin-react eslint-plugin-
jsx-a11y
```

There are some rules of Airbnb React/JSX Style Guide that I prefer not to use or change the default values a little bit, but it depends whether you keep them or remove them.

You can check all the ESLint rules on the official website (`https://eslint.org/docs/rules`) and all the special React ESLint rules at `https://github.com/yannickcr/eslint-plugin-react/tree/master/docs/rules`.

The rules that I prefer not to use or I prefer to change the default values of are as follows:

- `comma-dangle`: off
- `arrow-parens`: off
- `max-len`: 120
- `no-param-reassign`: off
- `function-paren-newline`: off
- `react/require-default-props`: off

How to do it...

To enable our ESLint, we need to create a `.eslintrc` file and add the rules we want to turn off:

1. Creating `.eslintrc` file. You need to create a new file called `.eslintrc` at the root level:

```
{
  "parser": "babel-eslint",
  "extends": "airbnb",
  "rules": {
    "arrow-parens": "off",
```

```
      "comma-dangle": "off",
      "function-paren-newline": "off",
      "max-len": [1, 120],
      "no-param-reassign": "off",
      "react/require-default-props": "off"
    }
  }
```

2. Add a script to run the linter. In your `package.json` file, you need to add a new script to run the linter:

```
{
  "name": "airbnb",
  "version": "0.1.0",
  "private": true,
  "engines": {
    "node": ">= 10.8"
  },
  "dependencies": {
    "eslint": "^4.18.2",
    "eslint-config-airbnb": "^16.1.0",
    "eslint-plugin-babel": "^4.1.2",
    "eslint-plugin-react": "^7.7.0",
    "prop-types": "^15.6.1",
    "react": "^16.2.0",
    "react-dom": "^16.2.0",
    "react-scripts": "1.1.0"
  },
  "scripts": {
    "start": "react-scripts start",
    "build": "react-scripts build",
    "test": "react-scripts test --env=jsdom",
    "eject": "react-scripts eject",
    "lint": "eslint --ext .jsx,.js src"
  }
}
```

3. Once you have added the `lint` script, you can run the linter validation with this command:

```
npm run lint
```

4. Now you can see the linter errors you have in your project:

```
→ airbnb git:(master) ✗ npm run lint

> events@0.1.0 lint /Users/czantany/projects/React16Cookbook/Chapter3/Recipe2/airbnb
> eslint --ext .jsx,.js src


/Users/czantany/projects/React16Cookbook/Chapter3/Recipe2/airbnb/src/components/App.js
   8:1  error  Component should be written as a pure function  react/prefer-stateless-function
  11:7  error  JSX not allowed in files with extension '.js'   react/jsx-filename-extension

/Users/czantany/projects/React16Cookbook/Chapter3/Recipe2/airbnb/src/components/Person/Person.js
  33:11  error    Expected a line break after this opening brace   object-curly-newline
  33:47  error    Expected a line break before this closing brace  object-curly-newline
  51:5   warning  Unexpected console statement                     no-console
  56:7   error    JSX not allowed in files with extension '.js'    react/jsx-filename-extension

/Users/czantany/projects/React16Cookbook/Chapter3/Recipe2/airbnb/src/index.js
  6:17  error  JSX not allowed in files with extension '.js'  react/jsx-filename-extension

/Users/czantany/projects/React16Cookbook/Chapter3/Recipe2/airbnb/src/shared/components/layout/Content.js
  8:5  error  JSX not allowed in files with extension '.js'  react/jsx-filename-extension

/Users/czantany/projects/React16Cookbook/Chapter3/Recipe2/airbnb/src/shared/components/layout/Footer.js
  4:3  error  JSX not allowed in files with extension '.js'  react/jsx-filename-extension

/Users/czantany/projects/React16Cookbook/Chapter3/Recipe2/airbnb/src/shared/components/layout/Header.js
  10:5  error  JSX not allowed in files with extension '.js'  react/jsx-filename-extension

✖ 10 problems (9 errors, 1 warning)
  2 errors, 0 warnings potentially fixable with the `--fix` option.
```

5. Now we need to fix the linter errors. The first error is Component should be written as a pure function `react/prefer-stateless-function`. That means our `App` component can be written in a functional component because we don't use any local state:

```
import React from 'react';
import Person from './Person/Person';
import Header from '../shared/components/layout/Header';
import Content from '../shared/components/layout/Content';
import Footer from '../shared/components/layout/Footer';
import './App.css';

const App = () => (
  <div className="App">
    <Header title="Personal Information" />

    <Content>
      <Person />
    </Content>

    <Footer />
```

```
    </div>
);

export default App;
```

File: src/components/App.js

6. Next, we have this error: JSX not allowed in files with extension '.js' /react/jsx-filename-extension. This error means that in the files where we use JSX code, we need to use the .jsx extension instead of .js. We have six files with this problem (App.js, Person.js, index.js, Content.js, Footer.js, and Header.js). We just need to rename the files and change the extension to .jsx (App.jsx, Person.jsx, Content.jsx, Footer.jsx, and Header.jsx). Due to react-scripts, we won't change our index.js to index.jsx for now. Otherwise, we will get an error like this:

```
→ airbnb git:(master) × npm start

> airbnb@0.1.0 start /Users/carlos.santana/projects/React16Cookbook/Chapter3/Recipe2/airbnb
> react-scripts start

Could not find a required file.
  Name: index.js
  Searched in: /Users/carlos.santana/projects/React16Cookbook/Chapter3/Recipe2/airbnb/src
npm ERR! code ELIFECYCLE
npm ERR! errno 1
npm ERR! airbnb@0.1.0 start: `react-scripts start`
npm ERR! Exit status 1
npm ERR!
npm ERR! Failed at the airbnb@0.1.0 start script.
npm ERR! This is probably not a problem with npm. There is likely additional logging output above.

npm ERR! A complete log of this run can be found in:
npm ERR!     /Users/carlos.santana/.npm/_logs/2018-03-11T23_44_15_117Z-debug.log
```

In Chapter 10, *Mastering Webpack 4.x*, we will be able to rename all our JSX files with the .jsx extension.

7. We need to suppress the lint error. We have to write this comment at the top of our index.js file:

```
/* eslint react/jsx-filename-extension: "off" */
import React from 'react';
...
```

8. Let's look at this error: *Expected a line break after this opening brace*/`object-curly-newline`, and this error: *Expected a line break before this closing brace*/`object-curly-newline`. In our `Person.jsx` file, we have this object in our `handleOnChange` method:

```
const { firstName, lastName, email, phone } = this.state;
```

9. The rule says we need to add a break-line before and after the object:

```
const {
  firstName,
  lastName,
  email,
  phone
} = this.state;
```

10. Now let's look at Warning: Unexpected console statement /no-console. The console.log generated a warning in our linter that won't affect us, but if you need to have a console and you want to avoid the warning, you can add an exception with an ESLint comment like so:

```
console.log('Data:', data); // eslint-disable-line no-console
```

11. More ESLint comments do the same thing:

```
// eslint-disable-next-line no-console
console.log('Data:', data);
```

12. If you want to disable the consoles in the entire file, then at the beginning of the file you can do this:

```
/* eslint no-console: "off" */
import React, { Component } from 'react';
...
```

13. *Error: 'document' is not defined/no-undef.* There are two ways to fix this error in our `index.jsx` where we are using the global object document. The first one is to add a special comment to specify that the document object is a global variable:

```
/* global document */
import React from 'react';
import ReactDOM from 'react-dom';
...
```

14. I don't like this way. I prefer to add a `globals` node into our `.eslintrc` file:

```
{
  "parser": "babel-eslint",
  "extends": "airbnb",
  "globals": {
    "document": "true"
  },
  "rules": {
    "arrow-parens": "off",
    "comma-dangle": "off",
    "function-paren-newline": "off",
    "max-len": [1, 120],
    "no-param-reassign": "off",
    "react/require-default-props": "off"
  }
}
```

How it works...

The linter validation is essential for any project. Sometimes, this is a topic of discussion because most developers do not like to follow standards, but once everyone gets familiar with this style guide everything is more comfortable, and you will deliver better quality code.

So far, we know how to run the linter validation in our Terminal, but you can also add the ESLint validator to your IDE (Atom and VSC). For this example, we are going to use Atom.

Installing Atom plugins

In Atom (on a Mac) you can go to **Preferences** | **+Install**, and then you can find the Atom plugins. I'll give you a list of the plugins I use to improve my IDE and increase my productivity:

- `linter-eslint`: Lint JS on the fly, using ESLint
- `editorconfig`: Helps developers maintain consistent coding styles between different editors
- `language-babel`: Supports React syntax
- `minimap`: A preview of the full source code
- `pigments`: A package for displaying colors in projects and files

- `sort-lines`: Sorts your lines
- `teletype`: Shares your workspace with team members and allows them to collaborate on code in real time

Once you have installed these, packages if you go to a file with lint errors, you will be able to see them:

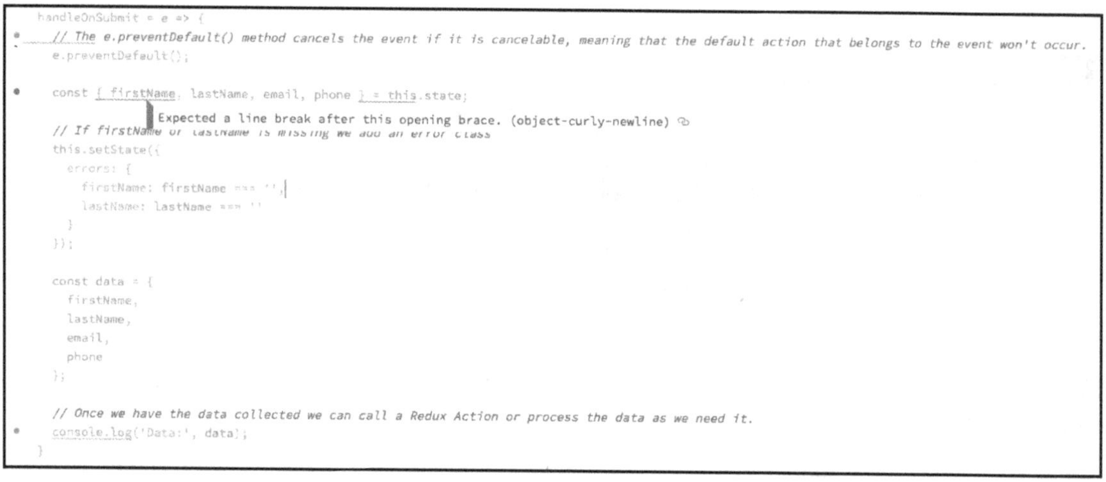

handleOnSubmit = e => {
// The e.preventDefault() method cancels the event if it is cancelable, meaning that the default action that belongs to the event won't occur.
e.preventDefault();
const { firstName, lastName, email, phone } = this.state;
Expected a line break after this opening brace. (object-curly-newline)
this.setState({
errors: {
firstName: firstName === '',
lastName: lastName === ''
const data = {
firstName,
lastName,
email,
phone
// Once we have the data collected we can call a Redux Action or process the data as we need it.
console.log('Data:', data);

Configuring EditorConfig

EditorConfig is also very useful for maintaining consistent coding styles when people in our team uses different editors. EditorConfig is supported by a lot of editors. You can check whether your editor is supported on the official website, `http://editorconfig.org`.

The configuration I use is this one; you need to create a file called `.editorconfig` in your `root` directory:

```
root = true

[*]
indent_style = space
indent_size = 2
end_of_line = lf
charset = utf-8
trim_trailing_whitespace = true
insert_final_newline = true

[*.html]
indent_size = 4
```

```
[*.css]
indent_size = 4

[*.md]
trim_trailing_whitespace = false
```

You can affect all the files with [*], and specific files with [*.extension].

There's more...

Running the linter validation in our IDE or with the Terminal is not enough to be sure that we are going to validate 100% of our code, and we are not going to inject any linter errors into our Git repositories. The most effective way to be 100% sure we are sending validated code to our Git repositories is to use Git hooks. That means you run the linter validator before performing a commit (pre-commit) or before a push (pre-push). I prefer to run the linter on the pre-commit and the unit tests on the pre-push (we are going to cover unit tests in `Chapter 12`, *Testing and Debugging*).

Husky is the package we are going to use to modify our Git hooks; you can install it with this command:

```
npm install husky
```

Once we have added this package, we need to alter our `package.json` and add new scripts:

```
{
  "name": "airbnb",
  "version": "0.1.0",
  "private": true,
  "dependencies": {
    "eslint": "^4.18.2",
    "eslint-config-airbnb": "^16.1.0",
    "eslint-plugin-babel": "^4.1.2",
    "eslint-plugin-jsx-a11y": "^6.0.3",
    "eslint-plugin-react": "^7.7.0",
    "husky": "^0.14.3",
    "prop-types": "^15.6.1",
    "react": "^16.2.0",
    "react-dom": "^16.2.0",
    "react-scripts": "1.1.0"
  },
  "scripts": {
    "start": "react-scripts start",
    "build": "react-scripts build",
```

```
      "test": "react-scripts test --env=jsdom",
      "eject": "react-scripts eject",
      "lint": "eslint --ext .jsx,.js src",
      "precommit": "npm run lint",
      "postmerge": "npm install",
      "postrewrite": "npm install",
    }
  }
```

We are using four scripts:

- `precommit`: Runs before a commit is performed.
- `postmerge`: Runs after performing a merge.
- `postrewrite`: This hook is called by commands that rewrite commits (git commit `--amend`, `git-rebase`; currently, `git-filter-branch` does not call it!).
- `*prepush`: I didn't add this Git hook at this moment, but this is useful for running our unit tests (`"prepush": "npm test"`), we are going to add this Git hook in `Chapter 12`, *Testing and Debugging*, when we cover the unit tests topic.

In this case, in our `precommit`, we will run our linter validator, and if the validator fails, the commit will not be executed until you fix all the linter errors. The postmerge and postrewrite hooks help us to sync our npm packages, so for example, if User A adds new npm packages, then User B pulls the new code and will automatically run the `npm install` command to install the new packages in the User B local machine.

Updating our title and meta tags with React Helmet

In all projects, it is vital to be able to change our site title and our meta tags with information on each specific page to be SEO friendly.

Getting ready

For this recipe, we need to install a package called `react-helmet`:

```
npm install react-helmet
```

How to do it...

React Helmet is the best way to handle the title and meta tags to improve the SEO on our websites:

1. Once we have installed the `react-helmet` package using the same component of `App.jsx`, we need to import React Helmet:

```
import Helmet from 'react-helmet';
```

2. We can change the title of our page by adding the title prop to the `Helmet` component like this:

```
<Helmet title="Person Information" />
```

3. If you start your application, you will see the title in your browser:

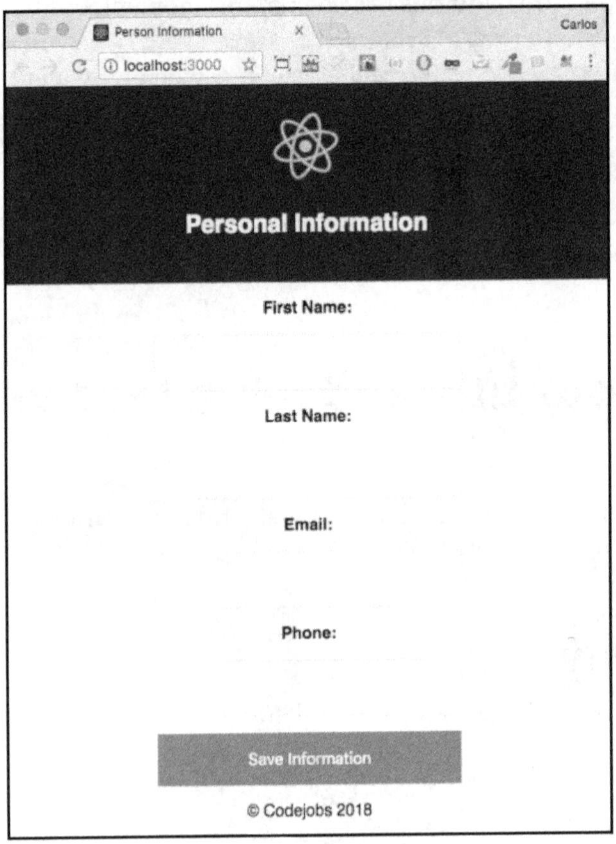

4. If you want to change your meta tags, you can do it like this:

```
<Helmet
  title="Person Information"
  meta={[
    { name: 'title', content: 'Person Information' },
    { name: 'description', content: 'This recipe talks about React
Helmet' }
  ]}
/>
```

How it works...

With that code, we are going to get this output:

```
<title>Person Information</title>
<meta name="title" content="Person Information" data-react-helmet="true">
<meta name="description" content="This recipe talks about React Helmet" data-react-helmet="true">
```

You can also do this if you want to add the HTML code directly into the `Helmet` component:

```
<Helmet>
  <title>Person Information</title>
  <meta name="title" content="Person Information" />
  <meta name="description" content="This recipe talks about React
Helmet" />
</Helmet>
```

You may have noticed that there is a flashing change on the title in the first load of the page, and this is because in our `index.html` file we have the title *React App* by default. You can change that by editing this file:

```
<head>
  <meta charset="utf-8">
  <meta name="viewport" content="width=device-width, initial-scale=1,
  shrink-to-fit=no">
  <meta name="theme-color" content="#000000">
  <link rel="manifest" href="%PUBLIC_URL%/manifest.json">
  <link rel="shortcut icon" href="%PUBLIC_URL%/favicon.ico">
  <title>Personal Information</title>
</head>
```

File: public/index.html

There's more...

So far, we have only changed our title in the main component (`<App />`), but in `Chapter 4`, *Adding Routes to Our Application with React Router V4,* we are going to be able to change our titles and meta tags in different components based on a route.

Also, in `Chapter 11`, *Implementing Server-Side Rendering,* we are going to learn how to implement server-side rendering in our application. You can also use React Helmet with server-side rendering, but you need to make some changes.

First, in your `index.html` (Note: this file will change to a JavaScript file in `Chapter 11`, *Implementing Server-Side Rendering;* Do not try to add this to your current `index.html` file) you will need to add something like this:

```
return `
  <head>
    <meta charset="utf-8">
    <title>Personal Information</title>
    ${helmet.title.toString()}
    ${helmet.meta.toString()}
    <link rel="shortcut icon" href="images/favicon.png"
    type="image/x-icon">
  </head>
`;
```

And with this, we are going to be able to update our titles and meta tags using server-side rendering.

4
Adding Routes to Our Application with React Router

In this chapter, the following recipes will be covered:

- Implementing React Router v4
- Creating nested routes and adding parameters to our paths

Introduction

In this chapter, we are going to learn how to add dynamic routes in our project using React Router v4.

Implementing React Router v4

React, unlike Angular, is a library instead of a framework, meaning specific functionalities, for example, routing or the `propTypes`, are not part of the React core. Instead, routing is handled by a third-party library called React Router.

Getting ready

We will use the code that we did in the *Implementing Airbnb React/JSX Style Guide* recipe in `Chapter 3`, *Handling Events, Binding, and Useful React Packages* (`Repository: Chapter03/Recipe4/airbnb`) to enable linter validation.

The first thing we need to do is to install React Router v4, and we can do it with this command:

```
npm install react-router-dom
```

You probably are confused about why we are installing `react-router-dom` instead of `react-router`. React Router contains all the common components of `react-router-dom` and `react-router-native`. That means that if you are using React for the web, you should use `react-router-dom`, and if you are using React Native, you need to use `react-router-native`. The `react-router-dom` package was created originally to contain version 4, and `react-router` was using version 3. `react-router-dom` has some improvements over `react-router`. They are listed here:

- Improved `<Link>` component (which renders an `<a>`).
- Includes `<BrowserRouter>`, which interacts with the browser's `window.history`.
- Includes `<NavLink>`, which is a `<Link>` wrapper that knows whether it's active or not.
- Includes `<HashRouter>`, which uses the hash in the URL to render the components. If you have one static page, you should use this component instead of `<BrowserRouter>`.

How to do it...

In this recipe, we are going to display some components based on the routes:

1. We need to create four functional components (`About`, `Contact`, `Home`, and `Error 404`) and name them as `index.jsx` in their directories.
2. Create the `Home` component:

```
import React from 'react';

const Home = () => (
  <div className="Home">
    <h1>Home</h1>
  </div>
);

export default Home;
```

File: src/components/Home/index.jsx

3. Create the `About` component:

```
import React from 'react';

const About = () => (
  <div className="About">
    <h1>About</h1>
  </div>
);

export default About;
```

File: src/components/About/index.jsx

4. Create the `Contact` component:

```
import React from 'react';

const Contact = () => (
  <div className="Contact">
    <h1>Contact</h1>
  </div>
);

export default Contact;
```

File: src/components/Contact/index.jsx

5. Create the `Error 404` component:

```
import React from 'react';

const Error404 = () => (
  <div className="Error404">
    <h1>Error404</h1>
  </div>
);

export default Error404;
```

File: src/components/Error/404.jsx

6. In our `src/index.js` file, we need to include our routes, which we are going to create in the next step. We need to import the `BrowserRouter` object from `react-router-dom`, and we can rename it Router:

```
import React from 'react';
import { render } from 'react-dom';
import { BrowserRouter as Router } from 'react-router-dom';
import './index.css';

// Routes
import AppRoutes from './routes';

render(
  <Router>
    <AppRoutes />
  </Router>,
  document.getElementById('root')
);
```

File: src/index.js

7. Now we need to create our `src/routes.jsx` file, to which we are going to import our `App` and `Home` components, and, using the `Route` component, we are going to add a route to execute our `Home` component when the user accesses root (/):

```
// Dependencies
import React from 'react';
import { Route } from 'react-router-dom';

// Components
import App from './components/App';
import Home from './components/Home';

const AppRoutes = () => (
  <App>
    <Route path="/" component={Home} />
  </App>
);

export default AppRoutes;
```

File: src/routes.jsx

8. After that, we need to modify our `App.jsx` file to render the route components as children:

```
import React from 'react';
import { element } from 'prop-types';
import Header from '../shared/components/layout/Header';
import Content from '../shared/components/layout/Content';
import Footer from '../shared/components/layout/Footer';
import './App.css';

const App = props => (
  <div className="App">
    <Header title="Routing" />

    <Content>
      {props.children}
    </Content>

    <Footer />
  </div>
);

App.propTypes = {
  children: element
};

export default App;
```

File: src/components/App.jsx

9. If you run your application, you will see the `Home` component in the root (`/`):

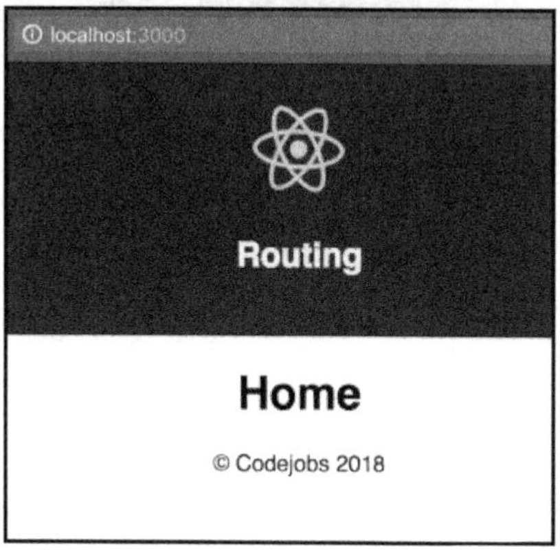

10. Now, let's add our `Error 404` when the user tries to access to any other route:

```
// Dependencies
import React from 'react';
import { Route } from 'react-router-dom';

// Components
import App from './components/App';
import Home from './components/Home';
import Error404 from './components/Error/404';

const AppRoutes = () => (
  <App>
    <Route path="/" component={Home} />
    <Route component={Error404} />
  </App>
);

export default AppRoutes;
```

File: src/routes.jsx

11. If you run the application, you will see that it is rendering both components (`Home` and `Error 404`). You are probably wondering why:

12. It's because we need to use the `<Switch>` component to execute just one component if it matches the path. For this, we need to import the `Switch` component and add it as a wrapper in our routes:

```
// Dependencies
import React from 'react';
import { Route, Switch } from 'react-router-dom';

// Components
import App from './components/App';
import Home from './components/Home';
import Error404 from './components/Error/404';

const AppRoutes = () => (
  <App>
    <Switch>
      <Route path="/" component={Home} />
      <Route component={Error404} />
    </Switch>
  </App>
);

export default AppRoutes;
```

File: src/routes.jsx

13. Now, if we go to the root (`/`) we will see our `Home` component, and the `Error404` won't be executed at the same time (it will just be executed the `Home` component), but if we go to `/somefakeurl`, we will see that the `Home` component is executed as well, and this is an issue:

14. To fix this problem, we need to add the exact prop in the route that we want to match exactly. The problem is that `/somefakeurl` will match our root (`/`), but if we want to be very specific about the paths, we need to add the exact prop to our `Home` route:

```
// Dependencies
import React from 'react';
import { Route, Switch } from 'react-router-dom';

// Components
import App from './components/App';
import Home from './components/Home';
import Error404 from './components/Error/404';

const AppRoutes = () => (
  <App>
    <Switch>
      <Route path="/" component={Home} exact />
      <Route component={Error404} />
    </Switch>
  </App>
);

export default AppRoutes;
```

15. Now if you go to `/somefakeurl`, you will be able to see the `Error404` component:

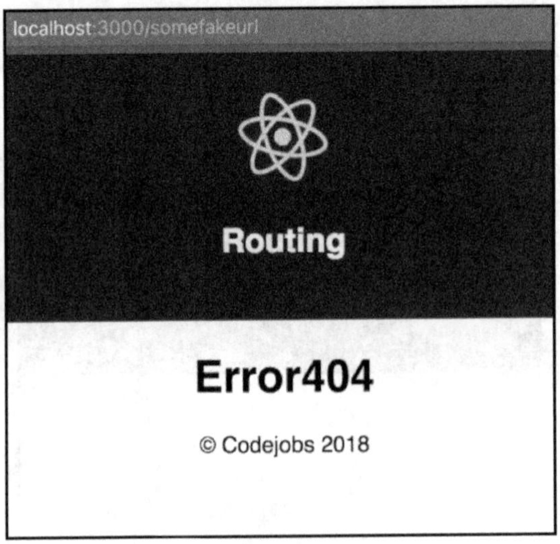

How it works...

As you can see, it is very easy to implement the React Router library. Now we can add more routes for our `About` (`/about`) and `Contact` (`/contact`) components:

```
// Dependencies
import React from 'react';
import { Route, Switch } from 'react-router-dom';

// Components
import App from './components/App';
import About from './components/About';
import Contact from './components/Contact';
import Home from './components/Home';
import Error404 from './components/Error/404';

const AppRoutes = () => (
  <App>
    <Switch>
      <Route path="/" component={Home} exact />
      <Route path="/about" component={About} exact />
      <Route path="/contact" component={Contact} exact />
      <Route component={Error404} />
    </Switch>
  </App>
);

export default AppRoutes;
```

If you go to `/about`, you will see this view:

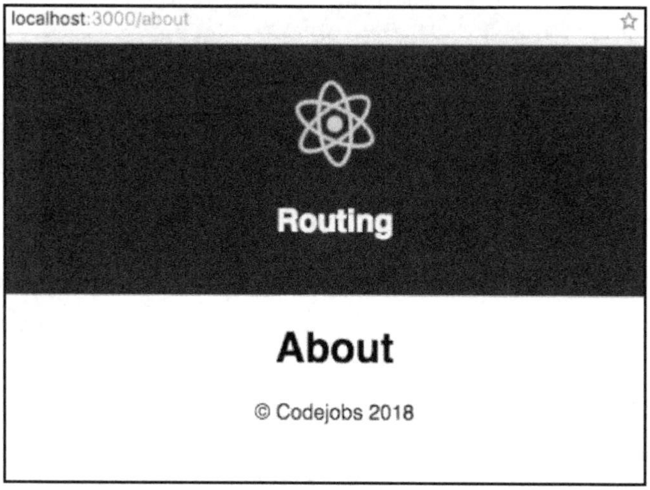

If you go to `/contact`, you will see this view:

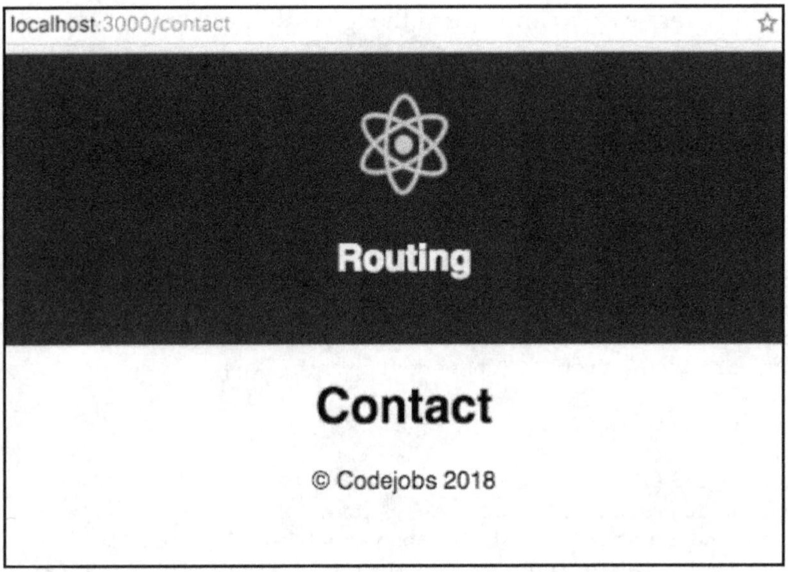

There's more...

So far, we have learned how to create simple routes in our project, but in the next recipe, we will learn how to include parameters within our routes, how to add nested routes, and how to navigate through our site using the `<Link>` component.

Adding parameters to our routes

For this recipe, we are going to use the same code as the last recipe, and we are going to add some parameters and show how to get them into our components.

How to do it...

In this recipe, we are going to create a simple `Notes` component to display all our notes when we visit the `/notes` route, but we will show one note when the user visits `/notes/:noteId` (we will filter the note using `noteId`):

1. We need to create a new component called Notes (`src/components/Notes/index.jsx`), and this is the skeleton of our `Notes` component:

```
import React, { Component } from 'react';
import './Notes.css';
class Notes extends Component {
  constructor() {
    super();
    // For now we are going to add our notes to our
    // local state, but normally this should come
    // from some service.
    this.state = {
      notes: [
        {
          id: 1,
          title: 'My note 1'
        },
        {
          id: 2,
          title: 'My note 2'
        },
        {
          id: 3,
          title: 'My note 3'
        },
      ]
    };
  }
  render() {
    return (
      <div className="Notes">
        <h1>Notes</h1>
      </div>
    );
  }
}
export default Notes;
```

File: src/components/Notes/index.jsx

2. The CSS file is as follows:

```
.Notes ul {
  list-style: none;
  margin: 0;
  margin-bottom: 20px;
  padding: 0;
}

.Notes ul li {
  padding: 10px;
}

.Notes a {
  color: #555;
  text-decoration: none;
}

.Notes a:hover {
  color: #ccc;
  text-decoration: none;
}
```

File: src/components/Notes/Notes.css

3. Once we have created our `Notes` component, we need to import it into our `src/routes.jsx` file:

```
// Dependencies
import React from 'react';
import { Route, Switch } from 'react-router-dom';

// Components
import App from './components/App';
import About from './components/About';
import Contact from './components/Contact';
import Home from './components/Home';
import Notes from './components/Notes';
import Error404 from './components/Error/404';

const AppRoutes = () => (
  <App>
    <Switch>
      <Route path="/" component={Home} exact />
      <Route path="/about" component={About} exact />
      <Route path="/contact" component={Contact} exact />
      <Route path="/notes" component={Notes} exact />
      <Route component={Error404} />
```

```
    </Switch>
  </App>
);

export default AppRoutes;
```

File: src/routes.jsx

4. Now we can see our Notes component if we go to the `/notes` URL:

5. Now that our `Notes` component is connected to React Router, let's render our notes as a list:

```
import React, { Component } from 'react';
import { Link } from 'react-router-dom';
import './Notes.css';

class Notes extends Component {
  constructor() {
    super();

    this.state = {
      notes: [
        {
          id: 1,
          title: 'My note 1'
        },
        {
          id: 2,
```

```
          title: 'My note 2'
        },
        {
          id: 3,
          title: 'My note 3'
        },
      ]
    };
  }

  renderNotes = notes => (
    <ul>
      {notes.map((note, key) => (
        <li key={key}>
          <Link to={`/notes/${note.id}`}>{note.title}</Link>
        </li>
      ))}
    </ul>
  );

  render() {
    const { notes } = this.state;

    return (
      <div className="Notes">
        <h1>Notes</h1>

        {this.renderNotes(notes)}
      </div>
    );
  }
}

export default Notes;
```

File: src/components/Notes/index.jsx

6. You may have noticed that we are using `<Link>` (this will generate an `<a>` tag) component that points to `/notes/notes.id`, and this is because we are going to add a new nested route into our `src/routes.jsx` file to match the `id` of the note:

```
// Dependencies
import React from 'react';
import { Route, Switch } from 'react-router-dom';

// Components
import App from './components/App';
import About from './components/About';
import Contact from './components/Contact';
import Home from './components/Home';
import Notes from './components/Notes';
import Error404 from './components/Error/404';

const AppRoutes = () => (
  <App>
    <Switch>
      <Route path="/" component={Home} exact />
      <Route path="/about" component={About} exact />
      <Route path="/contact" component={Contact} exact />
      <Route path="/notes" component={Notes} exact />
      <Route path="/notes/:noteId" component={Notes} exact />
      <Route component={Error404} />
    </Switch>
  </App>
);

export default AppRoutes;
```

File: src/routes.jsx

7. React Router has a special prop called `match`, which is an object that includes all the information about our executed route, and if we have parameters, we are going to be able to see them in the `match` object, like this:

```
render() {
  // Let's see what contains our props object.
  console.log(this.props);

  // We got the noteId param from match object.
  const { match: { params: { noteId } } } = this.props;
  const { notes } = this.state;
  // By default our selectedNote is false
  let selectedNote = false;
```

```
    if (noteId > 0) {
      // If the note id is higher than 0 then we filter it from our
      // notes array.
      selectedNote = notes.filter(
        note => note.id === Number(noteId)
      );
    }

    return (
      <div className="Notes">
        <h1>Notes</h1>
        {/* We render our selectedNote or all notes */}
        {this.renderNotes(selectedNote || notes)}
      </div>
    );
  }
```

File: src/components/Notes/index.jsx

8. The `match` prop looks like this.

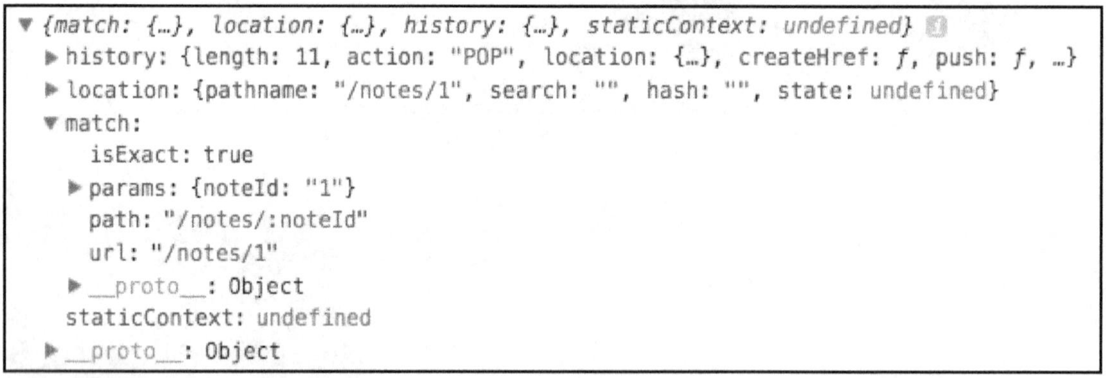
{match: {…}, location: {…}, history: {…}, staticContext: undefined}
history: {length: 11, action: "POP", location: {…}, createHref: f, push: f, …}
location: {pathname: "/notes/1", search: "", hash: "", state: undefined}
match:
isExact: true
params: {noteId: "1"}
path: "/notes/:noteId"
url: "/notes/1"
__proto__: Object
staticContext: undefined
__proto__: Object

How it works...

The `match` object contains a lot of useful information. React Router also includes the object's history and location. As you can see, we can get all the parameters we pass within our routes in the `match` object.

If you run the application and go to `/notes` URL, you will see this view:

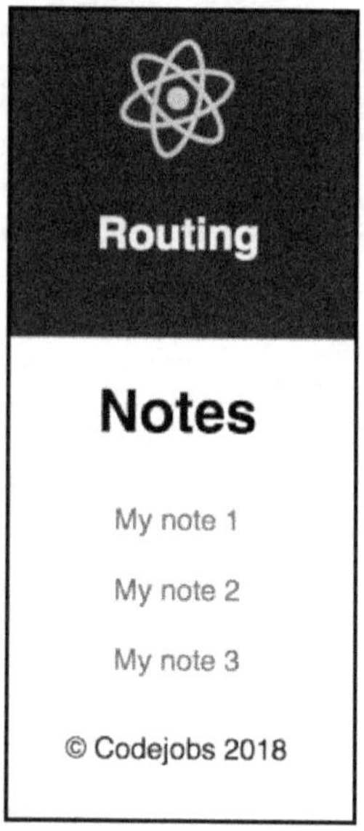

If you click on any link (I clicked on My note 2), you will see this view:

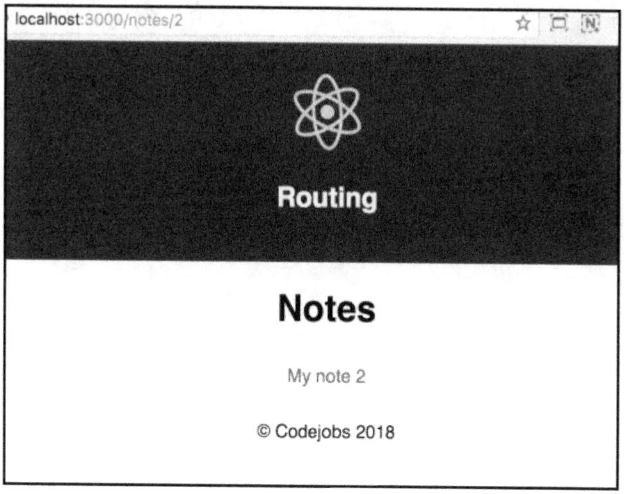

After this, we can add a menu in our `Header` component to access all our routes:

```
import React from 'react';
import PropTypes from 'prop-types';
import { Link } from 'react-router-dom';
import logo from '../../images/logo.svg';

// We created a component with a simple arrow function.
const Header = props => {
  const {
    title = 'Welcome to React',
    url = 'http://localhost:3000'
  } = props;

  return (
    <header className="App-header">
      <a href={url}>
        <img src={logo} className="App-logo" alt="logo" />
      </a>
      <h1 className="App-title">{title}</h1>

      <ul>
        <li><Link to="/">Home</Link></li>
        <li><Link to="/about">About</Link></li>
        <li><Link to="/notes">Notes</Link></li>
        <li><Link to="/contact">Contact</Link></li>
      </ul>
    </header>
  );
};

// Even with Functional Components we are able to validate our PropTypes.
Header.propTypes = {
  title: PropTypes.string.isRequired,
  url: PropTypes.string
};

export default Header;
```

File: src/shared/components/layout/Header.jsx

After that, we need to modify our `src/components/App.css` file to style our menu. Just add the following code at the end of the CSS file:

```
.App-header ul {
  margin: 0;
  padding: 0;
  list-style: none;
}

.App-header ul li {
  display: inline-block;
  padding: 0 10px;
}

.App-header ul li a {
  color: #fff;
  text-decoration: none;
}

.App-header ul li a:hover {
  color: #ccc;
}
```

File: src/components/App.css

Now you can see the menu like this:

5
Mastering Redux

In this chapter, the following recipes will be covered:

- Creating a Redux store
- Making action creators and dispatching actions
- Implementing Firebase with Redux

Introduction

Redux is a predictable state container for JavaScript apps. That means Redux can be used with vanilla JavaScript or frameworks/libraries such as Angular and jQuery. Redux is mainly a library responsible for issuing state updates and responses to actions. Redux is widely used with React. Instead of directly modifying the state of the application, the modification is handled by emitting events called actions. These events are functions (also known as action creators) that always return two key properties, a `type` (which indicates the type of action being performed, and the types should typically be defined as string constants) and a `payload` (the data you want to pass within the action). These functions emit events that are subscribed to by the reducers. The reducers are pure functions written to decide how each action will transform the state of the application. All state changes are handled in a single place: the Redux Store.

Without Redux, complex patterns are needed to communicate changes between our application components. Redux simplifies this by broadcasting state changes to components by using an application store. Within a React Redux application, components will subscribe to the store while the store broadcasts changes to the components. This diagram describes perfectly how Redux works:

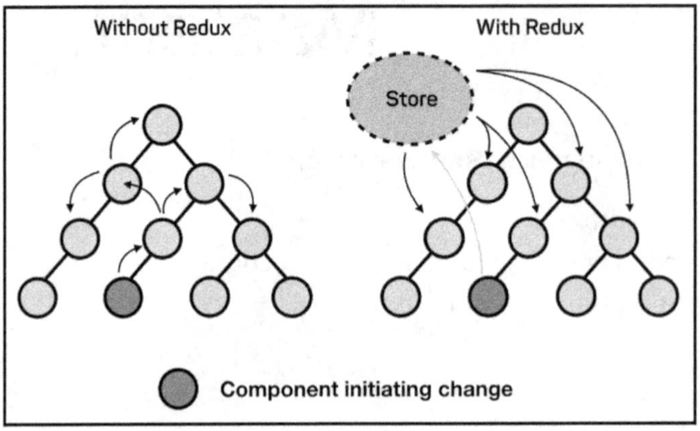

Redux proposes to handle our Redux state as immutable. However, the objects and arrays in JavaScript are not, which can cause us to mutate the state by mistake directly.

These are the three principles of Redux:

- **Single source of truth:** The state of your whole application is stored in an object tree within a single store.
- **The state is read-only:** The only way to change the state is to emit an action, an object describing what happened.
- **Changes are made with pure functions:** To specify how the state tree is transformed by actions, you write pure reducers.

This information was extracted from the Official site of Redux. To read more, visit `https://redux.js.org/introduction/three-principles`.

What is an action?

Actions are payloads of information that send data from your application to your store. They are the only source of information for the store. You send them to the store using `store.dispatch()`. The actions are simple JavaScript objects and must have a property called `type` that indicates the type of the action being performed and a `payload` that is the information contained in action.

What is immutability?

Immutability is a fundamental concept in Redux. To change the state, a new object must be returned.

These are the immutable types in JavaScript:

- Number
- String
- Boolean
- Undefined
- Null

These are the mutable types in JavaScript:

- Arrays
- Functions
- Objects

Why immutability?

- **More clarity**: We know who changed the state (the reducer)
- **Better performance**
- **Easy debugging:** We can use Redux DevTools (we are going to cover that topic in `Chapter 12`, *Testing and Debugging*)

We can work with immutability in the following ways:

- ES6:
    - `Object.assign`
    - `Spread` operator (...)
- Libraries:
    - `Immutable.js`
    - `Lodash` (merge and extend)

What is a reducer?

A reducer resembles a meat grinder. In the meat grinder, we add the ingredients on top (state and action), and at the other end we get the result (a new state):

In technical terms, the reducer is a pure function that receives two parameters (the current state and the action), and you return a new immutable state depending on the action.

Types of components

Container:

- Focuses on how things work
- Is connected to Redux
- Dispatches Redux actions
- Is generated by `react-redux`

Presentational:

- Focuses on how things look
- Is not connected to Redux
- Receives data or functions via props
- Most of the time are Stateless

Redux Flow

The Redux Flow starts when we call an action from the UI (`React` component). This action will send the information (`type` and `payload`) to the store, which interacts with the reducers to update the state based on the action type. Once the state is updated by the reducer, it returns the value to the store, and then the store sends the new value to our React application:

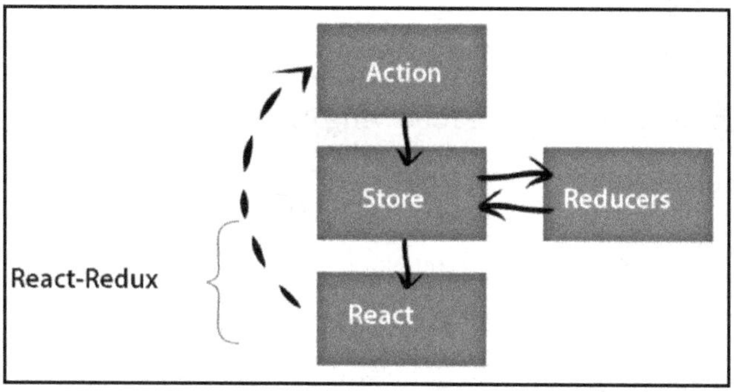

Creating a Redux Store

A store holds the whole state of your application, and the only way to change the state inside is by dispatching an action. A store is not a class; it is just an object with a few methods on it.

The store methods are as follows:

- `getState()`: Returns the current state of your application
- `dispatch(action)`: Dispatches an action and is the only way to trigger a state change
- `subscribe(listener)`: Adds a change listener that is called any time an action is dispatched
- `replaceReducer(nextReducer)`: Replaces the reducer that is currently used by the store to calculate the state

Getting ready

To work with Redux, we need to install the following packages:

```
npm install redux react-redux
```

How to do it...

First, we need to create a file for our store at `src/shared/redux/configureStore.js`:

1. Let's go ahead and write the following code:

```
// Dependencies
import { createStore } from 'redux';

// Root Reducer
import rootReducer from '../reducers';

export default function configureStore(initialState) {
  return createStore(
    rootReducer,
    initialState
  );
}
```

File: src/shared/redux/configureStore.js

2. The second thing we need to do is to create our `initialState` variable in our `public/index.html` file. For now, we will create a device state to detect whether the user is using a mobile or a desktop:

```
<body>
  <div id="root"></div>

  <script>
    // Detecting the user device
    const isMobile = /iPhone|Android/i.test(navigator.userAgent);

    // Creating our initialState
    const initialState = {
      device: {
        isMobile
      }
    };

    // Saving our initialState to the window object
```

```
    window.initialState = initialState;
  </script>
</body>
```

File: public/index.html

3. We need to create a `reducers` directory in our shared folder. The first reducer we need to create is `deviceReducer`:

```
export default function deviceReducer(state = {}) {
  return state;
}
```

File: src/shared/reducers/deviceReducer.js

4. Once we have created `deviceReducer`, we need to create an `index.js` file, where we are going to import all our reducers and combine them into a `rootReducer`:

```
// Dependencies
import { combineReducers } from 'redux';

// Shared Reducers
import device from './deviceReducer';

const rootReducer = combineReducers({
  device
});

export default rootReducer;
```

File: src/shared/reducers/index.js

5. Now let's modify our `src/index.js` file. We need to create our Redux Store and pass it to our provider:

```
import React from 'react';
import { render } from 'react-dom';
import { BrowserRouter as Router } from 'react-router-dom';
import { Provider } from 'react-redux';
import './index.css';

// Redux Store
import configureStore from './shared/redux/configureStore';

// Routes
import AppRoutes from './routes';
```

```
// Configuring Redux Store
const store = configureStore(window.initialState);

// DOM
const rootElement = document.getElementById('root');

// App Wrapper
const renderApp = Component => {
  render(
    <Provider store={store}>
      <Router>
        <Component />
      </Router>
    </Provider>,
    rootElement
  );
};

// Rendering our App
renderApp(AppRoutes);
```

6. Now we can edit our `Home` component. We need to connect our component to Redux using `connect` from `react-redux`, and then, using `mapStateToProps`, we are going to retrieve the device's state:

```
import React from 'react';
import { bool } from 'prop-types';
import { connect } from 'react-redux';

const Home = props => {
  const { isMobile } = props;

  return (
    <div className="Home">
      <h1>Home</h1>

      <p>
        You are using:
        <strong>{isMobile ? 'mobile' : 'desktop'}</strong>
      </p>
    </div>
  );
};

Home.propTypes = {
  isMobile: bool
};
```

```
function mapStateToProps(state) {
  return {
    isMobile: state.device.isMobile
  };
}

function mapDispatchToProps() {
  return {};
}

export default connect(mapStateToProps, mapDispatchToProps)(Home);
```

How it works...

If you followed all the steps correctly, you should be able to see this view using Chrome in your desktop:

And if you activate the Chrome Device Emulator, or if you use a real device or the iPhone simulator, you will see this view:

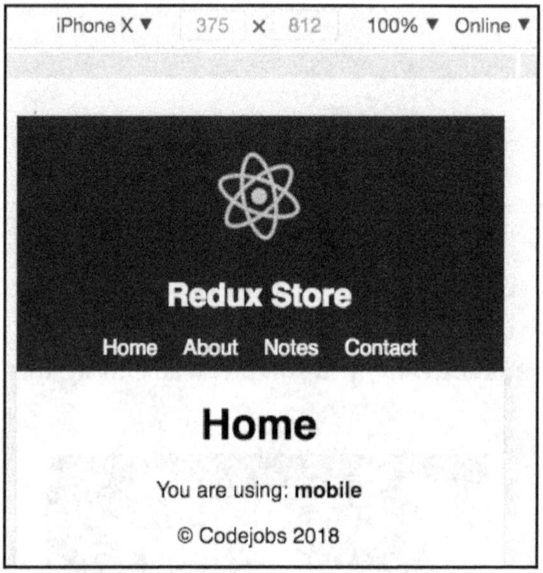

What is mapStateToProps?

The `mapStateToProps` function typically confuses many people, but it is easy to understand. It takes a piece of the state (from the store), and it passes it into your component as a `prop`. In other words, the parameter that receives `mapStateToProps` is the Redux state, and inside you will have all the reducers you have defined in `rootReducer`, and then you return an object with the data you need to send to your component. Here's an example:

```
function mapStateToProps(state) {
  return {
    isMobile: state.device.isMobile
  };
}
```

As you can see, the state has a `device` node, which is our `deviceReducer`; there are other ways to do this that, most of the time, confuse many people. One way is by using ES6 destructuring and arrow functions something like this:

```
const mapStateToProps = ({ device }) => ({
  isMobile: device.isMobile
});
```

Also, there is another way to do it directly in the `connect` middleware. Usually, this can be confusing, to begin with, but once you get used to it, it's the way to go. I typically do this:

```
export default connect(({ device }) => ({
  isMobile: device.isMobile
}), null)(Home);
```

After we map our Redux state to the props, we can retrieve the data like this:

```
const { isMobile } = props;
```

As you can see, for the second parameter, `mapDispatchToProps`, I directly sent a null value since we are not dispatching an action in this component yet. In the next recipe, I am going to talk about `mapDispatchToProps`.

Making action creators and dispatching actions

Actions are the most crucial pieces of Redux; they are responsible for triggering state updates in our Redux Store. In this recipe, we are going to display the top 100 cryptocurrencies listed on `http://www.coinmarketcap.com` using their public API.

Getting ready

For this recipe, we need to install Axios (a promise-based HTTP client for the browser and Node.js) and Redux Thunk (a thunk is a function that wraps an expression to delay its evaluation):

```
npm install axios redux-thunk
```

How to do it...

We are going to use the same code we created in the last recipe (`Repository: /Chapter05/Recipe1/store`) and add some modifications:

1. First, we need to create new folders: `src/actions`, `src/reducers`, `src/components/Coins`, and `src/shared/utils`.

2. The first file we need to create is`src/actions/actionTypes.js`, where we need to add our constants for our actions:

```
export const FETCH_COINS_REQUEST = 'FETCH_COINS_REQUEST';
export const FETCH_COINS_SUCCESS = 'FETCH_COINS_SUCCESS';
export const FETCH_COINS_ERROR = 'FETCH_COINS_ERROR';
```

File: src/actions/actionTypes.js

3. Maybe you are wondering why we need to create a constant with the same name as the string. It is because, when using constants, we can't have duplicate constant names (we will get an error if we repeat one by mistake). Another reason is that the actions are used in two files, in the actual actions file and then in our reducer. To avoid repeating the strings, I decided to create the `actionTypes.js` file and write our constants once.
4. I like to divide my actions into three parts: `request`, `received`, and `error`. I called those main actions base actions, and we need to create a file for these actions in `src/shared/redux/baseActions.js`:

```
// Base Actions
export const request = type => ({
  type
});

export const received = (type, payload) => ({
  type,
  payload
});

export const error = type => ({
  type
});
```

File: src/shared/redux/baseActions.js

5. After we have built our `baseActions.js` file, we need to create another file for our actions, and this should be inside `src/actions/coinsActions.js`. For this recipe, we will use the public API from `CoinMarketCap` (`https://api.coinmarketcap.com/v1/ticker/`):

```
// Dependencies
import axios from 'axios';

// Action Types
import {
```

```
  FETCH_COINS_REQUEST,
  FETCH_COINS_SUCCESS,
  FETCH_COINS_ERROR
} from './actionTypes';

// Base Actions
 import { request, received, error } from
'../shared/redux/baseActions';

export const fetchCoins = () => dispatch => {
  // Dispatching our request action
  dispatch(request(FETCH_COINS_REQUEST));

  // Axios Data
  const axiosData = {
    method: 'GET',
    url: 'https://api.coinmarketcap.com/v1/ticker/',
    headers: {
      Accept: 'application/json',
      'Content-Type': 'application/json'
    }
  };

  // If everything is correct we dispatch our received action
  // otherwise our error action.
  return axios(axiosData)
    .then(response => dispatch(received(FETCH_COINS_SUCCESS,
response.data)))
    .catch(err => {
      // eslint-disable-next-line no-console
      console.log('AXIOS ERROR:', err.response);
      dispatch(error(FETCH_COINS_ERROR));
    });
};
```

File: src/actions/coinsActions.js

6. Once we have our actions file ready, we need to create our reducer file to update our Redux state based on our actions. Let's create a file in `src/reducers/coinsReducer.js`:

```
// Action Types
import {
  FETCH_COINS_SUCCESS,
  FETCH_SINGLE_COIN_SUCCESS
} from '../actions/actionTypes';

// Utils
```

```
import { getNewState } from '../shared/utils/frontend';

// Initial State
const initialState = {
  coins: []
};

export default function coinsReducer(state = initialState, action)
{
  switch (action.type) {
    case FETCH_COINS_SUCCESS: {
      const { payload: coins } = action;

      return getNewState(state, {
        coins
      });
    }

    default:
      return state;
  }
};
```

File: src/reducers/coinsReducer.js

7. Then we need to add our reducer to our `combineReducers` in `src/shared/reducers/index.js`:

```
// Dependencies
import { combineReducers } from 'redux';

// Components Reducers
import coins from '../../reducers/coinsReducer';

// Shared Reducers
import device from './deviceReducer';

const rootReducer = combineReducers({
  coins,
  device
});

export default rootReducer;
```

File: src/shared/reducers/index.js

8. As you can see, I included the `getNewState` util; this is a basic function that performs an `Object.assign`, but is more explicit and easy to understand, so let's create our `utils` file at `src/shared/utils/frontend.js`. The `isFirstRender` function is required for our component to validate whether our data is empty or not the first time we try to render:

```
export function getNewState(state, newState) {
  return Object.assign({}, state, newState);
}

export function isFirstRender(items) {
  return !items || items.length === 0 || Object.keys(items).length
=== 0;
}
```

File: src/shared/utils/frontend.js

9. Now we need to create a `Container` component at `src/components/Coins/index.js`. In the introduction, I mentioned there are two types of components: `container` and `presentational`. The container must be connected to Redux and should not have any JSX code, just our `mapStateToProps` and `mapDispatchToProps`, and then on the export, we can pass the `presentational` component that we are going to render, passing as props the values of the actions and our Redux state. To create our `mapDispatchToProps` function, we need to use the `bindActionCreators` method from our Redux library. This will bind our `dispatch` method to all the actions we pass. There are different ways to do this without `bindActionCreators`, but using this method is considered good practice:

```
// Dependencies
import { connect } from 'react-redux';
import { bindActionCreators } from 'redux';

// Components
import Coins from './Coins';

// Actions
import { fetchCoins } from '../../actions/coinsActions';
// Mapping our Redux State to Props
const mapStateToProps = ({ coins }) => ({
  coins
});
// Binding our fetchCoins action.
const mapDispatchToProps = dispatch => bindActionCreators(
  {
```

```
      fetchCoins
    },
    dispatch
  );

export default connect(
  mapStateToProps,
  mapDispatchToProps
)(Coins);
```

File: src/components/Coins/index.js

10. The `Coins` component that we are importing in our container is as follows:

```
// Dependencies
import React, { Component } from 'react';
import { array } from 'prop-types';

// Utils
import { isFirstRender } from '../../shared/utils/frontend';

// Styles
import './Coins.css';

class Coins extends Component {
  static propTypes = {
    coins: array
  };

  componentWillMount() {
    const { fetchCoins } = this.props;
    // Fetching coins action.
    fetchCoins();
  }

  render() {
    const { coins: { coins } } = this.props;
    // If the coins const is an empty array,
    // then we return null.
    if (isFirstRender(coins)) {
      return null;
    }
```

```
    return (
      <div className="Coins">
        <h1>Top 100 Coins</h1>

        <ul>
          {coins.map((coin, key) => (
            <li key={key}>
              <span className="left">
                {coin.rank} {coin.name} {coin.symbol}
              </span>
              <span className="right">${coin.price_usd}</span>
            </li>
          ))}
        </ul>
      </div>
    );
  }
}

export default Coins;
```

File: src/components/Coins/Coins.jsx

11. And the CSS for this component is as follows:

```
.Coins ul {
    margin: 0 auto;
    margin-bottom: 20px;
    padding: 0;
    list-style: none;
    width: 300px;
}

.Coins ul a {
    display: block;
    color: #333;
    text-decoration: none;
    background: #5ed4ff;
}

.Coins ul a:hover {
    color: #333;
    text-decoration: none;
    background: #baecff;
}

.Coins ul li {
    border-bottom: 1px solid black;
```

```
        text-align: left;
        padding: 10px;
        display: flex;
        justify-content: space-between;
    }
```

File: src/components/Coins/Coins.css

12. In our `src/shared/redux/configureStore.js` file, we need to import `redux-thunk` and use the `applyMiddleware` method to use this library in our Redux Store:

```
// Dependencies
import { createStore, applyMiddleware } from 'redux';
import thunk from 'redux-thunk';

// Root Reducer
import rootReducer from '../reducers';

export default function configureStore(initialState) {
  const middleware = [
    thunk
  ];

  return createStore(
    rootReducer,
    initialState,
    applyMiddleware(...middleware)
  );
}
```

File: src/shared/redux/configureStore.js

13. Let's add the link to `/coins` in our `Header` component:

```
import React from 'react';
import PropTypes from 'prop-types';
import { Link } from 'react-router-dom';
import logo from '../../images/logo.svg';

// We created a component with a simple arrow function.
const Header = props => {
  const {
    title = 'Welcome to React',
    url = 'http://localhost:3000'
  } = props;

  return (
    <header className="App-header">
      <a href={url}>
        <img src={logo} className="App-logo" alt="logo" />
      </a>
      <h1 className="App-title">{title}</h1>

      <ul>
        <li><Link to="/">Home</Link></li>
        <li><Link to="/about">About</Link></li>
        <li><Link to="/coins">Coins</Link></li>
        <li><Link to="/notes">Notes</Link></li>
        <li><Link to="/contact">Contact</Link></li>
      </ul>
    </header>
  );
};

// Even with Functional Components we are able to validate our
PropTypes.
Header.propTypes = {
  title: PropTypes.string.isRequired,
  url: PropTypes.string
};

export default Header;
```

File: src/shared/components/layout/Header.jsx

14. Finally, the last piece of the puzzle is to add our component (container) to our `src/routes.jsx` file:

```
// Dependencies
import React from 'react';
import { Route, Switch } from 'react-router-dom';

// Components
import App from './components/App';
import About from './components/About';
import Coins from './components/Coins';
import Contact from './components/Contact';
import Home from './components/Home';
import Notes from './components/Notes';
import Error404 from './components/Error/404';

const AppRoutes = () => (
  <App>
    <Switch>
      <Route path="/" component={Home} exact />
      <Route path="/about" component={About} exact />
      <Route path="/coins" component={Coins} exact />
      <Route path="/contact" component={Contact} exact />
      <Route path="/notes" component={Notes} exact />
      <Route path="/notes/:noteId" component={Notes} exact />
      <Route component={Error404} />
    </Switch>
  </App>
);

export default AppRoutes;
```

File: src/routes.jsx

How it works...

If you open the API (`https://api.coinmarketcap.com/v1/ticker/`) you will see the JSON object like this:


```
[
  {
    "id": "bitcoin",
    "name": "Bitcoin",
    "symbol": "BTC",
    "rank": "1",
    "price_usd": "7393.92",
    "price_btc": "1.0",
    "24h_volume_usd": "5101960000.0",
    "market_cap_usd": "125378331744",
    "available_supply": "16956950.0",
    "total_supply": "16956950.0",
    "max_supply": "21000000.0",
    "percent_change_1h": "-0.13",
    "percent_change_24h": "0.16",
    "percent_change_7d": "-7.06",
    "last_updated": "1522824568"
  },
  {
    "id": "ethereum",
    "name": "Ethereum",
    "symbol": "ETH",
    "rank": "2",
    "price_usd": "406.993",
    "price_btc": "0.0553014",
    "24h_volume_usd": "1275330000.0",
    "market_cap_usd": "40131471569.0",
    "available_supply": "98604820.0",
    "total_supply": "98604820.0",
    "max_supply": null,
    "percent_change_1h": "-0.1",
    "percent_change_24h": "2.13",
    "percent_change_7d": "-10.5",
    "last_updated": "1522824553"
  },
```

We will get an array of objects with the top 100 coins in `https://coinmarketcap.com`. If you followed all the steps correctly, you would be able to see this view:

Implementing Firebase with Redux

Firebase is a Backend-as-a-Service (BaaS) that is part of the Google Cloud Platform. One of the most popular services of Firebase is the Realtime Database, which uses a WebSocket to sync your data. Firebase also offers services for file storage, authentication (social media and email/password authentication), hosting, and more.

You can use Firebase mainly for real-time applications, but you can also use it as your regular database for non-real-time applications if you want to. Firebase is supported by many languages (such as JavaScript, Java, Python, and Go) and platforms such as Android, iOS, and the web.

Firebase is free but, of course, if you need more capacity, they have different plans depending on your project's requirements. You can check out the prices at `https://firebase.google.com/pricing`.

For this recipe, we are going to use Firebase's free service to show some popular phrases. That means you will need to create an account using your Google email at `https://firebase.google.com`.

Getting ready

Once you are registered on Firebase, you need to create a new project by clicking on **Add project** in your Firebase console:

I'll name my project `codejobs`; of course, you can name it as you want:

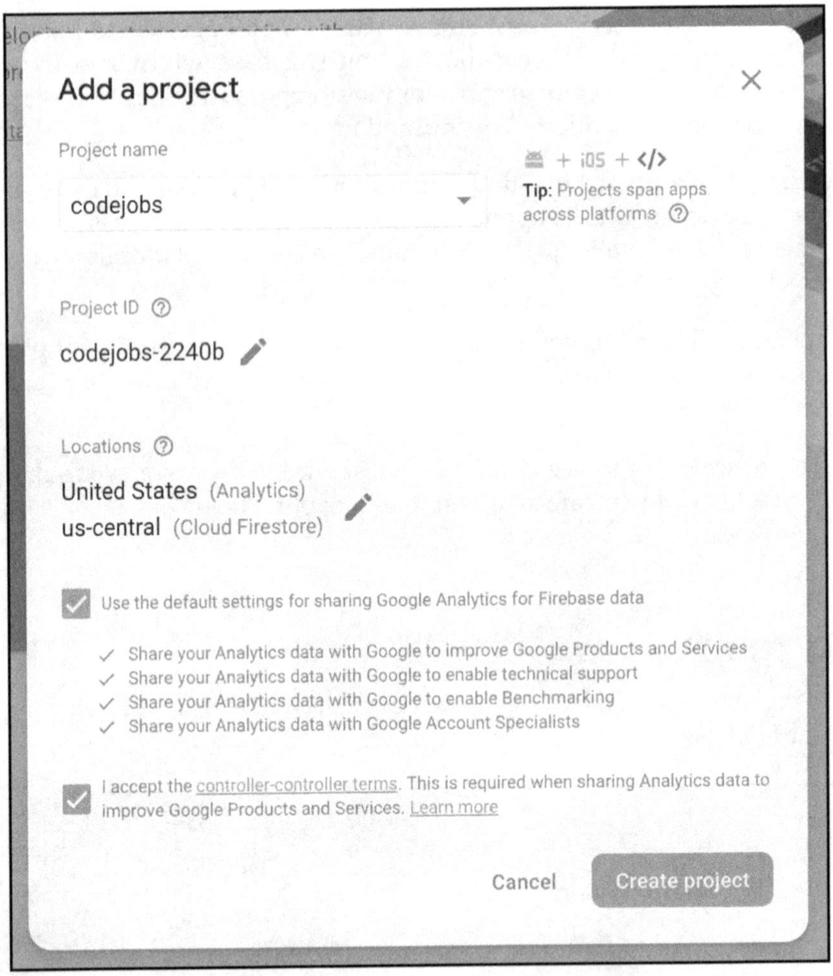

As you can see, Firebase automatically added a random code to our Project ID, but you can edit it if you want to make sure the Project ID does not exist, and after you must accept the terms and conditions and click on **Create Project** button:

Now you must select the **Add Firebase to your web app** option, and you will get information about your application:

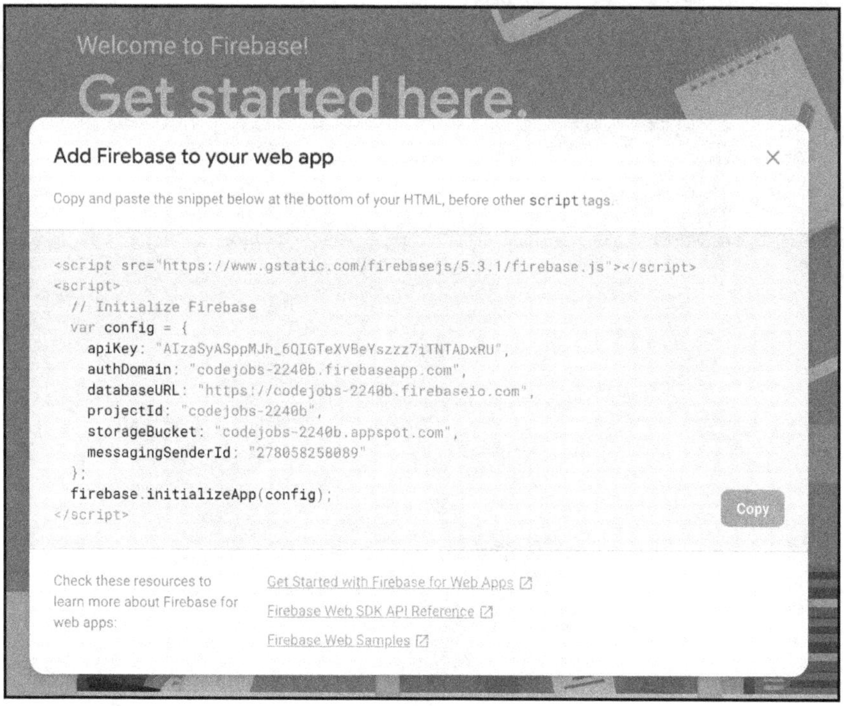

Do not share this information with anyone. I'm sharing this with you because I want to show you the way to connect your application to Firebase.

Now go to **Develop** | **Database** in your dashboard and click on the **Create database** button:

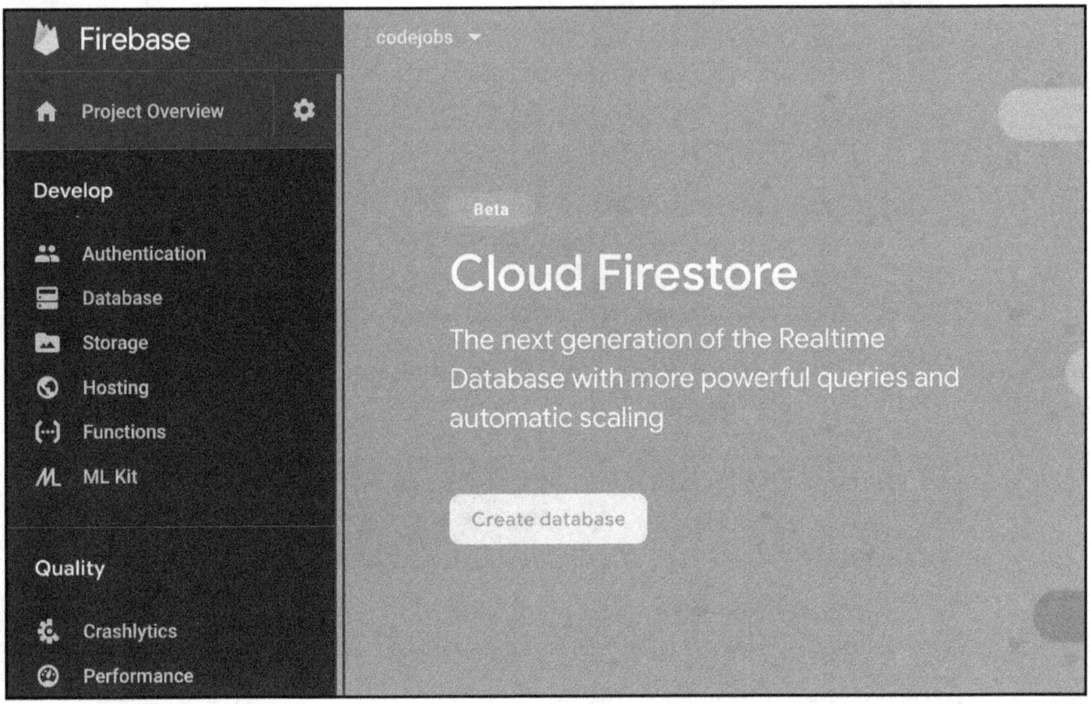

After that, choose the **Start** option in locked mode and click on the **Enable** button:

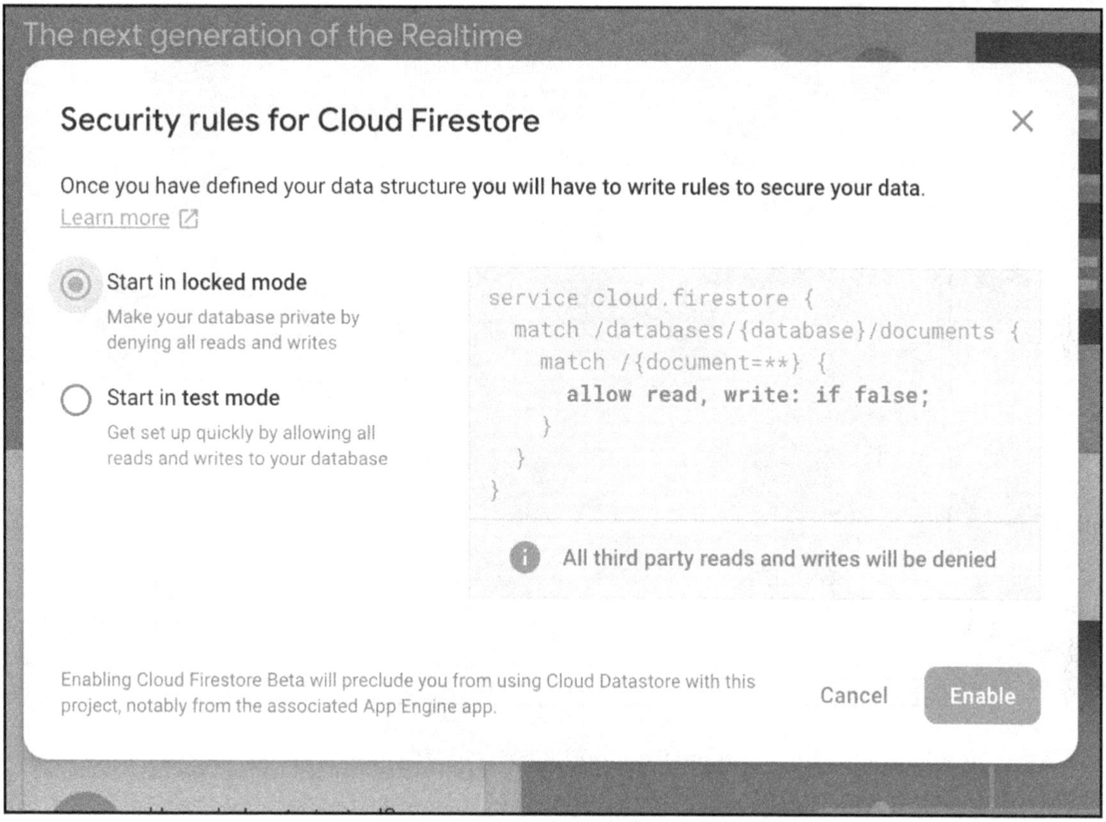

Then, at the top of the page, select the dropdown and choose the **Realtime Database** option:

Once we have our Realtime Database created, let's import some data. To do this, you can select the **Import JSON** option in the dropdown:

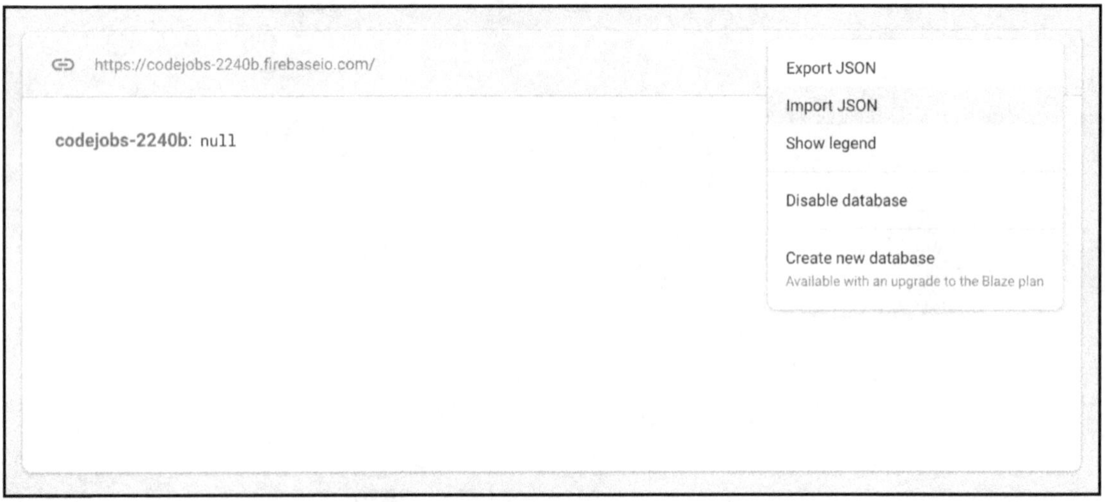

Let's create a basic JSON file to import our phrases data:

```
{
  "phrases": [
    {
      "phrase": "A room without books is like a body without a
     soul.",
      "author": "Marcus Tullius Cicero"
    },
    {
      "phrase": "Two things are infinite: the universe and human
      stupidity; and I'm not sure about the universe.",
      "author": "Albert Einstein"
    },
    {
      "phrase": "You only live once, but if you do it right, once is
       enough.",
      "author": "Mae West"
    },
    {
      "phrase": "If you tell the truth, you don't have to remember
       anything.",
      "author": "Mark Twain"
    },
    {
      "phrase": "Be yourself; everyone else is already taken.",
      "author": "Oscar Wilde"
    }
  ]
}
```

File: src/data/phrases.json

Save this file in a data directory and then import it into your Firebase database:

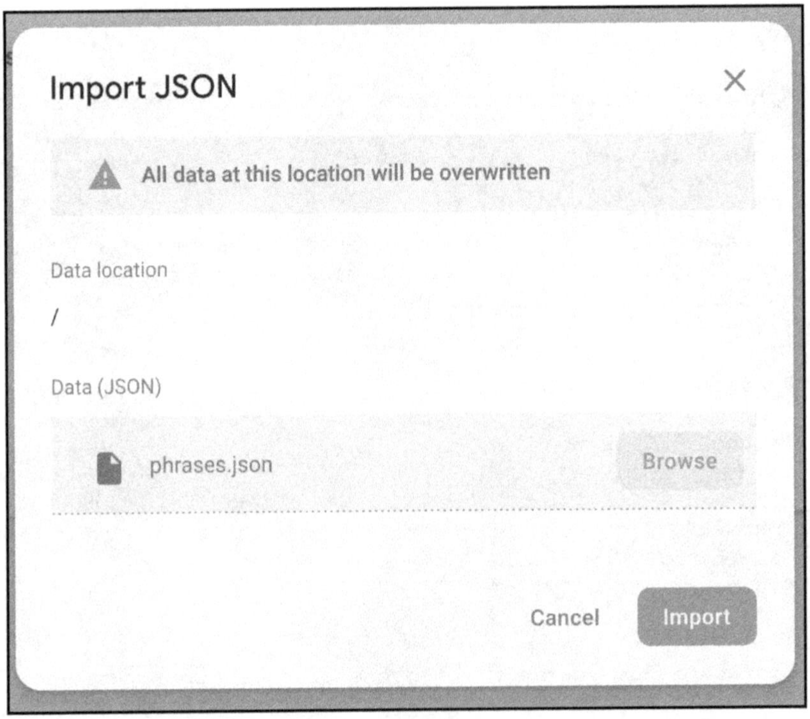

TIP

As you can see in the red warning, All data at this location will be overwritten. This means that if you have any old data in the database, it will be replaced, so be careful with importing new data into your database.

If you did everything correctly, you should see the imported data like this:

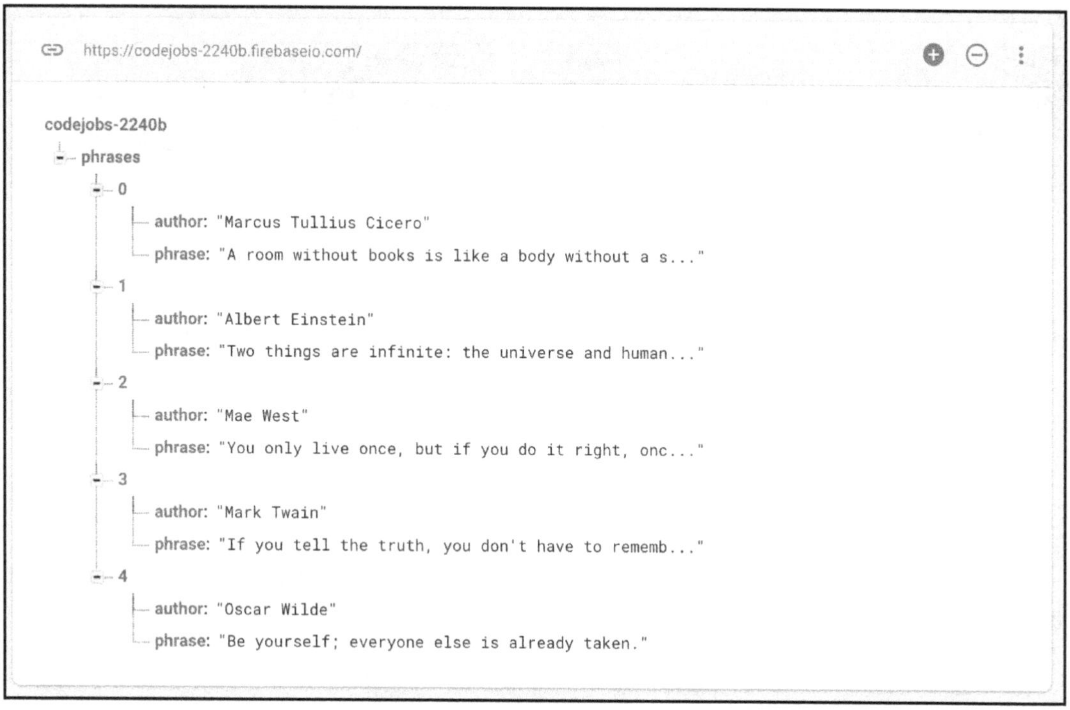
https://codejobs-2240b.firebaseio.com/
codejobs-2240b
phrases
0
author: "Marcus Tullius Cicero"
phrase: "A room without books is like a body without a s..."
1
author: "Albert Einstein"
phrase: "Two things are infinite: the universe and human..."
2
author: "Mae West"
phrase: "You only live once, but if you do it right, onc..."
3
author: "Mark Twain"
phrase: "If you tell the truth, you don't have to rememb..."
4
author: "Oscar Wilde"
phrase: "Be yourself; everyone else is already taken."

Now we need to alter our permissions to be able to read and write in our database. If you go to the **Rules** tab, you will see something like this:

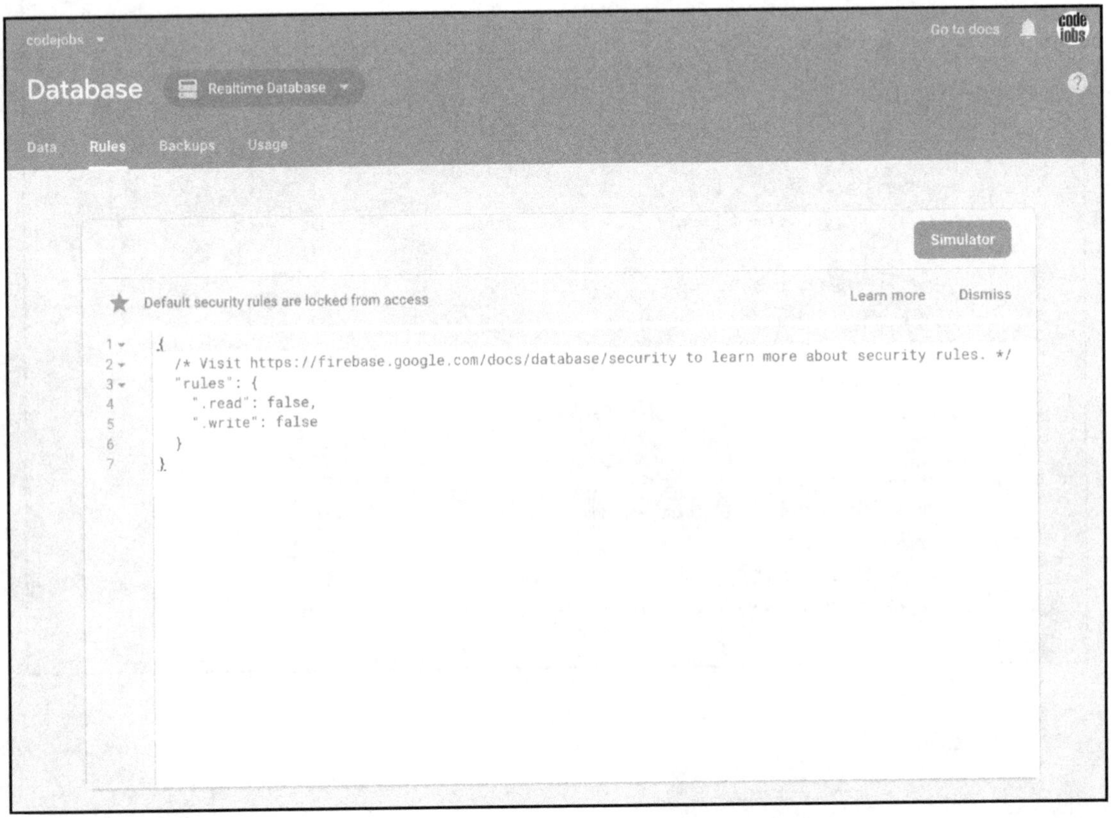

For now, let's change them to true and then click on the **Publish** button:

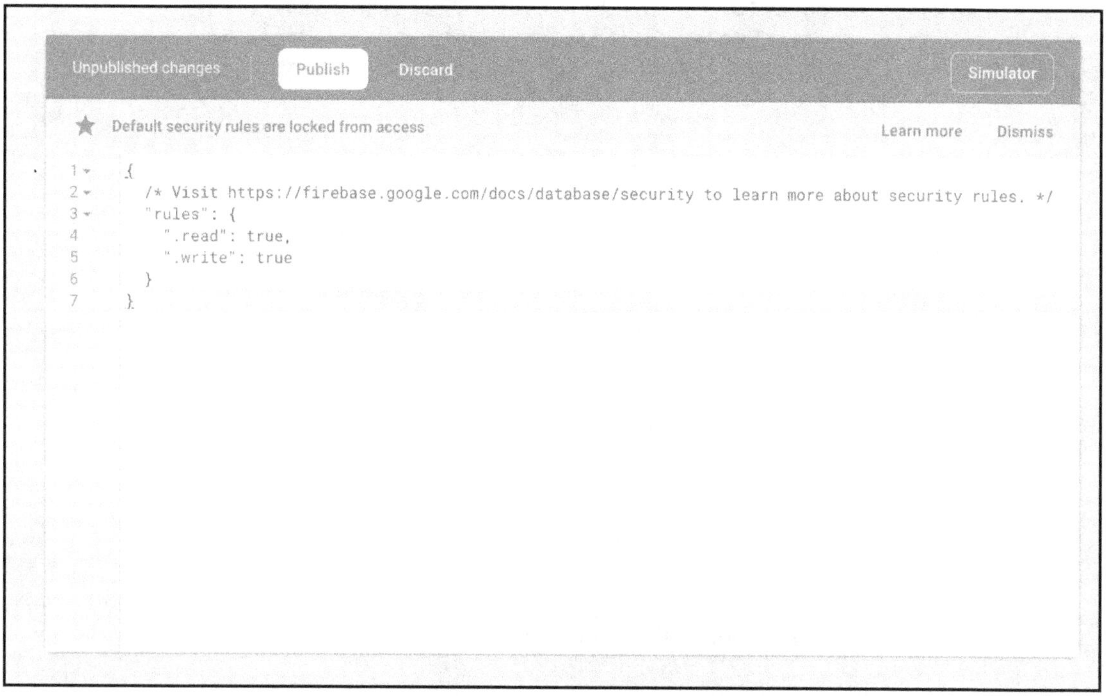

Finally, we have finished all the needed steps on Firebase. Now let's create the Firebase application in React. We will re-use the last recipe of the `CoinMarketCap` (`Repository: Chapter05/Recipe2/coinmarketcap`). The first thing we need to do is to install the firebase dependency:

```
npm install firebase
```

How to do it...

I removed some components from the last recipe, and I just focused on the Phrases application. Let's create it by following these steps:

1. Copy your project configuration and replace it in the file:

```
export const fbConfig = {
  ref: 'phrases',
  app: {
    apiKey: 'AIzaSyASppMJh_6QIGTeXVBeYszzz7iTNTADxRU',
```

```
      authDomain: 'codejobs-2240b.firebaseapp.com',
      databaseURL: 'https://codejobs-2240b.firebaseio.com',
      projectId: 'codejobs-2240b',
      storageBucket: 'codejobs-2240b.appspot.com',
      messagingSenderId: '278058258089'
    }
  };
```

File: src/config/firebase.js

2. After this, we need to create a file to manage our Firebase database, and we will export our `ref` (our phrases table):

```
import firebase from 'firebase';
import { fbConfig } from '../../config/firebase';

firebase.initializeApp(fbConfig.app);

export default firebase.database().ref(fbConfig.ref);
```

File: src/shared/firebase/database.js

3. Let's prepare everything for our component. First, go to the `routes` file and add the `Phrases` container to the root path of your router:

```
// Dependencies
import React from 'react';
import { Route, Switch } from 'react-router-dom';

// Components
import App from './components/App';
import Error404 from './components/Error/404';
import Phrases from './components/Phrases';

const AppRoutes = () => (
  <App>
    <Switch>
      <Route path="/" component={Phrases} exact />
      <Route component={Error404} />
    </Switch>
  </App>
);

export default AppRoutes;
```

File: src/routes.jsx

4. Now let's create our `actionTypes` file:

```
export const FETCH_PHRASE_REQUEST = 'FETCH_PHRASE_REQUEST';
export const FETCH_PHRASE_SUCCESS = 'FETCH_PHRASE_SUCCESS';

export const ADD_PHRASE_REQUEST = 'ADD_PHRASE_REQUEST';

export const DELETE_PHRASE_REQUEST = 'DELETE_PHRASE_REQUEST';
export const DELETE_PHRASE_SUCCESS = 'DELETE_PHRASE_SUCCESS';

export const UPDATE_PHRASE_REQUEST = 'UPDATE_PHRASE_REQUEST';
export const UPDATE_PHRASE_SUCCESS = 'UPDATE_PHRASE_SUCCESS';
export const UPDATE_PHRASE_ERROR = 'UPDATE_PHRASE_ERROR';
```

File: src/actions/actionTypes.js

5. Now, in our actions, we are going to perform four tasks (fetch, add, delete, and update) just like a CRUD (Create, Read, Update and Delete):

```
// Firebase Database
import database from '../shared/firebase/database';

// Action Types
import {
  FETCH_PHRASE_REQUEST,
  FETCH_PHRASE_SUCCESS,
  ADD_PHRASE_REQUEST,
  DELETE_PHRASE_REQUEST,
  DELETE_PHRASE_SUCCESS,
  UPDATE_PHRASE_REQUEST,
  UPDATE_PHRASE_SUCCESS,
  UPDATE_PHRASE_ERROR
} from './actionTypes';

// Base Actions
import { request, received } from '../shared/redux/baseActions';

export const fetchPhrases = () => dispatch => {
  // Dispatching our FETCH_PHRASE_REQUEST action
  dispatch(request(FETCH_PHRASE_REQUEST));

  // Listening for added rows
  database.on('child_added', snapshot => {
    dispatch(received(
      FETCH_PHRASE_SUCCESS,
      {
        key: snapshot.key,
        ...snapshot.val()
```

```
      }
    ));
  });

  // Listening for updated rows
  database.on('child_changed', snapshot => {
    dispatch(received(
      UPDATE_PHRASE_SUCCESS,
      {
        key: snapshot.key,
        ...snapshot.val()
      }
    ));
  });

  // Lisetining for removed rows
  database.on('child_removed', snapshot => {
    dispatch(received(
      DELETE_PHRASE_SUCCESS,
      {
        key: snapshot.key
      }
    ));
  });
};

export const addPhrase = (phrase, author) => dispatch => {
  // Dispatching our ADD_PHRASE_REQUEST action
  dispatch(request(ADD_PHRASE_REQUEST));

  // Adding a new element by pushing to the ref.
  // NOTE: Once this is executed the listener
  // will be on fetchPhrases (child_added).
  database.push({
    phrase,
    author
  });
}

export const deletePhrase = key => dispatch => {
  // Dispatching our DELETE_PHRASE_REQUEST action
  dispatch(request(DELETE_PHRASE_REQUEST));

  // Removing element by key
  // NOTE: Once this is executed the listener
  // will be on fetchPhrases (child_removed).
  database.child(key).remove();
}
```

```
export const updatePhrase = (key, phrase, author) => dispatch =>
{
  // Dispatching our UPDATE_PHRASE_REQUEST action
  dispatch(request(UPDATE_PHRASE_REQUEST));

  // Collecting our data...
  const data = {
    phrase,
    author
  };

  // Updating an element by key and data
  database
    // First we select our element by key
    .child(key)
    // Updating the data in this point
    .update(data)
    // Returning the updated data
    .then(() => database.once('value'))
    // Getting the actual values of the snapshat
    .then(snapshot => snapshot.val())
    .catch(error => {
      // If there is an error we dispatch our error action
      dispatch(request(UPDATE_PHRASE_ERROR));

      return {
        errorCode: error.code,
        errorMessage: error.message
      };
    });
};
```

File: src/actions/phrasesActions.js

In Firebase, we don't use a regular ID. Instead, Firebase uses a key value as an ID. The imported data is like a basic array, with keys 0, 1, 2, 3, 4, and so on, so for that data, each key is used as an ID. But when we create data through Firebase, the keys are going to be unique string values with random code, such as `-lg4fgFQkfm`.

6. After we have added our actions, we can create our reducer file:

```
// Action Types
import {
  FETCH_PHRASE_SUCCESS,
  DELETE_PHRASE_SUCCESS,
  UPDATE_PHRASE_SUCCESS,
```

```
} from '../actions/actionTypes';
// Utils
import { getNewState } from '../shared/utils/frontend';

// Initial State
const initialState = {
  phrases: []
};

export default function phrasesReducer(state = initialState,
action) {
  switch (action.type) {
    case FETCH_PHRASE_SUCCESS: {
      const { payload: phrase } = action;

      const newPhrases = [...state.phrases, phrase];

      return getNewState(state, {
        phrases: newPhrases
      });
    }

    case DELETE_PHRASE_SUCCESS: {
      const { payload: deletedPhrase } = action;

      const filteredPhrases = state.phrases.filter(
        phrase => phrase.key !== deletedPhrase.key
      );

      return getNewState(state, {
        phrases: filteredPhrases
      });
    }

    case UPDATE_PHRASE_SUCCESS: {
      const { payload: updatedPhrase } = action;

      const index = state.phrases.findIndex(
        phrase => phrase.key === updatedPhrase.key
      );

      state.phrases[index] = updatedPhrase;

      return getNewState({}, {
        phrases: state.phrases
      });
    }
```

```
      default:
       return state;
    }
  };
```

File: src/reducers/phrasesReducer.js

7. Let's now create our Redux container. We will include all the actions we will dispatch in our component and connect Redux to get the phrases state:

```
// Dependencies
import { connect } from 'react-redux';
import { bindActionCreators } from 'redux';

// Components
import Phrases from './Phrases';

// Actions
import {
  addPhrase,
  deletePhrase,
  fetchPhrases,
  updatePhrase
} from '../../actions/phrasesActions';

const mapStateToProps = ({ phrases }) => ({
  phrases: phrases.phrases
});

const mapDispatchToProps = dispatch => bindActionCreators(
  {
    addPhrase,
    deletePhrase,
    fetchPhrases,
    updatePhrase
  },
  dispatch
);

export default connect(
  mapStateToProps,
  mapDispatchToProps
)(Phrases);
```

File: src/components/Phrases/index.js

8. Then our `Phrases` component will be as follows:

```
// Dependencies
import React, { Component } from 'react';
import { array } from 'prop-types';

// Styles
import './Phrases.css';

class Phrases extends Component {
  static propTypes = {
    phrases: array
  };

  state = {
    phrase: '',
    author: '',
    editKey: false
  };

  componentWillMount() {
    this.props.fetchPhrases();
  }

  handleOnChange = e => {
    const { target: { name, value } } = e;

    this.setState({
      [name]: value
    });
  }

  handleAddNewPhrase = () => {
    if (this.state.phrase && this.state.author) {
      this.props.addPhrase(
        this.state.phrase,
        this.state.author
      );
      // After we created the new phrase we clean the states
      this.setState({
        phrase: '',
        author: ''
      });
    }
  }

  handleDeleteElement = key => {
    this.props.deletePhrase(key);
```

```
}

handleEditElement = (key, phrase, author) => {
  this.setState({
    editKey: key,
    phrase,
    author
  });
}

handleUpdatePhrase = () => {
  if (this.state.phrase && this.state.author) {
    this.props.updatePhrase(
      this.state.editKey,
      this.state.phrase,
      this.state.author
    );

    this.setState({
      phrase: '',
      author: '',
      editKey: false
    });
  }
}

render() {
  const { phrases } = this.props;

  return (
    <div className="phrases">
      <div className="add">
        <p>Phrase: </p>

        <textarea
          name="phrase"
          value={this.state.phrase}
          onChange={this.handleOnChange}
        ></textarea>

        <p>Author</p>
        <input
          name="author"
          type="text"
          value={this.state.author}
          onChange={this.handleOnChange}
        />
```

```
          <p>
            <button
              onClick={
                this.state.editKey
                  ? this.handleUpdatePhrase
                  : this.handleAddNewPhrase
              }
            >
              {this.state.editKey
                ? 'Edit Phrase'
                : 'Add New Phrase'}
            </button>
          </p>
        </div>

        {phrases && phrases.map(({ key, phrase, author }) => (
          <blockquote key={key} className="phrase">
            <p className="mark">
              "
            </p>

            <p className="text">
              {phrase}
            </p>

            <hr />

            <p className="author">
              {author}
            </p>

            <a
              onClick={() => {
                this.handleDeleteElement(key);
              }}
            >
              X
            </a>
            <a
              onClick={
                () => this.handleEditElement(key, phrase, author)
              }
            >
              Edit
            </a>
          </blockquote>
        ))}
      </div>
```

```
    );
  }
}

export default Phrases;
```

File: src/components/Phrases/Phrases.jsx

9. Finally, our styles file is as follows:

```
hr {
  width: 98%;
  border: 1px solid white;
}

.phrase {
  background-color: #2db2ff;
  border-radius: 17px;
  box-shadow: 2px 2px 2px 2px #E0E0E0;
  color: white;
  font-size: 20px;
  margin-top: 25px;
  overflow: hidden;
  border-left: none;
  padding: 20px;
}

.mark {
  color: white;
  font-family: "Times New Roman", Georgia, Serif;
  font-size: 100px;
  font-weight: bold;
  margin-top: -20px;
  text-align: left;
  text-indent: 20px;
}

.text {
  font-size: 30px;
  font-style: italic;
  margin: 0 auto;
  margin-top: -65px;
  text-align: center;
  width: 90%;
}

.author {
  font-size: 30px;
```

```
}

textarea {
  width: 50%;
  font-size: 30px;
  padding: 10px;
  border: 1px solid #333;
}

input {
  font-size: 30px;
  border: 1px solid #333;
}

a {
  cursor: pointer;
  float: right;
  margin-right: 10px;
}
```

File: src/components/Phrases/Phrases.css

How it works...

The key to understanding how Firebase works with Redux is that you need to know that Firebase uses a WebSocket to sync the data, and that means the data is streaming in real time. The way to detect data changes is by using the `database.on()` method.

In the `fetchPhrases()` action, we have three Firebase listeners:

- `database.on('child_added')`: It has two functionalities. The first one brings the data from Firebase (the first time) row by row. The second functionality is to detect when a new row is added to the database and updates the data in real time.
- `database.on('child_changed')`: It detects changes in existing rows. This works when we perform an update of a row.
- `database.on('child_removed')`: Detects when a row is removed.

There is another method called `database.once('value')`, which does the same thing as `child_added` but returns the data in an array, and just once. That means it does not detect dynamic changes like `child_added`.

If you run the application, you will see this view:

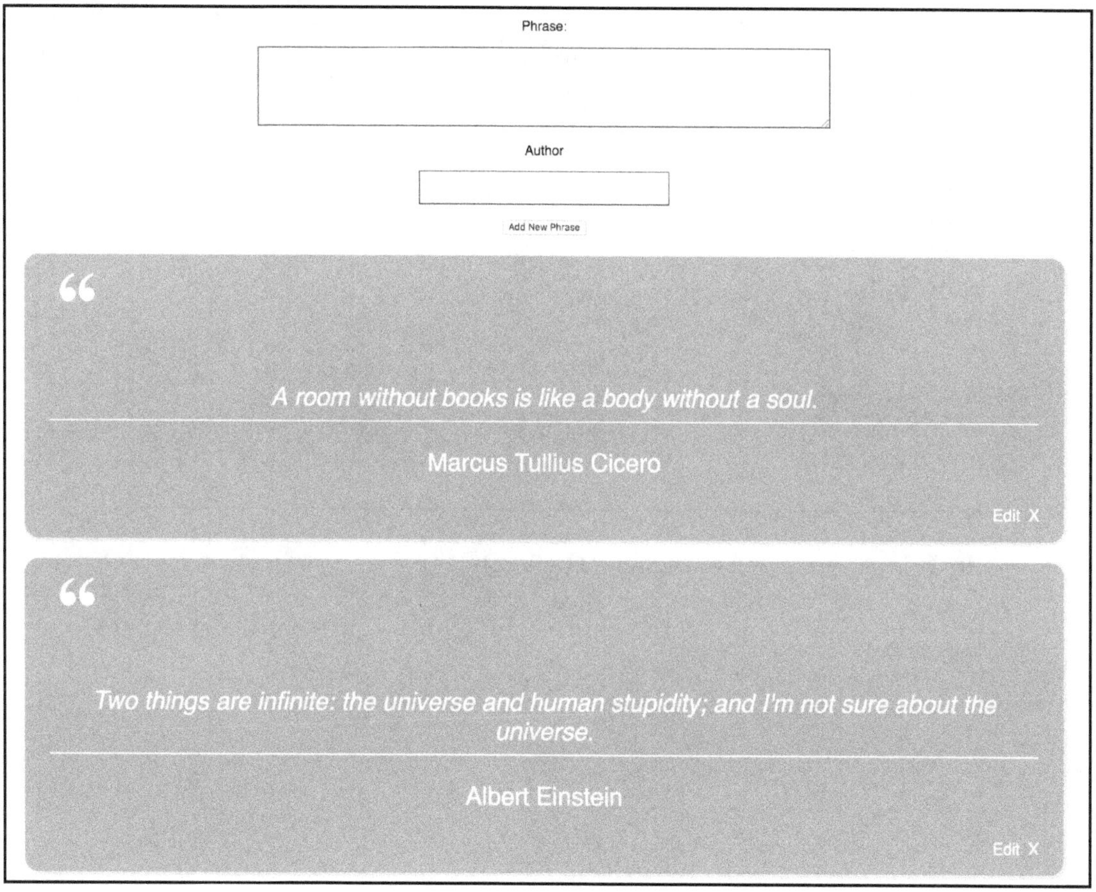

Phrase:
Author
Add New Phrase
A room without books is like a body without a soul.
Marcus Tullius Cicero
Edit X
Two things are infinite: the universe and human stupidity; and I'm not sure about the universe.
Albert Einstein
Edit X

The blockquotes are too big to put all of them in, but our last one is this:

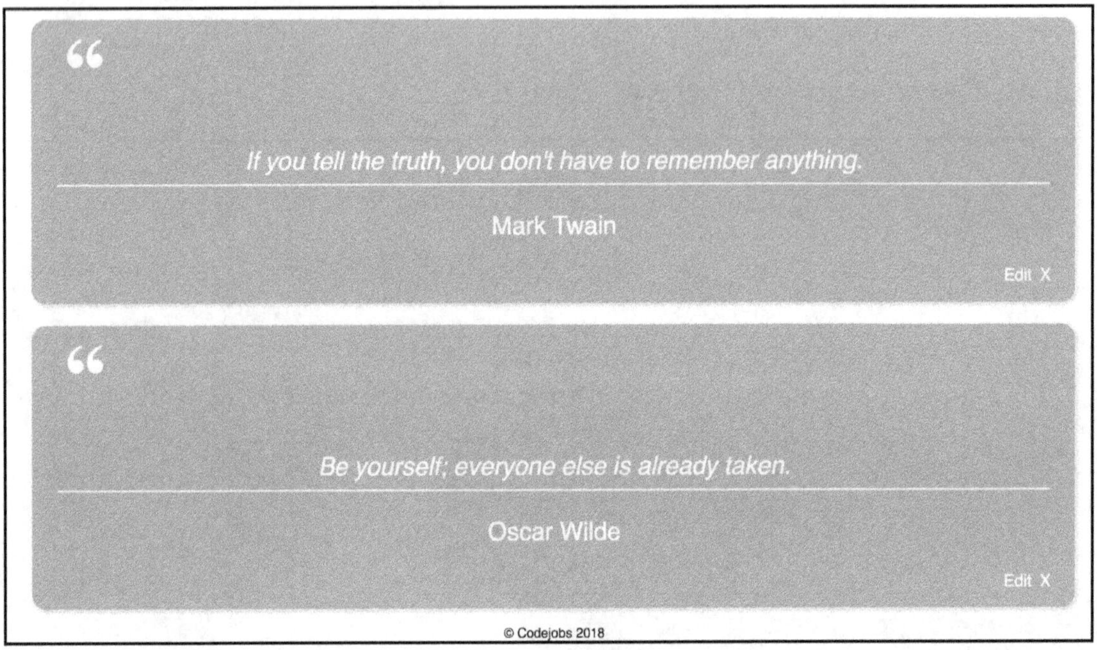
If you tell the truth, you don't have to remember anything.
Mark Twain
Edit X
Be yourself; everyone else is already taken.
Oscar Wilde
Edit X
© Codejobs 2018

Let's modify our `phrases.json` and add a new row:

```
{
  "phrases": [
    {
      "phrase": "A room without books is like a body without a
      soul.",
      "author": "Marcus Tullius Cicero"
    },
    {
      "phrase": "Two things are infinite: the universe and human
       stupidity; and
       I'm not sure about the universe.",
      "author": "Albert Einstein"
    },
    {
      "phrase": "You only live once, but if you do it right, once is
      enough.",
      "author": "Mae West"
    },
    {
      "phrase": "If you tell the truth, you don't have to remember
```

```
          anything.",
          "author": "Mark Twain"
        },
        {
          "phrase": "Be yourself; everyone else is already taken.",
          "author": "Oscar Wilde"
        },
        {
          "phrase": "Hasta la vista, baby!",
          "author": "Terminator"
        }
      ]
    }
```

If we go to Firebase and import the JSON again, we will see that, in real time, the data will be updated without refreshing the page:

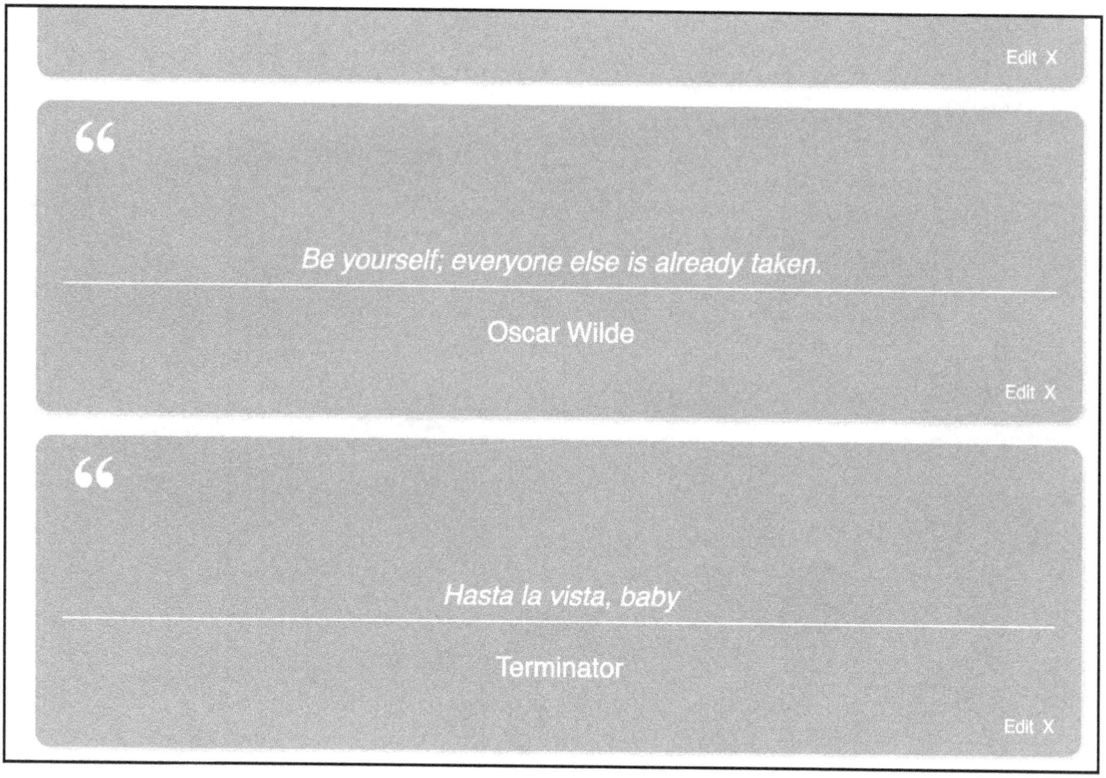

Now, if you see an `X` link to remove phrases, let's remove the first one (Marcus Tullius Cicero). If you open the Firebase page in another tab, you will see that the data is being deleted in real time:

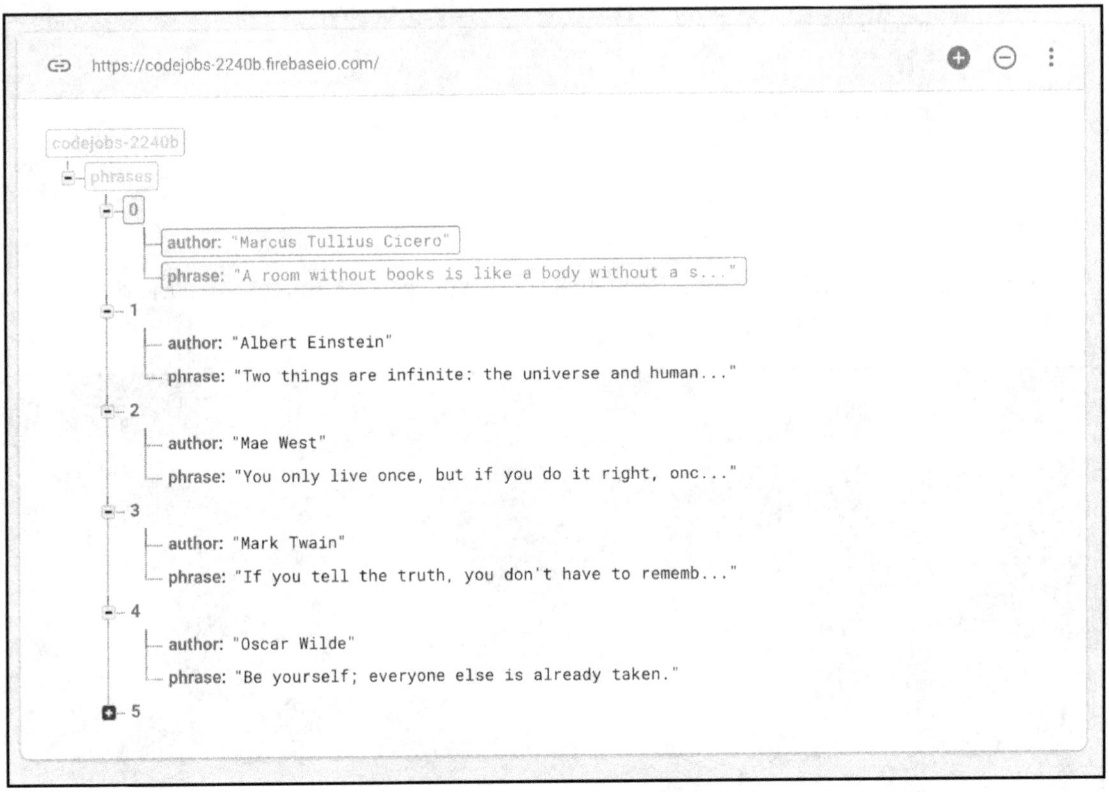
https://codejobs-2240b.firebaseio.com/
codejobs-2240b
phrases
0
author: "Marcus Tullius Cicero"
phrase: "A room without books is like a body without a s..."
1
author: "Albert Einstein"
phrase: "Two things are infinite: the universe and human..."
2
author: "Mae West"
phrase: "You only live once, but if you do it right, onc..."
3
author: "Mark Twain"
phrase: "If you tell the truth, you don't have to rememb..."
4
author: "Oscar Wilde"
phrase: "Be yourself; everyone else is already taken."
5

Also, if you add a new row (using textarea and input), you will see that reflected in real time:

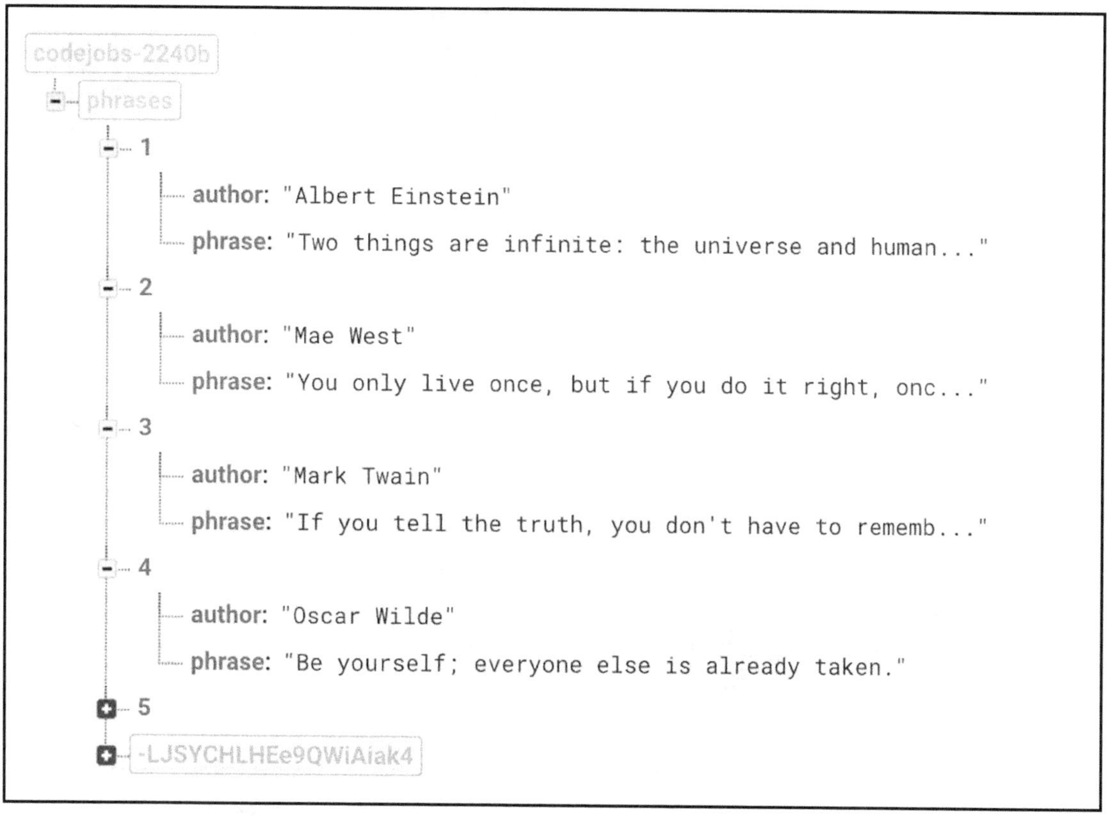
codejobs-2240b
phrases
1
author: "Albert Einstein"
phrase: "Two things are infinite: the universe and human..."
2
author: "Mae West"
phrase: "You only live once, but if you do it right, onc..."
3
author: "Mark Twain"
phrase: "If you tell the truth, you don't have to rememb..."
4
author: "Oscar Wilde"
phrase: "Be yourself; everyone else is already taken."
5
-LJSYCHLHEe9QWiAiak4

As I mentioned before, when we add new data from our React application, instead of importing a JSON Firebase will generate unique keys for the new data. In this case for the new phrase I added, the `-LJSYCHLHEe9QWiAiak4` key was created.

Even if we update a row, we can see that the change was reflected in real time:

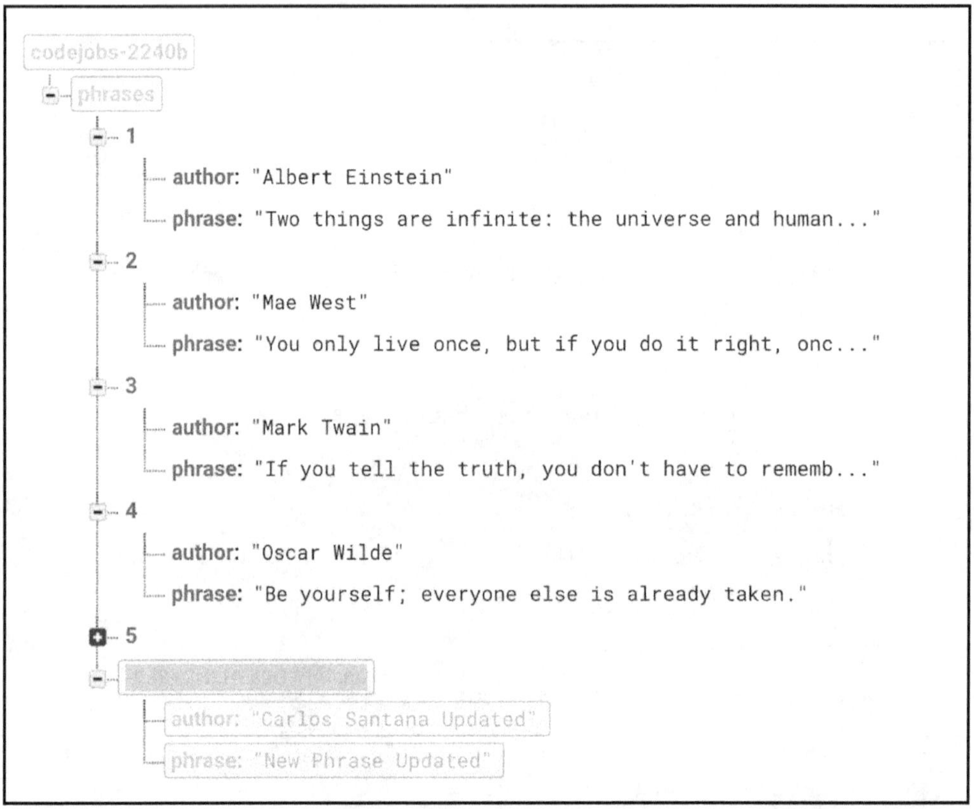
codejobs-2240b
phrases
1
author: "Albert Einstein"
phrase: "Two things are infinite: the universe and human..."
2
author: "Mae West"
phrase: "You only live once, but if you do it right, onc..."
3
author: "Mark Twain"
phrase: "If you tell the truth, you don't have to rememb..."
4
author: "Oscar Wilde"
phrase: "Be yourself; everyone else is already taken."
5
author: "Carlos Santana Updated"
phrase: "New Phrase Updated"

As you can see, all the operations are easy to implement, and with Firebase we saved a lot of time that would otherwise have been spent working on a backend service. Firebase is awesome!

6
Creating Forms with Redux Form

In this chapter, the following recipes will be covered:

- Creating a controlled form with the local state
- Building a form using Redux Form
- Implementing validation in a form

Introduction

Forms are a fundamental part of any web application, and in the following recipes, we are going to learn how to use forms with and without Redux Form.

Creating a controlled form with the local state

For this recipe, we are going to create a simple Todo List to use a form using our local state.

Getting ready

For this recipe, we need to install the `uuid` package to generate random IDs, as shown in the following code:

```
npm install uuid
```

How to do it...

Let's create our controlled form by following these steps:

1. First, for the Todo List, we will create a new component called `Todo` into `src/components/Todo/index.jsx`. The skeleton we will use is shown in the following code:

```
import React, { Component } from 'react';
import uuidv4 from 'uuid/v4';
import './Todo.css';

class Todo extends Component {
  constructor() {
    super();

    // Initial state...
    this.state = {
      task: '',
      items: []
    };
  }

  render() {
    return (
      <div className="Todo">
        <h1>New Task:</h1>

        <form onSubmit={this.handleOnSubmit}>
          <input value={this.state.task} />
        </form>
      </div>
    );
  }
}

export default Todo;
```

File: src/components/Todo/index.jsx

2. Remember that we need to add the component to our `src/routes.jsx`, as shown in the following code:

```
// Dependencies
import React from 'react';
import { Route, Switch } from 'react-router-dom';

// Components
import App from './components/App';
import About from './components/About';
import Coins from './components/Coins';
import Contact from './components/Contact';
import Home from './components/Home';
import Notes from './components/Notes';
import Todo from './components/Todo';
import Error404 from './components/Error/404';

const AppRoutes = () => (
  <App>
    <Switch>
      <Route path="/" component={Home} exact />
      <Route path="/about" component={About} exact />
      <Route path="/coins" component={Coins} exact />
      <Route path="/contact" component={Contact} exact />
      <Route path="/notes" component={Notes} exact />
      <Route path="/notes/:noteId" component={Notes} exact />
      <Route path="/todo" component={Todo} exact />
      <Route component={Error404} />
    </Switch>
  </App>
);

export default AppRoutes;
```

File: src/routes.jsx

3. If you go to `/todo` you will see the input, but you will probably notice that it is not possible to write anything on it, and this is because we are connecting our local state (`this.state.task`) to our input value, but we need an `onChange` function to update our state, as demonstrated in the following code:

```
import React, { Component } from 'react';
import uuidv4 from 'uuid/v4';
import './Todo.css';

class Todo extends Component {
  constructor() {
```

```
    super();

    // Initial state...
    this.state = {
      task: '',
      items: []
    };
  }

  handleOnChange = e => {
    const { target: { value } } = e;
    // Updating our task state with the input value...
    this.setState({
      task: value
    });
  }

  render() {
    return (
      <div className="Todo">
        <h1>New Task:</h1>

        <form onSubmit={this.handleOnSubmit}>
          <input
            value={this.state.task}
            onChange={this.handleOnChange}
          />
        </form>
      </div>
    );
  }
}

export default Todo;
```

File: src/components/Todo/index.jsx

4. Now we can write anything in our input, as shown in the following screenshot:

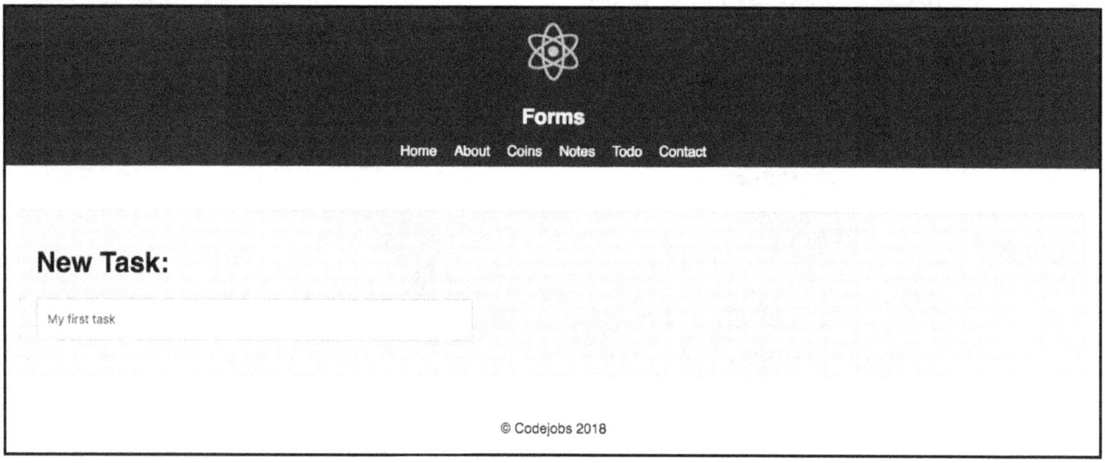

5. To save the item written in our input, we need to add an `onSubmit` function in our `form` tag, where we need to update our local state to push the item to the `items` array. Also, we need to include our `List` component, where we are going to display all the items. The complete code is as follows:

```
import React, { Component } from 'react';
import uuidv4 from 'uuid/v4';
import List from './List';
import './Todo.css';

class Todo extends Component {
  constructor() {
    super();

    // Initial state...
    this.state = {
      task: '',
      items: []
    };
  }

  handleOnChange = e => {
    const { target: { value } } = e;

    // Updating our task state with the input value...
    this.setState({
      task: value
    });
```

```
    }

    handleOnSubmit = e => {
      // Prevent default to avoid the actual form submit...
      e.preventDefault();

      // Once is submitted we reset the task value and we push
      // task to the items array.
      this.setState({
        task: '',
        items: [
          ...this.state.items,
          {
            id: uuidv4(),
            task: this.state.task,
            complete: false
          }
        ]
      });
    }

    render() {
      return (
        <div className="Todo">
          <h1>New Task:</h1>

          <form onSubmit={this.handleOnSubmit}>
            <input
              value={this.state.task}
              onChange={this.handleOnChange}
            />
          </form>

          <List items={this.state.items} />
        </div>
      );
    }
  }

  export default Todo;
```

File: src/components/Todo/index.jsx

6. Our `List` component will be a functional component where we will render a list of items, as shown in the following code:

```
import React from 'react';

const List = props => (
  <ul>
    {props.items.map((item, key) => (
      <li key={key}>
        {item.task}
      </li>
    ))}
  </ul>
);

export default List;
```

File: src/components/Todo/List.jsx

7. Finally, we need to add our CSS file, as shown in the following code:

```
.Todo {
    background-color: #f5f5f5;
    border-radius: 4px;
    border: 1px solid #e3e3e3;
    box-shadow: inset 0 1px 1px rgba(0,0,0,.05);
    margin-bottom: 20px;
    margin: 50px auto;
    min-height: 20px;
    padding: 19px;
    text-align: left;
    width: 70%;
}

.Todo ul {
    margin: 20px 0px;
    padding: 0;
    list-style: none;
}

.Todo ul li {
    background-color: #fff;
    border: 1px solid #ddd;
    display: flex;
    justify-content: space-between;
    margin-bottom: -1px;
    padding: 10px 15px;
    position: relative;
```

```
}

.Todo form input {
    background-color: #fff;
    border-radius: 4px;
    border: 1px solid #ccc;
    box-shadow: inset 0 1px 1px rgba(0,0,0,.075);
    color: #555;
    font-size: 14px;
    height: 34px;
    line-height: 34px;
    padding: 6px 12px;
    width: 40%;
}

.Todo form button {
    background: #2ba6cb;
    border: 1px solid #1e728c;
    box-shadow: 0 1px 0 rgba(255, 255, 255, 0.5) inset;
    color: white;
    cursor: pointer;
    display: block;
    font-size: 14px;
    font-weight: bold;
    line-height: 1;
    margin: 20px auto;
    padding: 10px 20px 11px;
    position: relative;
    text-align: center;
    text-decoration: none;
}
```

File: src/components/Todo/Todo.css

8. Our Todo List will look as shown in the following screenshot:

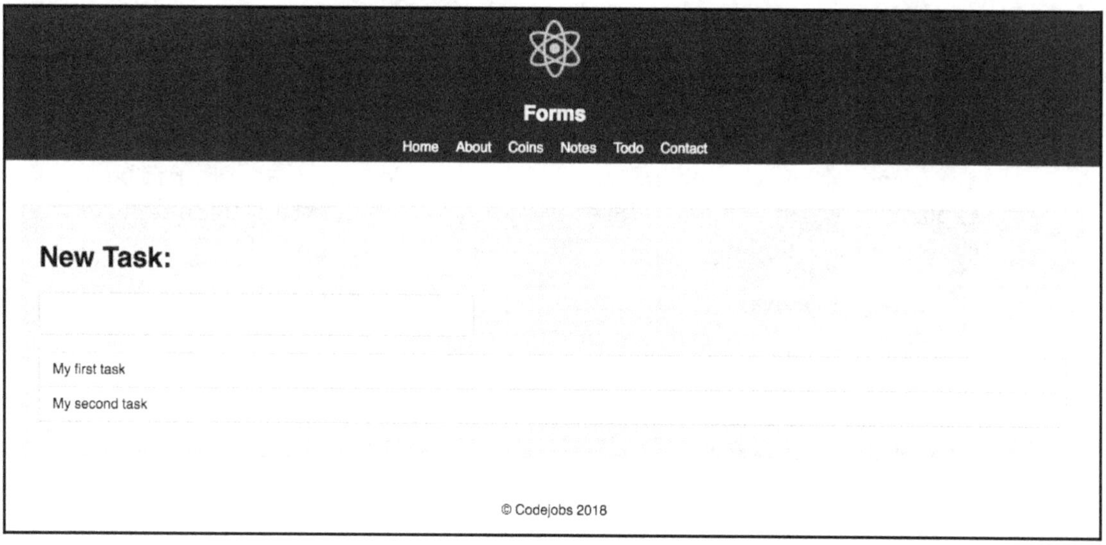

How it works...

As you can see, the only way to retrieve the values from input forms is by using the local state with an `onChange` function to update the value of the input. If you connect a state to the input value, but you don't add an `onChange` callback to update it, you won't be able to write anything, since the Virtual DOM is not being updated, and the only way to do so is by updating our local state.

Building a form using Redux Form

Redux Form is typically used for large forms or steps forms because it has a Redux state to keep the values through the entire form. Also, Redux Form is handy to validate the data and efficiently handle the submission.

Getting ready

For this recipe, we need to install Redux Form as follows:

```
npm install redux-form
```

How to do it...

For this recipe, we are going to make the same Todo List, but this time using Redux Form:

1. Once we've installed Redux Form, we need to do some modifications to the code of the last recipe to implement Redux Form. The first thing we need to do is to add a reducer for our forms. For this, we need to import a reducer from `redux-form`, and we can change the name of the variable to `formReducer` to be more explicit, and then add the reducer as a form into our `combineReducers`, as shown in the following code:

```
// Dependencies
import { combineReducers } from 'redux';
import { reducer as formReducer } from 'redux-form';

// Components Reducers
import coins from '../../reducers/coinsReducer';

// Shared Reducers
import device from './deviceReducer';

const rootReducer = combineReducers({
  coins,
  device,
  form: formReducer
});

export default rootReducer;
```

File: src/shared/reducers/index.js

2. Normally, all the forms we create with Redux Form need their component, and so that means we need to create a component to handle our Todo Form. As we need to create a file called `TodoForm.jsx` into our `Todo` folder, the code of our component is as follows:

```
import React, { Component } from 'react';
import { Field, reduxForm } from 'redux-form';

class TodoForm extends Component {
  // Functional component to render an input...
  renderInput = ({ input }) => <input {...input} type="text" />;

  // This function is useful to handle our
  onSubmit = values => {
    const { addTask, dispatch, reset } = this.props;
```

```
    // Resetting our form, this will clear our input...
    dispatch(reset('todo'));

    // Executing our addTask method and
    // passing the form values.
    addTask(values);
  }

  render() {
    // handleSubmit is part of Redux Form
    // to handle the onSubmit event
    const { handleSubmit } = this.props;

    return (
      <form onSubmit={handleSubmit(this.onSubmit)}>
        {/* Field is a Redux Form Component, we need to pass the
         name of the input and the component we are using to
         render it */}
        <Field
          name="task"
          component={this.renderInput}
        />
      </form>
    )
  }
}
// With this we named our form reducer for this specific form
(todo).
export default reduxForm({
  form: 'todo'
})(TodoForm);
```

File: src/components/Todo/TodoForm.jsx

3. Redux Form contains many useful props to handle our data in the forms. I market the props we are going to use for this recipe (`addTask` is a prop passed from another component, so that one is not properly part of Redux Form), you can see the all the props by adding a console in your render method `console.log(this.props);`, as shown in the following screenshot:

```
▼Object
» ▶addTask: f (values)
   anyTouched: false
  ▶array: {insert: f, move: f, pop: f, push: f, remove: f, …}
  ▶asyncValidate: f (name, value, trigger)
   asyncValidating: false
  ▶autofill: f ()
  ▶blur: f ()
  ▶change: f ()
  ▶clearAsyncError: f ()
  ▶clearFields: f ()
  ▶clearSubmit: f ()
  ▶clearSubmitErrors: f ()
  ▶destroy: f ()
   dirty: false
» ▶dispatch: f (action)
   error: undefined
   form: "todo"
» ▶handleSubmit: f (submitOrEvent)
   initialValues: undefined
  ▶initialize: f ()
   initialized: false
   invalid: false
   pristine: true
   pure: true
» ▶reset: f ()
  ▶resetSection: f ()
  ▶submit: f ()
   submitFailed: false
   submitSucceeded: false
   submitting: false
  ▶touch: f ()
   triggerSubmit: undefined
  ▶untouch: f ()
   valid: true
   warning: undefined
   ref: (...)
```

4. Now let's modify our `Todo` component to include the `TodoForm` component, and receive the data through our `addTask` method, as shown in the following code:

```
import React, { Component } from 'react';
import uuidv4 from 'uuid/v4';
import List from './List';
import TodoForm from './TodoForm';
import './Todo.css';
class Todo extends Component {
  constructor() {
    super();

    // Initial state...
    this.state = {
      items: []
    };
  }

  addTask = values => {
    // This values are coming from our
    // onSubmit method in our TodoForm.
    const { task } = values;

    this.setState({
      items: [
        ...this.state.items,
        {
          id: uuidv4(),
          task,
          complete: false
        }
      ]
    });
  }

  render() {
    return (
      <div className="Todo">
        <h1>New Task:</h1>

        <TodoForm addTask={this.addTask} />
        <List items={this.state.items} />
      </div>
    );
  }
}
export default Todo;
```

How it works...

As you can see, Redux Form is easy to implement:

1. On the first step, we connected our Redux Form reducer to our store
2. In the second step, we create our `TodoForm` component, where we render our form fields, connect our form reducer to the store, and where we send back the values to the `addTask` callback
3. In the last step, we render our `TodoForm` and send the `addTask` callback, which handles the task value to insert it into the local state

In the end, we are going to see the same result as the last recipe, but now using Redux Form, as shown in the following screenshot:

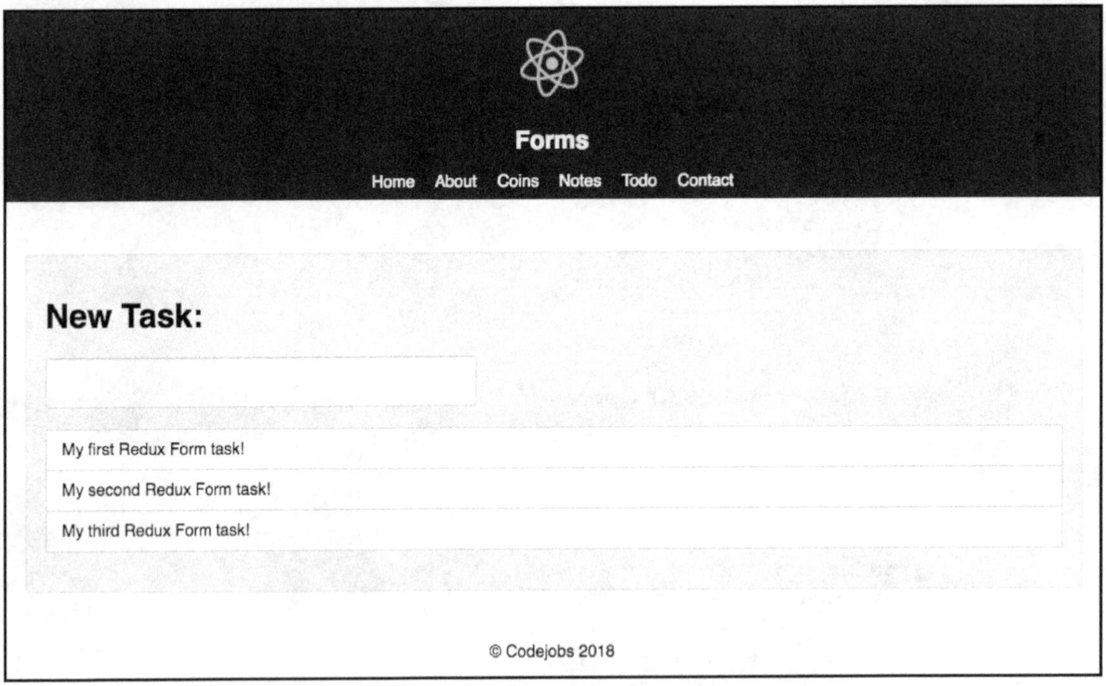

Implementing validation in a form

The last part of our Redux Form implementation is the validation. Using the previous recipe, let's add validation of the input task.

How to do it...

The validations are needed in any form, so let's add some validations to our fields:

1. First, we need to modify our `TodoForm.jsx` and we need to create a `validate` function, where we need to validate if our task is not empty. We then need to create a `renderError` method to render our error message if we try to add an empty task, as shown in the following code:

```
import React, { Component } from 'react';
import { Field, reduxForm } from 'redux-form';
import './TodoForm.css';

class TodoForm extends Component {
  renderInput = ({ input }) => <input {...input} type="text" />;

  onSubmit = values => {
    const { addTask, dispatch, reset } = this.props;

    // Resetting our form...
    dispatch(reset('todo'));

    addTask(values);
  }

  renderError(field) {
    const { meta: { submitFailed, error } } = field;

    if (submitFailed && error) {
      return (
        <div className="error">
          {error}
        </div>
      );
    }

    return null;
  }

  render() {
```

```
    const { handleSubmit, submitting } = this.props;

    return (
      <form onSubmit={handleSubmit(this.onSubmit)}>
        <Field name="task" component={this.renderInput} />
        <Field name="task" component={this.renderError} />
      </form>
    );
  }
}

const validate = values => {
  const errors = {};

  if (!values.task) {
    errors.task = 'Task cannot be empty!';
  }

  return errors;
}

export default reduxForm({
  validate,
  form: 'todo'
})(TodoForm);
```

File: src/components/Todo/TodoForm.jsx

2. Next, we need to create a `TodoForm.css` to add some styles to our error message, as shown in the following code:

```
.error {
  color: red;
  font-size: small;
  margin-top: 10px;
}
```

File: src/components/Todo/TodoForm.css

How it works...

If we try to add a new task without any value and press *Enter* to submit the form, we are going to see the view shown in the following screenshot:

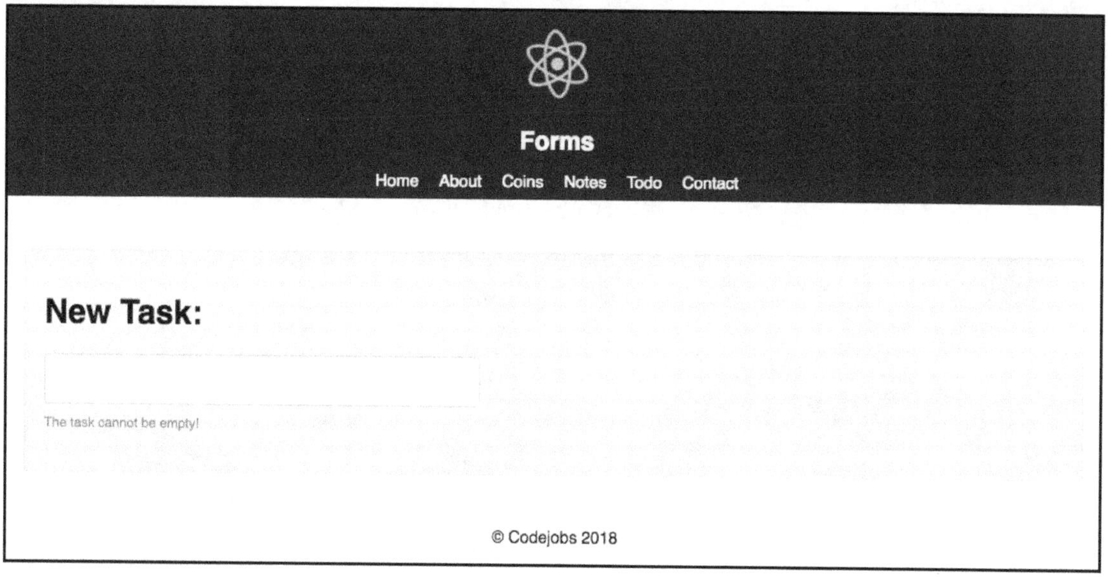

7 Animations with React

In this chapter, the following recipes will be covered:

- Animating a todo list with ReactCSSTransitionGroup
- Using react-animations library
- Creating our first animation with React pose

Introduction

Animations are very common in any web application. Since CSS3, animations have become widespread and easy to implement. The most common use of animations are transitions, where you can change CSS properties and define the duration or delay. React can handle animations using an animation add-on called `ReactCSSTransitionGroup`. In the following recipes, we are going to use `ReactCSSTransitionGroup` to create some animations. `ReactCSSTransitionGroup` is an add-on component for implementing basic CSS animations and transitions smoothly.

Animating a todo list with ReactCSSTransitionGroup

In this recipe, we are going to animate a todo list using `ReactCSSTransitionGroup`.

Getting Ready

For this recipe, we need to install the `react-addons-css-transition-group` package:

```
npm install react-addons-css-transition-group
```

How to do it...

We are going to make a Todo list with some animations:

1. First, let's create our `Todo` component:

```
import React, { Component } from 'react';
import uuidv4 from 'uuid/v4';
import List from './List';
import './Todo.css';

class Todo extends Component {
  constructor() {
    super();

    // Initial state...
    this.state = {
      task: '',
      items: []
    };
  }

  componentWillMount() {
    // Setting default tasks...
    this.setState({
      items: [
        {
          id: uuidv4(),
          task: 'Default Task 1',
          completed: false
        },
        {
          id: uuidv4(),
          task: 'Default Task 2',
          completed: true
        },
        {
          id: uuidv4(),
          task: 'Default Task 3',
          completed: false
```

```
        }
      ]
    });
  }

  handleOnChange = e => {
    const { target: { value } } = e;

    // Updating our task state with the input value...
    this.setState({
      task: value
    });
  }

  handleOnSubmit = e => {
    // Prevent default to avoid the actual form submit...
    e.preventDefault();

    // Once is submited we reset the task value and we push the
    // new task to the items array.
    this.setState({
      task: '',
      items: [
        ...this.state.items,
        {
          id: uuidv4(),
          task: this.state.task,
          complete: false
        }
      ]
    });
  }

  markAsCompleted = id => {
    // Finding the task by id...
    const foundTask = this.state.items.find(
      task => task.id === id
    );

    // Updating the completed status...
    foundTask.completed = true;

    // Updating the state with the new updated task...
    this.setState({
      items: [
        ...this.state.items,
        ...foundTask
      ]
```

```
    });
  }

  removeTask = id => {
    // Filtering the tasks by removing the specific task id...
    const filteredTasks = this.state.items.filter(
      task => task.id !== id
    );

    // Updating items state...
    this.setState({
      items: filteredTasks
    });
  }

  render() {
    return (
      <div className="Todo">
        <h1>New Task:</h1>

        <form onSubmit={this.handleOnSubmit}>
          <input
            value={this.state.task}
            onChange={this.handleOnChange}
          />
        </form>

        <List
          items={this.state.items}
          markAsCompleted={this.markAsCompleted}
          removeTask={this.removeTask}
        />
      </div>
    );
  }
}

export default Todo;
```

File: src/components/Todo/index.jsx

2. Now, in our `List` component, we need to include `ReactCSSTransitionGroup` and use it as a wrapper in our list elements. We need to specify the name of our transition using the `transitionName` prop, and `transitionAppear` adds a transition at the first animation mount. By default, it is `false`:

```
import React from 'react';
import ReactCSSTransitionGroup from 'react-addons-css-transition-
group';
import './List.css';

const List = props => (
  <ul>
    <ReactCSSTransitionGroup
      transitionName="todo"
      transitionAppear={true}
    >
      {props.items.map((item, key) => (
        <li
          key={key}
          className={`${item.completed ? 'completed' : 'pending'}`}
        >
          {item.task}

          <div className="actions">
            <span
              className={item.completed ? 'hide' : 'done'}
              onClick={() => props.markAsCompleted(item.id)}
            >
              <i className="fa fa-check"></i>
            </span>

            <span
              className="trash"
              onClick={() => props.removeTask(item.id)}
            >
              <i className="fa fa-trash"></i>
            </span>
          </div>
        </li>
      ))}
    </ReactCSSTransitionGroup>
  </ul>
);

export default List;
```

File: src/components/Todo/List.jsx

3. Now, using `transitionName`, we will add some styles using the special classes that are created by `ReactCSSTransitionGroup`:

```
.todo-enter {
    opacity: 0.01;
}

.todo-enter.todo-enter-active {
    opacity: 1;
    transition: opacity 0.5s ease;
}

.todo-leave {
    opacity: 1;
}

.todo-leave.todo-leave-active {
    opacity: 0.01;
    transition: opacity .5s ease-in;
}

.todo-appear {
    opacity: 0.01;
    transition: opacity .5s ease-in;
}

.todo-appear.todo-appear-active {
    opacity: 1;
}
```

File: src/components/Todo/List.css

How it works...

We need to include the elements we want to animate inside our `ReactCSSTransitionGroup` component. Every time we add an item to our Todo list, we can see that our special classes (`.todo-enter` and `.todo-enter-active`) are being injected for a second to start our animation:

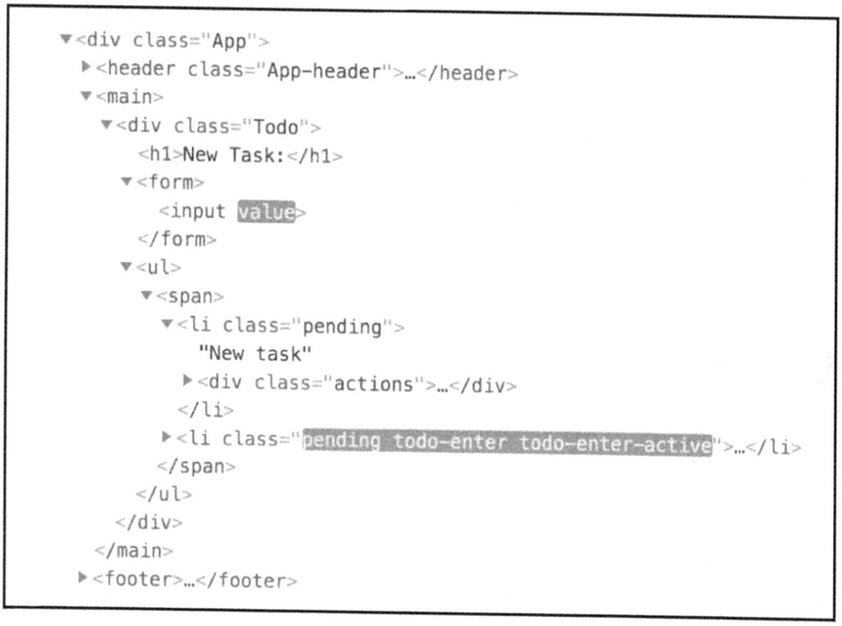

```
▼<div class="App">
  ▶<header class="App-header">…</header>
  ▼<main>
    ▼<div class="Todo">
       <h1>New Task:</h1>
      ▼<form>
         <input value>
       </form>
      ▼<ul>
        ▼<span>
          ▼<li class="pending">
             "New task"
            ▶<div class="actions">…</div>
           </li>
          ▶<li class="pending todo-enter todo-enter-active">…</li>
         </span>
       </ul>
     </div>
   </main>
  ▶<footer>…</footer>
```

And if we remove an item, we will see the `.todo-leave` and `.todo-leave-active` classes for a second:

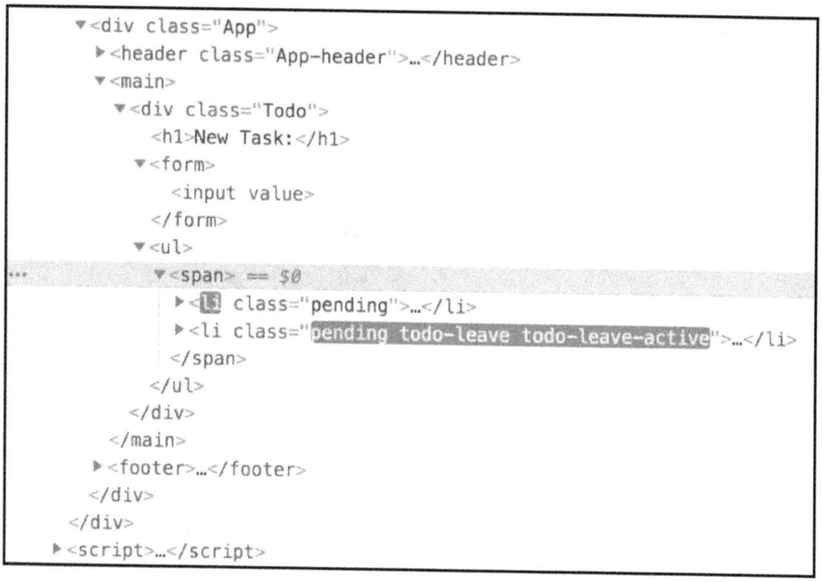

```
    ▼<div class="App">
      ▶<header class="App-header">…</header>
      ▼<main>
        ▼<div class="Todo">
           <h1>New Task:</h1>
          ▼<form>
             <input value>
           </form>
          ▼<ul>
...         ▼<span> == $0
              ▶<li class="pending">…</li>
              ▶<li class="pending todo-leave todo-leave-active">…</li>
             </span>
           </ul>
         </div>
       </main>
      ▶<footer>…</footer>
     </div>
   </div>
  ▶<script>…</script>
```

As you can see, using ReactCSSTransitionGroup helps us to handle the states of our animations. You can use this to create better animations in your React application.

Using react-animations library

In this recipe, we are going to learn how to use the library react-animations.

Getting ready

For this recipe, we need to install the following packages:

```
npm install react-animations radium
```

How to do it...

Let's do some animation:

1. We need to use Radium to create our inline styles to use our animations from the react-animations package. First, let's create our component:

```
import React, { Component } from 'react';
import { fadeIn } from 'react-animations';
import Radium, { StyleRoot } from 'radium';

const styles = {
  fadeIn: {
    animation: 'x 1s',
    animationName: Radium.keyframes(fadeIn, 'fadeIn')
  }
};

class Animations extends Component {
  render() {
    return (
      <StyleRoot>
        <div className="Animations" style={styles.fadeIn}>
          <h1>This text will be animated</h1>
        </div>
      </StyleRoot>
    );
  }
}
```

```
export default Animations;
```

File: src/components/Animations/index.jsx

2. In this example, we are using the `fadeIn` animation. We need to import the animation we want to use from `react-animations`, add the animation to our `Radium` styles, then use `<StyleRoot>` as a wrapper for our animation, and finally specify the inline style, `fadeIn`.
3. If you want to use another animation, for example, `bounce`, then you need to add the bounce animation and create a style for it:

```
import React, { Component } from 'react';
import { fadeIn, bounce } from 'react-animations';
import Radium, { StyleRoot } from 'radium';

const styles = {
  fadeIn: {
    animation: 'x 1s',
    animationName: Radium.keyframes(fadeIn, 'fadeIn')
  },
  bounce: {
    animation: 'x 1s',
    animationName: Radium.keyframes(bounce, 'bounce')
  }
};

class Animations extends Component {
  render() {
    return (
      <StyleRoot>
        <div className="Animations" style={styles.bounce}>
          <h1>This text will be animated</h1>
        </div>
      </StyleRoot>
    );
  }
}

export default Animations;
```

File: src/components/Animations/index.jsx

There's more...

As you can see, using animations from `react-animations` is very easy. There are a lot more animations:

- `bounce`
- `fadeIn`
- `fadeOut`
- `flash`
- `flip`
- `rollIn`
- `rollOut`
- `rotateIn`
- `rotateOut`
- `rubberBand`
- `shake`
- `swing`
- `zoomIn`
- `zoomOut`

To see all the available animations, visit the official repository at `https://github.com/FormidableLabs/react-animations`.

Creating our first animation with React Pose

React Pose is a declarative motion system for HTML, SVG, and React. It is a very cool library with which you can do amazing animations with React.

Getting ready

For this recipe, we will need to install the following packages and update our `react` and `react-dom` to be `16.4.2` or higher:

```
npm install react react-dom react-pose styled-components
```

How to do it...

Follow these steps to create a React pose animation:

1. First, let's create our component structure:

```
import React, { Component } from 'react';
import posed from 'react-pose';
import styled from 'styled-components';
import './Animations.css';

class Animations extends Component {
  render() {
    return (
      <div class="Animations">

      </div>
    );
  }
}

export default Animations;
```

File: src/components/Animations/index.jsx

2. The second thing we need to do is to create our first posed `div` with the states of our animation (`normal` and `hover`) and create a styled `div` using `styled-components`:

```
import React, { Component } from 'react';
import posed from 'react-pose';
import styled from 'styled-components';
import './Animations.css';

// Creating our posed div
const Circle = posed.div({
  normal: {
    scale: 1 // Normal state
  },
  hover: {
    scale: 3 // Hover state
  }
});

// Creating styled component
const StyledCircle = styled(Circle)`
  color: white;
```

```
  cursor: pointer;
  background: blue;
  line-height: 80px;
  border-radius: 50%;
  height: 80px;
  width: 80px;
`;

class Animations extends Component {
  render() {
    return (
      <div class="Animations">

      </div>
    );
  }
}

export default Animations;
```

File: src/components/Animations/index.jsx

3. Now we need to add our `StyledCircle` component into our `render` method:

```
render() {
  return (
    <div class="Animations">
      <StyledCircle
        pose={this.state.hover ? 'hover' : 'normal'}
        onMouseEnter={this.handleMouseEnter}
        onMouseLeave={this.handleMouseLeave}
        onClick={this.handleClick}
        style={{ background: this.state.bg }}
      >
        Click me!
      </StyledCircle>
    </div>
  );
}
```

File: src/components/Animations/index.jsx

4. As you can see, we need to create some event methods, and we are going to use the local state to change the size of the circle and the color when the user clicks:

```
import React, { Component } from 'react';
import posed from 'react-pose';
import styled from 'styled-components';
import './Animations.css';

const Circle = posed.div({
  normal: {
    scale: 1 // Normal state
  },
  hover: {
    scale: 3 // Hover state
  }
});

// Creating styled component
const StyledCircle = styled(Circle)`
  color: white;
  cursor: pointer;
  background: blue;
  line-height: 80px;
  border-radius: 50%;
  height: 80px;
  width: 80px;
`;

class Animations extends Component {
  state = {
    bg: 'blue',
    hover: false
  };

  handleMouseEnter = () => {
    this.setState({
      hover: true
    });
  }

  handleMouseLeave = () => {
    this.setState({
      hover: false
    });
  }

  handleClick = () => {
    // Choosing a random color...
```

```
    const colors = ['red', 'green', 'gray', 'orange', 'black',
'pink'];

    this.setState({
      bg: colors[Math.floor(Math.random() * colors.length)]
    });
  }

  render() {
    return (
      <div class="Animations">
        <StyledCircle
          pose={this.state.hover ? 'hover' : 'normal'}
          onMouseEnter={this.handleMouseEnter}
          onMouseLeave={this.handleMouseLeave}
          onClick={this.handleClick}
          style={{ background: this.state.bg }}
        >
          Click me!
        </StyledCircle>
      </div>
    );
  }
}

export default Animations;
```

File: src/components/Animations/index.jsx

How it works...

Our first view is going to be a blue circle with the label **Click me!**:

If we hover over the circle, we are going to see the pose animation, which increases the scale of the circle:

Finally, if we click on the circle, we are going to see the that our circle change its background color randomly:

There's more...

We can even combine the animations from `react-animations` library. For example, if we want to flip the circle when the user clicks on it, then we can do this:

```
import React, { Component } from 'react';
import posed from 'react-pose';
import styled, { keyframes } from 'styled-components';
import { flip } from 'react-animations';
import './Animations.css';

const flipAnimation = keyframes`${flip}`;

const Circle = posed.div({
  normal: {
    scale: 1 // Normal state
  },
  hover: {
    scale: 3 // Hover state
  }
});

// Creating styled component
const StyledCircle = styled(Circle)`
  color: white;
  cursor: pointer;
  background: blue;
  line-height: 80px;
  border-radius: 50%;
  height: 80px;
  width: 80px;
`;

class Animations extends Component {
  state = {
    style: {
      background: 'blue'
    },
    hover: false
  };

  handleMouseEnter = () => {
    this.setState({
      hover: true
    });
  }

  handleMouseLeave = () => {
```

```
      this.setState({
        hover: false
      });
    }

    handleClick = () => {
      // Choosing a random color...
      const colors = ['red', 'green', 'gray', 'orange', 'black', 'pink'];

      this.setState({
        style: {
          animation: `1s ${flipAnimation}`,
          background: colors[Math.floor(Math.random() * colors.length)]
        }
      });
    }

    render() {
      return (
        <div className="Animations">
          <StyledCircle
            pose={this.state.hover ? 'hover' : 'normal'}
            onMouseEnter={this.handleMouseEnter}
            onMouseLeave={this.handleMouseLeave}
            onClick={this.handleClick}
            style={this.state.style}
           >
             Click me!
           </StyledCircle>
         </div>
      );
    }
  }

  export default Animations;
```

File: src/components/Animations/index.jsx

8

Creating an API with Node.js Using MongoDB and MySQL

In this chapter, the following recipes will be covered:

- Creating a basic API with Express
- Building a database with MongoDB
- Building a database with MySQL
- Adding access tokens to secure our API

Introduction

From the Node.js official website (`https://nodejs.org`):

> *Node.js is a JavaScript runtime built on Chrome's V8 JavaScript engine. Node.js uses an event-driven, non-blocking I/O model that makes it lightweight and efficient. Node.js' package ecosystem, npm, is the largest ecosystem of open source libraries in the world.*

Node.js is widely used as a backend for web applications because it is easy to create an API and its performance is better than technologies such as Java, PHP, or Ruby. Usually, the most popular way to use Node.js is by using a framework called Express.

From Express official website (`https://expressjs.com`):

> *Express is a minimal and flexible Node.js web application framework that provides a robust set of features for web and mobile applications.*

Creating a basic API with Express

Express is the most popular Node.js framework and is easy to install and to use. In this recipe we are going to create, configure, and install a basic API using Express.

Getting ready

First, we need to install Node. You need to go to the official website, `www.nodejs.org`, and then download Node.js. There are two versions: the **LTS** (**Long Term Support**) version and the current version, which has the latest features. In my opinion, it is always better to choose the LTS version, but it's up to you.

Once you have installed Node, you can check which version you have by running this command in your Terminal:

```
node -v
v10.8.0
```

Also, Node includes Node Package Manager (npm) by default. You can check which version you have with this command:

```
npm -v
6.3.0
```

Now we need to install Express. To do this, there is a package called `express-generator`, which will allow us to create an Express application with a simple command. We need to install it globally:

```
npm install -g express-generator
```

After we installed `express-generator`, we can create an Express application. I usually prefer to create a directory called `projects` inside my home folder on my Mac, or if you use Windows, you can make it at `C:\projects`:

```
express my-first-express-app
```

Once you run the command, you will see something like this:

```
[→ projects express my-first-express-app

  warning: the default view engine will not be jade in future releases
  warning: use `--view=jade' or `--help' for additional options


   create : my-first-express-app/
   create : my-first-express-app/public/
   create : my-first-express-app/public/javascripts/
   create : my-first-express-app/public/images/
   create : my-first-express-app/public/stylesheets/
   create : my-first-express-app/public/stylesheets/style.css
   create : my-first-express-app/routes/
   create : my-first-express-app/routes/index.js
   create : my-first-express-app/routes/users.js
   create : my-first-express-app/views/
   create : my-first-express-app/views/error.jade
   create : my-first-express-app/views/index.jade
   create : my-first-express-app/views/layout.jade
   create : my-first-express-app/app.js
   create : my-first-express-app/package.json
   create : my-first-express-app/bin/
   create : my-first-express-app/bin/www

   change directory:
     $ cd my-first-express-app

   install dependencies:
     $ npm install

   run the app:
     $ DEBUG=my-first-express-app:* npm start
```

If you follow the instructions to run the application, you will see the Express application running at `http://localhost:3000`:

```
cd my-first-express-app
npm install
npm start
```

You will see this view:

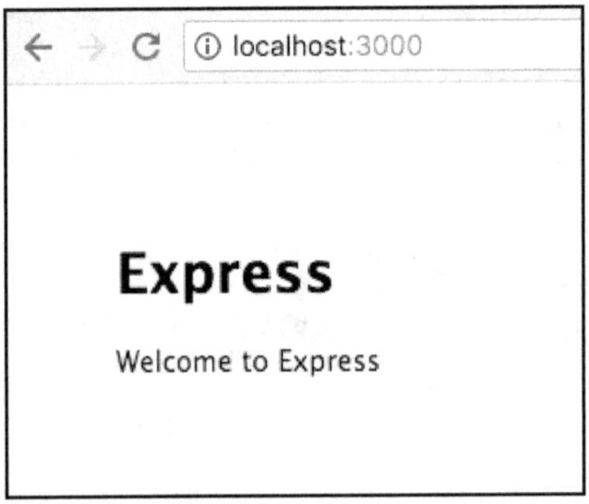

How to do it...

The code generated by default with `express-generator` is ES5 code, using `var`, `require`, `module.exports`, and so on:

1. The first thing we need to do is convert this code to be ES6. To do this, let's first modify our `app.js` file. This is the original code of this file:

```
var createError = require('http-errors');
var express = require('express');
var path = require('path');
var cookieParser = require('cookie-parser');
var logger = require('morgan');

var indexRouter = require('./routes/index');
var usersRouter = require('./routes/users');

var app = express();

// view engine setup
app.set('views', path.join(__dirname, 'views'));
app.set('view engine', 'jade');

app.use(logger('dev'));
app.use(express.json());
app.use(express.urlencoded({ extended: false }));
app.use(cookieParser());
app.use(express.static(path.join(__dirname, 'public')));
```

```
app.use('/', indexRouter);
app.use('/users', usersRouter);

// catch 404 and forward to error handler
app.use(function(req, res, next) {
  next(createError(404));
});

// error handler
app.use(function(err, req, res, next) {
  // set locals, only providing error in development
  res.locals.message = err.message;
  res.locals.error = req.app.get('env') === 'development' ? err :
{};

  // render the error page
  res.status(err.status || 500);
  res.render('error');
});

module.exports = app;
```

File: app.js

2. Migrating to ES6, we should have this code:

```
import createError from 'http-errors';
import express from 'express';
import path from 'path';
import cookieParser from 'cookie-parser';
import logger from 'morgan';

import indexRouter from './routes/index';
import usersRouter from './routes/users';

const app = express();

// view engine setup
app.set('views', path.join(__dirname, 'views'));
app.set('view engine', 'jade');

app.use(logger('dev'));
app.use(express.json());
app.use(express.urlencoded({ extended: false }));
app.use(cookieParser());
app.use(express.static(path.join(__dirname, 'public')));

app.use('/', indexRouter);
```

```
app.use('/users', usersRouter);

// catch 404 and forward to error handler
app.use((req, res, next) => {
  next(createError(404));
});

// error handler
app.use((err, req, res, next) => {
  // set locals, only providing error in development
  res.locals.message = err.message;
  res.locals.error = req.app.get('env') === 'development' ? err : {};

  // render the error page
  res.status(err.status || 500);
  res.render('error');
});

// Listening port
app.listen(3000);
```

File: app.js

3. Now let's remove our `bin/www` directory because we had added `app.listen(3000);` at the end of our file, and then you need to modify the `start` script in `package.json`:

```
"scripts": {
  "start": "node app.js"
}
```

File: package.json

4. If you try to run your application with `npm start` you will get this error:

```
➜  my-first-express-app git:(master) ✗ npm start

> my-first-express-app@0.0.0 start /Users/czantany/projects/React16Cookbook/Chapter8/Recipe1/my-first-express-app
> node app.js

/Users/czantany/projects/React16Cookbook/Chapter8/Recipe1/my-first-express-app/app.js:1
(function (exports, require, module, __filename, __dirname) { import createError from 'http-errors';
                                                              ^^^^^^

SyntaxError: Unexpected token import
    at createScript (vm.js:80:10)
    at Object.runInThisContext (vm.js:152:10)
    at Module._compile (module.js:605:28)
    at Object.Module._extensions..js (module.js:652:10)
    at Module.load (module.js:560:32)
    at tryModuleLoad (module.js:503:12)
    at Function.Module._load (module.js:495:3)
    at Function.Module.runMain (module.js:682:10)
    at startup (bootstrap_node.js:191:16)
    at bootstrap_node.js:613:3
npm ERR! code ELIFECYCLE
npm ERR! errno 1
npm ERR! my-first-express-app@0.0.0 start: `node app.js`
npm ERR! Exit status 1
npm ERR!
npm ERR! Failed at the my-first-express-app@0.0.0 start script.
npm ERR! This is probably not a problem with npm. There is likely additional logging output above.

npm ERR! A complete log of this run can be found in:
npm ERR!     /Users/czantany/.npm/_logs/2018-04-11T04_35_47_178Z-debug.log
```

5. This error is because our ES6 code does not work directly with Node. We need to use Babel to compile our file and be able to write ES6 code. For this, we need to install `babel-cli` globally and also the `babel-preset-es2015` package:

```
npm install -g babel-cli
npm install babel-preset-es2015
```

→ babel-preset-env ✓

6. To make it work, we need to create a new file called `.babelrc` and add our `es2015` preset:

```
{
  "presets": ["es2015"]
}
```

→ { "presets": ["env"] }

File: .babelrc

7. Now you need to change your `start` script again and switch `node` to `babel-node`:

```
"scripts": {
  "start": "babel-node app.js"
}
```

File: package.json

8. If you run `npm start` in your terminal, you should be able to run the application now.
9. After we have changed our code to ES6, we have another issue. If you modify a file and you save it in the application, it will not refresh. Also, if for some reason our application crashes, then our server will stop working. The way to fix this is by using a Node watcher. The most popular one is `nodemon`:

```
npm install nodemon
```

10. You need to modify your `start` script for this:

```
"scripts": {
  "start": "nodemon app.js --exec babel-node"
}
```

File: package.json

11. Now if you make any changes to your application (for example, in the `routes/index.js` file, you can change the text `Express` on line 6 for any other content), you will see how the server restarts itself and refreshes the site:

```
→ my-first-express-app git:(master) ✗ npm start

> my-first-express-app@0.0.0 start /Users/czantany/projects/React16Cookbook/Chapter8/Recipe1/my-first-express-app
> nodemon app.js --exec babel-node

[nodemon] 1.17.3
[nodemon] to restart at any time, enter `rs`
[nodemon] watching: *.*
[nodemon] starting `babel-node app.js`
GET / 304 189.684 ms - -
GET /stylesheets/style.css 304 1.370 ms - -
[nodemon] restarting due to changes...
[nodemon] starting `babel-node app.js`
GET / 200 193.477 ms - 173
GET /stylesheets/style.css 304 1.379 ms - -
```

12. As you can see, the first message in green says `starting babel-node app.js`, and then when it detects a change, it says restarting due to changes... Now we can see the changes reflected in our site:

13. Because our Express application was created to be an API instead of a regular website, we need to remove many things that are superfluous, such as the `views` folder and the template engine, and we need to make some structural changes to make it easier to handle. Let's see what our `app.js` file looks like now:

```
// Dependencies
import express from 'express';
import path from 'path';

// Controllers
import apiController from './controllers/api';

// Express Application
const app = express();

// Middlewares
app.use(express.json());
app.use(express.urlencoded({ extended: false }));

// Routes
app.use('/api', apiController);

// Listening port
app.listen(3000);
```

File: app.js

14. As you can see, I renamed the `routes` directory to `controllers`, and also I deleted the `users.js` file that was in that folder, and I renamed the `index.js` as `api.js`. Let's create an API to handle a blog:

```
import express from 'express';

const router = express.Router();
// Mock data, this should come from a database....
const posts = [
  {
    id: 1,
    title: 'My blog post 1',
    content: '<p>Content</p>',
    author: 'Carlos Santana'
  },
  {
    id: 2,
    title: 'My blog post 2',
    content: '<p>Content</p>',
    author: 'Cristina Rojas'
  },
  {
    id: 3,
    title: 'My blog post 3',
    content: '<p>Content</p>',
    author: 'Carlos Santana'
  }
];

router.get('/', (req, res, next) => {
  res.send(`
    <p>API Endpoints:</p>
    <ul>
      <li>/api/posts</li>
      <li>/api/post/:id</li>
    </ul>
  `);
});

router.get('/posts', (req, res, next) => {
  res.json({
    response: posts
  });
});

router.get('/post/:id', (req, res, next) => {
  const { params: { id } } = req;
```

```
    const singlePost = posts.find(post => post.id === Number(id));

    if (!singlePost) {
      res.send({
        error: true,
        message: 'Post not found'
      });
    }

    res.json({
      response: [singlePost]
    });
  });

  export default router;
```

File: controllers/api.js

How it works...

Now let's test our new API:

1. If we go to `http://localhost:3000/api`, we are going to display a list of the endpoints. This is optional, but it is useful as a reference for developers:

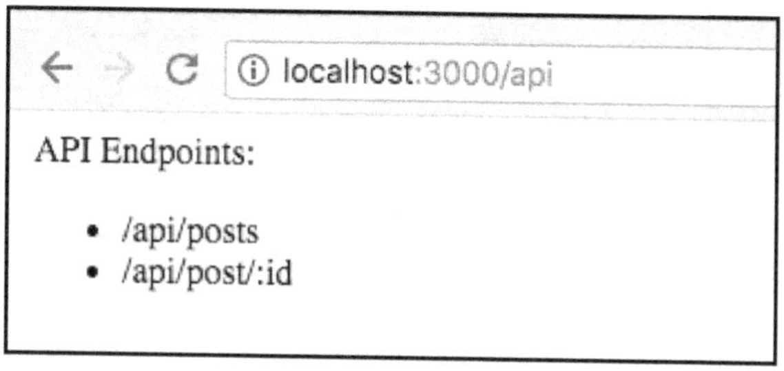

2. If you go to `http://localhost:3000/api/posts`, you will see all the posts:

```
{
  "response": [
    {
      "id": 1,
      "title": "My blog post 1",
      "content": "<p>Content</p>",
      "author": "Carlos Santana"
    },
    {
      "id": 2,
      "title": "My blog post 2",
      "content": "<p>Content</p>",
      "author": "Cristina Rojas"
    },
    {
      "id": 3,
      "title": "My blog post 3",
      "content": "<p>Content</p>",
      "author": "Carlos Santana"
    }
  ]
}
```

3. Also, if you hit `http://localhost:3000/api/post/1`, you will get the first post of the list:

```
{
  "response": [
    {
      "id": 1,
      "title": "My blog post 1",
      "content": "<p>Content</p>",
      "author": "Carlos Santana"
    }
  ]
}
```

4. Finally, if you try to get a post that does not exist in our data (`http://localhost:3000/api/post/99`), then we will return an error:

```
{
  "error": true,
  "message": "Post not found"
}
```

Building a database with MongoDB

MongoDB is the most popular NoSQL database. It is free (open source) and document-oriented. In this recipe, we are going to install MongoDB, create a database, create a document, and insert some data to display information with Node.js using the Mongoose library.

Getting ready

First, we need to install MongoDB. In this recipe, I'm going to show you the easiest way to install it using Mac, and I'll give you some links to install it if you have Linux or Windows.

> **From the MongoDB official documentation** (`https://docs.mongodb.com/manual/tutorial/install-mongodb-on-os-x`): "Starting in version 3.0, MongoDB only supports MacOS version 10.7 (Lion) and later on Intel x86-64."

Installing MongoDB Community Edition manually (the hard way)

This installation works for Mac and Linux:

1. Download the binary files for the version you want of MongoDB from `https://www.mongodb.com/download-center#community`.

2. Extract the files from the downloaded file; you can use the terminal and use this command:

```
tar -zxvf mongodb-osx-ssl-x86_64-3.6.3.tgz
```

3. Copy the extracted folder to the location from which MongoDB will run:

```
mkdir -p mongodb
cp -R -n mongodb-osx-ssl-x86_64-3.6.3/ mongodb
```

4. Ensure the location of the binaries is in the `PATH` variable. You can add the following line in your shell's `rc` file, such as `~/.bashrc` or `~/.bash_profile`:

```
export PATH=<your-mongodb-install-directory>/bin:$PATH
```

Installing MongoDB Community Edition with Homebrew (the easy way)

Homebrew is a package manager for Mac (*also known as the missing package manager for macOS*) and is easy to install. Go to the official website (https://brew.sh), and there you will find a command that you should run to install it, which is as follows:

```
/usr/bin/ruby -e "$(curl -fsSL
https://raw.githubusercontent.com/Homebrew/install/master/install)"
```

1. If you have Homebrew already installed, or if you just installed it, then the first thing you need to do is to update the package database with this command:

```
brew update
```

2. Now we need to install MongoDB using this command:

```
brew install mongodb
```

3. If you want to install the latest development version of MongoDB, then you should run this command (I don't recommend it because it may have some bugs that are not fixed yet, but it is up to you):

```
brew install mongodb --devel
```

Running MongoDB

Before we start MongoDB for the first time, we need to create a directory in which the *mongod* process will write the data:

1. By default, the mongod process uses the `/data/db` directory. To create this folder, you can use the following command:

   ```
   mkdir -p /data/db
   ```

2. Now we need to set permissions for the data directory:

   ```
   chmod -R 777 /data
   ```

3. In a new terminal (or tab) you need to run the following:

   ```
   mongod
   ```

4. If you didn't get an error, you could start the Mongo shell on the same host machine as *mongod* (in a new terminal or tab):

   ```
   mongo --host 127.0.0.1:127017
   ```

> **TIP** If you get an error like this: *Error: Port number 127017 out of range parsing HostAndPort from "127.0.0.1:127017"*, then just run `mongo` without `--host` flag.

5. Finally, if you want to stop MongoDB, press *Ctrl* + *C* in the terminal that `mongod` is running.
6. If everything works, you should see this in your Terminal:

```
[→ projects mongo --host 127.0.0.1:27017
MongoDB shell version v3.6.3
connecting to: mongodb://127.0.0.1:27017/
MongoDB server version: 3.6.3
Welcome to the MongoDB shell.
For interactive help, type "help".
For more comprehensive documentation, see
        http://docs.mongodb.org/
Questions? Try the support group
        http://groups.google.com/group/mongodb-user
Server has startup warnings:
2018-04-12T23:04:44.496-0700 I CONTROL  [initandlisten]
2018-04-12T23:04:44.496-0700 I CONTROL  [initandlisten] ** WARNING: Access control is not enabled for the database.
2018-04-12T23:04:44.496-0700 I CONTROL  [initandlisten] **          Read and write access to data and configuration is unrestricted.
2018-04-12T23:04:44.496-0700 I CONTROL  [initandlisten]
2018-04-12T23:04:44.496-0700 I CONTROL  [initandlisten] ** WARNING: This server is bound to localhost.
2018-04-12T23:04:44.496-0700 I CONTROL  [initandlisten] **          Remote systems will be unable to connect to this server.
2018-04-12T23:04:44.496-0700 I CONTROL  [initandlisten] **          Start the server with --bind_ip <address> to specify which IP
2018-04-12T23:04:44.496-0700 I CONTROL  [initandlisten] **          addresses it should serve responses from, or with --bind_ip_all to
2018-04-12T23:04:44.497-0700 I CONTROL  [initandlisten] **          bind to all interfaces. If this behavior is desired, start the
2018-04-12T23:04:44.497-0700 I CONTROL  [initandlisten] **          server with --bind_ip 127.0.0.1 to disable this warning.
2018-04-12T23:04:44.497-0700 I CONTROL  [initandlisten]
2018-04-12T23:04:44.497-0700 I CONTROL  [initandlisten]
2018-04-12T23:04:44.497-0700 I CONTROL  [initandlisten] ** WARNING: soft rlimits too low. Number of files is 256, should be at least 1000
```

How to do it...

First, we need to create a new database:

1. To create a new database or switch to an existing database, you need to run: `use <name of the database>`. Let's create a blog database:

```
use blog
```

2. Now we need to create a collection called *posts*, and you need to save the data directly in JSON format using the `db.<your-collection-name>.save({})` command:

```
db.posts.save({ title: 'Post 1', slug: 'post-1', content:
'<p>Content</p>' })
```

3. As you can see, I'm not adding any `id` value, and that is because MongoDB automatically creates a unique ID for each row called `_id`, which is a random hash. If you want to see the data that you just saved, you need to use the `find()` method without any parameters:

```
db.posts.find()
```

4. You should see your data like this:

```
> db.posts.find()
{ "_id" : ObjectId("5ad2e0074fa0d047639da615"), "title" : "Post 1", "slug" : "post-1", "content" : "<p>Content</p>" }
```

5. Now let's suppose you add a new row for Post 2 and you want to find that specific row by specifying the slug (post-2). You can do it like this:

```
db.posts.find({ slug: 'post-2' })
```

6. You should see this:

```
> db.posts.find()
{ "_id" : ObjectId("5ad2e0074fa0d047639da615"), "title" : "Post 1", "slug" : "post-1", "content" : "<p>Content</p>" }
{ "_id" : ObjectId("5ad2e6ed4fa0d047639da616"), "title" : "Post 2", "slug" : "post-2", "content" : "<p>Content</p>" }
> db.posts.find({ slug: 'post-2' })
{ "_id" : ObjectId("5ad2e6ed4fa0d047639da616"), "title" : "Post 2", "slug" : "post-2", "content" : "<p>Content</p>" }
```

7. Now let's change the Post 2 title to My Updated Post 2. To do this, we need to update our row as follows:

```
db.posts.update({ slug: "post-2" }, { $set: { title: "My Updated
Post 2" }})
```

8. The first parameter is the query to find the row we want to update, and the second one modifies the fields using `$set`.
9. Finally, if we want to remove a specific row, we can do it as follows:

```
db.posts.remove({ "_id": ObjectId("5ad2e6ed4fa0d047639da616") })
```

10. The recommended way to remove a row is by specifying the `_id` directly to avoid deleting other rows by mistake but is also possible to delete a row by any other field. For example, let's say you want to remove Post 1 using the slug. You can do it like this:

```
db.posts.remove({ "slug": "post-1" })
```

11. Now that you have learned how to do basic operations with MongoDB let's implement MongoDB into Node.js using the Mongoose library, which is an **Object Document Mapper** (**ODM**) for Node. We need to install some extra packages for this recipe:

```
npm install mongoose body-parser slug
```

12. Using the same code as the previous recipe (`Repository: Chapter08/Recipe1/my-first-express-app`), we are going to connect Mongoose to Node.js. The first thing we need to do is to modify `app.js`:

```
// Dependencies
import express from 'express';
import path from 'path';
import mongoose from 'mongoose';
import bodyParser from 'body-parser';

// Controllers
import apiController from './controllers/api';

// Express Application
const app = express();

// Middlewares
app.use(bodyParser.json());
app.use(bodyParser.urlencoded({ extended: false }));
```

```
// Mongoose Connection (blog is our database)
mongoose.connect('mongodb://localhost/blog');

// Routes
app.use('/api', apiController);

// Listening port
app.listen(3000);
```

File: app.js

13. Now that we have Mongoose connected to our database we need to create a model to handle our blog posts. To do this, you will need to create a `src/models/blog.js` file:

```
// Dependencies
import mongoose, { Schema } from 'mongoose';
import slug from 'slug';

// Defining the post schema...
const postSchema = new Schema({
  title: String,
  slug: { type: String, unique: true },
  content: { type: String, required: true },
  author: String,
  createdAt: Date
});

// Adding a custom method...
postSchema.methods.addAuthor = function(author) {
  /**
   * NOTE: Probably you are thinking, why I'm using function
   * and not an arrow function?
   * Is because arrow functions does not bind their own context
   * that means this actually refers to the originating context
   */
  this.author = author;

  return this.author;
};
//Before save we create the slug and we add the current date...
postSchema.pre('save', function(next) {
  this.slug = slug(this.title, { lower: 'on' });
  this.createdAt = Date.now();

  next();
});
```

```
// Creating our Model...
const Post = mongoose.model('Post', postSchema);

export default Post;
```

File: src/models/blog.js

14. Now to handle our model we need to create a new controller (`src/controllers/blog.js`) where we are going to add methods to save, update, remove, find all posts, or find a single post:

```
// Dependencies
import slugFn from 'slug';
import Post from '../models/blog';

export function createPost(title, content, callback) {
  // Creating a new post...
  const newPost = new Post({
    title,
    content
  });

  // Adding the post author...
  newPost.addAuthor('Carlos Santana');

  // Saving the post into the database...
  newPost.save(error => {
    if (error) {
      console.log(error);
      callback(error, true);
    }

    console.log('Post saved correctly!');
    callback(newPost);
  });
}

// Updating a post...
export function updatePost(slug, title, content, callback) {
  const updatedPost = {
    title,
    content,
    slug: slugFn(title, { lower: 'on' })
  };
```

```
    Post.update({ slug }, updatedPost, (error, affected) => {
      if (error) {
        console.log(error);
        callback(error, true);
      }

      console.log('Post updated correctly!');
      callback(affected);
    });
  }

  // Removing a post by slug...
  export function removePost(slug, callback) {
    Post.remove({ slug }, error => {
      if (error) {
        console.log(error);
        callback(error, true);
      }

      console.log('Post removed correctly!');
      callback(true);
    });
  }

  // Find all posts...
  export function findAllPosts(callback) {
    Post.find({}, (error, posts) => {
      if (error) {
        console.log(error);

        return false;
      }

      console.log(posts);
      callback(posts);
    });
  }

  // Find a single post by slug...
  export function findBySlug(slug, callback) {
    Post.find({ slug }, (error, post) => {
      if (error) {
        console.log(error);

        return false;
      }

      console.log(post);
```

```
    callback(post);
  });
}
```

File: src/controllers/blog.js

15. Finally, we are going to modify our API controller (`src/controllers/api.js`) to remove the fake data we created in the last recipe and get the data from the actual MongoDB database:

```
import express from 'express';
import {
  createPost,
  findAllPosts,
  findBySlug,
  removePost,
  updatePost
} from './blog';

const router = express.Router();
// GET Endpoints
router.get('/', (req, res, next) => {
  res.send(`
    <p>API Endpoints:</p>
    <ul>
      <li><a href="/api/posts">/api/posts</a></li>
      <li><a href="/api/post/1">/api/post/:id</a></li>
    </ul>
  `);
});

router.get('/posts', (req, res, next) => {
  findAllPosts(posts => {
    res.json({
      response: posts
    });
  });
});

router.get('/post/:slug', (req, res, next) => {
  const { params: { slug } } = req;

  findBySlug(slug, singlePost => {
    console.log('single', singlePost);
    if (!singlePost || singlePost.length === 0) {
      res.send({
        error: true,
        message: 'Post not found'
```

```
        });
      } else {
        res.json({
          response: [singlePost]
        });
      }
    });
  });
  // POST Endpoints
  router.post('/post', (req, res, next) => {
    const { title, content } = req.body;

    createPost(title, content, (data, error = false) => {
      if (error) {
        res.json({
          error: true,
          message: data
        });
      } else {
        res.json({
          response: {
            saved: true,
            post: data
          }
        });
      }
    });
  });

  // DELETE Endpoints
  router.delete('/post/:slug', (req, res, next) => {
    const { params: { slug } } = req;

    removePost(slug, (removed, error) => {
      if (error) {
        res.json({
          error: true,
          message: 'There was an error trying to remove this
          post...'
        });
      } else {
        res.json({
          response: {
            removed: true
          }
        })
      }
    });
```

```
});

// PUT Endpoints
router.put('/post/:slug', (req, res, next) => {
  const { params: { slug }, body: { title, content } } = req;

  updatePost(slug, title, content, (affected, error) => {
    if (error) {
      res.json({
        error: true,
        message: 'There was an error trying to update the post'
      });
    } else {
      res.json({
        response: {
          updated: true,
          affected
        }
      })
    }
  });
});

export default router;
```

File: src/controllers/api.js

How it works...

You need to install Postman (`https://www.getpostman.com`) or any other REST client to test the API. Mainly for a `POST`, `PUT` and `DELETE` methods, the GET method can be easily verified on any browser.

GET method endpoints

GET /posts. This endpoint can be tested with your browser. Go to `http://localhost:3000/api/posts`. I have manually inserted three rows:


```
{
  "response": [
    {
      "_id": "5ad6e225187dd792b33652ce",
      "title": "My blog post 1",
      "content": "<p>Content</p>",
      "author": "Carlos Santana",
      "slug": "my-blog-post-1",
      "createdAt": "2018-04-18T06:13:57.943Z",
      "__v": 0
    },
    {
      "_id": "5ad6e22d187dd792b33652cf",
      "title": "My blog post 2",
      "content": "<p>Content</p>",
      "author": "Carlos Santana",
      "slug": "my-blog-post-2",
      "createdAt": "2018-04-18T06:14:05.894Z",
      "__v": 0
    },
    {
      "_id": "5ad6e232187dd792b33652d0",
      "title": "My blog post 3",
      "content": "<p>Content</p>",
      "author": "Carlos Santana",
      "slug": "my-blog-post-3",
      "createdAt": "2018-04-18T06:14:10.310Z",
      "__v": 0
    }
  ]
}
```


If you want to test it on Postman, then write the same URL (`http://localhost:3000/api/posts`), select the `GET` method, and click on the Send button:

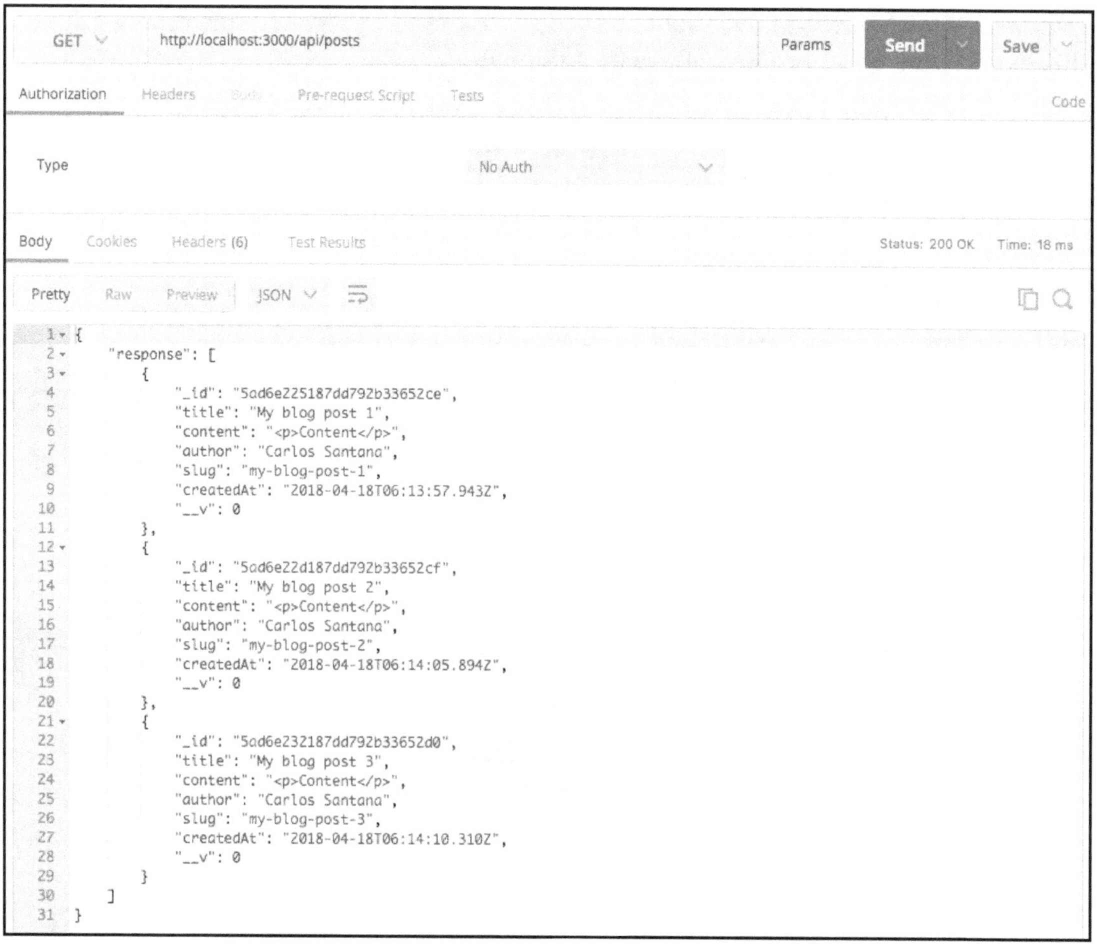
GET
http://localhost:3000/api/posts
Params
Send
Save
Authorization
Headers
Pre-request Script
Tests
Code
Type
No Auth
Body
Cookies
Headers (6)
Test Results
Status: 200 OK
Time: 18 ms
Pretty
Raw
Preview
JSON
{
"response": [
{
"_id": "5ad6e225187dd792b33652ce",
"title": "My blog post 1",
"content": "<p>Content</p>",
"author": "Carlos Santana",
"slug": "my-blog-post-1",
"createdAt": "2018-04-18T06:13:57.943Z",
"__v": 0
},
{
"_id": "5ad6e22d187dd792b33652cf",
"title": "My blog post 2",
"content": "<p>Content</p>",
"author": "Carlos Santana",
"slug": "my-blog-post-2",
"createdAt": "2018-04-18T06:14:05.894Z",
"__v": 0
},
{
"_id": "5ad6e232187dd792b33652d0",
"title": "My blog post 3",
"content": "<p>Content</p>",
"author": "Carlos Santana",
"slug": "my-blog-post-3",
"createdAt": "2018-04-18T06:14:10.310Z",
"__v": 0
}
]
}

GET /post/:slug. This endpoint is also a `GET`, and you need to pass the slug (friendly URL) on the URL. For example, the slug of the first row, My blog post 1, is my-blog-post-1. A slug is a friendly URL that has the same value of a title but in lowercase, without special characters, and with the spaces replaced with dashes (-). In our model, we defined our slug as a unique field. That means there cannot be more than one post with the same slug.

Let's go to `http://localhost:3000/api/post/my-blog-post-1` in the browser. If the slug exists in the database you will see the information:

```
{
  "response": [
    [
      {
        "_id": "5ad6e225187dd792b33652ce",
        "title": "My blog post 1",
        "content": "<p>Content</p>",
        "author": "Carlos Santana",
        "slug": "my-blog-post-1",
        "createdAt": "2018-04-18T06:13:57.943Z",
        "__v": 0
      }
    ]
  ]
}
```

But if you try to find a slug that does not exist in the database you will get this error:

```
// http://localhost:3000/api/post/my-fake-post

{
  "error": true,
  "message": "Post not found"
}
```

POST method endpoints

The `POST` method is typically used when we want to insert new data into our database.

POST /post. For this endpoint, we need to use Postman to be able to send the data through the body. To do this, you need to select the POST method in Postman. Use the URL `http://localhost:3000/api/post`, then click on Headers, and you need to add the header `Content-Type` with the value `application/x-www-form-urlencoded`:

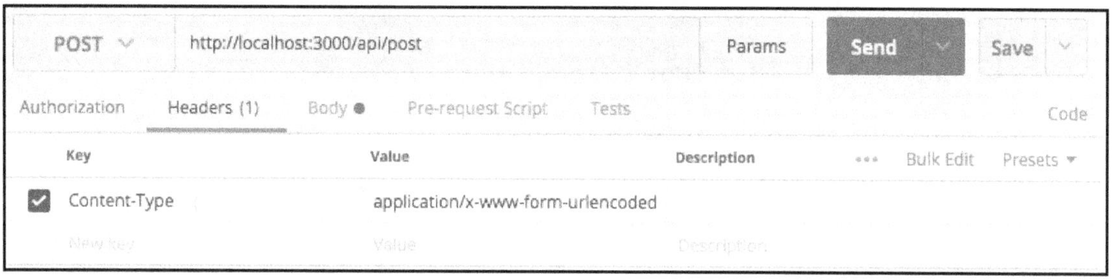

After you set the header, then go to the **Body** tab and select the **raw** option, and you can send the information like this:

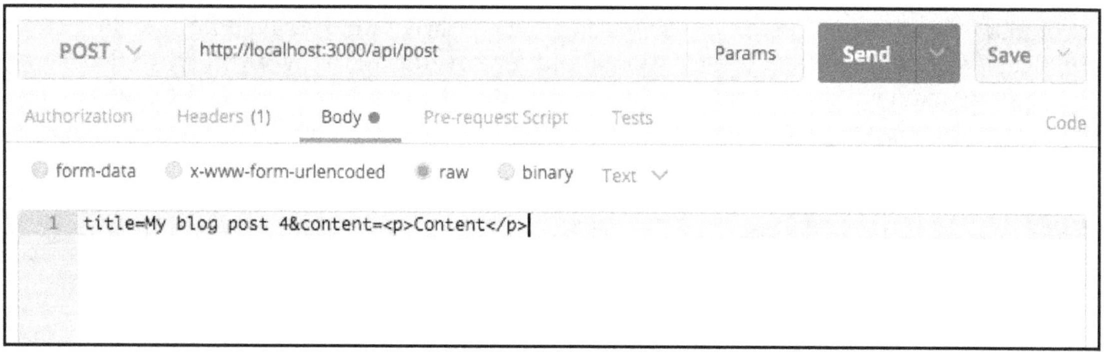

Now you can hit the **Send** button and see the response that the service returns:

Body
Cookies
Headers (6)
Test Results
Status: 200 OK
Time: 90 ms
Pretty
Raw
Preview
JSON
{
"response": {
"saved": true,
"post": {
"_id": "5ad6f589dda9fcc3e2236009",
"title": "My blog post 4",
"content": "<p>Content</p>",
"author": "Carlos Santana",
"slug": "my-blog-post-4",
"createdAt": "2018-04-18T07:36:41.761Z",
"__v": 0
}
}
}

If you did everything correctly, you should get a response with the saved node set to true and the *post* node containing information about the saved post. Now if you try to hit the *Send* button again with the same data (the same title), it will cause an error because, as you remember, our slug must be unique:

Body
Cookies
Headers (6)
Test Results
Status: 200 OK
Time: 41 ms
Pretty
Raw
Preview
JSON
{
"error": true,
"message": {
"code": 11000,
"index": 0,
"errmsg": "E11000 duplicate key error collection: blog.posts index: slug_1 dup key: { : \"my-blog-post-4\" }",
"op": {
"_id": "5ad6f649dda9fcc3e223600a",
"title": "My blog post 4",
"content": "<p>Content</p>",
"author": "Carlos Santana",
"slug": "my-blog-post-4",
"createdAt": "2018-04-18T07:39:53.449Z",
"__v": 0
}
}
}

You are probably wondering what the `__v` is if we haven't added that node directly. That is the `versionKey`, which is a property set on each document when it's first created by Mongoose. This key's value contains the internal revision of the document. You can change or remove the name of this document property. The default is `__v`.

If you want to change it, you can do something like this when you are defining a new schema:

```
// If you want to change the name of the versionKey
new Schema({...}, { versionKey: '_myVersion' });
```

Or if you want to remove it, you can pass `false` to the `versionKey`, but I don't recommend doing that because you won't have control on the version changes every time you update a document:

```
// If you want to remove it you can do:
new Schema({...}, { versionKey: false });
```

DELETE method endpoints

The `DELETE` method, as the name implies, is for deleting rows in a database.

DELETE /post/:slug. In Postman, we need to select the `DELETE` method, and in the URL you need to pass the slug of the post you want to remove. For example, let's remove the post my-blog-post-2. If you remove it correctly you should get a response with the removed node set to true:

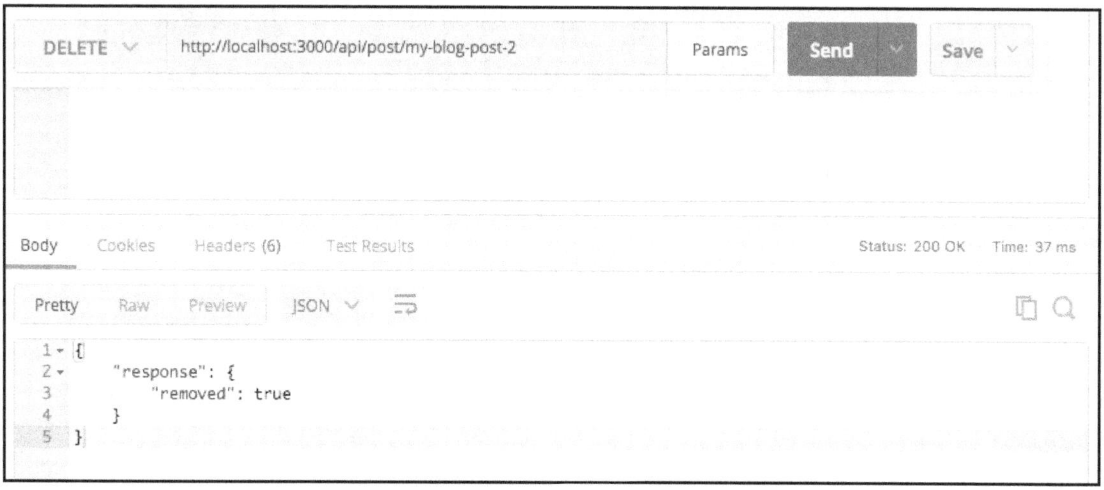

If you want to verify the post was deleted, you can go to the `/posts` endpoint again, and you will see that is not in the JSON anymore:


```
// http://localhost:3000/api/posts

{
  "response": [
    {
      "_id": "5ad6e225187dd792b33652ce",
      "title": "My blog post 1",
      "content": "<p>Content</p>",
      "author": "Carlos Santana",
      "slug": "my-blog-post-1",
      "createdAt": "2018-04-18T06:13:57.943Z",
      "__v": 0
    },
    {
      "_id": "5ad6e232187dd792b33652d0",
      "title": "My blog post 3",
      "content": "<p>Content</p>",
      "author": "Carlos Santana",
      "slug": "my-blog-post-3",
      "createdAt": "2018-04-18T06:14:10.310Z",
      "__v": 0
    },
    {
      "_id": "5ad6f589dda9fcc3e2236009",
      "title": "My blog post 4",
      "content": "<p>Content</p>",
      "author": "Carlos Santana",
      "slug": "my-blog-post-4",
      "createdAt": "2018-04-18T07:36:41.761Z",
      "__v": 0
    }
  ]
}
```

PUT method endpoints

The last method is `PUT`, and it is typically used to update a row in a database.

PUT /post/:slug. In Postman you need to select the PUT method, then the URL of the post you want to edit. Let's edit my-blog-post-3; the URL will be `http://localhost:3000/api/post/my-blog-post-3`. On the Headers tab, like in the `POST` method, you need to add a `Content-Type` header with the value application/x-www-form-urlencoded. In the Body tab, you send the new data you want to replace, in this case, a new title and new content:

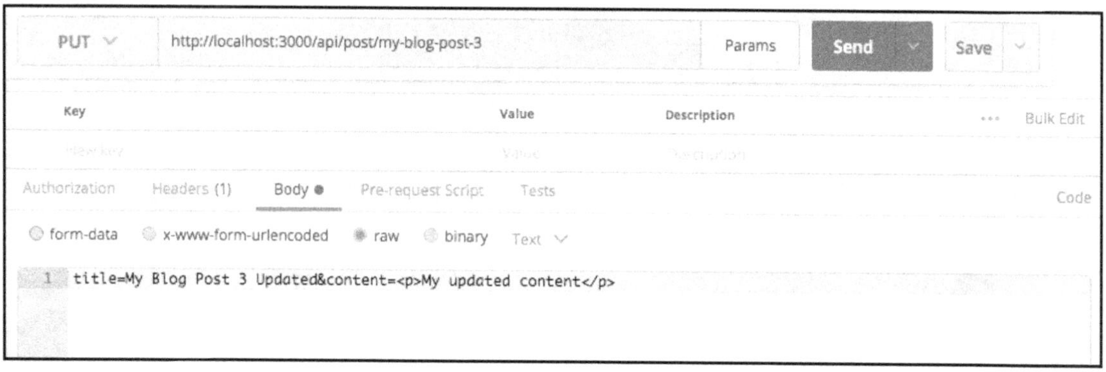

If everything works fine, you should get this response:

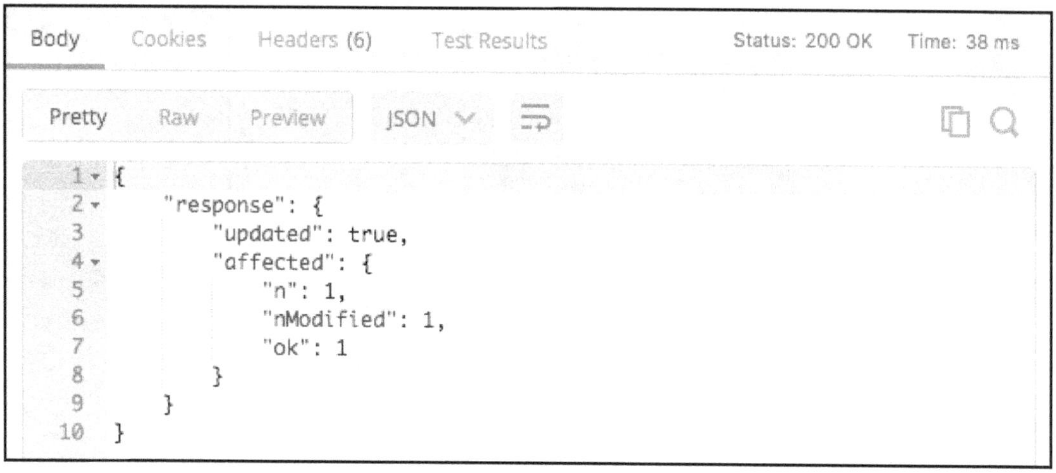

Again, if you want to verify the post was updated correctly then go to the `/posts` endpoint in your browser:


```
{
  "response": [
    {
      "_id": "5ad6e225187dd792b33652ce",
      "title": "My blog post 1",
      "content": "<p>Content</p>",
      "author": "Carlos Santana",
      "slug": "my-blog-post-1",
      "createdAt": "2018-04-18T06:13:57.943Z",
      "__v": 0
    },
    {
      "_id": "5ad6e232187dd792b33652d0",
      "title": "My Blog Post 3 Updated",
      "content": "<p>My updated content</p>",
      "author": "Carlos Santana",
      "slug": "my-blog-post-3-updated",
      "createdAt": "2018-04-18T06:14:10.310Z",
      "__v": 0
    },
    {
      "_id": "5ad6f589dda9fcc3e2236009",
      "title": "My blog post 4",
      "content": "<p>Content</p>",
      "author": "Carlos Santana",
      "slug": "my-blog-post-4",
      "createdAt": "2018-04-18T07:36:41.761Z",
      "__v": 0
    }
  ]
}
```


As you can see, the post title, content, and slug were updated correctly.

Building a database with MySQL

MySQL is the most popular database. It's an open source Relational Database Management System (RDBMS). MySQL normally is a central component of the LAMP (Linux, Apache, MySQL, PHP/ Python/ Perl) stack; many bundles include MySQL:

- AMPPS (Max, Linux, and Windows) – `https://www.ampps.com`
- XAMPP (Mac, Linux, and Windows) – `https://www.apachefriends.org`
- WAMP Server (Windows) – `http://www.wampserver.com`
- MAMP (Mac) – `https://www.mamp.info`

Other developers prefer to install it individually. If you want to do this, you can download MySQL directly from the official website: `https://dev.mysql.com/downloads/mysql/`.

In this recipe, I'm going to use MySQL Workbench to execute the SQL queries. You can download it from `https://www.mysql.com/products/workbench/`. Feel free to use any other MySQL administrator, or if you prefer the terminal, you can use MySQL commands directly.

Here are more MySQL GUI tools:

- phpMyAdmin – `https://www.phpmyadmin.net`
- Sequel Pro – `https://www.sequelpro.com`
- Navicat – `https://www.navicat.com`

Getting ready

To work with MySQL on Node, we need to install the sequelize and mysql2 packages:

```
npm install sequelize mysql2 slug
```

How to do it...

1. The first thing we need to do is to create a database, which we will name as blog, and use it:

```
CREATE DATABASE blog;
USE blog;
```

2. Now that we have our database ready let's work on the MySQL implementation with Node.js. There are many ways to use MySQL with Node, but for this recipe, we will use a package called *Sequelize*, which is a robust ORM for MySQL and other databases such as SQLite, Postgres, and MsSQL.
3. The first thing we need to do is to create a config file to add our database configuration (host, database, user, password, etc). To do this, you need to create a file called `config/index.js`:

```
export default {
  db: {
    dialect: 'mysql', // 'mysql'|'sqlite'|'postgres'|'mssql'
    host: 'localhost', // Your host, by default is localhost
    database: 'blog', // Your database name
    user: 'root', // Your MySQL user, by default is root
    password: '123456' // Your Db password, sometimes by default
                       //is empty.
  }
};
```

File: config/index.js

4. We can re-use the same API controller we used in the MongoDB recipe:

```
import express from 'express';
import {
  createPost,
  findAllPosts,
  findBySlug,
  removePost,
  updatePost
} from './blog';

const router = express.Router();

// GET Methods
router.get('/', (req, res, next) => {
  res.send(`
    <p>API Endpoints:</p>
    <ul>
      <li><a href="/api/posts">/api/posts</a></li>
      <li><a href="/api/post/1">/api/post/:id</a></li>
    </ul>
  `);
});

router.get('/posts', (req, res, next) => {
  findAllPosts(posts => {
```

```
    res.json({
      response: posts
    });
  });
});

router.get('/post/:slug', (req, res, next) => {
  const { params: { slug } } = req;

  findBySlug(slug, singlePost => {
    console.log('single', singlePost);
    if (!singlePost || singlePost.length === 0) {
      res.send({
        error: true,
        message: 'Post not found'
      });
    } else {
      res.json({
        response: [singlePost]
      });
    }
  });
});

// POST Methods
router.post('/post', (req, res, next) => {
  const { title, content } = req.body;

  createPost(title, content, (data, error = false) => {
    if (error) {
      res.json({
        error: true,
        details: error
      });
    } else {
      res.json({
        response: {
          saved: true,
          post: data
        }
      });
    }
  });
});

// DELETE Methods
router.delete('/post/:slug', (req, res, next) => {
  const { params: { slug } } = req;
```

```
    removePost(slug, (removed, error) => {
      if (error) {
        res.json({
          error: true,
          message: 'There was an error trying to remove this
post...'
        });
      } else {
        res.json({
          response: {
            removed: true
          }
        })
      }
    });
  });

  // PUT Methods
  router.put('/post/:slug', (req, res, next) => {
    const { params: { slug }, body: { title, content } } = req;

    updatePost(slug, title, content, (affected, error) => {
      if (error) {
        res.json({
          error: true,
          message: 'There was an error trying to update the post'
        });
      } else {
        res.json({
          response: {
            updated: true,
            affected
          }
        })
      }
    });
  });

  export default router;
```

File: controllers/api.js

5. Now we need to create our blog model (`models/blog.js`). Let's build it in sections; the first thing is the connection to our database:

```
// Dependencies
import Sequelize from 'sequelize';
import slug from 'slug';

// Configuration
import config from '../config';

// Connecting to the database
const db = new Sequelize(config.db.database, config.db.user,
config.db.password, {
  host: config.db.host,
  dialect: config.db.dialect,
  operatorsAliases: false
});
```

File: models/blog.js

6. After we created our database connection, let's create our Post model. We will create a table called posts with the following fields: `id`, `title`, `slug`, `content`, `author`, and `createdAt`, but Sequelize by default will automatically create an extra field called `updatedAt` when you add a `DATE` field, which will change every time we update a row:

```
// This will remove the extra response
const queryType = {
  type: Sequelize.QueryTypes.SELECT
};

// Defining our Post model...
const Post = db.define('posts', {
  id: {
    type: Sequelize.INTEGER,
    autoIncrement: true,
    primaryKey: true
  },
  title: {
    type: Sequelize.STRING,
    allowNull: false,
    validate: {
      notEmpty: {
        msg: 'The title is empty',
      }
    }
  },
```

```
    slug: {
      type: Sequelize.STRING,
      allowNull: false,
      unique: true,
      validate: {
        notEmpty: {
          msg: 'The slug is empty',
        }
      }
    },
    content: {
      type: Sequelize.TEXT,
      allowNull: false,
      validate: {
        notEmpty: {
          msg: 'The content is empty'
        }
      }
    },
    author: {
      type: Sequelize.STRING,
      allowNull: false,
      validate: {
        notEmpty: {
          msg: 'Who is the author?',
        }
      }
    },
    createdAt: {
      type: Sequelize.DATE,
      defaultValue: Sequelize.NOW
    },
  });
```

File: models/blog.js

7. One of the coolest things of sequelize is that we can add a validation with a custom message when a field is empty (`notEmpty`). Now we are going to add a method to create a new post:

```
// Creating new post...
export function createPost(title, content, callback) {
  // .sync({ force: true }), if you pass force this will
  // drop the table every time.
  db
    .sync()
    .then(() => {
      Post.create({
```

```
        title,
        slug: title ? slug(title, { lower: 'on' }) : '',
        content,
        author: 'Carlos Santana'
      }).then(insertedPost => {
        console.log(insertedPost);
        callback(insertedPost.dataValues);
      }).catch(error => {
        console.log(error);
        callback(false, error);
      });
    });
}
```

File: models/blog.js

8. Now we need a method to update a post:

```
// Updating a post...
export function updatePost(slg, title, content, callback) {
  Post.update(
    {
      title,
      slug: slug(title, { lower: 'on' }),
      content
    },
    {
      where: { slug: slg }
    }
  ).then(rowsUpdated => {
    console.log('UPDATED', rowsUpdated);
    callback(rowsUpdated);
  }).catch(error => {
    console.log(error);
    callback(false, error);
  });
}
```

File: models/blog.js

9. Also, we need a method to delete a post by its slug:

```
// Removing a post by slug...
export function removePost(slug, callback) {
  Post.destroy({
    where: {
      slug
    }
  }).then(rowDeleted => {
    console.log('DELETED', rowDeleted);
    callback(rowDeleted);
  }).catch(error => {
    console.log(error);
    callback(false, error);
  });
}
```

File: models/blog.js

10. Sequelize also supports SQL queries directly. Let's create two methods, one to find all the posts and the other to find a post by slug using SQL queries:

```
// Find all posts...
export function findAllPosts(callback) {
  db.query('SELECT * FROM posts', queryType).then(data => {
    callback(data);
  });
}

// Find a single post by slug...
export function findBySlug(slug, callback) {
  db.query(`SELECT * FROM posts WHERE slug = '${slug}'`,
queryType).then(data => {
    callback(data);
  });
}
```

File: models/blog.js

11. The `queryType` variable that we defined at the beginning of the file is to avoid getting a second response from Sequelize. By default, if you don't pass this `queryType` Sequelize will return the result in a multidimensional array (the first object is the result and the second one is the metadata object). Let's put all the pieces together:

```
// Dependencies
import Sequelize from 'sequelize';
```

```
import slug from 'slug';

// Configuration
import config from '../config';

// Connecting to the database
const db = new Sequelize(config.db.database, config.db.user,
config.db.password, {
  host: config.db.host,
  dialect: config.db.dialect,
  operatorsAliases: false // This is to avoid the warning:
 //sequelize
 //deprecated String based operators are now deprecated.
});

// This will remove the extra metadata object
const queryType = {
  type: Sequelize.QueryTypes.SELECT
};

// Defining our Post model...
const Post = db.define('posts', {
  id: {
    type: Sequelize.INTEGER,
    autoIncrement: true,
    primaryKey: true
  },
  title: {
    type: Sequelize.STRING,
    allowNull: false,
    validate: {
      notEmpty: {
        msg: 'The title is empty',
      }
    }
  },
  slug: {
    type: Sequelize.STRING,
    allowNull: false,
    unique: true,
    validate: {
      notEmpty: {
        msg: 'The slug is empty',
      }
    }
  },
  content: {
    type: Sequelize.TEXT,
```

```
      allowNull: false,
      validate: {
        notEmpty: {
          msg: 'The content is empty'
        }
      }
    },
    author: {
      type: Sequelize.STRING,
      allowNull: false,
      validate: {
        notEmpty: {
          msg: 'Who is the author?',
        }
      }
    },
    createdAt: {
      type: Sequelize.DATE,
      defaultValue: Sequelize.NOW
    },
  });

  // Creating new post...
  export function createPost(title, content, callback) {
    db
      .sync()
      .then(() => {
        Post.create({
          title,
          slug: title ? slug(title, { lower: 'on' }) : '',
          content,
          author: 'Carlos Santana'
        }).then(insertedPost => {
          console.log(insertedPost);
          callback(insertedPost.dataValues);
        }).catch((error) => {
          console.log(error);
          callback(false, error);
        });
      });
  }

  // Updating a post...
  export function updatePost(slg, title, content, callback) {
    Post.update(
      {
        title,
        slug: slug(title, { lower: 'on' }),
```

```
        content
      },
      {
        where: { slug: slg }
      }
    ).then(rowsUpdated => {
      console.log('UPDATED', rowsUpdated);
      callback(rowsUpdated);
    }).catch(error => {
      console.log(error);
      callback(false, error);
    });
  }

  // Removing a post by slug...
  export function removePost(slug, callback) {
    Post.destroy({
      where: {
        slug
      }
    }).then(rowDeleted => {
      console.log('DELETED', rowDeleted);
      callback(rowDeleted);
    }).catch(error => {
      console.log(error);
      callback(false, error);
    });
  }

  // Find all posts...
  export function findAllPosts(callback) {
    db.query('SELECT * FROM posts', queryType).then(data => {
      callback(data);
    });
  }

  // Find a single post by slug...
  export function findBySlug(slug, callback) {
    db.query(`SELECT * FROM posts WHERE slug = '${slug}'`,
queryType).then(data => {
      callback(data);
    });
  }
```

File: models/blog.js

How it works...

It will work in the same way as the MongoDB recipe, just with minor differences in the results. To test the API, you will need to install Postman (`https://www.getpostman.com`).

POST method endpoints

The POST method is typically used when we want to insert new data into our database.

POST /post. For this endpoint, we need to use Postman to send the data through the request body. To do this, you need to select the POST method in Postman. Enter the URL `http://localhost:3000/api/post`, then click on Headers, and you need to add a `Content-Type` header with a value of `application/x-www-form-urlencoded`:

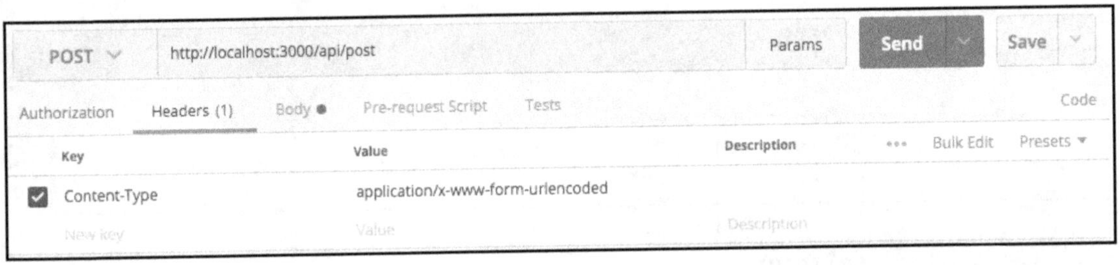

After you set the header, go to the `Body` tab and select the `raw` option, and you can send the information like this:

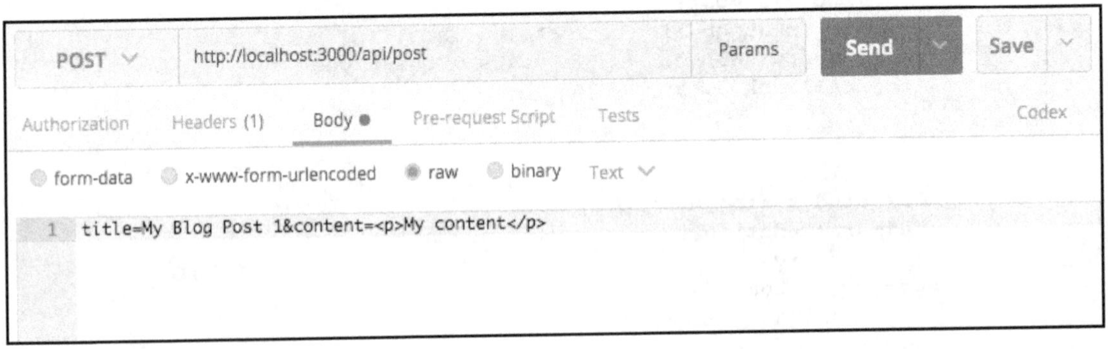

Now you can hit the Send button and see the response that the service returns:

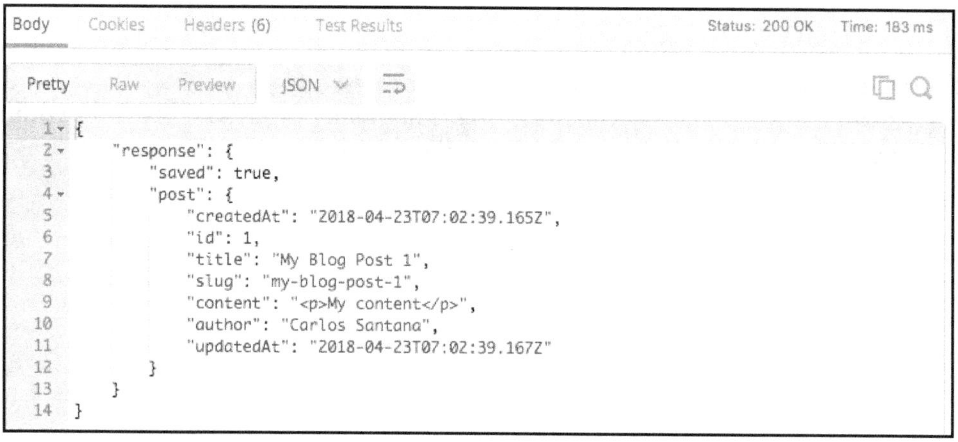
Body
Cookies
Headers (6)
Test Results
Status: 200 OK
Time: 183 ms
Pretty
Raw
Preview
JSON
{
"response": {
"saved": true,
"post": {
"createdAt": "2018-04-23T07:02:39.165Z",
"id": 1,
"title": "My Blog Post 1",
"slug": "my-blog-post-1",
"content": "<p>My content</p>",
"author": "Carlos Santana",
"updatedAt": "2018-04-23T07:02:39.167Z"
}
}
}

If you did everything correctly, you should get a response with the saved node set to true and the post node with information about the saved post. If you try to hit the *Send* button again with the same data (the same title), it will cause an error because, as you remember, our slug must be unique:

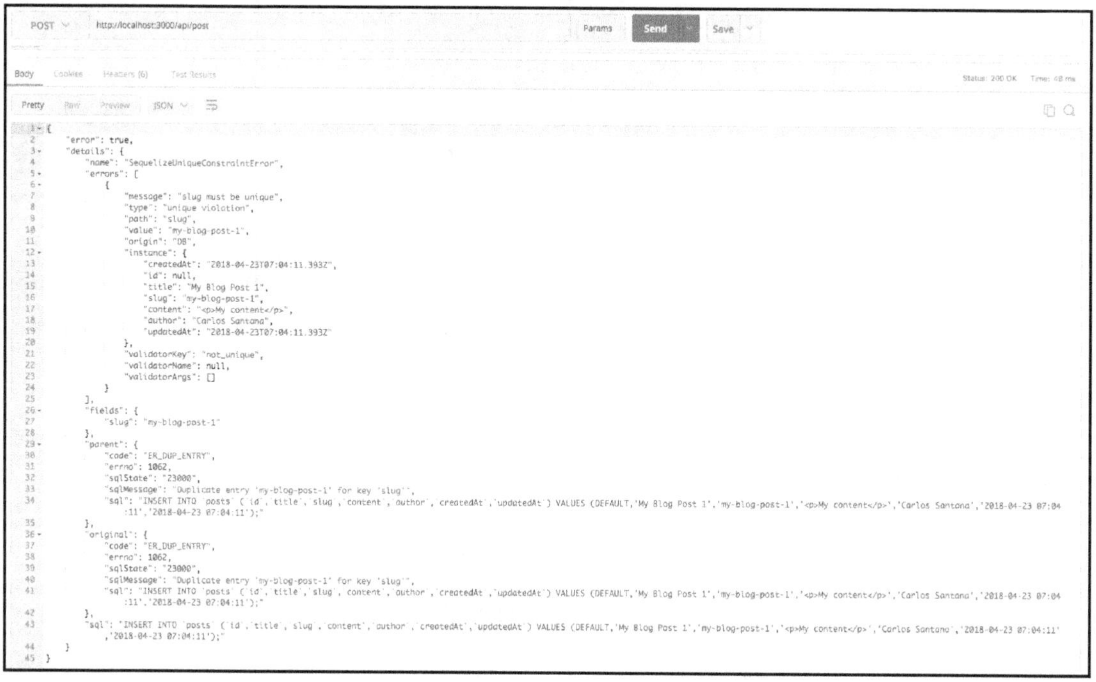
POST
http://localhost:3000/api/post
Params
Send
Save

The text in this image is not relevant. The purpose of the image is to give you a glimpse of how the error looks like. Try in your Postman, and you will see the same error as the image.

GET method endpoints

GET /posts. This endpoint can be tested with your browser. Go to `http://localhost:3000/api/posts`. I have manually inserted three rows with the `createPost` method:


```
{
  "response": [
    {
      "id": 1,
      "title": "My Blog Post 1",
      "slug": "my-blog-post-1",
      "content": "<p>My content</p>",
      "author": "Carlos Santana",
      "createdAt": "2018-04-23T07:07:23.000Z",
      "updatedAt": "2018-04-23T07:07:23.000Z"
    },
    {
      "id": 2,
      "title": "My Blog Post 2",
      "slug": "my-blog-post-2",
      "content": "<p>My content</p>",
      "author": "Carlos Santana",
      "createdAt": "2018-04-23T07:07:31.000Z",
      "updatedAt": "2018-04-23T07:07:31.000Z"
    },
    {
      "id": 3,
      "title": "My Blog Post 3",
      "slug": "my-blog-post-3",
      "content": "<p>My content</p>",
      "author": "Carlos Santana",
      "createdAt": "2018-04-23T07:07:37.000Z",
      "updatedAt": "2018-04-23T07:07:37.000Z"
    }
  ]
}
```


If you want to test it on Postman, then write the same URL (`http://localhost:3000/api/posts`), select the `GET` method, and click on the **Send** button:

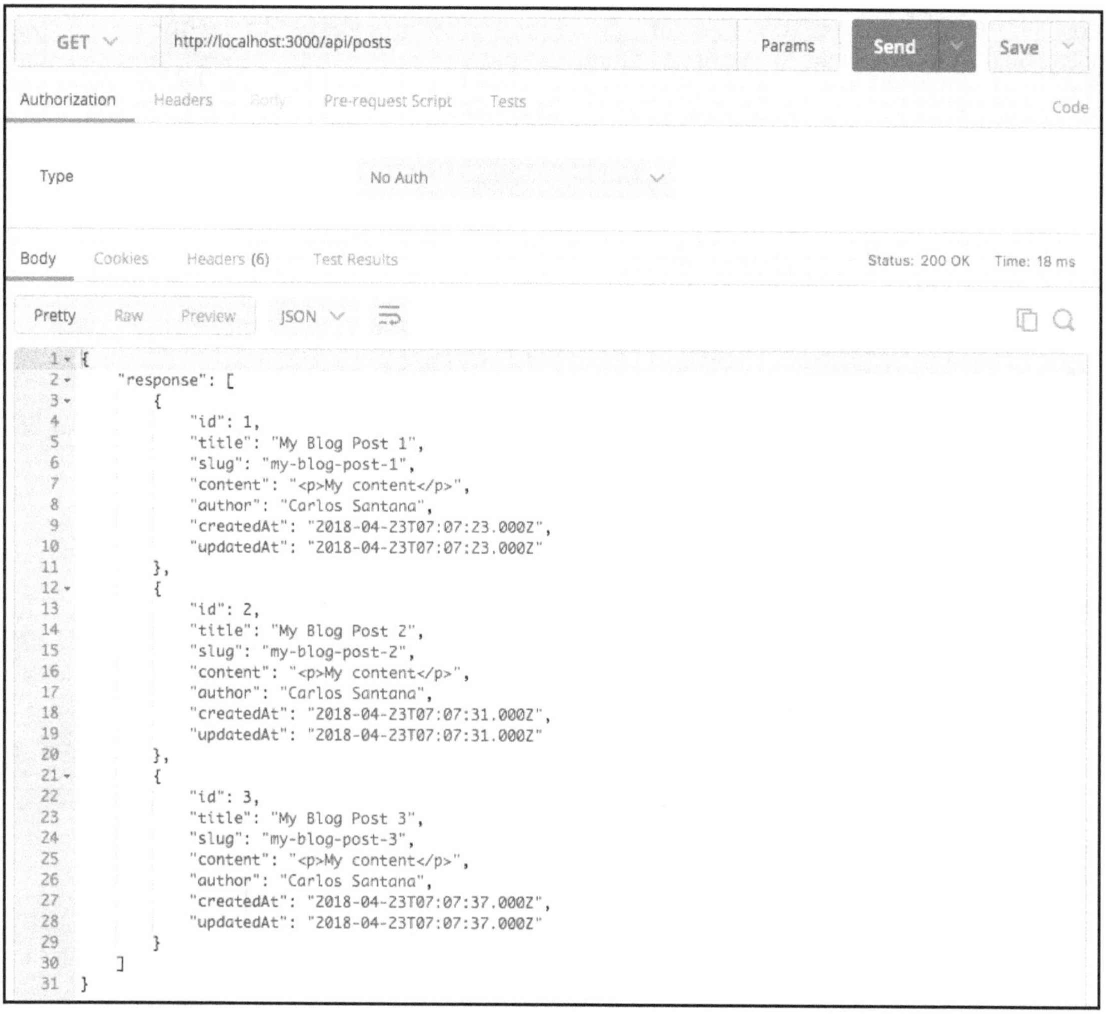
GET
http://localhost:3000/api/posts
Params
Send
Save
Authorization
Headers
Pre-request Script
Tests
Code
Type
No Auth
Body
Cookies
Headers (6)
Test Results
Status: 200 OK
Time: 18 ms
Pretty
Raw
Preview
JSON
{
"response": [
{
"id": 1,
"title": "My Blog Post 1",
"slug": "my-blog-post-1",
"content": "<p>My content</p>",
"author": "Carlos Santana",
"createdAt": "2018-04-23T07:07:23.000Z",
"updatedAt": "2018-04-23T07:07:23.000Z"
},
{
"id": 2,
"title": "My Blog Post 2",
"slug": "my-blog-post-2",
"content": "<p>My content</p>",
"author": "Carlos Santana",
"createdAt": "2018-04-23T07:07:31.000Z",
"updatedAt": "2018-04-23T07:07:31.000Z"
},
{
"id": 3,
"title": "My Blog Post 3",
"slug": "my-blog-post-3",
"content": "<p>My content</p>",
"author": "Carlos Santana",
"createdAt": "2018-04-23T07:07:37.000Z",
"updatedAt": "2018-04-23T07:07:37.000Z"
}
]
}

GET /post/:slug

This endpoint is also a GET, and you need to pass the slug (the friendly URL) in the URL. For example, the slug of the first row, My blog post 1, is my-blog-post-1. A slug is a friendly URL that has the same value as the title but in lowercase, without special characters and the spaces are replaces with dashes (-). In our model, we defined our slug as a unique field, which means that there cannot be more than one post with the same slug.

Let's go to `http://localhost:3000/api/post/my-blog-post-1` in the browser. If the slug exists in the database you will see the information:

```
{
  "response": [
    [
      {
        "id": 1,
        "title": "My Blog Post 1",
        "slug": "my-blog-post-1",
        "content": "<p>My content</p>",
        "author": "Carlos Santana",
        "createdAt": "2018-04-23T07:07:23.000Z",
        "updatedAt": "2018-04-23T07:07:23.000Z"
      }
    ]
  ]
}
```

But if you try to view a slug that does not exist in the database you will get this error:

```
// http://localhost:3000/api/post/my-fake-post

{
  "error": true,
  "message": "Post not found"
}
```

DELETE method endpoints

The `DELETE` method, as the name implies, is for deleting rows in a database.

DELETE /post/:slug. In Postman, we need to select the `DELETE` method, and in the URL you need to pass the slug of the post you want to remove. For example, let's remove my-blog-post-2. If you remove it correctly you should get a response with the removed node with a value of true:

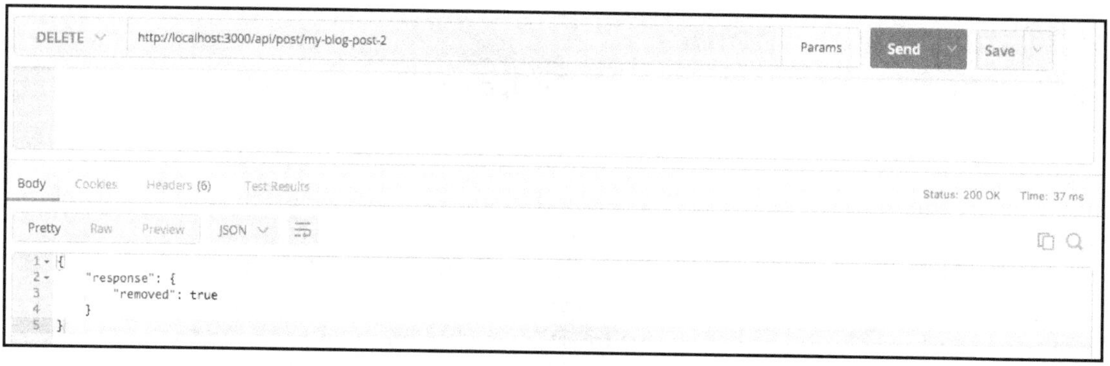

If you want to verify the post was deleted, you can go to the `/posts` endpoint again, and you will see that is not in the JSON anymore:


```
{
  "response": [
    {
      "id": 1,
      "title": "My Blog Post 1",
      "slug": "my-blog-post-1",
      "content": "<p>My content</p>",
      "author": "Carlos Santana",
      "createdAt": "2018-04-23T07:07:23.000Z",
      "updatedAt": "2018-04-23T07:07:23.000Z"
    },
    {
      "id": 3,
      "title": "My Blog Post 3",
      "slug": "my-blog-post-3",
      "content": "<p>My content</p>",
      "author": "Carlos Santana",
      "createdAt": "2018-04-23T07:07:37.000Z",
      "updatedAt": "2018-04-23T07:07:37.000Z"
    }
  ]
}
```

PUT method endpoints

The last method is `PUT`, and it is usually used to update a row in a database.

```
PUT /post/:slug
```

In Postman, you need to select the PUT method first, then the URL of the post you want to edit. Let's edit my-blog-post-3; so the URL will be `http://localhost:3000/api/post/my-blog-post-3`. In the Headers tab, you need to add, as in the POST method, the `Content-Type` header with the value `application/x-www-form-urlencoded`. The last part is the **Body** tab, where you can send the new data you want to replace, in this case, a new title and new content:

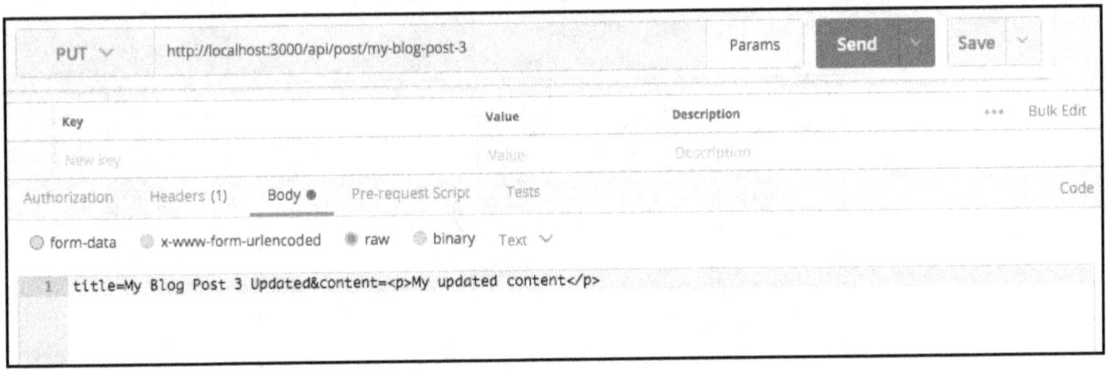

If everything works fine, you should get this response:

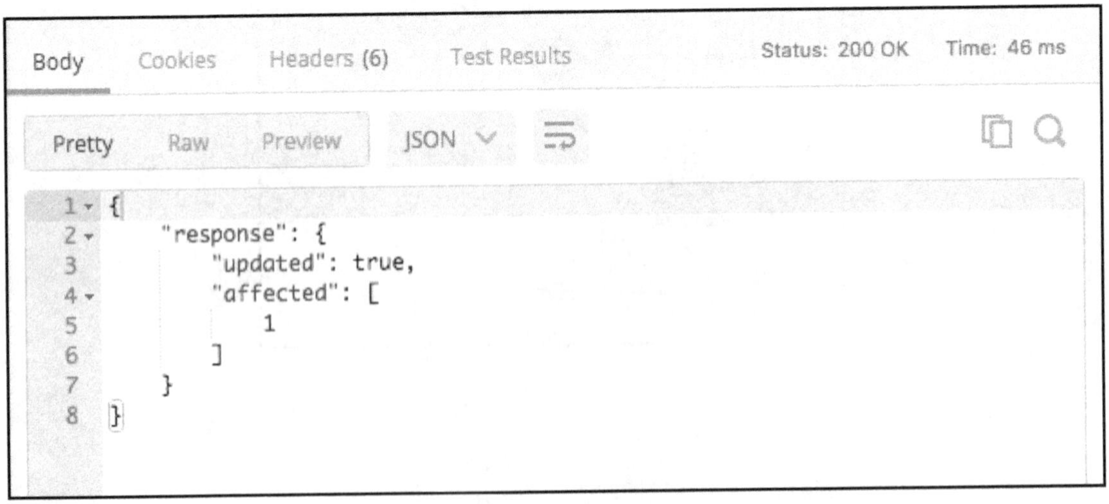

Again, if you want to verify the post was updated correctly, then go to the `/posts` endpoint in your browser:


```
{
  "response": [
    {
      "id": 1,
      "title": "My Blog Post 1",
      "slug": "my-blog-post-1",
      "content": "<p>My content</p>",
      "author": "Carlos Santana",
      "createdAt": "2018-04-23T07:07:23.000Z",
      "updatedAt": "2018-04-23T07:07:23.000Z"
    },
    {
      "id": 3,
      "title": "My Blog Post 3 Updated",
      "slug": "my-blog-post-3-updated",
      "content": "<p>My updated content</p>",
      "author": "Carlos Santana",
      "createdAt": "2018-04-23T07:07:37.000Z",
      "updatedAt": "2018-04-23T07:16:08.000Z"
    }
  ]
}
```


As you can see, the post title, content, and slug were updated correctly.

Adding access tokens to secure our API

The APIs that we created in the last two recipes is public. That means everyone can access and get the information from our server, but what happens if you want to add a security layer on the API and get the information for registered users on your platform? We need to add access token validation to protect our API, and to do this; we have to use **JSON Web Tokens** (**JWT**).

Getting ready

For this recipe, you need to install JWT for Node.js:

```
npm install jsonwebtoken
```

How to do it...

We will mostly use the same code that we created for the MySQL recipe and add a security layer to validate our access tokens:

1. The first thing we need to do is to modify our config file (`config/index.js`), add a security node with the `secretKey` we are going to use to create our tokens, and add the expiration time of the token:

```
export default {
  db: {
    dialect: 'mysql', // The database engine you want to use
    host: 'localhost', // Your host, by default is localhost
    database: 'blog', // Your database name
    user: 'root', // Your MySQL user, by default is root
    password: '123456' // Your MySQL password
  },
  security: {
    secretKey: 'C0d3j0bs', // Secret key
    expiresIn: '1h' // Expiration can be: 30s, 30m, 1h, 7d, etc.
  }
};
```

File: config/index.js

2. The next step is to create a `db.js` file in our model's folder to separate our database connection and share it between our models. Before, we just had the blog model, but now we are going to create a user model file as well:

```
// Configuration
import config from '../config';
import Sequelize from 'sequelize';

export const db = new Sequelize(
  config.db.database,
  config.db.user,
  config.db.password,
  {
    host: config.db.host,
```

```
        dialect: config.db.dialect,
        operatorsAliases: false
      }
    );
```

File: models/db.js

3. Now we need to create a table for users and save a record for our user:

```
CREATE TABLE users (
  id int(11) UNSIGNED NOT NULL AUTO_INCREMENT,
  username varchar(255) NOT NULL,
  password varchar(255) NOT NULL,
  email varchar(255) NOT NULL,
  fullName varchar(255) NOT NULL,
  PRIMARY KEY (`id`)
);
```

4. We can insert a user with this command, change the username and password. In this recipe, we are going to use the SHA1 algorithm to encrypt our passwords:

```
INSERT INTO users (id, username, password, email, fullName)
VALUES (
  NULL,
  'czantany',
  SHA1('123456'),
  'carlos@milkzoft.com',
  'Carlos Santana'
);

// The SHA1 hash generated for the 123456 password is
// 7c4a8d09ca3762af61e59520943dc26494f8941b
```

5. After we have created our user table and we have a registered user, let's create our user model with a `login` method:

```
// Dependencies
import Sequelize from 'sequelize';

// Db Connection
import { db } from './db';

// This will remove the extra response
const queryType = {
  type: Sequelize.QueryTypes.SELECT
};

// Login
```

```
export function login(username, password, callback) {
  db.query(`
    SELECT id, username, email, fullName
    FROM users
    WHERE username = '${username}' AND password = '${password}'
  `, queryType).then(data => callback(data));
}
```

File: models/user.js

6. The next step is to modify our API controller, add a `login` endpoint to generate our token, and add a function to validate the token. Then we are going to protect one of our endpoints (`/api/posts`):

```
// Dependencies
import express from 'express';
import jwt from 'jsonwebtoken';

// Models
import {
  createPost,
  findAllPosts,
  findBySlug,
  removePost,
  updatePost
} from '../models/blog';
import { login } from '../models/user';

// Configuration
import config from '../config';

// Extracting the secretKey and the expiresIn
const { security: { secretKey, expiresIn } } = config;

const router = express.Router();

// Token Validation
const validateToken = (req, res, next) => {
  if (req.headers['access-token']) {
    // The token should come as 'Bearer <access-token>'
    req.accessToken = req.headers['access-token'].split(' ')[1];
  // We just need the token that's why we split the string by
   //space
    // and we got the token in the position 1 of the array
    //generated
    // by the split method.
    return next();
```

```
  } else {
    res.status(403).send({
      error: 'You must send an access-token header...'
    });
  }
}

// POST login - This will generate a new token
router.post('/login', (req, res) => {
  const { username, password } = req.body;

  login(username, password, data => {
    if (Object.keys(data).length === 0) {
      res.status(403).send({ error: 'Invalid login' });
    }

    // Creating the token with the
    // user data + secretKey + expiration time
    jwt.sign({ data }, secretKey, { expiresIn }, (error,
    accessToken) => {
      res.json({
        accessToken
      });
    });
  });
});

// We pass validateToken as middleware and then we verify with
//  req.accessToken
  router.get('/posts', validateToken, (req, res, next) => {
    jwt.verify(req.accessToken, secretKey, (error, userData) => {
      if (error) {
        console.log(error);
        res.status(403).send({ error: 'Invalid token' });
      } else {
        findAllPosts(posts => {
          res.json({
            response: posts,
            user: userData
          });
        });
      }
    });
  });
  // From here all the others endpoints are public...
  router.get('/post/:slug', (req, res, next) => {
    const { params: { slug } } = req;
```

```
    findBySlug(slug, singlePost => {
      console.log('single', singlePost);
      if (!singlePost || singlePost.length === 0) {
        res.send({
          error: true,
          message: 'Post not found'
        });
      } else {
        res.json({
          response: [singlePost]
        });
      }
    });
  });

// POST Methods
router.post('/post', (req, res, next) => {
  const { title, content } = req.body;

  createPost(title, content, (data, error = false) => {
    if (error) {
      res.json({
        error: true,
        details: error
      });
    } else {
      res.json({
        response: {
          saved: true,
          post: data
        }
      });
    }
  });
});

// DELETE Methods
router.delete('/post/:slug', (req, res, next) => {
  const { params: { slug } } = req;

  removePost(slug, (removed, error) => {
    if (error) {
      res.json({
        error: true,
        message: 'There was an error trying to remove this
        post...'
      });
    } else {
```

```
        res.json({
          response: {
            removed: true
          }
        });
      }
    });
  });

  // PUT Methods
  router.put('/post/:slug', (req, res, next) => {
    const { params: { slug }, body: { title, content } } = req;

    updatePost(slug, title, content, (affected, error) => {
      if (error) {
        res.json({
          error: true,
          message: 'There was an error trying to update the post'
        });
      } else {
        res.json({
          response: {
            updated: true,
            affected
          }
        });
      }
    });
  });

  export default router;
```

File: controllers/api.js

How it works...

If you want to test the security of your API, the first thing you need to do is to execute the *POST* `/api/login` method to get a new token. As before, we can do this with Postman.

You need to select the POST method and then write the URL `http://localhost:3000/api/login` and add a `Content-Type` header with the value `application/x-www-form-urlencoded` to be able to send data through the request body:

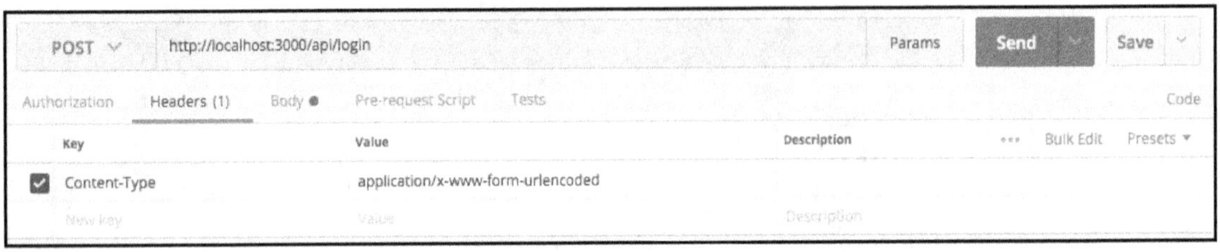

Then, on the *Body* tab, we need to send our data (username and password) with the information of the user that we have in the database. Here we are doing this process manually, but eventually, this information should come from a login form on your website:

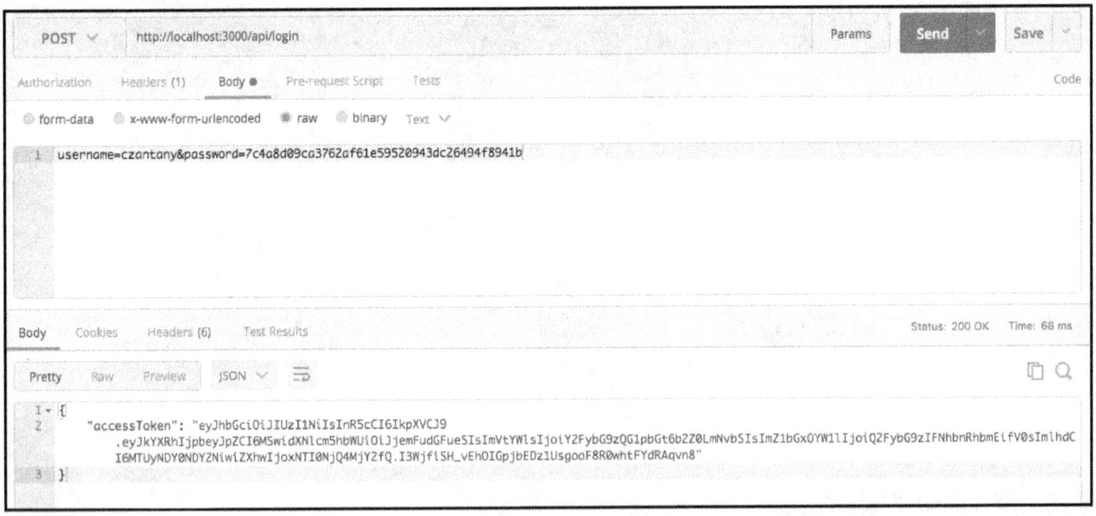

If you passed the correct information for your user you should get the `accessToken`, but if for some reason the login fails or the user or password is incorrect, you will get an error like this:

Once you get the new `accessToken` (remember that this token will be valid just for 1 hour; after the expiration time you will need to create a new one) you need to copy the token and then send it as header (as an access token with the format `Bearer <access-token>`) in the protected endpoint we have (`/api/posts`):

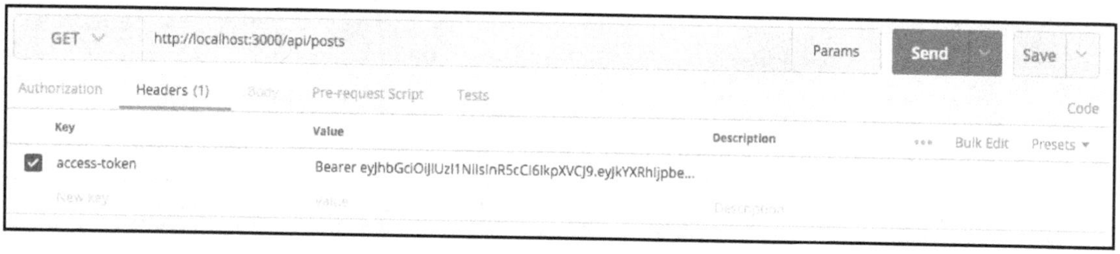

It is crucial that you send the correct format, Bearer[SPACE]<access-token>. Remember, we are using a space to get the token. If you did everything correctly, you should get the response from the service with the posts from the blog and the user information (this can maybe be in a different endpoint, but for this example, I just added the user data here).

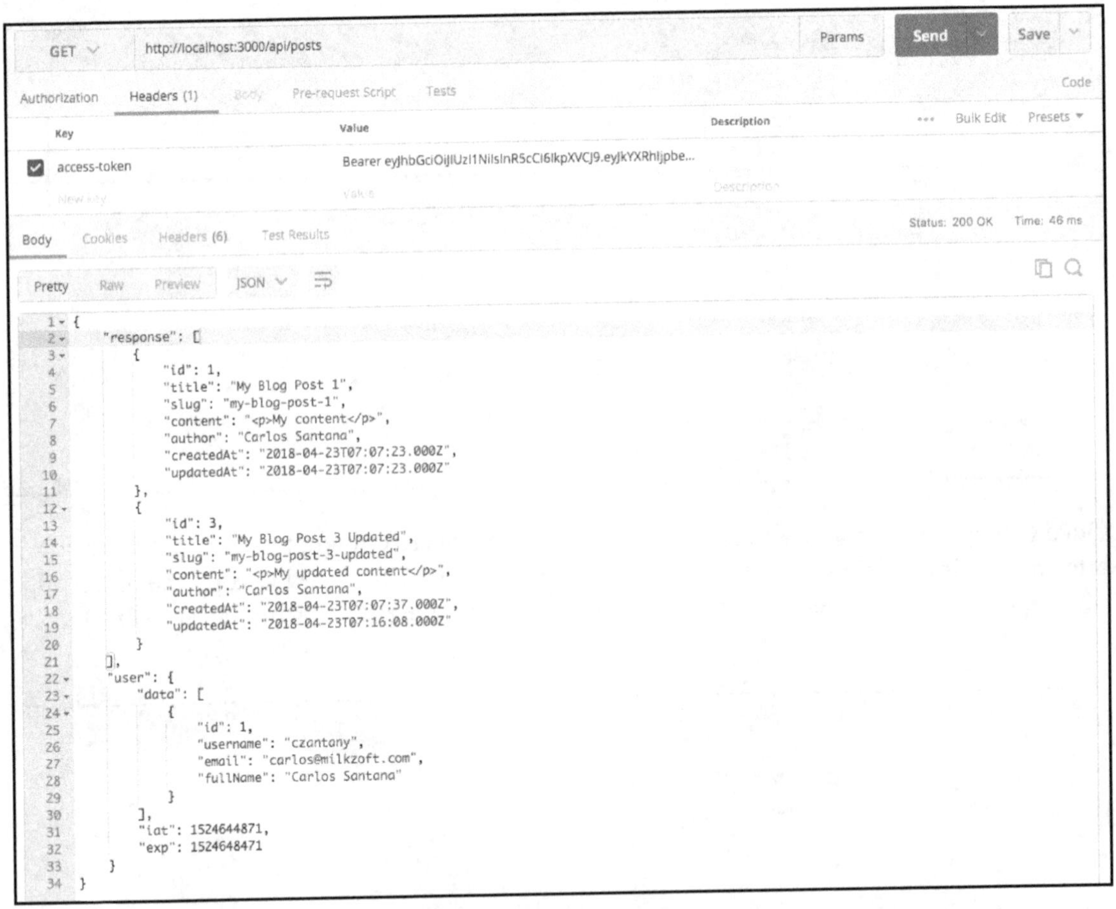

As you can see in the user data, we are getting the information from the database plus two new fields: `iat` (issued at) and `exp` (token expiration). But what happens if our token expires or the user sends an incorrect access-token? In these scenarios, we will return an error:

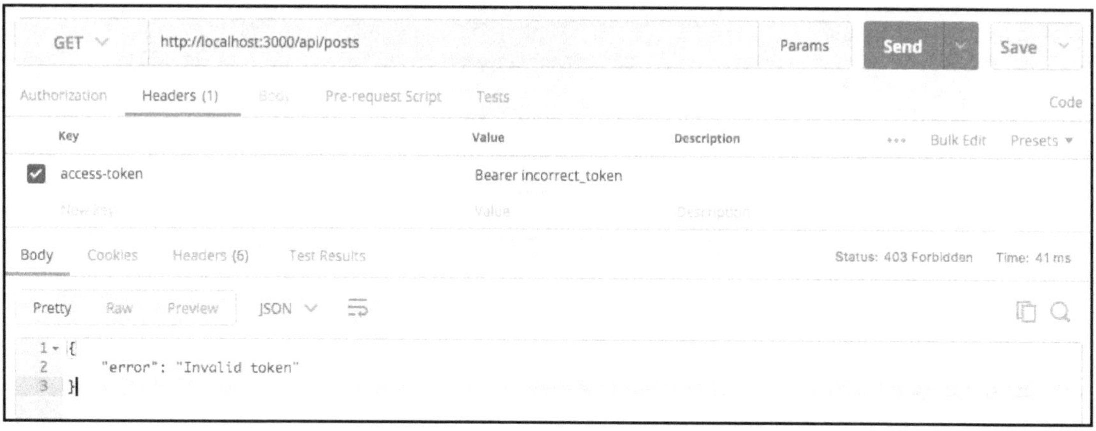

There's more...

As you can see, token validation is easy to implement and adds a security layer for our API when we are working with private data. You will probably ask where the best place is to save the generated access token. Some people save the access token in cookies or sessions, but I don't recommend this because there are some associated security issues. My recommendation is to use local storage to save it only while the user is connected to the site, and then remove it after the user closes the browser, but again this will depend on the type of security you want to add to your platform.

9
Apollo and GraphQL

In this chapter, the following recipes will be covered:

- Creating our first GraphQL server
- Creating a Twitter timeline with Apollo and GraphQL

Introduction

GraphQL is an application-layer query language that can be used with any database. It is also open source (MIT license) and was created by Facebook. It mainly differs from REST in that GraphQL does not use endpoints, but queries instead, and is supported by most server languages, such as JavaScript (Node.js), Go, Ruby, PHP, Java, and Python.

We'll now look at the main differences between GraphQL and REST.

GraphQL:

- The queries are readable
- You can evolve the API without versions
- Type system
- You can avoid doing multiple round trips to fetch related data
- It's easy to limit the set of data we need

REST:

- In REST, everything is a resource
- REST is schemaless
- You need versions to evolve the API
- It's hard to limit the set of data we need
- If you need data from different resources, you need to make multiple requests

Creating our first GraphQL server

For this recipe, we are going to create a contacts list in which we will save the name, phone, and email addresses of our friends.

Getting ready

The first thing we need to do is to create a directory for our project and initialize a new `package.json` file installing `express`, `graphql`, and `express-graphql`:

```
mkdir contacts-graphql
cd contacts-graphql
npm init --yes
npm install express graphql express-graphql babel-preset-env
npm install -g babel-cli
```

We need to install `babel-preset-env` and `babel-cli` to use ES6 syntax in Node. Also, we need to create a `.babelrc` file :

```
{
  "presets": ["env"]
}
```

File: .babelrc

How to do it...

Let's create our first GraphQL server:

1. First, we need to create an `index.js` file for our Express server:

```
import express from 'express';

const app = express();

app.listen(3000, () => console.log('Running server on port 3000'));
```

File: index.js

2. If you run `babel-node index.js` in your terminal, you should be able to see the node server running on port 3000:

```
→ contacts-graphql git:(master) × babel-node index.js
Running server on port 3000
```

3. Now we need to include our `express-graphql` library and import the `buildSchema` method from `graphql`:

```
import express from 'express';
import expressGraphQL from 'express-graphql';
import { buildSchema } from 'graphql';

const app = express();

app.listen(3000, () => console.log('Running server on port 3000'));
```

File: index.js

4. Once we have our `expressGraphQL` and `buildSchema`, let's create our first GraphQL server with our first query:

```
// Dependencies
import express from 'express';
import expressGraphQL from 'express-graphql';
import { buildSchema } from 'graphql';

// Express Application
const app = express();

// Creating our GraphQL Schema
const schema = buildSchema(`
  type Query {
    message: String
  }
`);

// Root has the methods we will execute to get the data
const root = {
  message: () => 'First message'
};

// GraphQL middleware
app.use('/graphql', expressGraphQL({
  schema,
  rootValue: root,
```

```
    graphiql: true // This enables the GraphQL browser's IDE
  }));

  // Running our server
  app.listen(3000, () => console.log('Running server on port
3000'));
```

File: index.js

5. Now let's create our data file for our contacts list. We can make a data directory and a `contacts.json` file:

```
{
  "contacts": [
    {
      "id": 1,
      "name": "Carlos Santana",
      "phone": "281-323-4146",
      "email": "carlos@milkzoft.com"
    },
    {
      "id": 2,
      "name": "Cristina",
      "phone": "331-251-5673",
      "email": "cristina@gmail.com"
    },
    {
      "id": 3,
      "name": "John Smith",
      "phone": "415-307-4382",
      "email": "john.smith@gmail.com"
    },
    {
      "id": 4,
      "name": "John Brown",
      "phone": "281-323-4146",
      "email": "john.brown@gmail.com"
    }
  ]
}
```

File: data/contacts.json

6. We will now need to add the methods to get the data (`getContact` and `getContacts`):

```
// Dependencies
import express from 'express';
import expressGraphQL from 'express-graphql';
import { buildSchema } from 'graphql';

// Contacts Data
import { contacts } from './data/contacts';

// Express Application
const app = express();

// Creating our GraphQL Schema
const schema = buildSchema(`
  type Query {
    contact(id: Int!): Contact
    contacts(name: String): [Contact]
  }

  type Contact {
    id: Int
    name: String
    phone: String
    email: String
  }
`);

// Data methods
const methods = {
  getContact: args => {
    const { id } = args;

    return contacts.filter(contact => contact.id === id)[0];
  },
  getContacts: args => {
    const { name = false } = args;

    // If we don't get a name we return all contacts
    if (!name) {
      return contacts;
    }

    // Returning contacts with same name...
    return contacts.filter(
      contact => contact.name.includes(name)
    );
```

```
  }
};

// Root has the methods we will execute to get the data
const root = {
  contact: methods.getContact,
  contacts: methods.getContacts
};

// GraphQL middleware
app.use('/graphql', expressGraphQL({
  schema,
  rootValue: root,
  graphiql: true // This enables the GraphQL GUI
}));

// Runnign our server
app.listen(3000, () => console.log('Running server on port 3000'));
```

File: index.js

How it works...

If you run the server and you go to the URL `http://localhost:3000/graphql`, you will see the GraphiQL IDE and, by default, the message query, if you click on the play button you will observe the data with the message "**First message**":

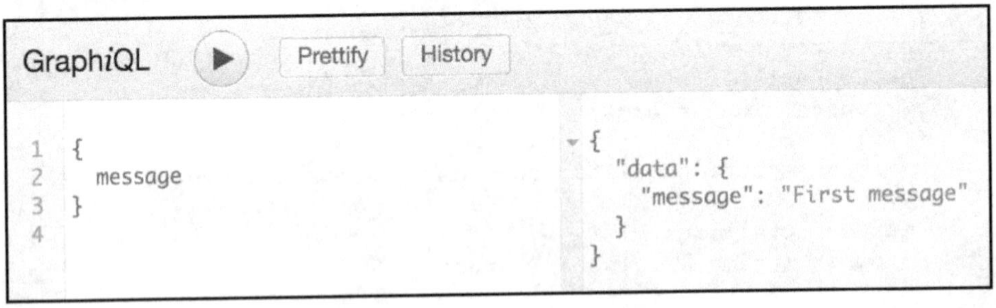

Now in the GraphiQL IDE, we need to create a query and add a query variable for our `contactId` to get a single contact:

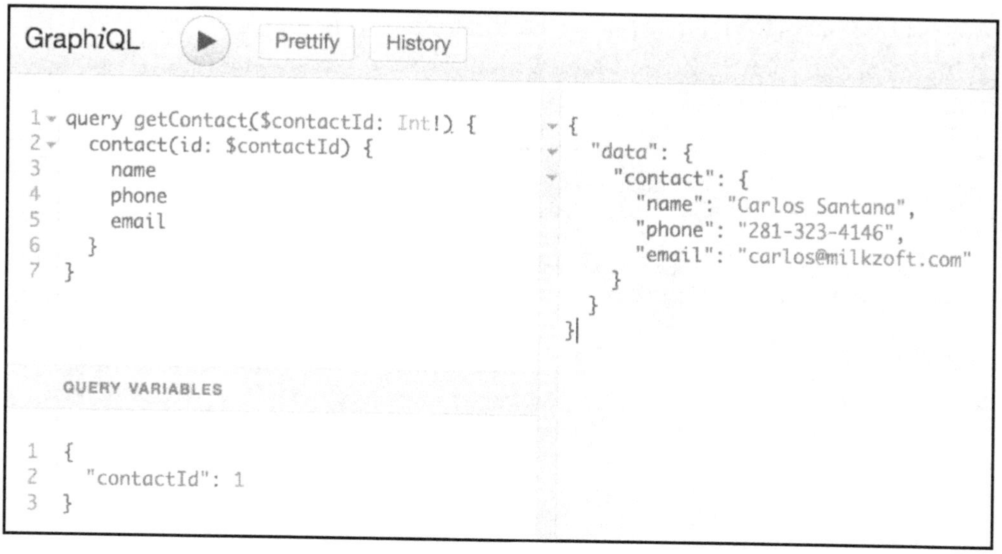
GraphiQL
Prettify
History
query getContact($contactId: Int!) {
contact(id: $contactId) {
name
phone
email
}
}
QUERY VARIABLES
{
"contactId": 1
}
{
"data": {
"contact": {
"name": "Carlos Santana",
"phone": "281-323-4146",
"email": "carlos@milkzoft.com"
}
}
}

Now for our `getContacts` query, we need to pass the `contactName` variable:

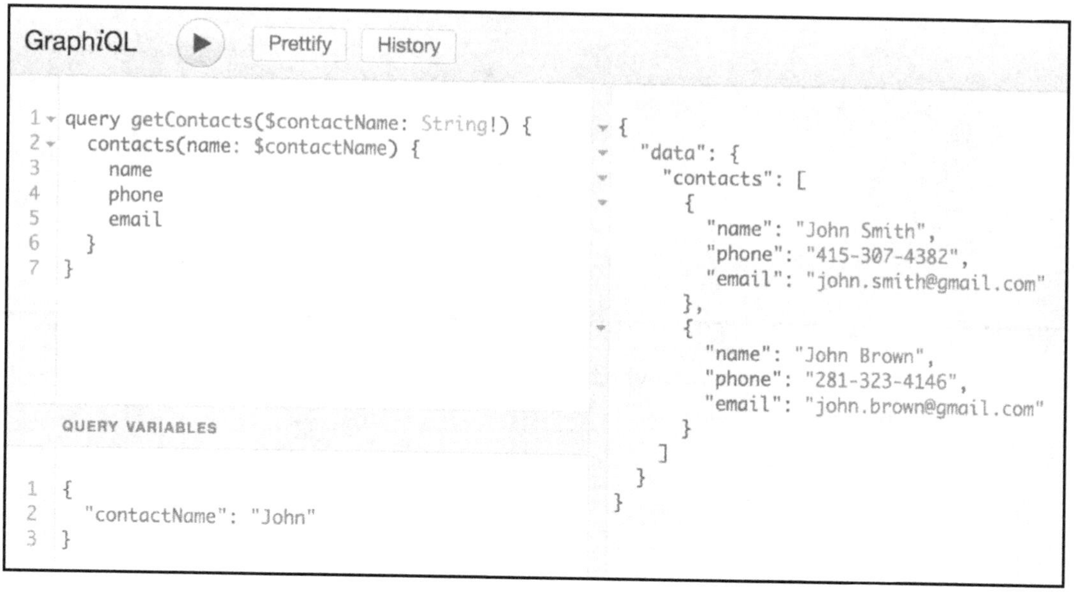
GraphiQL
Prettify
History
query getContacts($contactName: String!) {
contacts(name: $contactName) {
name
phone
email
}
}
QUERY VARIABLES
{
"contactName": "John"
}
{
"data": {
"contacts": [
{
"name": "John Smith",
"phone": "415-307-4382",
"email": "john.smith@gmail.com"
},
{
"name": "John Brown",
"phone": "281-323-4146",
"email": "john.brown@gmail.com"
}
]
}
}

As you can see, if we send John as the `contactName`, the query will return the two rows we have with the names John Smith and John Brown. Also, if we send an empty value, we are going to get all the contacts:

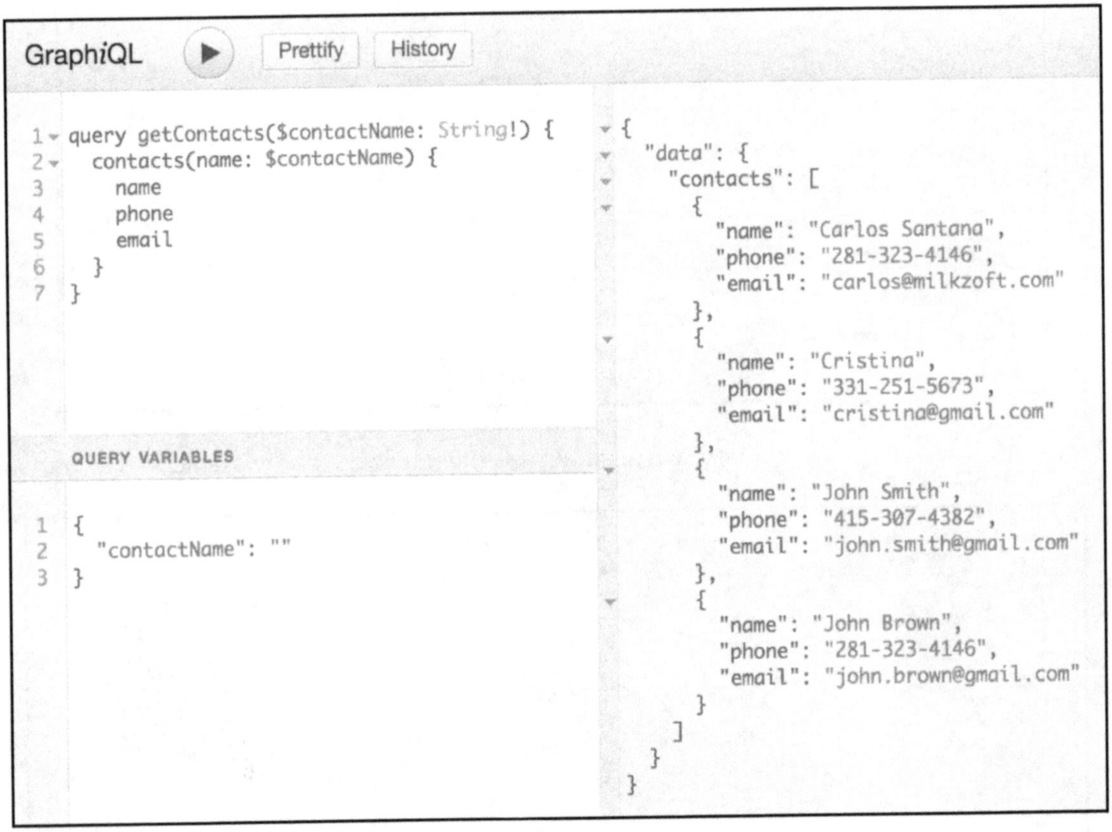
GraphiQL
Prettify
History
query getContacts($contactName: String!) {
contacts(name: $contactName) {
name
phone
email
}
}
QUERY VARIABLES
{
"contactName": ""
}
{
"data": {
"contacts": [
{
"name": "Carlos Santana",
"phone": "281-323-4146",
"email": "carlos@milkzoft.com"
},
{
"name": "Cristina",
"phone": "331-251-5673",
"email": "cristina@gmail.com"
},
{
"name": "John Smith",
"phone": "415-307-4382",
"email": "john.smith@gmail.com"
},
{
"name": "John Brown",
"phone": "281-323-4146",
"email": "john.brown@gmail.com"
}
]
}
}

Also, we can start using fragments, which are used to share fields between `queries`, `mutations`, and `subscriptions`:

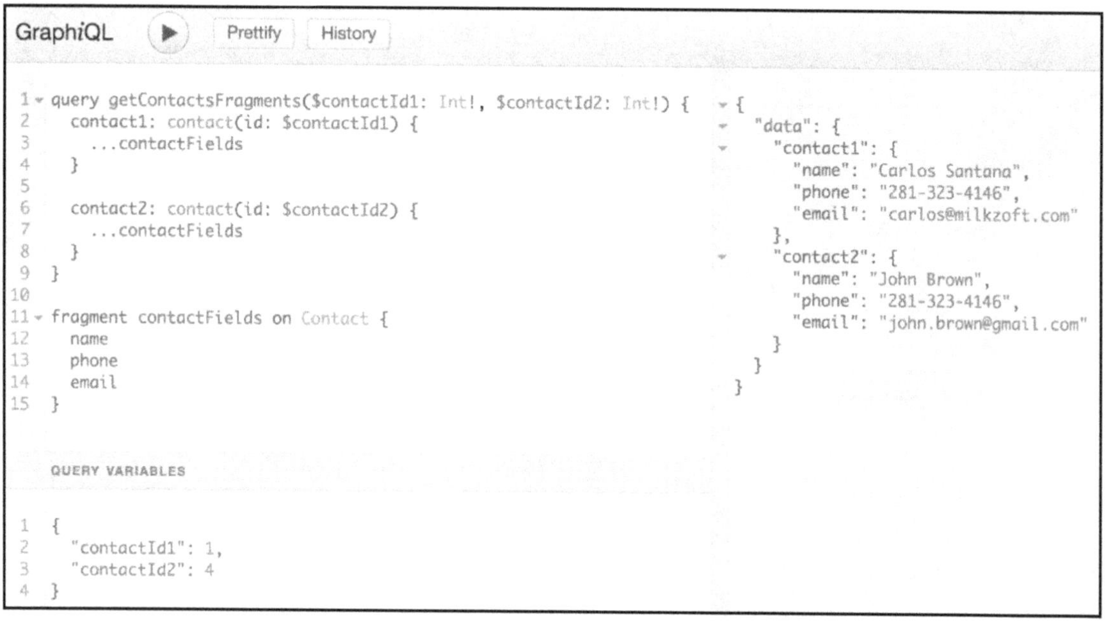

GraphiQL
Prettify
History
query getContactsFragments($contactId1: Int!, $contactId2: Int!) {
contact1: contact(id: $contactId1) {
...contactFields
}
contact2: contact(id: $contactId2) {
...contactFields
}
}
fragment contactFields on Contact {
name
phone
email
}
QUERY VARIABLES
{
"contactId1": 1,
"contactId2": 4
}
{
"data": {
"contact1": {
"name": "Carlos Santana",
"phone": "281-323-4146",
"email": "carlos@milkzoft.com"
},
"contact2": {
"name": "John Brown",
"phone": "281-323-4146",
"email": "john.brown@gmail.com"
}
}
}

As you can see, we define our fragment with the fields we want to get and then in both queries (`contact1` and `contact2`), we re-use the same fragment (`contactFields`). In the query variables, we pass the values of the contacts we want to get data.

There's more...

Mutations are also essential because they help us to modify our data. Let's implement a mutation and update a contact by passing the ID and the fields we want to change.

We need to add our mutation definition and create the function to update our contact; our code should look like this:

```
// Dependencies
import express from 'express';
import expressGraphQL from 'express-graphql';
import { buildSchema } from 'graphql';

// Contacts Data
import { contacts } from './data/contacts';

// Express Application
const app = express();
```

```
// Creating our GraphQL Schema
const schema = buildSchema(`
  type Query {
    contact(id: Int!): Contact
    contacts(name: String): [Contact]
  }

  type Mutation {
    updateContact(
      id: Int!,
      name: String!,
      phone: String!,
      email: String!
    ): Contact
  }

  type Contact {
    id: Int
    name: String
    phone: String
    email: String
  }
`);

// Data methods
const methods = {
  getContact: args => {
    const { id } = args;

    return contacts.filter(contact => contact.id === id)[0];
  },
  getContacts: args => {
    const { name = false } = args;

    // If we don't get a name we return all contacts
    if (!name) {
      return contacts;
    }

    // Returning contacts with same name...
    return contacts.filter(contact => contact.name.includes(name));
  },
  updateContact: ({ id, name, phone, email }) => {
    contacts.forEach(contact => {
      if (contact.id === id) {
        // Updating only the fields that has new values...
        contact.name = name || contact.name;
        contact.phone = phone || contact.phone;
```

```
            contact.email = email || contact.email;
          }
        });

        return contacts.filter(contact => contact.id === id)[0];
      }
    };

    // Root has the methods we will execute to get the data
    const root = {
      contact: methods.getContact,
      contacts: methods.getContacts,
      updateContact: methods.updateContact
    };

    // GraphQL middleware
    app.use('/graphql', expressGraphQL({
      schema,
      rootValue: root,
      graphiql: true // This enables the GraphQL GUI
    }));

    // Running our server
    app.listen(3000, () => console.log('Running server on port 3000'));
```

File: index.js

Now let's create our mutation in GraphiQL and update a contact:

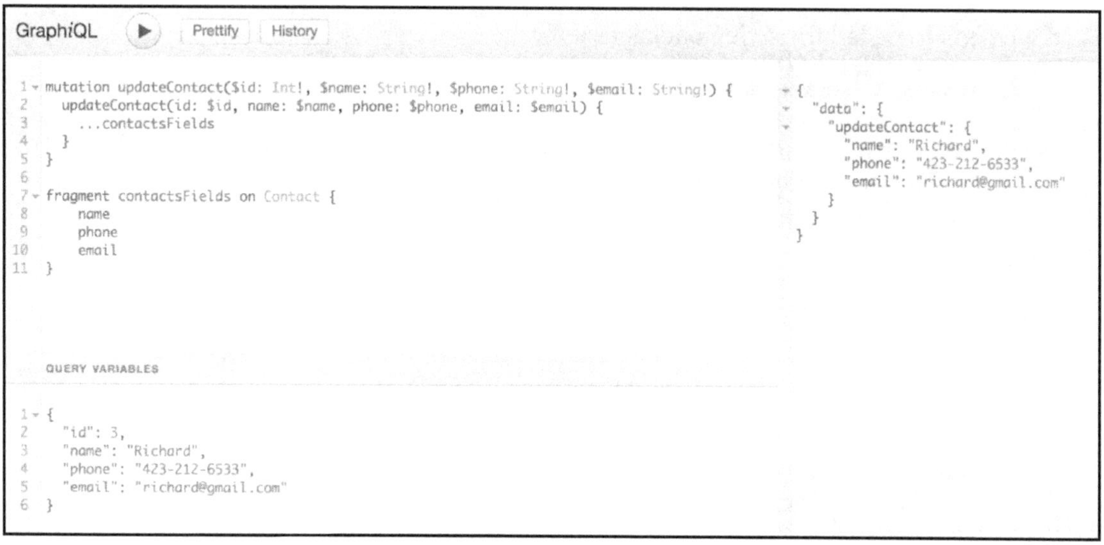

Creating a Twitter timeline with Apollo and GraphQL

Apollo is an open source infrastructure for GraphQL. There are other libraries for handling GraphQL, such as Relay and Universal React Query Library (URQL). The main problem with these libraries is that they are mainly for React applications, while Apollo can work with any other technology or framework.

Getting ready

For this recipe, we are going to create a new React application using `create-react-app`:

```
create-react-app apollo
```

We need to eject the configuration by executing the following command:

```
npm run eject
```

The `eject` command will bring all the configuration of `react-scripts` to your local project (Webpack configuration).

Now we need to install the following packages:

```
npm install apollo-boost graphql graphql-tag moment mongoose react-
apollo
```

And we need to install these dev packages as well:

```
npm install --save-dev babel-preset-react babel-preset-stage-0
```

Then we need to add a `resolutions` node to specify the exact version of GraphQL we are going to use. This is to avoid version conflicts. The current version of `graphql` is `0.13.2`. Of course, you will need to specify the latest version of GraphqQL at the time you're reading this:

```
"resolutions": {
  "graphql": "0.13.2"
}
```

Also, we need to remove the `babel` node in our `package.json`.

```
"babel": {
  "presets": [
    "react-app"
  ]
}
```

File: package.json

Then, finally, we need to create a `.babelrc` file with this:

```
{
  "presets": ["react", "stage-0"]
}
```

File: .babelrc

Before we jump to the actual recipe, we need to create first our GraphQL backend server to create all the queries and mutations we will need to complete this project. We'll see how to do that in the following sections.

Creating our GraphQL backend server

Let's get started with the backend server:

1. First, inside the `apollo` project (the one we created with `create-react-app`), we need to create a new directory called `backend`, initialize a `package.json` file, and create inside the `src` folder:

```
cd apollo
mkdir backend
cd backend
npm init -y
mkdir src
```

2. Now we need to install these dependencies:

```
npm install cors express express-graphql graphql graphql-tools
mongoose nodemon babel-preset-es2015

npm install -g babel-cli
```

→ babel-preset-env

3. In our `package.json` file, we need to modify our start script to use `nodemon`:

```
"scripts": {
  "start": "nodemon src/app.js --watch src --exec babel-node
  --presets es2015"
}
```

File: package.json

4. Then we need to create our `app.js` file, in which we are going to create our GraphQL middleware:

```
// Dependencies
import express from 'express';
import expressGraphQL from 'express-graphql';
import cors from 'cors';
import graphQLExpress from 'express-graphql';
import { makeExecutableSchema } from 'graphql-tools';

// Query
import { typeDefs } from './types/Query';
import { resolvers } from './types/Resolvers';

// Defining our schema with our typeDefs and resolvers
const schema = makeExecutableSchema({
  typeDefs,
  resolvers
});

// Intializing our express app
const app = express();

// Using cors
app.use(cors());

// GraphQL Middleware
app.use('/graphiql', graphQLExpress({
  schema,
  pretty: true,
  graphiql: true
}));
```

```
// Listening port 5000
app.listen(5000);

console.log('Server started on port 5000');
```

File: src/app.js

5. As you can see, we have included our typeDefs and resolvers from `types` folder, so let's create that directory and create our Query file:

```
export const typeDefs = [`
  # Scalar Types (custom type)
  scalar DateTime

  # Tweet Type (should match our Mongo schema)
  type Tweet {
    _id: String
    tweet: String
    author: String
    createdAt: DateTime
  }

  # Query
  type Query {
    # This query will return a single Tweet
    getTweet(_id: String): Tweet

    # This query will return an array of Tweets
    getTweets: [Tweet]
  }

  # Mutations
  type Mutation {
    # DateTime is a custom Type
    createTweet(
      tweet: String,
      author: String,
      createdAt: DateTime
    ): Tweet
    # Mutation to delete a Tweet
    deleteTweet(_id: String): Tweet
    # Mutation to update a Tweet (! means mandatory).
    updateTweet(
      _id: String!,
      tweet: String!
    ): Tweet
  }
```

```
  # Schema
  schema {
    query: Query
    mutation: Mutation
  }
`];
```

File: src/types/Query.js

6. After we have created our Query file, we need to add our resolvers. These are the functions that are executed for each Query and Mutation. We are also going to define our custom `DateTime` type using `GraphQLScalarType`:

```
// Dependencies
import { GraphQLScalarType } from 'graphql';
// TweetModel (Mongo Schema)
import TweetModel from '../model/Tweet';
// Resolvers
export const resolvers = {
  Query: {
    // Receives an _id and returns a single Tweet.
    getTweet: _id => TweetModel.getTweet(_id),
    // Gets an array of Tweets.
    getTweets: () => TweetModel.getTweets()
  },
  Mutation: {
    // Creating a Tweet passing the args (Tweet object), the _ is
    // the root normally is undefined
    createTweet: (_, args) => TweetModel.createTweet(args),
    // Deleting a Tweet passing in the args the _id of the Tweet
    // we want to remove
    deleteTweet: (_, args) => TweetModel.deleteTweet(args),
    // Updating a Tweet passing the new values of the Tweet we
    // want to update
    updateTweet: (_, args) => TweetModel.updateTweet(args)
  },
  // This DateTime will return the current date.
  DateTime: new GraphQLScalarType({
    name: 'DateTime',
    description: 'Date custom scalar type',
    parseValue: () => new Date(),
    serialize: value => value,
    parseLiteral: ast => ast.value
  })
};
```

File: src/types/Resolvers.js

7. Finally, we need to create our tweet model:

```
// Dependencies
import mongoose from 'mongoose';

// Connecting to Mongo
mongoose.Promise = global.Promise;
mongoose.connect('mongodb://localhost:27017/twitter', {
  useNewUrlParser: true
});

// Getting Mongoose Schema
const Schema = mongoose.Schema;

// Defining our Tweet schema
const tweetSchema = new Schema({
  tweet: String,
  author: String,
  createdAt: Date,
});

// Creating our Model
const TweetModel = mongoose.model('Tweet', tweetSchema);

export default {
  // Getting all the tweets and sorting descending
  getTweets: () => TweetModel.find().sort({ _id: -1 }),
  // Getting a single Tweet using the _id
  getTweet: _id => TweetModel.findOne({ _id }),
  // Saving a Tweet
  createTweet: args => TweetModel(args).save(),
  // Removing a Tweet by _id
  deleteTweet: args => {
    const { _id } = args;

    TweetModel.remove({ _id }, error => {
      if (error) {
        console.log('Error Removing:', error);
      }
    });

    // Even when we removed a tweet we need to return the object
    // of the tweet
    return args;
  },
  // Updating a Tweet (just the field tweet will be updated)
  updateTweet: args => {
    const { _id, tweet } = args;
```

```
      // Searching by _id and then update tweet field.
      TweetModel.update({ _id }, {
        $set: {
          tweet
        }
      },
      { upsert: true }, error => {
        if (error) {
          console.log('Error Updating:', error);
        }
      });

      // This is hard coded for now
      args.author = 'codejobs';
      args.createdAt = new Date();

      // Returning the updated Tweet
      return args;
    }
  };
```

File: src/model/Tweet.js

You need to have MongoDB installed and running to use this project. If you don't know how to do this, you can look at `Chapter 8`, *Creating an API with Node.js Using MongoDB and MySQL.*

8. Now for the moment of truth! If you followed all the steps correctly you should see the GraphiQL IDE working if you go to `http://localhost:5000/graphiql`, but it's possible you'll get this error:

```
{
  "errors": [
    {
      "message": "Cannot use GraphQLSchema \"[object Object]\"
from another module or realm.\n\nEnsure that there is only one
instance of \"graphql\" in the node_modules\ndirectory. If
different versions of \"graphql\" are the dependencies of
other\nrelied on modules, use \"resolutions\" to ensure only one
version is installed.\n\nhttps://yarnpkg.com/en/docs/selective-
version-resolutions\n\nDuplicate \"graphql\" modules cannot be
used at the same time since different\nversions may have different
capabilities and behavior. The data from one\nversion used in the
function from another could produce confusing and\nspurious
results."
    }
  ]
}
```

9. Usually, this error means that we are using `graphql` in two projects (frontend and backend) and npm does not know which version will use which. This is a tricky error, but I will show you how to fix it. First, we remove the `node_modules` folder from both of our projects (frontend and backend). Then we need to add a `resolutions` node in both of the `package.json` files:

```
"resolutions": {
  "graphql": "0.13.2"
}
```

10. At the same time, we also need to remove the caret (`^`) from the `graphql` version in both `package.json` files.
11. Now we must delete the `package-lock.json` and `yarn.lock` files (if you have them).
12. Before we install the dependencies again, it's a good idea to update npm to the latest version:

```
npm install -g npm
```

13. After that, just to be safe, let's remove the npm cache:

```
npm cache clean --force
```

14. And now you run `npm install` again (first on the backend), and after you run the project with `npm start`, if everything works fine you should see the GraphiQL IDE working properly:

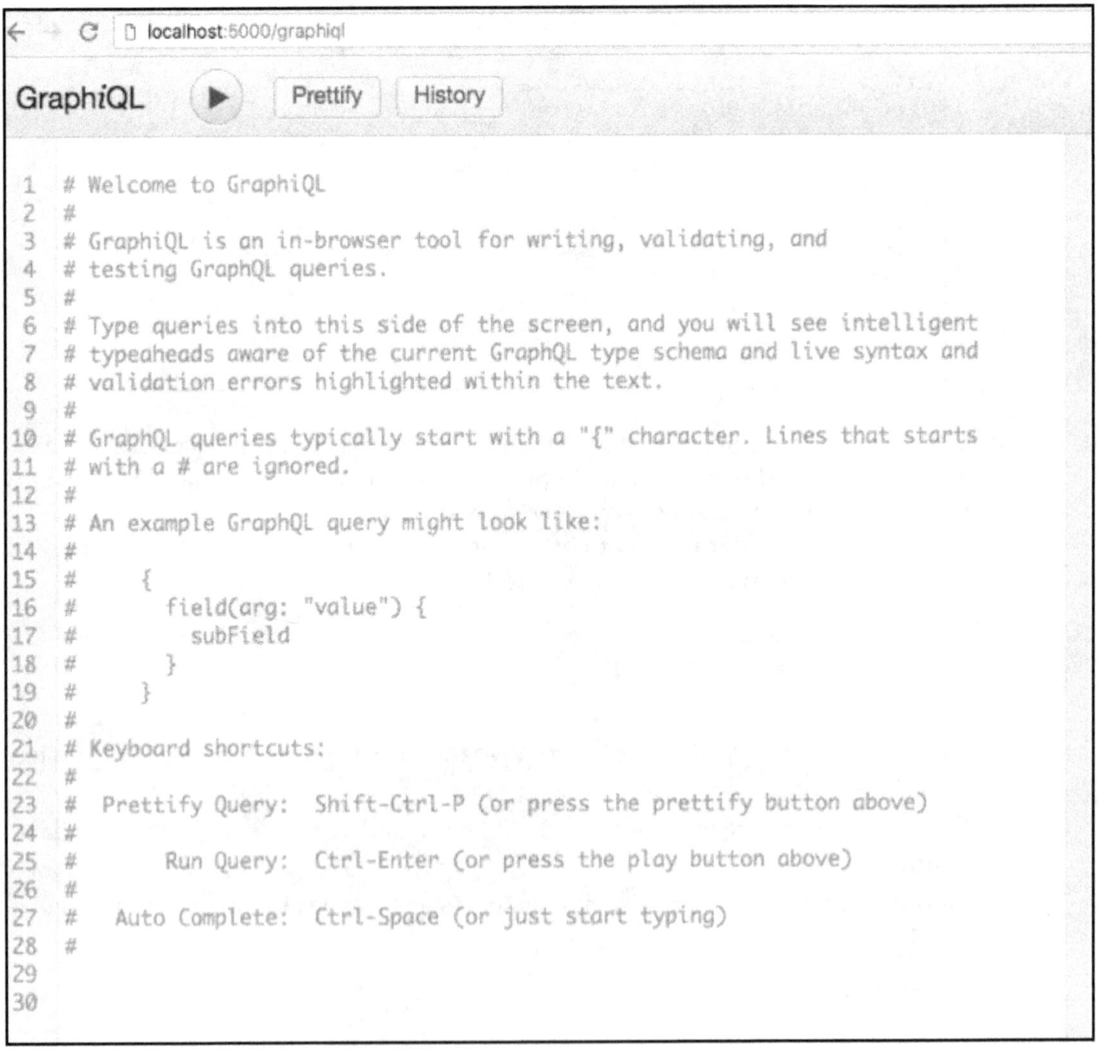

How to do it...

Now that we have our backend ready, let's start working on our frontend:

1. The first file we need to modify is the `index.js` file:

```
// Dependencies
import React from 'react';
import { render } from 'react-dom';
import ApolloClient from 'apollo-boost';
import { ApolloProvider } from 'react-apollo';

// Components
import App from './App';

// Styles
import './index.css';

// Apollo Client
const client = new ApolloClient({
  uri: 'http://localhost:5000/graphiql' // Backend endpoint
});

// Wrapping the App with ApolloProvider
const AppContainer = () => (
  <ApolloProvider client={client}>
    <App />
  </ApolloProvider>
);

// Root
const root = document.getElementById('root');

// Rendering the AppContainer
render(<AppContainer />, root);
```

File: src/index.js

2. We connect our backend endpoint to `ApolloClient`, and we wrapped our `<App />` component with `<ApolloProvider>` (yes, this is similar to Redux Provider). Now let's modify our `App.js` file to include our main component (`Tweets`):

```
// Dependencies
import React, { Component } from 'react';

// Components
import Tweets from './components/Tweets';
```

```
// Styles
import './App.css';

class App extends Component {
  render() {
    return (
      <div className="App">
        <Tweets />
      </div>
    );
  }
}

export default App;
```

File: src/App.js

3. The first thing we need to do is create our GraphQL queries and mutations. To do this, we need to create a new directory called `graphql` and other two directories inside it, one for `mutations` and the other for `queries`:

```
// Dependencies
import gql from 'graphql-tag';

// getTweets query
export const QUERY_GET_TWEETS = gql`
  query getTweets {
    getTweets {
      _id
      tweet
      author
      createdAt
    }
  }
`;
```

File: src/graphql/queries/index.js

4. Yes, you see it properly, it's not a typo! The function is called without parentheses and using only backticks (`` gql`YOUR QUERY HERE` ``). The `getTweets` query is already defined in our backend. We are executing the `getTweets` query, and we will get the fields (`_id`, `tweet`, `author`, and `createdAt`). Now let's create our mutations:

```
// Dependencies
import gql from 'graphql-tag';

// createTweet Mutation
export const MUTATION_CREATE_TWEET = gql`
  mutation createTweet(
    $tweet: String,
    $author: String,
    $createdAt: DateTime
  ) {
    createTweet(
      tweet: $tweet,
      author: $author,
      createdAt: $createdAt
    ) {
      _id
      tweet
      author
      createdAt
    }
  }
`;

// deleteTweet Mutation
export const MUTATION_DELETE_TWEET = gql`
  # ! means mandatory
  mutation deleteTweet($_id: String!) {
    deleteTweet(
      _id: $_id
    ) {
      _id
      tweet
      author
      createdAt
    }
  }
`;

// updateTweet Mutation
export const MUTATION_UPDATE_TWEET = gql`
  mutation updateTweet(
```

```
      $_id: String!,
      $tweet: String!
    ) {
      updateTweet(
        _id: $_id,
        tweet: $tweet
      ) {
        _id
        tweet
        author
        createdAt
      }
    }
  `;
```

File: src/graphql/mutations/index.js

5. I always like to do refactors and improve things, that's why I created two helpers for the `Query` and `Mutation` components from `react-apollo`. First, let's create two directories, `shared` and `shared/components`. First, this is our Query component:

```
// Dependencies
import React, { Component } from 'react';
import { Query as ApolloQuery } from 'react-apollo';

class Query extends Component {
  render() {
    const {
      query,
      render: Component
    } = this.props;

    return (
      <ApolloQuery query={query}>
        {({ loading, error, data }) => {
          if (loading) {
            return <p>Loading...</p>;
          }

          if (error) {
            return <p>Query Error: {error}</p>
          }

          return <Component data={data || false} />;
        }}
      </ApolloQuery>
```

```
      );
    }
  }

  export default Query;
```

File: src/shared/components/Query.js

6. Our Mutation component should be like this:

```
// Dependencies
import React, { Component } from 'react';
import { Mutation as ApolloMutation } from 'react-apollo';

class Mutation extends Component {
  render() {
    const {
      mutation,
      query,
      children,
      onCompleted
    } = this.props;

    return (
      <ApolloMutation
        mutation={mutation}
        update={(cache, { data }) => {
          // Getting the mutation and query name
          const {
            definitions: [{ name: { value: mutationName } }]
          } = mutation;
          const {
            definitions: [{ name: { value: queryName } }]
          } = query;

          // Getting cachedData from previous query
          const cachedData = cache.readQuery({ query });

          // Getting current data (result of the mutation)
          const current = data[mutationName];

          // Initializing our updatedData
          let updatedData = [];

          // Lower case mutation name
          const mutationNameLC = mutationName.toLowerCase();

          // If the mutation includes "delete" or "remove"
```

```
          if (mutationNameLC.includes('delete')
            || mutationNameLC.includes('remove')) {
            // Removing the current tweet by filtering
            // from the cachedData
            updatedData = cachedData[queryName].filter(
              row => row._id !== current._id
            );
          } else if (mutationNameLC.includes('create')
            || mutationNameLC.includes('add')) {
            // Create or add action injects the current
            // value in the array
            updatedData = [current, ...cachedData[queryName]];
          } else if (mutationNameLC.includes('edit')
            || mutationNameLC.includes('update')) {
            // Edit or update actions will replace the old values
            // with the new ones
            const index = cachedData[queryName].findIndex(
              row => row._id === current._id
            );
            cachedData[queryName][index] = current;
            updatedData = cachedData[queryName];
          }

          // Updating our data to refresh the tweets list
          cache.writeQuery({
            query,
            data: {
              [queryName]: updatedData
            }
          });
        }}
        onCompleted={onCompleted}
      >
        {/**
          * Here we render the content of the
          * component (children)
          */}
        {children}
      </ApolloMutation>
    );
  }
}

export default Mutation;
```

File: src/shared/components/Mutation.js

7. Once we have our helpers ready, let's create our components for Tweets, Tweet, and CreateTweet. This is our `Tweets` component:

```
// Dependencies
import React, { Component } from 'react';

// Components
import Tweet from './Tweet';
import CreateTweet from './CreateTweet';
import Query from '../shared/components/Query';

// Queries
import { QUERY_GET_TWEETS } from '../graphql/queries';

// Styles
import './Tweets.css';

class Tweets extends Component {
  render() {
    return (
      <div className="tweets">
        {/* Rendering CreateTweet component */}
        <CreateTweet />

        {/**
          * Executing QUERY_GET_TWEETS query and render our Tweet
          * component
          */}
        <Query query={QUERY_GET_TWEETS} render={Tweet} />
      </div>
    );
  }
}

export default Tweets;
```

File: src/components/Tweets.js

8. This is our `Tweet` component:

```
// Dependencies
import React, { Component } from 'react';
import moment from 'moment';

// Components
import Mutation from '../shared/components/Mutation';

// Queries
import {
  MUTATION_DELETE_TWEET,
  MUTATION_UPDATE_TWEET
} from '../graphql/mutations';

import { QUERY_GET_TWEETS } from '../graphql/queries';

// Images (those are temporary images and exists on the repository)
import TwitterLogo from './twitter.svg';
import CodejobsAvatar from './codejobs.png';

class Tweet extends Component {
  // Local State
  state = {
    currentTweet: false
  };

  // Enabling a textarea for edit a Tweet
  handleEditTweet = _id => {
    const { data: { getTweets: tweets } } = this.props;

    const selectedTweet = tweets.find(tweet => tweet._id === _id);

    const currentTweet = {
      [_id]: selectedTweet.tweet
    };

    this.setState({
      currentTweet
    });
  }

  // Handle Change for textarea
  handleChange = (value, _id) => {
    const { currentTweet } = this.state;

    currentTweet[_id] = value;
```

```
    this.setState({
      currentTweet
    });
  }

  // Delete tweet mutation
  handleDeleteTweet = (mutation, _id) => {
    // Sending variables
    mutation({
      variables: {
        _id
      }
    });
  }

  // Update tweet mutation
  handleUpdateTweet = (mutation, value, _id) => {
    // Sending variables
    mutation({
      variables: {
        _id,
        tweet: value
      }
    });
  }

  render() {
    // Getting the data from getTweets query
    const { data: { getTweets: tweets } } = this.props;

    // currentTweet state
    const { currentTweet } = this.state;

    // Mapping the tweets
    return tweets.map(({
      _id,
      tweet,
      author,
      createdAt
    }) => (
      <div className="tweet" key={`tweet-${_id}`}>
        <div className="author">
          {/* Rendering our Twitter Avatar (this is hardcoded) */}
          <img src={CodejobsAvatar} alt="Codejobs" />

          {/* Rendering the author */}
          <strong>{author}</strong>
        </div>
```

```
<div className="content">
  <div className="twitter-logo">
    {/* Rendering the Twitter Logo */}
    <img src={TwitterLogo} alt="Twitter" />
  </div>

  {/**
    * If there is no currentTweet being edited then
    * we display the tweet as a text otherwise we
    * render a textarea with the tweet to be edited
    */}
  {!currentTweet[_id]
    ? tweet
    : (
      <Mutation
        mutation={MUTATION_UPDATE_TWEET}
        query={QUERY_GET_TWEETS}
        onCompleted={() => {
          // Once the mutation is completed we clear our
          // currentTweet state
          this.setState({
            currentTweet: false
          });
        }}
      >
        {(updateTweet) => (
          <textarea
            autoFocus
            className="editTextarea"
            value={currentTweet[_id]}
            onChange={(e) => {
              this.handleChange(
                e.target.value,
                _id
              );
            }}
            onBlur={(e) => {
              this.handleUpdateTweet(
                updateTweet,
                e.target.value,
                _id
              );
            }}
          />
        )}
      </Mutation>
    )
  }
```

```
          </div>

          <div className="date">
            {/* Rendering the createdAt date (MMM DD, YYYY) */}
            {moment(createdAt).format('MMM DD, YYYY')}
          </div>

          {/* Rendering edit icon */}
          <div
            className="edit"
            onClick={() => {
              this.handleEditTweet(_id);
            }}
          >
            <i className="fa fa-pencil" aria-hidden="true" />
          </div>

          {/* Mutation for delete a tweet */}
          <Mutation
            mutation={MUTATION_DELETE_TWEET}
            query={QUERY_GET_TWEETS}
          >
            {(deleteTweet) => (
              <div
                className="delete"
                onClick={() => {
                  this.handleDeleteTweet(deleteTweet, _id);
                }}
              >
                <i className="fa fa-trash" aria-hidden="true" />
              </div>
            )}
          </Mutation>
        </div>
      ));
    }
  }

export default Tweet;
```

File: src/components/Tweet.js

9. Our `CreateTweet` component is as follows:

```
// Dependencies
import React, { Component } from 'react';
import Mutation from '../shared/components/Mutation';
```

```
// Images (this image is on the repository)
import CodejobsAvatar from './codejobs.png';

// Queries
import { MUTATION_CREATE_TWEET } from '../graphql/mutations';
import { QUERY_GET_TWEETS } from '../graphql/queries';

class CreateTweet extends Component {
  // Local state
  state = {
    tweet: ''
  };

  // Handle change for textarea
  handleChange = e => {
    const { target: { value } } = e;

    this.setState({
      tweet: value
    })
  }

  // Executing createTweet mutation to add a new Tweet
  handleSubmit = mutation => {
    const tweet = this.state.tweet;
    const author = '@codejobs';
    const createdAt = new Date();

    mutation({
      variables: {
        tweet,
        author,
        createdAt
      }
    });
  }

  render() {
    return (
      <Mutation
        mutation={MUTATION_CREATE_TWEET}
        query={QUERY_GET_TWEETS}
        onCompleted={() => {
          // On mutation completed we clean the tweet state
          this.setState({
            tweet: ''
          });
        }}
```

```
        >
          {(createTweet) => (
            <div className="createTweet">
              <header>
                Write a new Tweet
              </header>

              <section>
                <img src={CodejobsAvatar} alt="Codejobs" />

                <textarea
                  placeholder="Write your tweet here..."
                  value={this.state.tweet}
                  onChange={this.handleChange}
                />
              </section>

              <div className="publish">
                <button
                  onClick={() => {
                    this.handleSubmit(createTweet);
                  }}
                >
                  Tweet it!
                </button>
              </div>
            </div>
          )}
        </Mutation>
      );
    }
  }

export default CreateTweet;
```

File: src/components/CreateTweet.js

10. Finally, but no less important, this is the file for the styles:

```
.tweet {
  margin: 20px auto;
  padding: 20px;
  border: 1px solid #ccc;
  height: 200px;
  width: 80%;
  position: relative;
}

.author {
  text-align: left;
  margin-bottom: 20px;
}

.author strong {
  position: absolute;
  top: 40px;
  margin-left: 10px;
}

.author img {
  width: 50px;
  border-radius: 50%;
}

.content {
  text-align: left;
  color: #222;
  text-align: justify;
  line-height: 25px;
}

.date {
  color: #aaa;
  font-size: 12px;
  position: absolute;
  bottom: 10px;
}

.twitter-logo img {
  position: absolute;
  right: 10px;
  top: 10px;
  width: 20px;
}
```

```
.createTweet {
  margin: 20px auto;
  background-color: #F5F5F5;
  width: 86%;
  height: 225px;
  border: 1px solid #AAA;
}

.createTweet header {
  color: white;
  font-weight: bold;
  background-color: #2AA3EF;
  border-bottom: 1px solid #AAA;
  padding: 20px;
}

.createTweet section {
  padding: 20px;
  display: flex;
}

.createTweet section img {
  border-radius: 50%;
  margin: 10px;
  height: 50px;
}

textarea {
  border: 1px solid #ddd;
  height: 80px;
  width: 100%;
}

.publish {
  margin-bottom: 20px;
}

.publish button {
  cursor: pointer;
  border: 1px solid #2AA3EF;
  background-color: #2AA3EF;
  padding: 10px 20px;
  color: white;
  border-radius: 20px;
  float: right;
  margin-right: 20px;
}
```

```
.delete {
  position: absolute;
  right: 10px;
  bottom: 10px;
  cursor: pointer;
}

.edit {
  position: absolute;
  right: 30px;
  bottom: 10px;
  cursor: pointer;
}
```

File: src/components/Tweets.css

How it works...

If you did everything correctly and you run the frontend and backend (each on a different terminal) then you can run the project at `http://localhost:3000`, and you should see this view:

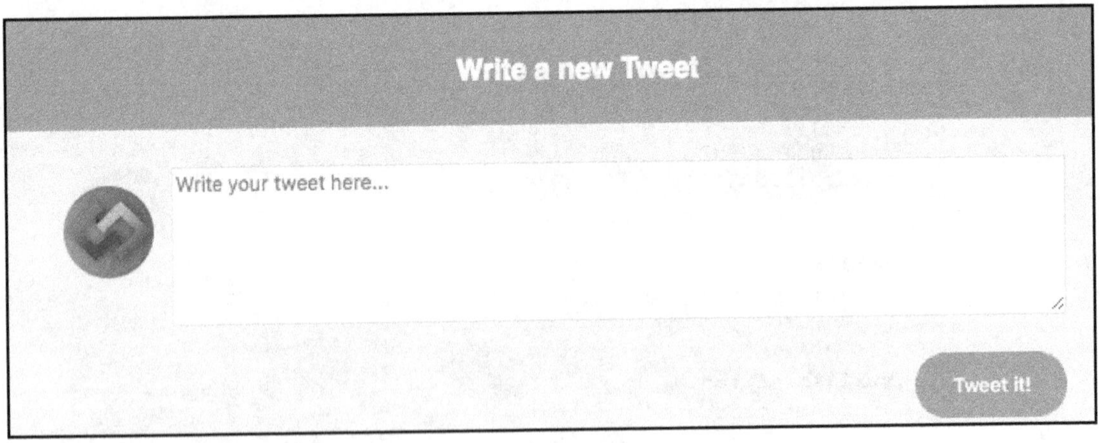

Now we can create new tweets by writing them in the text area and clicking on the **Tweet it!** button:

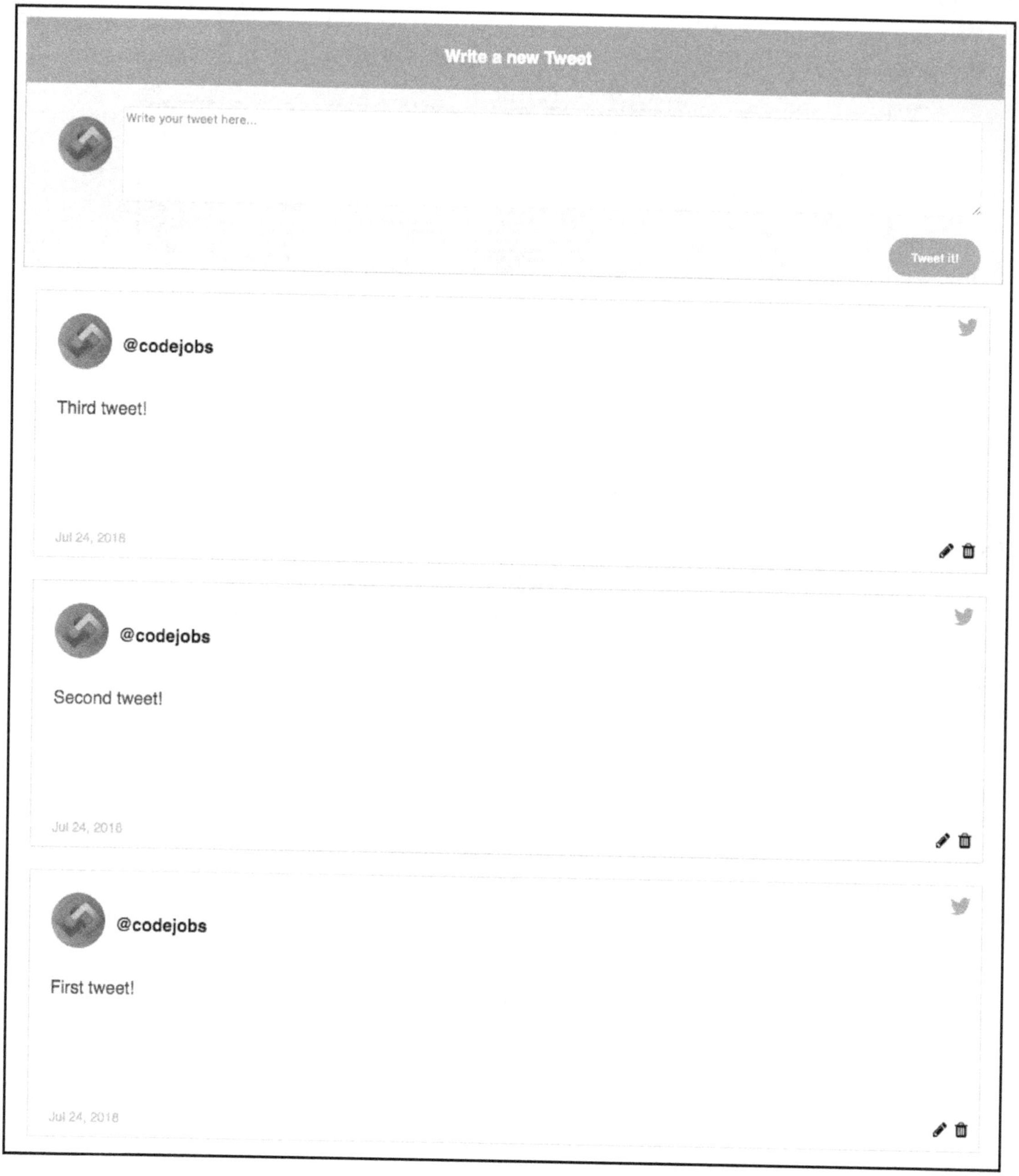
Write a new Tweet
Write your tweet here...
Tweet it!
@codejobs
Third tweet!
Jul 24, 2016
@codejobs
Second tweet!
Jul 24, 2016
@codejobs
First tweet!
Jul 24, 2016

As you can see, the order of tweets is descending. This means that the newest tweets are posted at the top. If you want to edit a tweet, you can click on the edit icon (the pencil):

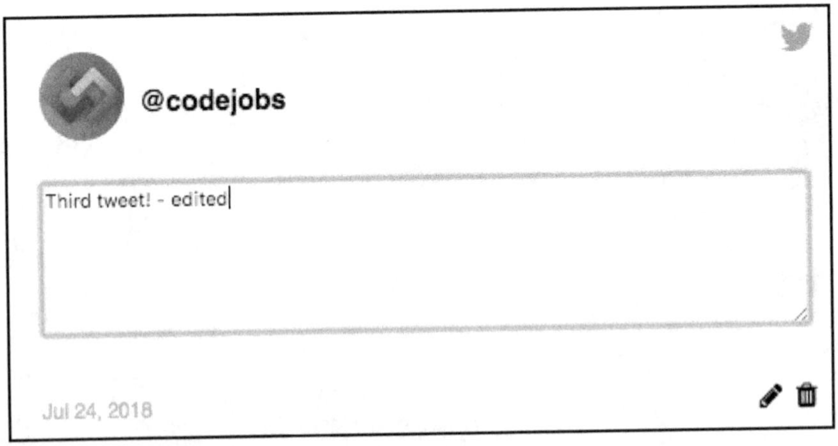

The way to save the changes is by removing the focus (onBlur) on the textarea, and now we can see the updated tweet:

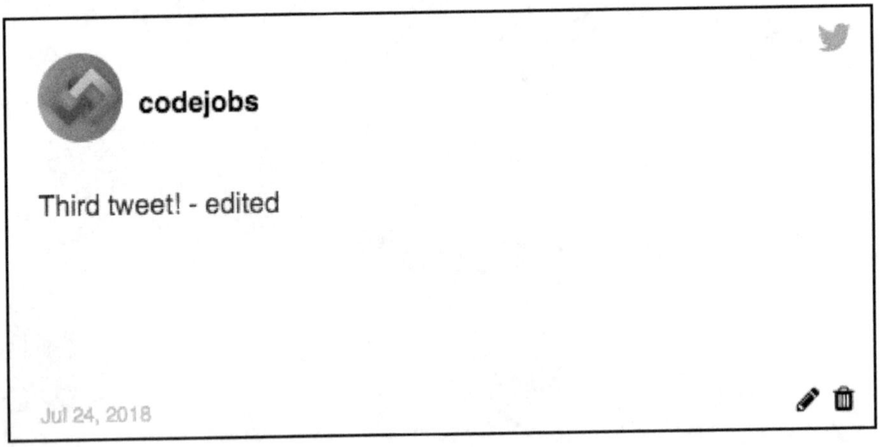

Finally, if you want to delete a tweet, then click on the trash icon (I have removed the second tweet):

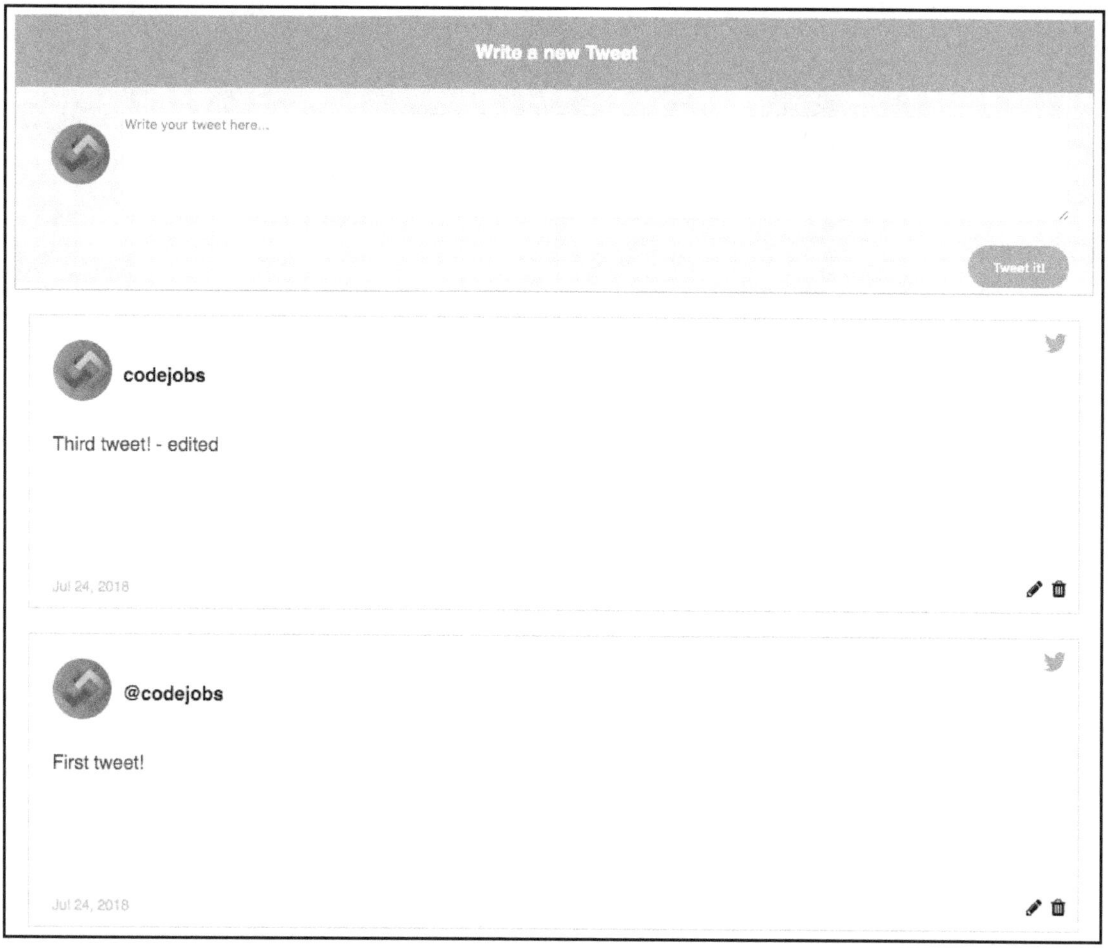

As you can see, the mutations are very easy to implement, and with the helpers, we have simplified this process.

> You're probably thinking that there's some way to use Redux with GraphQL, but let me tell you that it is possible that GraphQL will replace Redux because we have access to the data through the ApolloProvider.

10
Mastering Webpack 4.x

In this chapter, the following recipes will be covered:

- Webpack 4 Zero Configuration
- Adding React to Webpack 4
- Adding Webpack Dev Server and Sass, Stylus, or LessCSS with React
- Webpack 4 Optimization – Splitting Bundles
- Implementing Node.js with React/Redux and Webpack 4

Introduction

From the Webpack 4 official website (`https://webpack.js.org`):

> *"Webpack is a static module bundler for modern JavaScript applications. When webpack processes your application, it internally builds a dependency graph which maps every module your project needs and generates one or more bundles. Since version 4, webpack does not require a configuration file to bundle your project. Nevertheless, it is incredibly configurable to fit your needs better."*

Webpack 4 Zero Configuration

Webpack 4 does not need a configuration file by default. In the older versions, you had to have a configuration file. If you need to customize Webpack 4 to your project's needs, you can still create a configuration file, which will be much easier to configure.

Getting Ready

For this recipe, you need to create a new folder and install the following packages:

```
mkdir webpack-zero-configuration
cd webpack-zero-configuration
npm install --save-dev webpack webpack-cli
```

In your Webpack folder, you need to create a `package.json` file, and for this, you can use the following command:

```
npm init -y
```

How to do it...

Let's now start the configuration:

1. Open `package.json`, and add a new `build` script:

```
{
  "name": "webpack-zero-configuration",
  "version": "1.0.0",
  "description": "Webpack 4 Zero Configuration",
  "main": "index.js",
  "scripts": {
    "build": "webpack"
  },
  "author": "Carlos Santana",
  "license": "MIT",
  "devDependencies": {
    "webpack": "^4.6.0",
    "webpack-cli": "^2.0.15"
  }
}
```

File: package.json

2. Run the build script in your terminal:

```
npm run build
```

3. You will see this error:

```
|→ webpack-zero-configuration git:(master) × npm run build

> webpack-zero-configuration@1.0.0 build /Users/czantany/projects/React16Cookbook/Chapter9/Recipe1/webpack-zero-configuration
> webpack

Hash: c5c39baed786921d7219
Version: webpack 4.6.0
Time: 42ms
Built at: 2018-04-29 23:36:29

WARNING in configuration
The 'mode' option has not been set, webpack will fallback to 'production' for this value. Set 'mode' option to 'development' or 'production' to enable defaults for each environment.
You can also set it to 'none' to disable any default behavior. Learn more: https://webpack.js.org/concepts/mode/

ERROR in Entry module not found: Error: Can't resolve './src' in '/Users/czantany/projects/React16Cookbook/Chapter9/Recipe1/webpack-zero-configuration'
npm ERR! code ELIFECYCLE
npm ERR! errno 2
npm ERR! webpack-zero-configuration@1.0.0 build: `webpack`
npm ERR! Exit status 2
npm ERR!
npm ERR! Failed at the webpack-zero-configuration@1.0.0 build script.
npm ERR! This is probably not a problem with npm. There is likely additional logging output above.

npm ERR! A complete log of this run can be found in:
npm ERR!     /Users/czantany/.npm/_logs/2018-04-30T06_36_29_286Z-debug.log
```

The error you get in the terminal will look like this: ERROR in Entry module not found: Error: Can't resolver'./src' in '/Users/czantany/projects/React16Cookbook/Chapter9/Recipe1/webpack-zero-configuration'

4. Because we're now in Webpack 4, by the default, the main entry point is `src/index.js`. Let's create this file to be able to build our first bundle:

```
console.log('Index file...');
```

File: src/index.js

5. If you re-run the build script, you will see that Webpack creates a new bundle file called `main.js` io the `dist` folder (again, this is by default):

```
|→ webpack-zero-configuration git:(master) × npm run build

> webpack-zero-configuration@1.0.0 build /Users/czantany/projects/React16Cookbook/Chapter9/Recipe1/webpack-zero-configuration
> webpack

Hash: 5d14a62e6fd3072d4312
Version: webpack 4.6.0
Time: 282ms
Built at: 2018-04-29 23:53:16
  Asset       Size  Chunks             Chunk Names
main.js  573 bytes       0  [emitted]  main
Entrypoint main = main.js
[0] ./src/index.js 30 bytes {0} [built]

WARNING in configuration
The 'mode' option has not been set, webpack will fallback to 'production' for this value. Set 'mode' option to 'development' or 'production' to enable defaults for each environment.
You can also set it to 'none' to disable any default behavior. Learn more: https://webpack.js.org/concepts/mode/
```

The warning let us know that we can choose the mode between production or development

6. There is a Warning message in the terminal: the `mode` option has not been set, webpack will fallback to production for this value. Set `mode` to `development` or `production` to enable defaults for each environment. You can also set it to `none` to disable any default behavior. You can learn more at https://webpack.js.org/concepts/mode/. By default, production mode is enabled, and that's why our bundle (`dist/main.js`) is minified and obfuscated, similar to the following:

```
!function(e){var n={};function r(t){if(n[t])return
n[t].exports;var o=n[t]={i:t,l:!1,exports:{}};return
e[t].call(o.exports,o,o.exports,r),o.l=!0,o.exports}r.m=e,r.c=n,r.d
=function(e,n,t){r.o(e,n)||Object.defineProperty(e,n,{configurable:
!1,enumerable:!0,get:t})},r.r=function(e){Object.defineProperty(e,"
__esModule",{value:!0})},r.n=function(e){var
n=e&&e.__esModule?function(){return e.default}:function(){return
e};return r.d(n,"a",n),n},r.o=function(e,n){return
Object.prototype.hasOwnProperty.call(e,n)},r.p="",r(r.s=0)}([functi
on(e,n){console.log("Index file...")}]);
```

File: dist/main.js

How it works...

Webpack 4 has two modes: production and development. In Webpack 3, you needed to create a config file for each one; now you can get the same result just with a single line. Let's add a script to get our application to start using the development mode:

```
{
  "name": "webpack-zero-configuration",
  "version": "1.0.0",
  "description": "Webpack 4 Zero Configuration",
  "main": "index.js",
  "scripts": {
    "build-development": "webpack --mode development",
    "build": "webpack --mode production"
  },
  "author": "Carlos Santana",
  "license": "MIT",
  "devDependencies": {
    "webpack": "^4.6.0",
    "webpack-cli": "^2.0.15"
  }
}
```

File: package.json

If you run the `npm run build-development` command, now you will see that the bundle is not compressed at all:

```
/******/ 	__webpack_require__.r = function(exports) {
/******/ 		Object.defineProperty(exports, '__esModule', { value: true });
/******/ 	};
/******/
/******/ 	// getDefaultExport function for compatibility with non-harmony modules
/******/ 	__webpack_require__.n = function(module) {
/******/ 		var getter = module && module.__esModule ?
/******/ 			function getDefault() { return module['default']; } :
/******/ 			function getModuleExports() { return module; };
/******/ 		__webpack_require__.d(getter, 'a', getter);
/******/ 		return getter;
/******/ 	};
/******/
/******/ 	// Object.prototype.hasOwnProperty.call
/******/ 	__webpack_require__.o = function(object, property) { return Object.prototype.hasOwnProperty.call(object, property); };
/******/
/******/ 	// __webpack_public_path__
/******/ 	__webpack_require__.p = "";
/******/
/******/
/******/ 	// Load entry module and return exports
/******/ 	return __webpack_require__(__webpack_require__.s = "./src/index.js");
/******/ })
/************************************************************************/
/******/ ({

/***/ "./src/index.js":
/*!**********************!*\
  !*** ./src/index.js ***!
  \**********************/
/*! no static exports found */
/***/ (function(module, exports) {

eval("console.log('Index file...');\n\n\n//# sourceURL=webpack:///./src/index.js?");

/***/ })

/******/ });
```

File: dist/main.js

As you can see, by default, Webpack 4 using production minifies the code and performs some optimizations for this environment, in Webpack 3, this configuration had to be done manually in a config file.

There's more...

If you want to implement Babel with Webpack 4 to transpile ES6 code, you need to use `babel-loader`, and you may need to install the following packages:

```
npm install --save-dev babel-loader babel-core babel-preset-env
```

1. Create a .babelrc file at the root of your project and then add this code:

```
{
  "presets": ["env"]
}
```

File: .babelrc

2. Add our `babel-loader` using a `webpack.config.js` file:

```
const webpackConfig = {
  module: {
    rules: [
      {
        test: /\.js$/,
        exclude: /node_modules/,
        use: 'babel-loader'
      }
    ]
  }
};

module.exports = webpackConfig;
```

File: webpack.config.js

3. Create a file called `src/numbers.js` and import it to our `src/index.js` to test our `babel-loader`:

```
export const numbers = ['one', 'two', 'three'];
```

File: src/numbers.js

4. In our `index.js` file, do the following:

```
import { numbers } from './numbers';
numbers.forEach(number => console.log(number));
```

File: src/index.js

5. Run the `npm run build` script, and if everything works fine, you should get this result:

```
→ webpack-zero-configuration git:(master) × npm run build

> webpack-zero-configuration@1.0.0 build /Users/carlos.santana/projects/React16Cookbook/Chapter9/Recipe1/webpack-zero-configuration
> webpack --mode production

Hash: 46ba3a2bd4d9c878a101
Version: webpack 4.6.0
Time: 335ms
Built at: 2018-04-30 15:41:02
  Asset       Size  Chunks             Chunk Names
main.js  615 bytes       0  [emitted]  main
Entrypoint main = main.js
[0] ./src/index.js + 1 modules 132 bytes {0} [built]
    | ./src/index.js 85 bytes [built]
    | ./src/numbers.js 47 bytes [built]
```

6. It is also possible to use `babel-loader` directly in the terminal without a config file, for this, we need to use the `--module-bind` flag to bind an extension to a loader:

```
{
  "name": "webpack-zero-configuration",
  "version": "1.0.0",
  "description": "Webpack 4 Zero Configuration",
  "main": "index.js",
  "scripts": {
    "build-development": "webpack --mode development --module-bind
   js=babel-loader",
    "build": "webpack --mode production --module-bind js=babel-
     loader"
  },
  "author": "Carlos Santana",
  "license": "MIT",
  "devDependencies": {
    "babel-core": "^6.26.3",
    "babel-loader": "^7.1.4",
    "babel-preset-env": "^1.6.1",
    "webpack": "^4.6.0",
    "webpack-cli": "^2.0.15"
  }
}
```

7. There are more flags to bind modules (if you want to learn more about Webpack CLI, you can visit the official site at `https://webpack.js.org/api/cli/`):
   - `--module-bind-post`: Bind an extension to a post-loader
   - `--module-bind-pre`: Bind an extension to a pre-loader

Adding React to Webpack 4

In this recipe, we are going to implement React with Webpack 4, but we will use a plugin called `html-webpack-plugin` to generate our `index.html` file to render our React application. In the next recipe, we will integrate Node.js to have more flexibility in our server-side before rendering the HTML code.

Getting Ready

For this recipe, you will need to install the following packages:

```
npm install react react-dom babel-preset-react
```

How to do it...

Here are the steps to add React to Webpack 4:

1. Using the same code of the last recipe, create a `.babelrc` file and add some presets:

```
{
  "presets": [
    "env",
    "react"
  ]
}
```

File: .babelrc

2. In our `webpack.config.js` file, where we have our `babel-loader`, we need to add the `.jsx` extension beside the `.js` extension to be able to apply `babel-loader` to our React components:

```
const webpackConfig = {
  module: {
    rules: [
      {
        test: /\.(js|jsx)$/,
        exclude: /node_modules/,
        use: 'babel-loader'
      }
    ]
  }
};

module.exports = webpackConfig;
```

File: webpack.config.js

3. After we added the `.jsx` extension to our `babel-loader`, we need to create the `src/components/App.jsx` file:

```
// Dependencies
import React from 'react';

// Components
import Home from './Home';

const App = props => (
  <div>
    <Home />
  </div>
);

export default App;
```

File: src/components/App.jsx

4. Creating the `Home` component:

```
import React from 'react';

const Home = () => <h1>Home</h1>;

export default Home;
```

File: src/components/Home/index.jsx

5. In our main `index.js` file, we need to include `react`, the `render` method from `react-dom` and our `App` component, and render the application:

```
// Dependencies
import React from 'react';
import { render } from 'react-dom';

// Components
import App from './components/App';

render(<App />, document.querySelector('#root'));
```

File: src/index.jsx

6. You may wonder where the `#root` div is since we have not created `index.html` yet. In this specific recipe, we are going to use the `html-webpack-plugin` plugin to process our HTML:

```
npm install --save-dev html-webpack-plugin
```

7. Open your `webpack.config.js` file. We need to add our `html-webpack-plugin` and create a plugins node in our config file:

```
const HtmlWebPackPlugin = require('html-webpack-plugin');

const webpackConfig = {
  module: {
    rules: [
      {
        test: /\.(js|jsx)$/,
        exclude: /node_modules/,
        use: 'babel-loader'
      }
    ]
  },
  plugins: [
    new HtmlWebPackPlugin({
```

```
      title: 'Codejobs',
      template: './src/index.html',
      filename: './index.html'
    })
  ]
};

module.exports = webpackConfig;
```

File: webpack.config.js

8. Create the `index.html` template at your `src` directory level:

```
<!DOCTYPE html>
<html>
  <head>
    <meta charset="UTF-8">
    <title><%= htmlWebpackPlugin.options.title %></title>
  </head>
  <body>
    <div id="root"></div>
  </body>
</html>
```

File: src/index.html

How it works...

As you can see, we can inject variables from the plugin using the `htmlWebpackPlugin.options` object between the `<%=` and `%>` delimiters. Now it's time to test our application, try to run the `npm run build` command:

```
→ webpack-react git:(master) × npm run build

> webpack-zero-configuration@1.0.0 build /Users/czantany/projects/React16Cookbook/Chapter9/Recipe2/webpack-react
> webpack --mode production

Hash: 84c31b85f4c06a4b03fa
Version: webpack 4.6.0
Time: 259ms
Built at: 2018-05-06 14:18:35

ERROR in Entry module not found: Error: Can't resolve './src' in '/Users/czantany/projects/React16Cookbook/Chapter9/Recipe2/webpack-react'
Child html-webpack-plugin for "index.html":
     1 asset
    Entrypoint undefined = ./index.html
    [0] (webpack)/buildin/module.js 497 bytes {0} [built]
    [1] (webpack)/buildin/global.js 489 bytes {0} [built]
    [3] ./node_modules/html-webpack-plugin/lib/loader.js!./src/index.html 418 bytes {0} [built]
        + 1 hidden module
npm ERR! code ELIFECYCLE
npm ERR! errno 2
npm ERR! webpack-zero-configuration@1.0.0 build: `webpack --mode production`
npm ERR! Exit status 2
npm ERR!
npm ERR! Failed at the webpack-zero-configuration@1.0.0 build script.
npm ERR! This is probably not a problem with npm. There is likely additional logging output above.

npm ERR! A complete log of this run can be found in:
npm ERR!     /Users/czantany/.npm/_logs/2018-05-06T21_18_35_624Z-debug.log
```

Big red error: Can't resolve `./src` directory, but what does it mean? Do you remember how we used the `.jsx` extension in our files? Even we added that extension to our `babel-loader` rule so why is not working? It's because we had to add a resolve node to our configuration and specified the file extensions we want to support. Otherwise, we have to use only the `.js` extension:

```
const HtmlWebPackPlugin = require('html-webpack-plugin');

const webpackConfig = {
  module: {
    rules: [
      {
        test: /\.(js|jsx)$/,
        exclude: /node_modules/,
        use: 'babel-loader'
      }
    ]
  },
  plugins: [
    new HtmlWebPackPlugin({
      title: 'Codejobs',
      template: './src/index.html',
```

```
      filename: './index.html'
    })
  ],
  resolve: {
    extensions: ['.js', '.jsx']
  }
};

module.exports = webpackConfig;
```

File: webpack.config.js

If you run `npm run build` again, now it should work:

```
➜ webpack-react git:(master) ✗ npm run build

> webpack-zero-configuration@1.0.0 build /Users/czantany/projects/React16Cookbook/Chapter9/Recipe2/webpack-react
> webpack --mode production

Hash: 80f8d65912ca45aa1f4a
Version: webpack 4.6.0
Time: 685ms
Built at: 2018-05-06 14:28:11
       Asset       Size  Chunks             Chunk Names
     main.js    106 KiB       0  [emitted]  main
./index.html  204 bytes          [emitted]
Entrypoint main = main.js
[16] ./src/index.jsx 452 bytes {0} [built]
    + 16 hidden modules
Child html-webpack-plugin for "index.html":
     1 asset
    Entrypoint undefined = ./index.html
    [0] (webpack)/buildin/module.js 497 bytes {0} [built]
    [1] (webpack)/buildin/global.js 489 bytes {0} [built]
    [3] ./node_modules/html-webpack-plugin/lib/loader.js!./src/index.html 418 bytes {0} [built]
        + 1 hidden module
```

After you run that command, you will see that you have two files in your dist directory: `index.html` and `main.js`. If you open your `index.html` file with Chrome, you should see the following result:

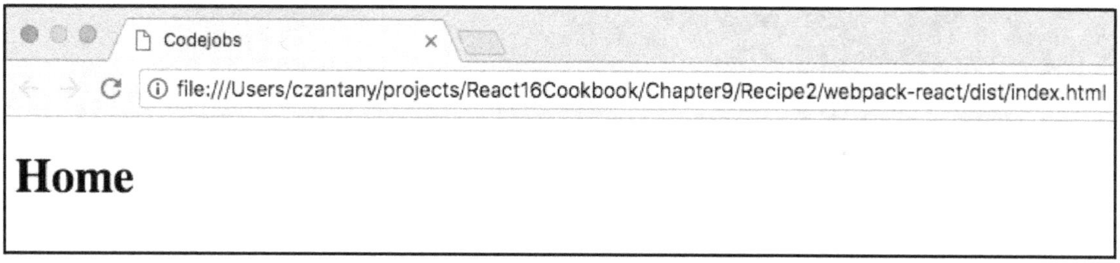

We can build our bundle, but it is 100% static. In the next recipe, we are going to add Webpack Dev Server to run our React Application in an actual server and refresh the server every time we make a change.

There's more...

I prefer to use ES6 code in all my projects, even in the configurations, and I like to break my Webpack configuration into separate files for better organization and an easier understanding of the configurations. If you have worked with Webpack before, you are aware that a `webpack.config.js` file can be huge and very hard to maintain, so let me explain how to do that:

1. Rename the `webpack.config.js` file to `webpack.config.babel.js`. When you add the `.babel` suffix on a `.js` file, this will be handled by Babel automatically.
2. Let's migrate our current ES5 code to ES6:

```
import HtmlWebPackPlugin from 'html-webpack-plugin';

export default {
  module: {
    rules: [
      {
        test: /\.(js|jsx)$/,
        exclude: /node_modules/,
        use: 'babel-loader'
      }
    ]
  },
  plugins: [
    new HtmlWebPackPlugin({
      title: 'Codejobs',
      template: './src/index.html',
      filename: './index.html'
    })
  ],
  resolve: {
    extensions: ['.js', '.jsx']
  }
};
```

File: webpack.config.babel.js

3. Create a folder called `webpack` and inside other called `configuration`.
4. Create an individual file for each node of our Webpack configuration and export it. For example, let's start by creating a file for our node module, so you should call `module.js`:

```
export default {
  rules: [
    {
      test: /\.(js|jsx)$/,
      exclude: /node_modules/,
      use: 'babel-loader'
    }
  ]
};
```

File: webpack/configuration/module.js

5. Let's create a file for our plugins (`plugins.js`):

```
import HtmlWebPackPlugin from 'html-webpack-plugin';

const plugins = [
  new HtmlWebPackPlugin({
    title: 'Codejobs',
    template: './src/index.html',
    filename: './index.html'
  })
];

export default plugins;
```

File: webpack/configuration/plugins.js

6. It's very useful to add our array of plugins into a constant because then we can add more plugins based on the environment (development or production), so now you can add plugins in a conditional way (using push).
7. The last node is resolve:

```
export default {
  extensions: ['.js', '.jsx']
}
```

File: webpack/configuration/resolve.js

8. We can import our files directly, but I prefer to use an `index.js` file and export all of them. This way, we only import the objects we need into our `webpack.config.babel.js` file:

```
// Configuration
import module from './module';
import plugins from './plugins';
import resolve from './resolve';

export {
  module,
  plugins,
  resolve
};
```

File: webpack/configuration/index.js

9. Our `webpack.config.babel.js` will be very clean:

```
import {
  module,
  plugins,
  resolve
} from './webpack/configuration';

export default {
  module,
  plugins,
  resolve
};
```

File: webpack.config.babel.js

Adding Webpack Dev Server and Sass, Stylus, or LessCSS with React

In the last recipe, we added React to Webpack 4, and we split our Webpack configuration, but in the end, we were just able to build our bundle and run the application as a static page. In this recipe, we are going to add the Webpack Dev Server to run our React Application in an actual server and restart the server every time we make a change. Also, we are going to implement CSS preprocessors such as Sass, Stylus, and LessCSS.

Getting Ready

For this recipe, you will need to install the following packages:

```
npm install webpack-dev-server css-loader extract-text-webpack-
plugin@v4.0.0-beta.0 style-loader
```

If you want to use Sass in your project, you have to install:

```
npm install sass-loader node-sass
```

If you prefer Stylus, you'll need the following:

```
npm install stylus-loader stylus
```

Or if you like LessCSS, install this:

```
npm install less-loader less
```

How to do it...

We will first add the Webpack Dev Server:

1. Once you installed the `webpack-dev-server` dependency, we need to add a new script to start the application in our `package.json`:

```
"scripts": {
  "start": "webpack-dev-server --mode development --open",
  "build-development": "webpack --mode development",
  "build": "webpack --mode production"
}
```

File: package.json

2. As you know, the `--mode` flag specifies the mode we want (the default is production), and the `--open` flag opens the browser when we start the application. Now you can run the application with the `npm start` command:

3. Your application was opened using port 8080, which is the default port of `webpack-dev-server`. If you want to change it, you can use the `--port` flag to specify which port you want to use:

```
"start": "webpack-dev-server --mode development --open --port 9999"
```

4. The cool thing about `webpack-dev-server` is that if you update any component, you will see the change reflected instantaneously. For example, let's modify our `Home` component:

```
import React from 'react';

const Home = () => <h1>Updated Home</h1>;

export default Home;
```

File: src/components/Home/index.jsx

5. You can see the reflected change in the same page without refreshing the page manually:

6. Let's add Sass, Stylus, or LessCSS to our project to have some styles in the application. You have to edit the file located at `webpack/configuration/module.js` and add `style-loader`, `css-loader`, and the loader we want for sass (`sass-loader`), stylus (`stylus-loader`), or less (`less-loader`):

```
export default {
  rules: [
    {
      test: /\.(js|jsx)$/,
      exclude: /node_modules/,
      use: 'babel-loader'
    },
    {
      test: /\.scss$/, // Can be: .scss or .styl or .less
      use: [
        {
          loader: 'style-loader'
        },
        {
          loader: 'css-loader',
          options: {
            // Enables CSS Modules
            modules: true,
            // Number of loaders applied before CSS loader
            importLoaders: 1,
            // Formatting CSS Class name
            localIdentName: '[name]_[local]_[hash:base64]',
            // Enable/disable sourcemaps
            sourceMap: true,
            // Enable/disable minification
            minimize: true
          }
        },
        {
          loader: 'sass-loader' // sass-loader or stylus-loader
                                // or less-loader
        }
      ]
    }
  ]
};
```

File: webpack/configuration/module.js

7. Using Sass, we can create the Home.scss file to add some styles:

```
$color: red;
.Home {
  color: $color;
}
```

File: src/components/Home/Home.scss

8. In the Home component, you can import the Sass file like this:

```
import React from 'react';
import styles from './Home.scss'; // For Sass
// import styles from './Home.styl'; // For Stylus
// import styles from './Home.less'; // For Less

const Home = () => <h1 className={styles.Home}>Updated Home</h1>;

export default Home;
```

File: src/component/Home/index.jsx

9. Each import line is for a different preprocessor. Use the line you want and remove the others. Sass generates this style:

10. If you want to use Stylus, create the `Home.styl` file and change the configuration in the `module.js` file from the Webpack configuration:

```
$color = green

.Home
  color: $color
```

File: src/components/Home/Home.styl

11. If you want to use Less CSS, do the necessary changes on the Webpack configuration and then use this file:

```
@color: blue;

.Home {
  color: @color;
}
```

File: src/components/Home/Home.less

How it works...

If you are curious, you probably already tried to see how it's rendering the stylesheet and how is the class name in our HTML. If you inspect the site, you will see something like this:

```
▼<head>
   <meta charset="UTF-8">
   <title>Codejobs</title>
   <link type="text/css" rel="stylesheet" href="blob:http://localhost:8080/296064a3-02c6-4485-a4f6-31e74b0c7b37">
 </head>
▼<body cz-shortcut-listen="true">
  ▼<div id="root">
    ▼<div>
       <h1 class="Home_Home_2kP8RGWU7MOaTbV8QA45HP">Updated Home</h1>
     </div>
   </div>
   <script type="text/javascript" src="main.js"></script>
 </body>
```

Dynamically is being inject a `<link>` tag with a temporal URL that contains our compiled css, and then our class name is "Home_Home_2kP..." this is because our configuration: `localIdentName: '[name]_[local]_[hash:base64]'`. With this, we are creating isolated styles, which means that we will never affect any other class if we use the same name.

There's more...

Let's implement CSS preprocessors such as Sass, Stylus, and LessCSS:

1. If you want to extract your CSS code to a `style.css` file and compress the code for production mode, you can use the `extract-text-webpack-plugin` package:

   ```
   npm install extract-text-webpack-plugin@v4.0.0-beta.0
   ```

2. We need to add this to our Webpack plugins:

   ```
   import HtmlWebPackPlugin from 'html-webpack-plugin';
   import ExtractTextPlugin from 'extract-text-webpack-plugin';

   const isProduction = process.env.NODE_ENV === 'production';

   const plugins = [
     new HtmlWebPackPlugin({
       title: 'Codejobs',
       template: './src/index.html',
       filename: './index.html'
   ```

```
    })
  ];

  if (isProduction) {
    plugins.push(
      new ExtractTextPlugin({
        allChunks: true,
        filename: './css/[name].css'
      })
    );
  }

  export default plugins;
```

File: webpack/configuration/plugins.js

3. As you can see, I'm pushing to the plugins array only if is production. This means we need to create a new script into our package.json to specify when we are going to use production:

```
"scripts": {
  "start": "webpack-dev-server --mode development --open",
  "start-production": "NODE_ENV=production webpack-dev-server --
  mode production",
  "build-development": "webpack --mode development",
  "build": "webpack --mode production"
}
```

4. Run `npm run start-production` in your terminal, and you will be able to start in production mode.
5. You will probably get some errors because we also need to add a rule for the Extract Text Plugin to our module node:

```
import ExtractTextPlugin from 'extract-text-webpack-plugin';

const isProduction = process.env.NODE_ENV === 'production';

const rules = [
  {
    test: /\.(js|jsx)$/,
    exclude: /node_modules/,
    use: 'babel-loader'
  }
];

if (isProduction) {
  rules.push({
```

```
        test: /\.scss/,
        use: ExtractTextPlugin.extract({
          fallback: 'style-loader',
          use: [
            'css-loader?minimize=true&modules=true&localIdentName=
            [name]_[local]_[hash:base64]',
            'sass-loader'
          ]
        })
      });
    } else {
      rules.push({
        test: /\.scss$/, // .scss - .styl - .less
        use: [
          {
            loader: 'style-loader'
          },
          {
            loader: 'css-loader',
            options: {
              modules: true,
              importLoaders: 1,
              localIdentName: '[name]_[local]_[hash:base64]',
              sourceMap: true,
              minimize: true
            }
          },
          {
            loader: 'sass-loader' // sass-loader, stylus-loader or
                                  //less-loader
          }
        ]
      });
    }

    export default {
      rules
    };
```

6. We are using Extract Text Plugin just for production. For any other environment, we use `style-loader`, `css-loader`, and `sass-loader` directly as before. That's why I love splitting the Webpack configuration into smaller files, as you can see, some of the files can be huge, so this helps us to be more organized. If you start the production mode with `npm run start-production`, you will see this CSS:

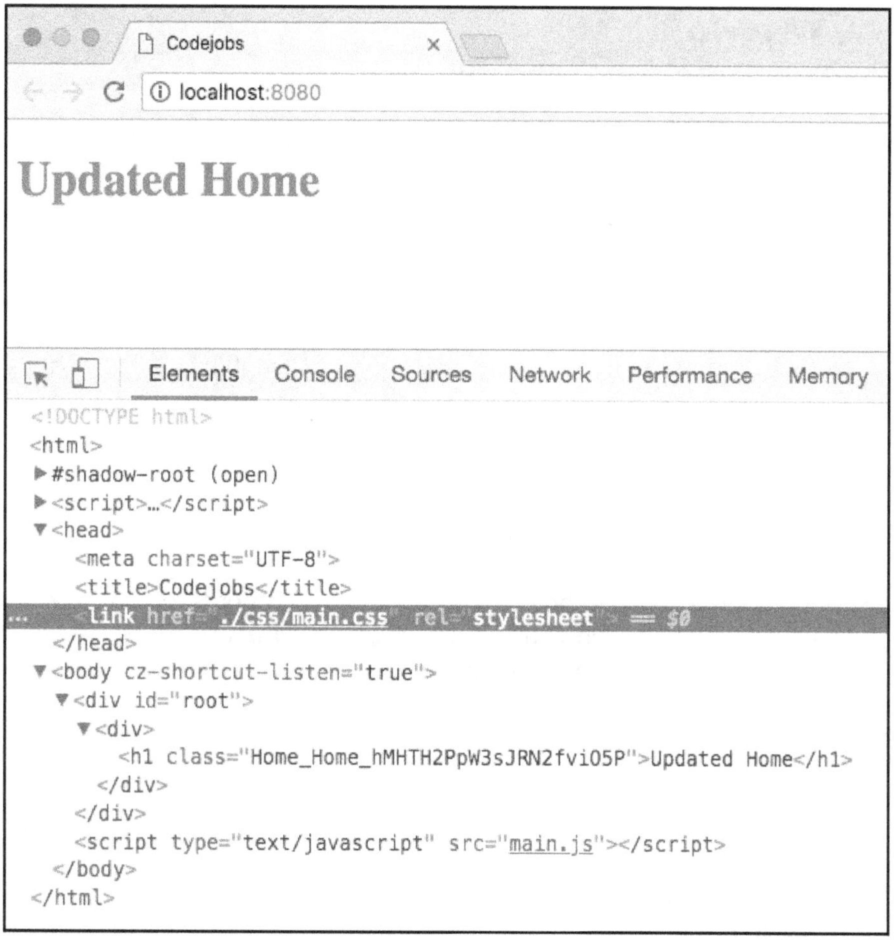

Webpack 4 Optimization – Splitting Bundles

Webpack 4 already has some optimizations presets for production mode, such as the code minification (before it was made with UglifyJS), but there are more things we can use to improve the performance of our application. In this recipe, we are going to learn how to split bundles (vendors and application bundles), add source maps, and implement the *BundleAnalyzerPlugin*.

Getting Ready

For this recipe, we need to install the following packages:

```
npm install webpack-bundle-analyzer webpack-notifier
```

How to do it...

Let's add a source map to our Webpack:

1. Create the `webpack/configuration/devtool.js` file:

```
const isProduction = process.env.NODE_ENV === 'production';

export default !isProduction ? 'cheap-module-source-map' : 'eval';
```

File: webpack/configuration/devtool.js

2. Split the bundles (using the new "optimization" Webpack node): one for our `/node_modules/` which will be the biggest one, and one for our React Application. You need to create the `optimization.js` file and add this code:

```
export default {
  splitChunks: {
    cacheGroups: {
      default: false,
      commons: {
        test: /node_modules/,
        name: 'vendor',
        chunks: 'all'
      }
    }
  }
}
```

File: webpack/configuration/optimization.js

3. Remember that you need to add those new files into `index.js`:

```
// Configuration
import devtool from './devtool';
import module from './module';
import optimization from './optimization';
import plugins from './plugins';
import resolve from './resolve';

export {
  devtool,
  module,
  optimization,
  plugins,
  resolve
};
```

File: webpack/configuration/index.js

4. Add the nodes to `webpack.config.babel.js`:

```
import {
  devtool,
  module,
  optimization,
  plugins,
  resolve
} from './webpack/configuration';

export default {
  devtool,
  module,
  plugins,
  optimization,
  resolve
};
```

File: webpack.config.babel.js

How it works...

Let's test this:

1. Just run the application with `npm start`. If you look at the HTML, you will see that it's automatically being injected into the `vendor.js` and `main.js` bundles:

```
▼<div id="root">
  ▼<div>
      <h1 class="Home_Home_hMHTH2PpW3sJRN2fvi05P">Updated Home</h1>
    </div>
  </div>
  <script type="text/javascript" src="vendor.js"></script>
  <script type="text/javascript" src="main.js"></script>
```

2. If you look at the **Network** tab, you can see the size of the files:

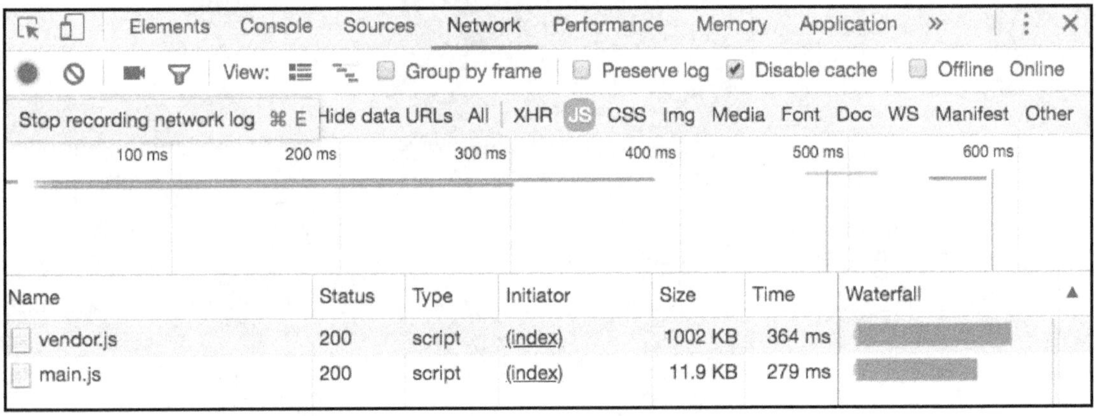

3. If you run the application with the production mode, you will notice that the bundles are smaller. Run the `npm run start-production` command:

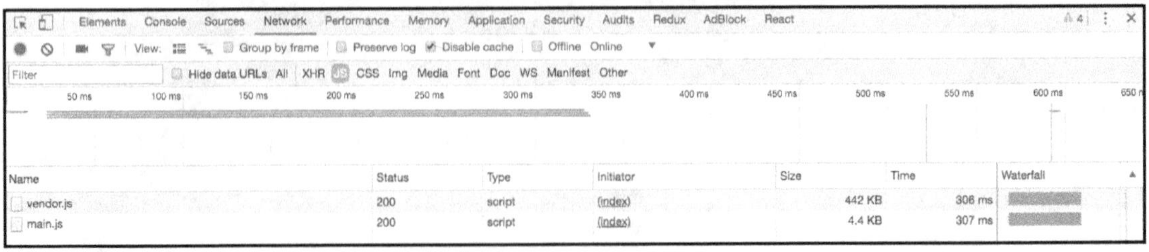

4. With this optimization, we are reducing the bundle sizes by 40%. In the next recipe, we are going to implement Node.js with Webpack and React, and we will be able to apply a GZip compression, which will help us to reduce the bundle sizes even more.
5. The `BundleAnalyzer` plugin can help us to see all the packages (`node_modules`) and our components sizes; this will give us an image of the bundles organizing by size (big squares mean big size and small squares mean small size). We can also implement the `WebpackNotifierPlugin` plugin, which is just a notification we can display every time our Webpack does a build:

```
import HtmlWebPackPlugin from 'html-webpack-plugin';
import ExtractTextPlugin from 'extract-text-webpack-plugin';
import WebpackNotifierPlugin from 'webpack-notifier';
import { BundleAnalyzerPlugin } from 'webpack-bundle-analyzer';

const isProduction = process.env.NODE_ENV === 'production';

const plugins = [
  new HtmlWebPackPlugin({
    title: 'Codejobs',
    template: './src/index.html',
    filename: './index.html'
  })
];

if (isProduction) {
  plugins.push(
    new ExtractTextPlugin({
      allChunks: true,
      filename: './css/[name].css'
    })
  );
} else {
  plugins.push(
    new BundleAnalyzerPlugin(),
    new WebpackNotifierPlugin({
      title: 'CodeJobs'
    })
  );
}

export default plugins;
```

File: webpack/configuration/plugins.js

6. `BundleAnalyzerPlugin` will be executed only on development mode; if you start the application (`npm start`), you will see that a new page is open and displays all the installed packages, specifying the size of each one:

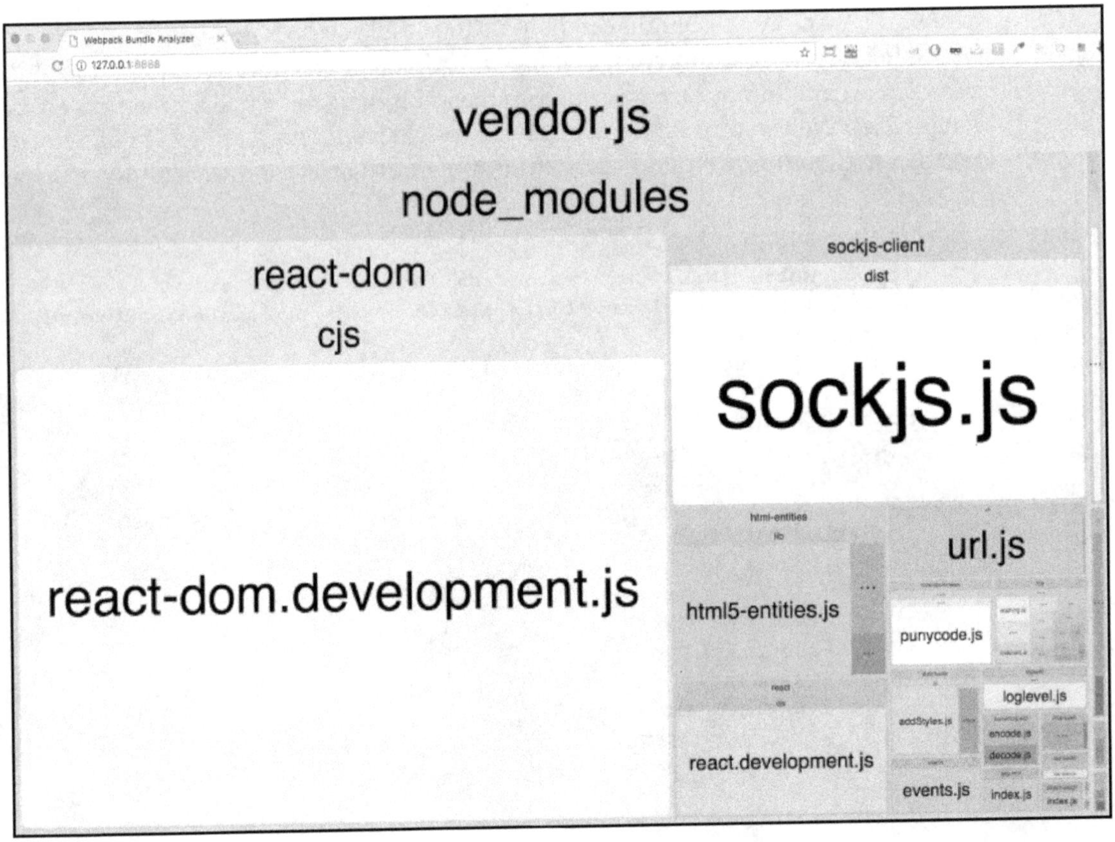

The purpose of this image is to show the sizes of the installed packages

7. The biggest one, of course, will be the vendor.js file, but we can also see our main.js components:

main.js
src
components
Home
Home.scss
App.jsx
index.jsx

8. You can see the fancy notification when you start your application:

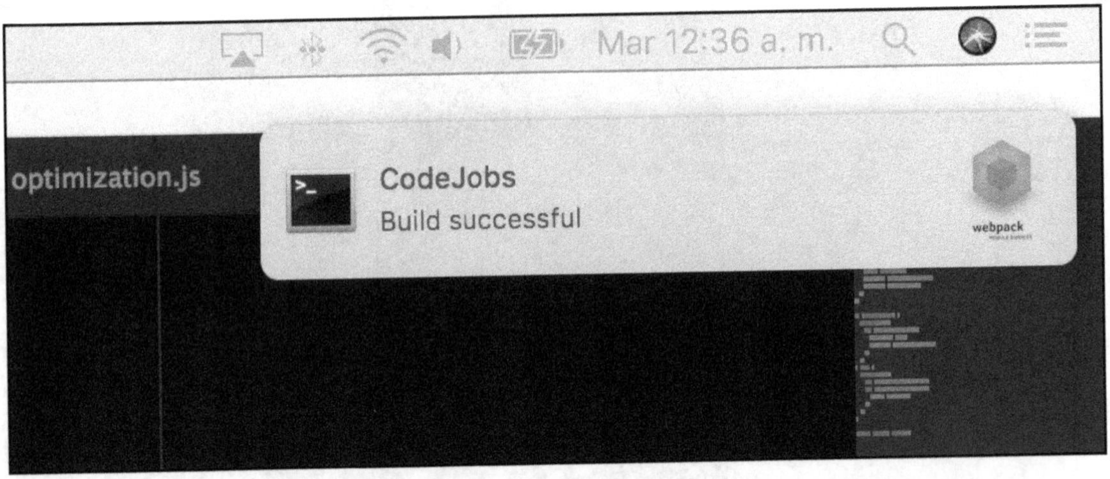

Implementing Node.js with React/Redux and Webpack 4

So far, in all the recipes, we have used React directly with `create-react-app` or Webpack 4. In this recipe, we are going to implement React and Redux using Node.js and Webpack 4; this will help us to have more robust applications.

Getting Ready

Using the same code of the last recipe, you will need to install all these packages:

```
npm install babel-cli express nodemon react-hot-loader react-router-dom
webpack-hot-middleware compression-webpack-plugin react-redux redux
```

How to do it...

Let's get started with the implementation:

1. Include the `react-hot-loader` plugin in our `.babelrc` file just for the development environment:

```
{
  "presets": ["env", "react"],
  "env": {
    "development": {
      "plugins": [
        "react-hot-loader/babel"
      ]
    }
  }
}
```

File: .babelrc

2. Create an Express Server; you need to create a file at `src/server/index.js`:

```
// Dependencies
import express from 'express';
import path from 'path';
import webpackDevMiddleware from 'webpack-dev-middleware';
import webpackHotMiddleware from 'webpack-hot-middleware';
import webpack from 'webpack';

// Webpack Configuration
import webpackConfig from '../../webpack.config.babel';

// Client Render
import clientRender from './render/clientRender';

// Utils
import { isMobile } from '../shared/utils/device';

// Environment
const isProduction = process.env.NODE_ENV === 'production';

// Express Application
const app = express();

// Webpack Compiler
const compiler = webpack(webpackConfig);
```

```
// Webpack Middleware
if (!isProduction) {
  // Hot Module Replacement
  app.use(webpackDevMiddleware(compiler));
  app.use(webpackHotMiddleware(compiler));
} else {
  // Public directory
  app.use(express.static(path.join(__dirname, '../../public')));

  // GZip Compression just for Production
  app.get('*.js', (req, res, next) => {
    req.url = `${req.url}.gz`;
    res.set('Content-Encoding', 'gzip');
    next();
  });
}

// Device Detection
app.use((req, res, next) => {
  req.isMobile = isMobile(req.headers['user-agent']);
  next();
});

// Client Side Rendering
app.use(clientRender());

// Disabling x-powered-by
app.disable('x-powered-by');

// Listen Port 3000...
app.listen(3000);
```

File: src/server/index.js

3. We included a device detection with Node.js to use in our `initialState` for Redux. we can create this util file for this purpose:

```
export function getCurrentDevice(ua) {
  return /mobile/i.test(ua) ? 'mobile' : 'desktop';
}
export function isDesktop(ua) {
  return !/mobile/i.test(ua);
}
export function isMobile(ua) {
  return /mobile/i.test(ua);
}
```

File: src/shared/utils/device.js

4. You will need the device reducer as well:

```
export default function deviceReducer(state = {}) {
  return state;
}
```

File: src/shared/reducers/deviceReducer.js

5. We need to create `index.js` in our reducers folders, in the place where we are going to combine our reducers:

```
// Dependencies
import { combineReducers } from 'redux';

// Shared Reducers
import device from './deviceReducer';

const rootReducer = combineReducers({
  device
});

export default rootReducer;
```

File: src/shared/reducers/index.js

6. Let's create our initialState file. This is where we are going to get the device information from the `req` object:

```
export default req => ({
  device: {
    isMobile: req.isMobile
  }
});
```

7. Redux needs a store to save all our reducers and our `initialState`; this will be our `configureStore`:

```
// Dependencies
import { createStore } from 'redux';

// Root Reducer
import rootReducer from '../reducers';

export default function configureStore(initialState) {
  return createStore(
    rootReducer,
    initialState
```

```
  );
}
```

File: src/shared/redux/configureStore.js

8. In the last recipes, we were using the `html-webpack-plugin` package to render the initial HTML template; now we have to do that in Node. For this, you need to create the `src/server/render/html.js` file:

```
// Dependencies
import serialize from 'serialize-javascript';

// Environment
const isProduction = process.env.NODE_ENV === 'production';

export default function html(options) {
  const { title, initialState } = options;
  let path = '/';
  let link = '';

  if (isProduction) {
    path = '/app/';
    link = `<link rel="stylesheet" href="${path}css/main.css" />`;
  }

  return `
    <!DOCTYPE html>
    <html>
      <head>
        <meta charset="utf-8">
        <title>${title}</title>
        ${link}
      </head>
      <body>
        <div id="root"></div>

        <script>
          window.initialState = ${serialize(initialState)};
        </script>
        <script src="${path}vendor.js"></script>
        <script src="${path}main.js"></script>
      </body>
    </html>
  `;
}
```

File: src/server/render/html.js

9. Create a function to render the HTML; I called this the `clientRender.js` file:

```
// HTML
import html from './html';

// Initial State
import initialState from './initialState';

export default function clientRender() {
  return (req, res) => res.send(html({
    title: 'Codejobs',
    initialState: initialState(req)
  }));
}
```

File: src/server/render/clientRender.js

10. After we've created our server files, we need to add our main entry file for the client. In this file, we are going to wrap our main `App` component inside the React Hot Loader App Container:

```
// Dependencies
import React from 'react';
import { render } from 'react-dom';
import { Provider } from 'react-redux';
import { AppContainer } from 'react-hot-loader';

// Redux Store
import configureStore from './shared/redux/configureStore';

// Components
import App from './client/App';

// Configuring Redux Store
const store = configureStore(window.initialState);

// Root element
const rootElement = document.querySelector('#root');

// App Wrapper
const renderApp = Component => {
  render(
    <AppContainer>
      <Provider store={store}>
        <Component />
      </Provider>
    </AppContainer>,
```

```
    rootElement
  );
};

// Rendering app
renderApp(App);

// Hot Module Replacement
if (module.hot) {
  module.hot.accept('./client/App', () => {
    renderApp(require('./client/App').default);
  });
}
```

File: src/index.jsx

11. Let's create a directory for our client files. The first file we need to create is `App.jsx`, where we are going to include our component's routes:

```
// Dependencies
import React from 'react';
import { BrowserRouter, Switch, Route } from 'react-router-dom';

// Components
import About from './components/About';
import Home from './components/Home';

const App = () => (
  <BrowserRouter>
    <Switch>
      <Route exact path="/" component={Home} />
      <Route exact path="/about" component={About} />
    </Switch>
  </BrowserRouter>
);

export default App;
```

File: src/client/App.jsx

12. To test our routes and our Redux state (`isMobile`), let's create the `About` component:

```
import React from 'react';
import { bool } from 'prop-types';
import { connect } from 'react-redux';
import styles from './About.scss';

const About = ({ isMobile }) => (
  <h1 className={styles.About}>About - {isMobile ? 'mobile' :
'desktop'}</h1>
);

About.propTypes = {
  isMobile: bool
};

export default connect(({ device }) => ({
  isMobile: device.isMobile
}))(About);
```

File: src/client/components/About/index.jsx

13. Add basic styles for this component:

```
$color: green;

.About {
  color: $color;
}
```

File: src/client/components/About/About.scss

14. When we want to use the React Hot Loader to refresh the page every time we make a change, we need to add an entry for our `webpack-hot-middleware` and one for `react-hot-loader` to connect to the **HMR** (**Hot Module Replacement**):

```
const isProduction = process.env.NODE_ENV === 'production';
const entry = [];

if (!isProduction) {
  entry.push(
    'webpack-hot-middleware/client?
     path=http://localhost:3000/__webpack_hmr&reload=true',
    'react-hot-loader/patch',
    './src/index.jsx'
  );
```

```
} else {
  entry.push('./src/index.jsx');
}

export default entry;
```

File: webpack/configuration/entry.js

15. Create the `output.js` file to specify where our Webpack should save the files:

```
// Dependencies
import path from 'path';

export default {
  filename: '[name].js',
  path: path.resolve(__dirname, '../../public/app'),
  publicPath: '/'
};
```

16. You need to import these files into our `index.js`:

```
// Configuration
import devtool from './devtool';
import entry from './entry';
import mode from './mode';
import module from './module';
import optimization from './optimization';
import output from './output';
import plugins from './plugins';
import resolve from './resolve';

export {
  devtool,
  entry,
  mode,
  module,
  optimization,
  output,
  plugins,
  resolve
};
```

File: webpack/configuration/index.js

17. We need to create a `mode.js` file as well, and handle the environment mode from our JS file because we are going to change our start script and we won't specify the mode directly anymore:

```
const isProduction = process.env.NODE_ENV === 'production';

export default !isProduction ? 'development' : 'production';
```

File: webpack/configuration/mode.js

18. Add `HotModuleReplacementPlugin` into our plugins file for development and `CompressionPlugin` for production:

```
import ExtractTextPlugin from 'extract-text-webpack-plugin';
import WebpackNotifierPlugin from 'webpack-notifier';
import { BundleAnalyzerPlugin } from 'webpack-bundle-analyzer';
import CompressionPlugin from 'compression-webpack-plugin';
import webpack from 'webpack';
const isProduction = process.env.NODE_ENV === 'production';
const plugins = [];
if (isProduction) {
  plugins.push(
    new ExtractTextPlugin({
      allChunks: true,
      filename: './css/[name].css'
    }),
    new CompressionPlugin({
      asset: '[path].gz[query]',
      algorithm: 'gzip',
      test: /\.js$/,
      threshold: 10240,
      minRatio: 0.8
    })
  );
} else {
  plugins.push(
    new webpack.HotModuleReplacementPlugin(),
    new BundleAnalyzerPlugin(),
    new WebpackNotifierPlugin({
      title: 'CodeJobs'
    })
  );
}
export default plugins;
```

File: webpack/configuration/plugins.js

19. In `package.json`, the new start script should look like this:

```
"scripts": {
  "build": "NODE_ENV=production webpack",
  "clean": "rm -rf public/app",
  "start": "npm run clean && NODE_ENV=development nodemon src/server --
watch src/server --exec babel-node --presets es2015",
  "start-production": "npm run clean && npm run build &&
NODE_ENV=production babel-node src/server --presets es2015"
}
```

File: package.json

If you use Windows, you have to use the `SET` keyword to specify `NODE_ENV`. For example, *`SET NODE_ENV=development`* or `SET NODE_ENV=production` otherwise won't work in your machine.

How it works...

We'll now see how it works:

1. Start the application with `npm start`.
2. You should see this page:

3. If you open the console of your browser, you will see that the HMR is now connected:

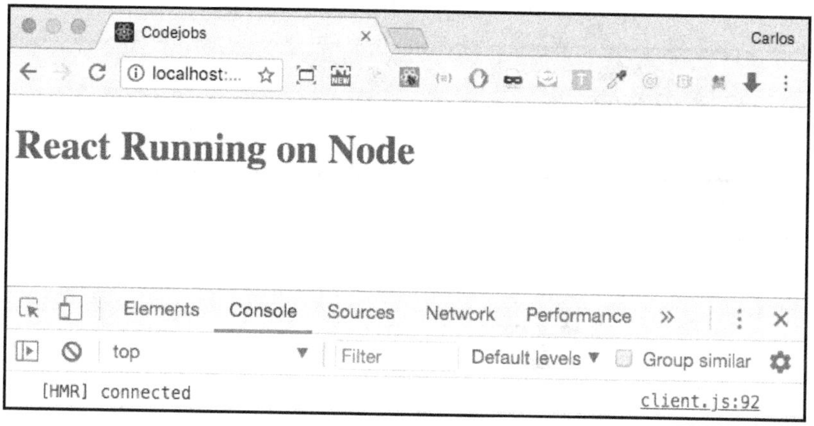

4. You can do a change in the `Home` component to see how the content is being updated without refresh:

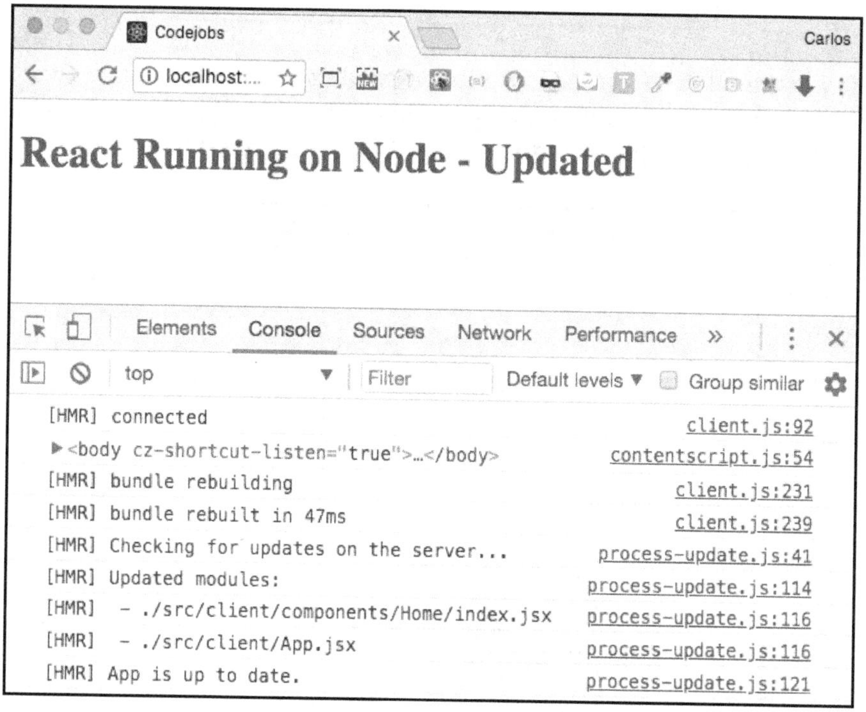

5. As you can see in the console, the HMR specify each event is occurring and give you the updated modules. If you open the Network tab, you will see the massive size of our bundles (*vendor.js = 1MB* and *main.js = 46.3KB*):

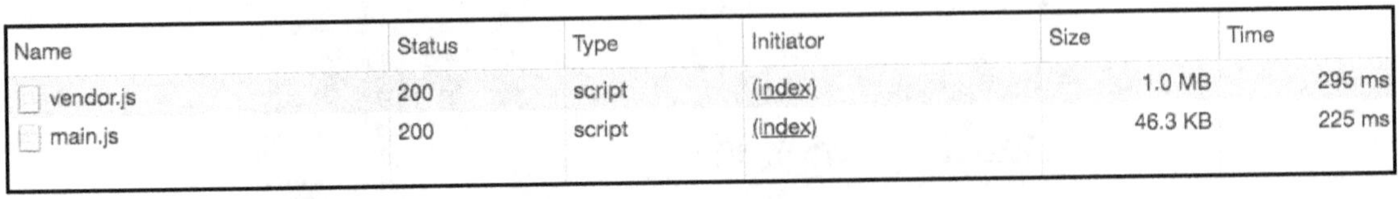
Name
Status
Type
Initiator
Size
Time
vendor.js
200
script
(index)
1.0 MB
295 ms
main.js
200
script
(index)
46.3 KB
225 ms

6. If you hit the `http://localhost:3000/about` URL, you will see the `About` component with the Redux state connected (`isMobile`):

7. If you want to run your application in production mode, execute `npm run start-production`. If everything works fine, you should see the same site but with smaller bundles (vendor.js: 262KB - 74% less and main.js: 5.2KB - 88% less):

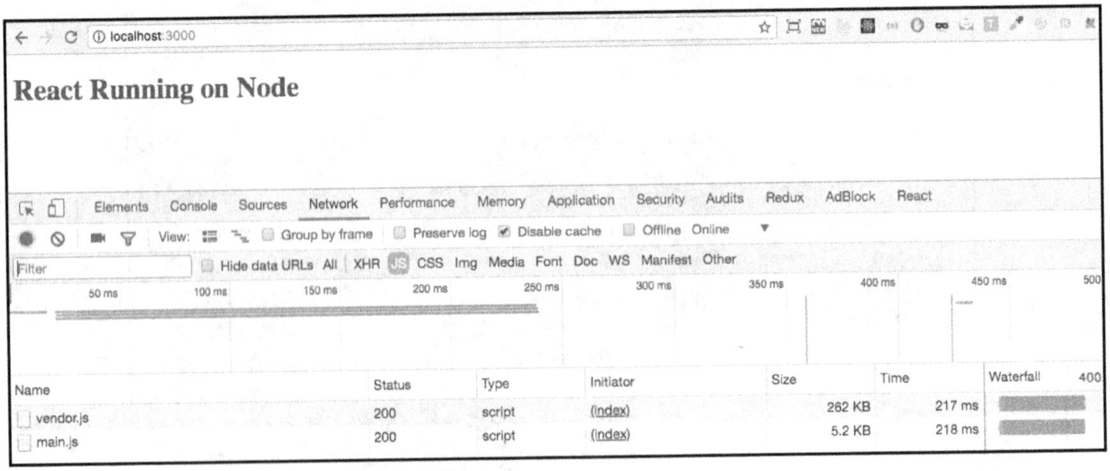

There's more...

I don't like to use relative paths in the imports, sometimes can be very difficult to calculate the depth of certain files. The `babel-plugin-module-resolver` package can help us to add a custom alias for our directories. For example:

```
// Instead of importing like this
import { isMobile } from '../../../shared/utils/device';

// Using module resolver you can use an alias like:
import { isMobile } from '@utils/device';
```

As you can see, using an alias is more consistent, and it does not matter in which path you are importing the util always will be the same path using the alias, it's cool, isn't it?

First, we need to install the package:

```
npm install babel-plugin-module-resolver
```

Then in our `.babelrc`, we can add our aliases for each path we want:

```
{
  "presets": ["env", "react"],
  "env": {
    "development": {
      "plugins": [
        "react-hot-loader/babel"
      ]
    }
  },
  "plugins": [
   ["module-resolver", {
     "root": ["./"],
     "alias": {
       "@App": "./src/client/App.jsx",
       "@client": "./src/client/",
       "@components": "./src/client/components",
       "@configureStore": "./src/shared/redux/configureStore.js",
       "@reducers": "./src/shared/reducers",
       "@server": "./src/server/",
       "@utils": "./src/shared/utils",
       "@webpack": "./webpack.config.babel.js"
     }
   }]
 ],
}
```

The `@` character is not necessary, but I like to use it to quickly identify whether I'm using an alias. Now you can modify some of the files we made in this recipe and replace the paths with the new aliases:

```
4 Chapter9/Recipe5/webpack-node-react/src/client/App.jsx                    View

@@ -3,8 +3,8 @@ import React from 'react';
 import { BrowserRouter, Switch, Route } from 'react-router-dom';

 // Components
-import About from './components/About';
-import Home from './components/Home';
+import About from '@components/About';
+import Home from '@components/Home';

 const App = () => (
   <BrowserRouter>
```

File: src/client/App.jsx

```
2 Chapter9/Recipe5/webpack-node-react/src/index.jsx                    View

@@ -5,7 +5,7 @@ import { Provider } from 'react-redux';
 import { AppContainer } from 'react-hot-loader';

 // Redux Store
-import configureStore from './shared/redux/configureStore';
+import configureStore from '@configureStore';

 // Components
 import App from './client/App';
```

File: src/index.jsx

```
4 Chapter9/Recipe5/webpack-node-react/src/server/index.js                View

@@ -6,13 +6,13 @@ import webpackHotMiddleware from 'webpack-hot-middleware';
 import webpack from 'webpack';

 // Webpack Configuration
-import webpackConfig from '../../webpack.config.babel';
+import webpackConfig from '@webpack';

 // Client Render
 import clientRender from './render/clientRender';

 // Utils
-import { isMobile } from '../shared/utils/device';
+import { isMobile } from '@utils/device';

 // Environment
 const isProduction = process.env.NODE_ENV === 'production';
```

File: src/server/index.js

```
2 Chapter9/Recipe5/webpack-node-react/src/shared/redux/configureStore.js   View

@@ -2,7 +2,7 @@
 import { createStore } from 'redux';

 // Root Reducer
-import rootReducer from '../reducers';
+import rootReducer from '@reducers';

 export default function configureStore(initialState) {
   return createStore(
```

File: src/shared/redux/configureStore.js

11
Implementing Server-Side Rendering

In this chapter, the following recipes will be covered:

- Implementing Server-Side Rendering
- Implementing promises with Server-Side Rendering
- Implementing Next.js

Introduction

React typically uses client-side rendering (CSR). This means that it dynamically injects the HTML code in the target `div` (it generally uses the `#app` or `#root` IDs), and that's why if you try to see the page's code directly (right-click—View Page Code) you will see something like this:

view-source:localhost:3000
<!DOCTYPE html>
<html>
<head>
<meta charset="utf-8">
<title>Codejobs</title>
</head>
<body>
<div id="root"></div>
<script>
window.initialState = {"device":{"isMobile":false}};
</script>
<script src="/vendor.js"></script>
<script src="/main.js"></script>
</body>
</html>

The only way to see the actual code is by inspecting the site with Chrome Dev Tools, or other tools, and here is the code generated by React using CSR:

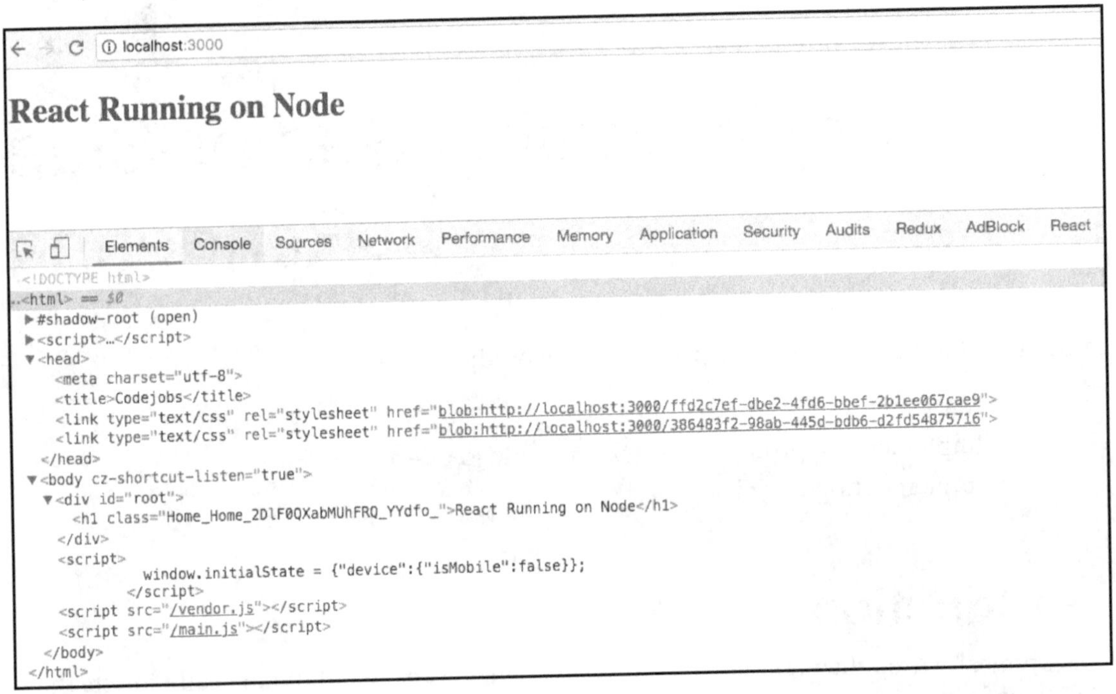

By inspecting the page, you can see the code that is injected into our `#root` div. *Server-side rendering (SSR)* is very useful for improving the *SEO* of our website and be indexed by the main search engines, such as *Google*, *Yahoo*, and *Bing*. You probably don't need to worry about *SSR* if you don't care too much about SEO. Currently, the Googlebot supports *CSR*, and it can index our site on *Google*, but if you care about SEO and you are worried about improving the SEO on other search engines, such as *Yahoo*, *Bing*, or *DuckDuckGo*, then using SSR is the way to go.

Implementing Server-Side Rendering

In this recipe, we will implement SSR in our project.

Getting ready

We are going to use the code from the last recipe (*Implementing Node.js with React/Redux and Webpack 4)* from `Chapter 10`, *Mastering Webpack 4.x*, and install some other dependencies:

```
npm install --save-dev webpack-node-externals webpack-dev-middleware
webpack-hot-middleware webpack-hot-server-middleware webpack-merge babel-
cli babel-preset-es2015
```

How to do it...

Let's now go through the steps of rendering:

1. First, we need to add our npm scripts to our `package.json` file:

```
"scripts": {
  "clean": "rm -rf dist/ && rm -rf public/app",
  "start": "npm run clean & NODE_ENV=development
  BABEL_ENV=development
  nodemon src/server --watch src/server --watch src/shared --
  exec babel-node --presets es2015",
  "start-analyzer": "npm run clean && NODE_ENV=development
  BABEL_ENV=development ANALYZER=true babel-node src/server"
}
```

File: package.json

2. Now we have to change our `webpack.config.js` file. Because we are going to implement SSR, we need to separate our Webpack configuration into a client configuration and server configuration, returning them as an array. The file should look like this:

```
// Webpack Configuration (Client & Server)
import clientConfig from './webpack/webpack.config.client';
import serverConfig from './webpack/webpack.config.server';

export default [
  clientConfig,
  serverConfig
];
```

File: webpack.config.js

3. Now we need to create a file for our client configuration inside our `webpack` folder. We need to call it `webpack.config.client.js`:

```
// Dependencies
import webpackMerge from 'webpack-merge';

// Webpack Configuration
import commonConfig from './webpack.config.common';
import {
  context,
  devtool,
  entry,
  name,
  output,
  optimization,
  plugins,
  target
} from './configuration';

// Type of Configuration
const type = 'client';

export default webpackMerge(commonConfig(type), {
  context: context(type),
  devtool,
  entry: entry(type),
  name: name(type),
  output: output(type),
  optimization,
  plugins: plugins(type),
  target: target(type)
});
```

File: webpack/webpack.config.client.js

4. Now the server config should be like this:

```
// Dependencies
import webpackMerge from 'webpack-merge';

// Webpack Configuration
import commonConfig from './webpack.config.common';

// Configuration
import {
  context,
  entry,
  externals,
```

```
  name,
  output,
  plugins,
  target
} from './configuration';

// Type of Configuration
const type = 'server';

export default webpackMerge(commonConfig(type), {
  context: context(type),
  entry: entry(type),
  externals: externals(type),
  name: name(type),
  output: output(type),
  plugins: plugins(type),
  target: target(type)
});
```

File: webpack/webpack.config.server.js

5. As you can see, in both files we are importing a common configuration file that contains a configuration that needs to be added to both the client and the server:

```
// Configuration
import { module, resolve, mode } from './configuration';
export default type => ({
  module: module(type),
  resolve,
  mode
});
```

File: webpack/webpack.config.common.js

6. We need to add new configuration files for Webpack nodes and also modify some of the files we already have. The first one we need to create is `context.js`. In this file (and some others) we are going to export a function with a type parameter, which can be *client* or *server*, and depending on that value we will return different configurations:

```
// Dependencies
import path from 'path';
export default type => type === 'server'
  ? path.resolve(__dirname, '../../src/server')
  : path.resolve(__dirname, '../../src/client');
```

File: webpack/configuration/context.js

7. The entry file is where we will add all the files that are going to be added to the bundle. Our entry file now should be like this:

```
// Environment
const isDevelopment = process.env.NODE_ENV !== 'production';

export default type => {
  if (type === 'server') {
    return './render/serverRender.js';
  }

  const entry = [];

  if (isDevelopment) {
    entry.push(
      'webpack-hot-middleware/client',
      'react-hot-loader/patch'
    );
  }

  entry.push('./index.jsx');

  return entry;
};
```

File: webpack/configuration/entry.js

8. We need to create a file called externals.js, which contains the modules we won't bundle (unless they are on the whitelist):

```
// Dependencies
import nodeExternals from 'webpack-node-externals';

export default () => [
  nodeExternals({
    whitelist: [/^redux\/(store|modules)/]
  })
];
```

File: webpack/configuration/externals.js

9. Also, we need to modify our `module.js` file to return our rules based on the environment or the configuration type:

```
// Dependencies
import ExtractTextPlugin from 'extract-text-webpack-plugin';

// Environment
const isDevelopment = process.env.NODE_ENV !== 'production';

export default type => {
  const rules = [
    {
      test: /\.(js|jsx)$/,
      use: 'babel-loader',
      exclude: /node_modules/
    }
  ];

  if (!isDevelopment || type === 'server') {
    rules.push({
      test: /\.scss$/,
      use: ExtractTextPlugin.extract({
        fallback: 'style-loader',
        use: [
          'css-loader?minimize=true&modules=true&localIdentName=
          [name]__[local]_[hash:base64]',
          'sass-loader'
        ]
      })
    });
  } else {
    rules.push({
      test: /\.scss$/,
      use: [
        {
          loader: 'style-loader'
        },
        {
          loader: 'css-loader',
          options: {
            modules: true,
            importLoaders: 1,
            localIdentName: '[name]__[local]_[hash:base64]',
            sourceMap: true,
            minimize: true
          }
        },
        {
```

```
            loader: 'sass-loader'
          }
        ]
      });
    }

    return {
      rules
    };
  };
```

File: webpack/configuration/module.js

10. Now we need to create a node for the name:

```
export default type => type;
```

File: webpack/configuration/name.js

11. For the output configuration, we need to return an object depending on the type of configuration (client or server):

```
// Dependencies
import path from 'path';

export default type => {
  if (type === 'server') {
    return {
      filename: 'server.js',
      path: path.resolve(__dirname, '../../dist'),
      libraryTarget: 'commonjs2'
    };
  }

  return {
    filename: '[name].bundle.js',
    path: path.resolve(__dirname, '../../public/app'),
    publicPath: '/'
  };
};
```

File: webpack/configuration/output.js

12. In our `plugins.js` file, we are validating whether the user has sent the `ANALYZER` variable to display the `BundleAnalyzerPlugin` just in that case and not every time we run our application in development mode:

```
// Dependencies
import CompressionPlugin from 'compression-webpack-plugin';
import ExtractTextPlugin from 'extract-text-webpack-plugin';
import webpack from 'webpack';
import WebpackNotifierPlugin from 'webpack-notifier';
import { BundleAnalyzerPlugin } from 'webpack-bundle-analyzer';

// Environment
const isDevelopment = process.env.NODE_ENV !== 'production';

// Analyzer
const isAnalyzer = process.env.ANALYZER === 'true';

export default type => {
  const plugins = [
    new ExtractTextPlugin({
      filename: '../../public/css/style.css'
    })
  ];

  if (isAnalyzer) {
    plugins.push(
      new BundleAnalyzerPlugin()
    );
  }

  if (isDevelopment) {
    plugins.push(
      new webpack.HotModuleReplacementPlugin(),
      new webpack.NoEmitOnErrorsPlugin(),
      new WebpackNotifierPlugin({
        title: 'CodeJobs'
      })
    );
  } else {
    plugins.push(
      new CompressionPlugin({
        asset: '[path].gz[query]',
        algorithm: 'gzip',
        test: /\.js$|\.css$|\.html$/,
        threshold: 10240,
        minRatio: 0.8
      })
    );
```

```
  }

  return plugins;
};
```

File: webpack/configuration/plugins.js

13. We need to specify our modules in our resolve file; the file should be like this:

```
// Dependencies
import path from 'path';

export default {
  extensions: ['.js', '.jsx'],
  modules: [
    'node_modules',
    path.resolve(__dirname, '../../src/client'),
    path.resolve(__dirname, '../../src/server')
  ]
};
```

File: webpack/configuration/resolve.js

14. The last configuration we need to create is the `target.js` file:

```
export default type => type === 'server' ? 'node' : 'web';
```

File: webpack/configuration/target.js

15. After we have configured our Webpack, we need to modify our `App.jsx` file, in which we need to create our routes for the client using the `<BrowserRouter>` component and `<StaticRouter>` for the server:

```
// Dependencies
import React from 'react';
import {
  BrowserRouter,
  StaticRouter,
  Switch,
  Route
} from 'react-router-dom';

// Components
import About from '@components/About';
import Home from '@components/Home';

export default ({ server, location, context = {} }) => {
```

```
    const routes = (
      <Switch>
        <Route exact path="/" component={Home} />
        <Route exact path="/about" component={About} />
      </Switch>
    );

    // Client Router
    let router = (
      <BrowserRouter>
        {routes}
      </BrowserRouter>
    );

    // Server Router
    if (server) {
      router = (
        <StaticRouter location={location} context={context}>
          {routes}
        </StaticRouter>
      );
    }

    return router;
  };
```

File: src/client/App.jsx

16. Now we need to modify our server file (`index.js`) to use our *clientRender* and *serverRender* middleware:

```
  // Dependencies
  import express from 'express';
  import path from 'path';
  import webpackDevMiddleware from 'webpack-dev-middleware';
  import webpackHotMiddleware from 'webpack-hot-middleware';
  import webpackHotServerMiddleware from 'webpack-hot-server-
middleware';
  import webpack from 'webpack';

  // Utils
  import { isMobile, isBot } from '@utils/device';

  // Client Render
  import clientRender from './render/clientRender';

  // Webpack Configuration
  import webpackConfig from '@webpack';
```

```
// Environment
const isProduction = process.env.NODE_ENV === 'production';

// Express Application
const app = express();

// Webpack Compiler
const compiler = webpack(webpackConfig);

// Public directory
app.use(express.static(path.join(__dirname, '../../public')));

// Device Detection
app.use((req, res, next) => {
  req.isMobile = isMobile(req.headers['user-agent']);
  // We detect if a search bot is accessing...
  req.isBot = isBot(req.headers['user-agent']);

  next();
});

// Webpack Middleware
if (!isProduction) {
  // Hot Module Replacement
  app.use(webpackDevMiddleware(compiler));
  app.use(webpackHotMiddleware(
    compiler.compilers.find(compiler => compiler.name ===
'client'))
  );
} else {
  // GZip Compression just for Production
  app.get('*.js', (req, res, next) => {
    req.url = `${req.url}.gz`;
    res.set('Content-Encoding', 'gzip');
    next();
  });
}

// Client Side Rendering
app.use(clientRender());

if (isProduction) {
  try {
    // eslint-disable-next-line
    const serverRender = require('../../dist/server.js').default;

    app.use(serverRender());
  } catch (e) {
```

```
      throw e;
    }
  }

  // For Server Side Rendering on Development Mode
  app.use(webpackHotServerMiddleware(compiler));

  // Disabling x-powered-by
  app.disable('x-powered-by');

  // Listen Port...
  app.listen(3000);
```

File: src/server/index.js

17. We need to modify our `clientRender.js` file. If we detect a search bot with the `isBot` function, we will return the `next()` middleware. Otherwise, we render the HTML and we execute the app with CSR:

```
  // HTML
  import html from './html';

  // Initial State
  import initialState from './initialState';

  export default function clientRender() {
    return (req, res, next) => {
      if (req.isBot) {
        return next();
      }

      res.send(html({
        title: 'Codejobs',
        initialState: initialState(req)
      }));
    };
  }
```

File: src/server/render/clientRender.js

18. Now let's create our `serverRender.js` file. Here, we need to render our `App` component using the `renderToString` method from `react-dom/server` library:

```
// Dependencies
import React from 'react';
import { renderToString } from 'react-dom/server';
import { Provider } from 'react-redux';

// Redux Store
import configureStore from '@configureStore';

// Components
import App from '../../client/App';

import html from './html';

// Initial State
import initialState from './initialState';

export default function serverRender() {
  return (req, res, next) => {
    // Configuring Redux Store
    const store = configureStore(initialState(req));

    const markup = renderToString(
      <Provider store={store}>
        <App
          server
          location={req.url}
        />
      </Provider>
    );

    res.send(html({
      title: 'Codejobs',
      markup,
      initialState: initialState(req)
    }));
  };
}
```

File: src/server/render/serverRender.js

How it works...

You can start the application by running the `npm start` command.

If you open the app at `http://localhost:3000` in your browser (Chrome, for example) and you right-click and then **View page source**, you will probably notice that we are not using SSR:

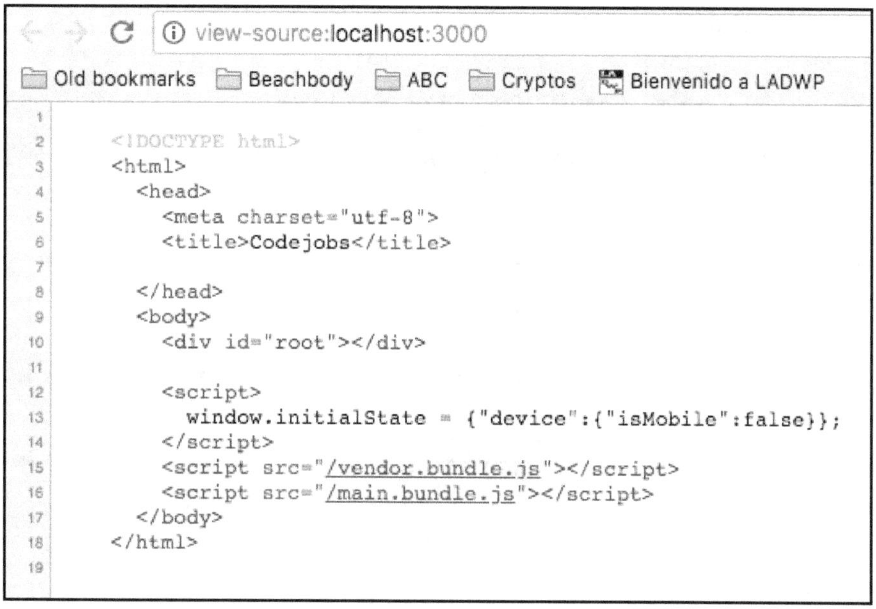

This is because we will only use SSR for search bots. The *isBot* function will detect all the search bots, and just for a test I added *curl* as a bot to test our SSR; this is the code of that function:

```
  export function isBot(ua) {
    const b =
/curl|bot|googlebot|google|baidu|bing|msn|duckduckgo|teoma|slurp|yandex|cra
wler|spider|robot|crawling/i;
    return b.test(ua);
  }
```

File: src/shared/utils/device.js

Open a new terminal while you have the application running in another terminal, and then execute the following command:

```
curl http://localhost:3000
```

```
➜ server-side-rendering git:(master) ✗ curl http://localhost:3000

    <!DOCTYPE html>
    <html>
      <head>
        <meta charset="utf-8">
        <title>Codejobs</title>

      </head>
      <body>
        <div id="root"><h1 class="Home__Home_fxZgbO4UV4SE3Z8dUhbk8" data-reactroot="">React Running on Node</h1></div>

        <script>
          window.initialState = {"device":{"isMobile":false}};
        </script>
        <script src="/vendor.bundle.js"></script>
        <script src="/main.bundle.js"></script>
      </body>
    </html>
```

As you can see, the HTML code inside the #root div is render it using the SSR.

Also, if you want to try to run `/about` in curl, you will see that also will render it using SSR:

```
➜ server-side-rendering git:(master) ✗ curl http://localhost:3000/about

    <!DOCTYPE html>
    <html>
      <head>
        <meta charset="utf-8">
        <title>Codejobs</title>

      </head>
      <body>
        <div id="root"><h1 class="About__About_2WIhNc2xQkmbHJlqJRlVlV" data-reactroot="">About - <!-- -->desktop</h1></div>

        <script>
          window.initialState = {"device":{"isMobile":false}};
        </script>
        <script src="/vendor.bundle.js"></script>
        <script src="/main.bundle.js"></script>
      </body>
    </html>
```

There is an extension for Chrome called User-Agent Switcher for C*hrome* where you can specify the user agent you want to use in your browser. In this way, you can add a special user agent for Googlebot, for example:

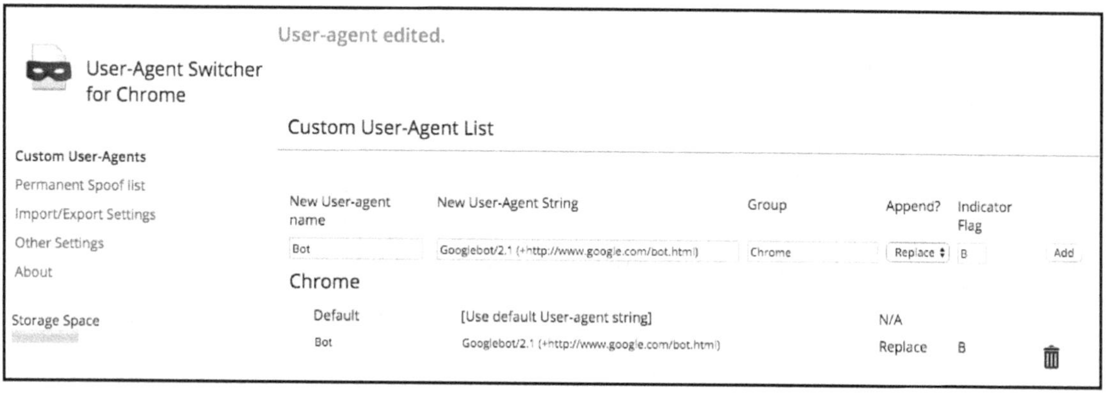

Then, if you select **Chrome** | **Bot** in User-Agent Switcher, you can see that the HTML code renders it as SSR when you do **View page source**:

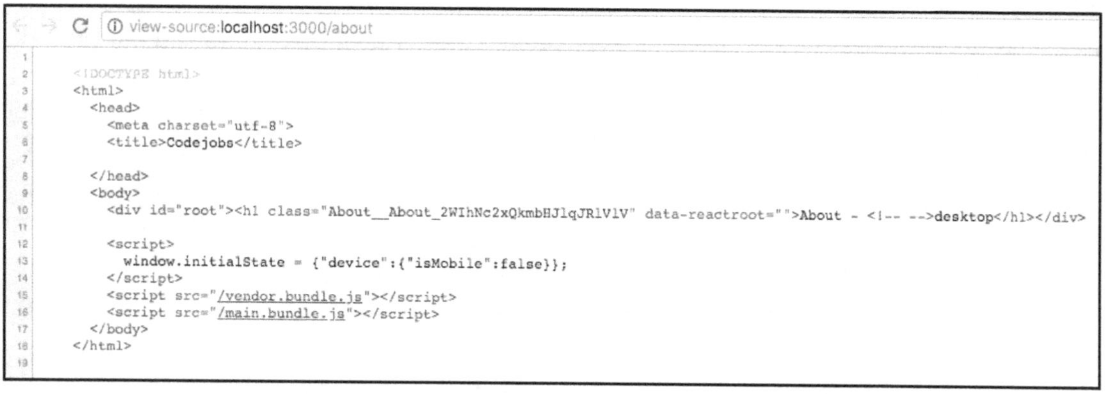

There's more...

When we are using SSR, we have to be very careful when we try to use the object window for the client. If you use it directly using SSR you will get a ReferenceError such as this:

```
ReferenceError: window is not defined
```

To solve this problem, you can validate that the window object exists, but this can be very repetitive. I prefer to create a function that can verify whether we are using a browser (client) or a server. You can do it like this:

```
export function isBrowser() {
  return typeof window !== 'undefined';
}
```

Then every time you need to use the window object, you can do something like this:

```
const store = isBrowser() ? configureStore(window.initialState) : {};
```

Implementing promises with Server-Side Rendering

In the last recipe, we saw how SSR works, but that recipe was limited to displaying the SSR with simple components. In this recipe, we will learn how to implement promises to connect our components to Redux, use an API to get data and render the components using SSR.

Getting ready

We are going to use the same code from the last recipe, but we will make some changes. In this recipe, we need to install these packages:

```
npm install axios babel-preset-stage-0 react-router-dom redux-devtools-extension redux-thunk
```

How to do it...

For this recipe, we are going to implement a basic todo list pulled from an API to show how to connect Redux to our application using SSR:

1. The first thing we need to do is to add a simple API to display a to-do list:

```
import express from 'express';

const router = express.Router();

// Mock data, this should come from a database....
```

```
const todo = [
  {
    id: 1,
    title: 'Go to the Gym'
  },
  {
    id: 2,
    title: 'Dentist Appointment'
  },
  {
    id: 3,
    title: 'Finish homework'
  }
];

router.get('/todo/list', (req, res, next) => {
  res.json({
    response: todo
  });
});

export default router;
```

File: src/server/controllers/api.js

2. The second step is to import this API controller into our `src/server/index.js` file and add it as middleware on the `/api` route:

```
...
// Controllers
import apiController from './controllers/api';
...
// Express Application
const app = express();

// Webpack Compiler
const compiler = webpack(webpackConfig);

// Routes
app.use('/api', apiController);
...
```

File: src/server/index.js

3. Previously, in our `serverRender.js` file, we rendered our `App` component directly. Now we need to get the promises from the components that have a static method called `initialAction`, save them into a promises array, resolve them, and then render our `App` method:

```
// Dependencies
import React from 'react';
import { renderToString } from 'react-dom/server';
import { Provider } from 'react-redux';
import { matchPath } from 'react-router-dom';

// Redux Store
import configureStore from '@configureStore';

// Components
import App from '../../client/App';

// HTML
import html from './html';

// Initial State
import initialState from './initialState';

// Routes
import routes from '@shared/routes';

export default function serverRender() {
  return (req, res, next) => {
    // Configuring Redux Store
    const store = configureStore(initialState(req));

    // Getting the promises from the components which has
    // initialAction.
    const promises = routes.paths.reduce((promises, route) => {
      if (matchPath(req.url, route) && route.component &&
route.component.initialAction) {
promises.push(Promise.resolve(store.dispatch(route.component.initia
lAction())));
      }

      return promises;
    }, []);

    // Resolving our promises
    Promise.all(promises)
      .then(() => {
        // Getting Redux Initial State
```

```
        const initialState = store.getState();

        // Rendering with SSR
        const markup = renderToString(
          <Provider store={store}>
            <App
              server
              location={req.url}
            />
          </Provider>
        );

        // Sending our HTML code.
        res.send(html({
          title: 'Codejobs',
          markup,
          initialState
        }));
      })
      .catch(e => {
        // eslint-disable-line no-console
        console.log('Promise Error: ', e);
      });
  };
}
```

File: src/server/render/serverRender.js

4. In this recipe, we need to change our folder structure a little bit in our client directory. Previously, we had a `components` directory and our components were inside. Now we are going to encapsulate our components as small applications, and inside we can create our actions, API, components, containers, and reducers. Our new structure should look like this:

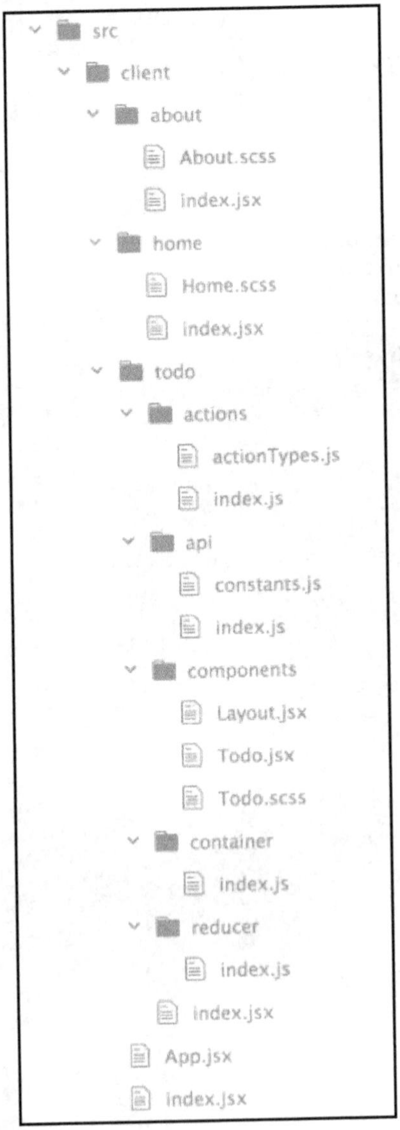

5. We will create a todo application. To do this, first we need to add our actions folder, and inside we need to make first our `actionTypes.js` file. In this file, we need to add our `FETCH_TODO` actions. I prefer to create an object with two functions, one for requests and the other for the success; you will see the advantage of this when we use this on our reducer and when we dispatch our actions:

```
// Actions
export const FETCH_TODO = {
  request: () => 'FETCH_TODO_REQUEST',
  success: () => 'FETCH_TODO_SUCCESS'
};
```

File: src/client/todo/actions/actionTypes.js

6. In our `index.js` file, we will create a fetchTodo action to retrieve our todo list items from our API:

```
// Base Actions
import { request, received } from '@baseActions';

// Api
import api from '../api';

// Action Types
import { FETCH_TODO } from './actionTypes';

export const fetchTodo = () => dispatch => {
  const action = FETCH_TODO;
  const { fetchTodo } = api;
  dispatch(request(action));

  return fetchTodo()
    .then(response => dispatch(received(action, response.data)));
};
```

File: src/client/todo/actions/index.js

7. As you can see, we are using two particular methods (request and received) from our base actions. These functions will help us to dispatch our actions easily (do you remember that we used the request and success methods in the actions?):

```
// Base Actions
export const request = ACTION => ({
  type: ACTION.request()
});

export const received = (ACTION, data) => ({
  type: ACTION.success(),
  payload: data
});
```

File: src/shared/redux/baseActions.js

8. Now let's create our `api` folder, where we need to add a `constants.js` file and our `index.js` file:

```
export const API = Object.freeze({
  TODO: 'api/todo/list'
});
```

File: src/client/todo/api/constants.js

9. In our `index.js` file, we have to create our Api class and add a static method called `fetchTodo`:

```
// Dependencies
import axios from 'axios';

// Configuration
import config from '@configuration';

// Utils
import { isBrowser } from '@utils/frontend';

// Constants
import { API } from './constants';

class Api {
  static fetchTodo() {
    // For Node (SSR) we have to specify our base domain
    // (http://localhost:3000/api/todo/list)
    // For Client Side Render just /api/todo/list.
    const url = isBrowser()
      ? API.TODO
```

```
        : `${config.baseUrl}/${API.TODO}`;

      return axios(url);
    }
  }

  export default Api;
```

File: src/client/todo/api/index.js

10. In our Todo container, we need to map our todo list and add the *fetchTodo* action to Redux. We will export a Layout component, to which we will add our other components and manipulate the way we want to display the layout:

```
// Dependencies
import { connect } from 'react-redux';
import { bindActionCreators } from 'redux';

// Components
import Layout from '../components/Layout';

// Actions
import { fetchTodo } from '../actions';

export default connect(({ todo }) => ({
  todo: todo.list
}), dispatch => bindActionCreators(
  {
    fetchTodo
  },
  dispatch
))(Layout);
```

File: src/client/todo/container/index.js

11. Our Layout component should be like this:

```
// Dependencies
import React from 'react';

// Shared Components
import Header from '@layout/Header';
import Content from '@layout/Content';
import Footer from '@layout/Footer';

// Componenets
import Todo from '../components/Todo';
```

```
const Layout = props => (
  <main>
    <Header {...props} />
    <Content>
      <Todo {...props} />
    </Content>
    <Footer {...props} />
  </main>
);
export default Layout;
```

File: src/client/todo/components/Layout.jsx

12. In this recipe, we are not going to see the layout components (Header, Content, and Footer) since they are very generic and we have used them in the past recipes. Now let's create our reducer file:

```
// Utils
import { getNewState } from '@utils/frontend';

// Action Types
import { FETCH_TODO } from '../actions/actionTypes';

// Initial State
const initialState = {
  list: []
};
export default function todoReducer(state = initialState, action)
{
  switch (action.type) {
    case FETCH_TODO.success(): {
      const { payload: { response = [] } } = action;

      return getNewState(state, {
        list: response
      });
    }

    default:
      return state;
  }
}
```

File: src/client/todo/reducer/index.js

13. Our Todo component will execute our fetchTodo action in the componentDidMount method, and then we render the Todo list into an HTML list; very simple:

```
// Dependencies
import React, { Component } from 'react';

// Utils
import { isFirstRender } from '@utils/frontend';

// Styles
import styles from './Todo.scss';

class Todo extends Component {
  componentDidMount() {
    const { fetchTodo } = this.props;

    fetchTodo();
  }

  render() {
    const {
      todo
    } = this.props;

    if (isFirstRender(todo)) {
      return null;
    }

    return (
      <div>
        <div className={styles.Todo}>
          <ol>
            {todo.map((item, key) =>
              <li key={key}>{item.title}</li>)}
          </ol>
        </div>
      </div>
    );
  }
}

export default Todo;
```

File: src/client/todo/components/Todo.jsx

14. Finally, we need to create an `index.jsx` file for our todo app, and in this file we are going to add our initialAction (this will return a promise) to execute our fetchTodo action and render this Todo list using SSR:

```
// Dependencies
import React from 'react';

// Actions
import { fetchTodo } from './actions';

// Main Container
import Container from './container';

// Main Component
const Main = props => <Container {...props} />;

// Initial Action
Main.initialAction = () => fetchTodo();

export default Main;
```

File: src/client/todo/index.jsx

How it works...

As you can see in our `serverRender.js` file, we get the promises and resolve them, and then we render our application using SSR.

If you want to test the application, you need to go to http://localhost:3000/todo in your browser.

Remember that in our app, we are just using SSR for search bots and curl, otherwise will use CSR. This is because the only reason we have to use SSR is to improve our SEO in Google, Yahoo, and Bing.

If we use CSR, the way we will execute our action is on the `componentDidMount()` method in our Todo component; and if we are using SSR, we will use the `initialAction` method, which returns a promise that will be resolved in `serverRender.js`.

If you open the page, you should see this:

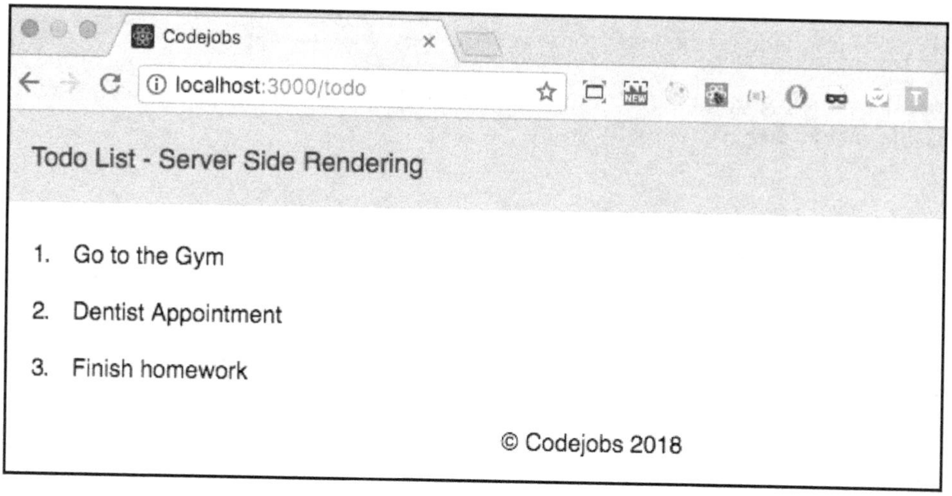

If you want to see whether the SSR is working, you can use the `curl` command and execute the same URL in your Terminal:

```
→ server-side-rendering-with-promises git:(master) curl http://localhost:3000/todo

    <!DOCTYPE html>
    <html>
      <head>
        <meta charset="utf-8">
        <title>Codejobs</title>

      </head>
      <body>
        <div id="root"><main data-reactroot=""><header class="Header__Header_3vPMdpb8PNwQOwc5kU7Rin"><a href="http://localhost:3000">T
odo List - Server Side Rendering</a></header><main><div><div class="Todo__Todo_cgxtjjuk1mPjlh79sXa9O"><ol><li>Go to the Gym</li><li>De
ntist Appointment</li><li>Finish homework</li></ol></div></div></main><footer class="Footer__Footer_33hOkW7mqICESUVpOT-1Zk">® Codejobs
 <!-- -->2018</footer></main></div>

        <script>
          window.initialState = {"todo":{"list":[{"id":1,"title":"Go to the Gym"},{"id":2,"title":"Dentist Appointment"},{"id":3,"titl
e":"Finish homework"}]},"device":{}};
        </script>
        <script src="/vendor.bundle.js"></script>
        <script src="/main.bundle.js"></script>
      </body>
    </html>
```

As you can see, the todo list reducer has been added to `initialState` and from there, we can render the list using SSR.

Implementing Next.js

Next.js is a minimalistic framework for server-rendered React applications.

In this recipe, we are going to learn how to implement Next.js with Sass, and we will also get data from a service using axios.

Getting ready

First, let's create a new directory called `nextjs`, initialize `package.json`, and finally create a new directory inside it:

```
mkdir nextjs
cd nextjs
npm init -y
mkdir src
```

Then we need to install some dependencies:

```
npm install next react react-dom axios node-sass @zeit/next-sass
```

How to do it...

Now that we have installed the dependencies, let's create our first Next.js application:

1. The first thing we need to do is to create some scripts in our package.json. In each script, we need to specify the `src` directory. Otherwise, it will try to start Next from the root instead of the `src` path:

```
"scripts": {
  "start": "next start src",
  "dev": "next src",
  "build": "next build src"
}
```

File: package.json

2. The main directory in Next is called `pages`. This is where we will include all the `pages` we want to render using Next:

```
cd src && mkdir pages
```

3. The first page we need to create is `index.jsx`:

```
const Index = () => <h1>Home</h1>;

export default Index;
```

File: src/pages/index.jsx

4. Now let's run our application using the dev script:

```
npm run dev
```

5. If everything works, you should see this in your terminal:

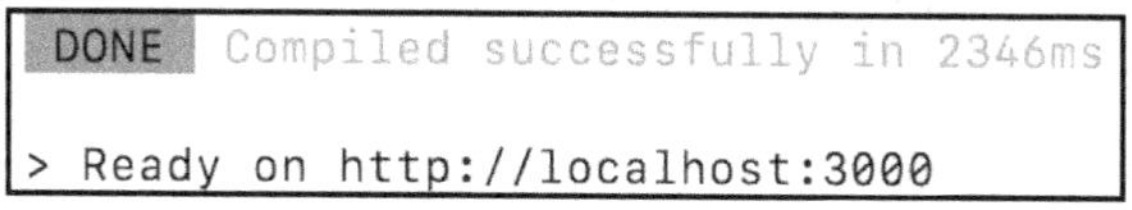

6. Open `http://localhost:3000`:

Next.js has its own Webpack configuration and hot reloading enabled. That means if you edit the index.js file you will see the changes reflected without refreshing the page.

7. Now let's create an About page to see how the routing works:

```
const About = () => <h1>About</h1>;

export default About;
```

File: src/pages/about.jsx

8. Now you will see the about page if you go to http://localhost:3000/about. As you can see, Next.js automatically creates a new route for each page we have created. This means we don't need to install React Router to handle the routing.

> TIP: In Next pages, it is not necessary to import React because it is automatically handled by Next as well.

9. Now we need to create a `next.config.js` file and import the withSass method to use Sass in our project. Unfortunately, this file needs to be written in ES5 syntax because the babel extension to use ES6 is not supported at the moment (`https://github.com/zeit/next.js/issues/2916`):

```
const withSass = require('@zeit/next-sass');

module.exports = withSass();
```

File: src/next.config.js

> TIP: In this file, we can also add custom Webpack configuration if we need it.

10. Then we need to create a special file in the `pages` directory called `_document.js`. This file is automatically handled by Next.js, and here we can define the head and body of our document:

```
import Document, { Head, Main, NextScript } from 'next/document';

export default class MyDocument extends Document {
  render() {
    return (
      <html>
        <Head>
          <title>Codejobs with Next</title>
```

```
            <link
              rel="stylesheet"
              href="/_next/static/style.css"
            />
          </Head>

          <body>
            <Main />
            <NextScript />
          </body>
        </html>
      );
    }
  }
```

File: src/pages/_document.js

TIP: The path to the CSS file (`/_next/static/style.css`) is by default; we should use that one to use styles in our project.

11. Now we can create some components to wrap up our pages. The first one we need to create is a navbar for menu options:

```
import Link from 'next/link';
import './Navbar.scss';

const Navbar = () => (
  <div className="navbar">
    <ul>
      <li>Codejobs</li>
      <li><Link href="/">Home</Link></li>
      <li><Link href="/about">About</Link></li>
    </ul>
  </div>
)
export default Navbar;
```

File: src/components/Navbar.jsx

TIP: The Link component is not the same as the React Router Link. There are a few differences; for example, the React Router Link uses the "to" prop and the Next Link uses "href" to specify the URL.

12. Now we can add Sass styles for our navbar:

```
.navbar {
  background: black;
  color: white;
  height: 60px;

  ul {
    padding: 0;
    margin: 0;
    list-style: none;

    li {
      display: inline-block;
      margin-left: 30px;
      text-align: center;

      a {
        display: block;
        color: white;
        line-height: 60px;
        width: 150px;

        &:hover {
          background: white;
          color: black;
        }
      }
    }
  }
}
```

File: src/components/Navbar.scss

13. Then we need to create our Layout component:

```
import Navbar from './Navbar';
import './Layout.scss';

const Layout = ({ children }) => (
  <div className="layout">
    <Navbar />

    <div className="wrapper">
      {children}
    </div>
  </div>
)
```

```
export default Layout;
```

File: src/components/Layout.jsx

14. The styles for our Layout are as follows:

```
body {
  font-family: verdana;
  padding: 0;
  margin: 0;
}

.layout {
  a {
    text-decoration: none;
  }

  .wrapper {
    margin: 0 auto;
    width: 96%;
  }
}
```

File: src/components/Layout.scss

15. Do you remember the recipe in `Chapter 5`, *Mastering Redux,* about listing the top 100 cryptocurrencies from CoinMarketCap (`Repository: Chapter05/Recipe2/coinmarketcap`)? In this recipe, we are going to do the same using Next.js. The first thing we need to do is to modify the page's `index.js` file and do an async `axios` request in the `getInitialProps` method:

```
import axios from 'axios';
import Layout from '../components/Layout';
import Coins from '../components/Coins';

const Index = ({ coins }) => (
  <Layout>
    <div className="index">
      <Coins coins={coins} />
    </div>
  </Layout>
);

Index.getInitialProps = async () => {
  const url = 'https://api.coinmarketcap.com/v1/ticker/';
  const res = await axios.get(url);
```

```
  return {
    coins: res.data
  };
};

export default Index;
```

File: src/pages/index.js

16. Now let's create the `Coins` component:

```
// Dependencies
import React, { Component } from 'react';
import { array } from 'prop-types';

// Styles
import './Coins.scss';

const Coins = ({ coins }) => (
  <div className="Coins">
    <h1>Top 100 Coins</h1>

    <ul>
      {coins.map((coin, key) => (
        <li key={key}>
          <span className="left">{coin.rank} {coin.name} <strong>
          {coin.symbol}</strong></span>
          <span className="right">${coin.price_usd}</span>
        </li>
      ))}
    </ul>
  </div>
);

Coins.propTypes = {
  coins: array
};

export default Coins;
```

File: src/components/Coins.jsx

17. The styles for the `Coins` component are as follows:

```
.Coins {
  h1 {
    text-align: center;
  }

  ul {
    margin: 0 auto;
    margin-bottom: 20px;
    padding: 0;
    list-style: none;
    width: 400px;

    li {
      border-bottom: 1px solid black;
      text-align: left;
      padding: 10px;
      display: flex;
      justify-content: space-between;

      a {
        display: block;
        color: #333;
        text-decoration: none;
        background: #5ed4ff;

        &:hover {
          color: #333;
          text-decoration: none;
          background: #baecff;
        }
      }
    }
  }
}
```

File: src/components/Coins.scss

How it works...

Now that we have created all the pages and components, let's test our Next application by running `npm run dev`:

Let's now see how it is rendering it in the HTML view:

Banzai! The HTML is rendered with SSR and is perfect for improving the SEO. As you can see, creating an application with Next is super fast, and we avoid a lot of configuration when enabling SSR.

12
Testing and Debugging

In this chapter, the following recipes will be covered:

- Testing our first component with Jest and Enzyme
- Testing a Redux Container, Actions, and Reducers
- Debugging a React application using React and Redux Dev Tools
- Simulating events

Introduction

Testing and debugging are very important for any project that wants to have high quality. Unfortunately, many developers do not care about testing (unit tests) because they think that will reduce the speed of the development and some of them leave it until the end of the project. In my personal experience, I can say that testing from the beginning of the project will save you time because, at the end, you will have fewer bugs to fix. React uses Jest to test its components, containers, actions, and reducers.

In the following recipes, we are also going to learn how to debug our React/Redux application.

Testing our first component with Jest and Enzyme

In this recipe, we are going to learn how to install and configure Jest in our project.

Getting ready

In this recipe, we need to install a few packages to test our React application:

```
npm install --save-dev jest jsdom enzyme enzyme-adapter-react-16 identity-
obj-proxy
```

How to do it...

After we've installed Jest, we need to configure it:

1. Add the `tests` scripts and the Jest configuration into our `package.json`:

```
{
  "name": "react-pro",
  "version": "1.0.0",
  "scripts": {
    "clean": "rm -rf dist/ && rm -rf public/app",
    "start": "npm run clean & NODE_ENV=development
    BABEL_ENV=development nodemon src/server --watch src/server --
    watch src/shared --exec babel-node --presets es2015",
    "start-analyzer": "npm run clean && NODE_ENV=development
    BABEL_ENV=development ANALYZER=true babel-node src/server",
    "test": "node scripts/test.js src --env=jsdom",
    "coverage": "node scripts/test.js src --coverage --env=jsdom"
  },
  "jest": {
    "setupTestFrameworkScriptFile": "
    <rootDir>/config/jest/setupTestFramework.js",
    "collectCoverageFrom": [
      "src/**/*.{js,jsx}"
    ],
    "setupFiles": [
      "<rootDir>/config/jest/browserMocks.js"
    ],
    "moduleNameMapper": {
      "^.+\\.(scss)$": "identity-obj-proxy"
    }
```

```
},
"author": "Carlos Santana",
"license": "MIT",
"dependencies": {
  "axios": "^0.18.0",
  "babel-preset-stage-0": "^6.24.1",
  "express": "^4.15.4",
  "react": "^16.3.2",
  "react-dom": "^16.3.2",
  "react-redux": "^5.0.6",
  "react-router-dom": "^4.2.2",
  "redux": "^4.0.0",
  "redux-devtools-extension": "^2.13.2",
  "redux-thunk": "^2.2.0"
},
"devDependencies": {
  "babel-cli": "^6.26.0",
  "babel-core": "^6.26.0",
  "babel-eslint": "^8.2.3",
  "babel-loader": "^7.1.2",
  "babel-plugin-module-resolver": "^3.1.1",
  "babel-preset-env": "^1.6.0",
  "babel-preset-es2015": "^6.24.1",
  "babel-preset-react": "^6.24.1",
  "compression-webpack-plugin": "^1.0.0",
  "css-loader": "^0.28.5",
  "enzyme": "^3.3.0",
  "enzyme-adapter-react-16": "^1.1.1",
  "eslint": "^4.5.0",
  "eslint-plugin-babel": "^5.1.0",
  "eslint-plugin-import": "^2.7.0",
  "eslint-plugin-jsx-a11y": "^6.0.2",
  "eslint-plugin-react": "^7.8.2",
  "eslint-plugin-standard": "^3.0.1",
  "extract-text-webpack-plugin": "4.0.0-beta.0",
  "husky": "^0.14.3",
  "identity-obj-proxy": "^3.0.0",
  "jest": "^23.1.0",
  "jsdom": "^11.11.0",
  "node-sass": "^4.5.3",
  "nodemon": "^1.17.4",
  "react-hot-loader": "^4.2.0",
  "redux-mock-store": "^1.5.1",
  "sass-loader": "^7.0.1",
  "style-loader": "^0.21.0",
  "webpack": "^4.8.3",
  "webpack-bundle-analyzer": "^2.9.0",
  "webpack-dev-middleware": "^3.1.3",
```

```
    "webpack-hot-middleware": "^2.18.2",
    "webpack-hot-server-middleware": "^0.5.0",
    "webpack-merge": "^4.1.0",
    "webpack-node-externals": "^1.6.0",
    "webpack-notifier": "^1.6.0"
  }
}
```

File: package.json

2. As you can see in our Jest configuration, we need to add the `setupTestFramework.js` file where we'll configure our enzyme to use it with Jest:

```
import { configure } from 'enzyme';
import Adapter from 'enzyme-adapter-react-16';

configure({ adapter: new Adapter() });
```

File: config/jest/setupTestFramework.js

3. In the `setupFiles` node, we can specify our `browserMocks.js` file, which is where we can mock any browser method we use in our App. For example, if you want to test `localStorage` in your app, this file is the proper place to mock it:

```
// Browser Mocks
const requestAnimationFrameMock = callback => {
  setTimeout(callback, 0);
};

Object.defineProperty(window, 'requestAnimationFrame', {
  value: requestAnimationFrameMock
});

const localStorageMock = (() => {
  let store = {}

  return {
    getItem: key => store[key] || null,
    setItem: (key, value) => store[key] = value.toString(),
    removeItem: key => delete store[key],
    clear: () => store = {}
  };
})();

Object.defineProperty(window, 'localStorage', {
  value: localStorageMock
```

```
});
```

File: config/jest/browserMocks.js

4. If you are using Sass, Stylus, or Less in your components, you need to specify the `moduleNameMapper` mode with a regex to match all the `.scss` files (or `.styl/.less`) in your project and handle those files with `identity-obj-proxy`, which is a package that mocks Webpack imports, such as CSS modules.
5. You may have noticed we added two new NPM scripts: one for test our app and the other to get the coverage (percentage of covered unit tests). For those, we are using a particular script, which is at `scripts/test.js`, let's create that file:

```
// Set the NODE_ENV to test
process.env.NODE_ENV = 'test';
// Requiring jest
const jest = require('jest');

// Getting the arguments from the terminal
const argv = process.argv.slice(2);
// Runing Jest passing the arguments
jest.run(argv);
```

File: scripts/test.js

6. Let's imagine we have this `Home` component:

```
import React from 'react';
import styles from './Home.scss';

const Home = props => (
  <h1 className={styles.Home}>Hello {props.name || 'World'}</h1>
);

export default Home;
```

File: src/client/home/index.jsx

7. If you want to test this component, you need to create a file with the same name but add the `.test` suffix in the file. In this case, our test file will be named `index.test.jsx`:

```
// Dependencies
import React from 'react';
import { shallow } from 'enzyme';

// Component to test...
import Home from './index';

describe('Home', () => {
  const subject = shallow(<Home />);
  const subjectWithProps = shallow(<Home name="Carlos" />);

  it('should render Home component', () => {
    expect(subject.length).toBe(1);
  });

  it('should render by default Hello World', () => {
    expect(subject.text()).toBe('Hello World');
  });

  it('should render the name prop', () => {
    expect(subjectWithProps.text()).toBe('Hello Carlos');
  });

  it('should has .Home class', () => {
    expect(subject.find('h1').hasClass('Home')).toBe(true);
  });
});
```

File: src/client/home/index.test.jsx

How it works...

If you want to test your application, you need to run the following command:

```
npm test
```

If your test is correct, you should see this result:

```
→ testing git:(master) ✗ npm test

> react-pro@1.0.0 test /Users/czantany/projects/React16Cookbook/Chapter11/Recipe1/testing
> node scripts/test.js src --env=jsdom

 PASS  src/client/home/index.test.jsx
  Home
    ✓ should render Home component (3ms)
    ✓ should render by default Hello World (3ms)
    ✓ should render the name prop (1ms)
    ✓ should has .Home class (3ms)

Test Suites: 1 passed, 1 total
Tests:       4 passed, 4 total
Snapshots:   0 total
Time:        1.183s
Ran all test suites matching /src/i.
```

The `PASS` label means that all of your tests in that file passed successfully; if you failed at least one test, you would see the `FAIL` label. Let's modify our `"should has .Home class` test. I'm going to change the value to `"Home2"` to force the fail:

```
➜ testing git:(master) ✗ npm test

> react-pro@1.0.0 test /Users/czantany/projects/React16Cookbook/Chapter11/Recipe1/testing
> node scripts/test.js src --env=jsdom

 FAIL  src/client/home/index.test.jsx
  Home
    ✓ should render Home component (3ms)
    ✓ should render by default Hello World (1ms)
    ✓ should render the name prop
    ✕ should has .Home class (9ms)

  ● Home › should has .Home class

    expect(received).toBe(expected) // Object.is equality

    Expected: true
    Received: false

      23 |
      24 |   it('should has .Home class', () => {
    > 25 |     expect(subject.find('h1').hasClass('Home2')).toBe(true);
         |                                                  ^
      26 |   });
      27 | });
      28 |

      at Object.<anonymous> (src/client/home/index.test.jsx:25:50)

Test Suites: 1 failed, 1 total
Tests:       1 failed, 3 passed, 4 total
Snapshots:   0 total
Time:        1.532s
Ran all test suites matching /src/i.
```

As you can see, now we got the `FAIL` label and specified with an X the failed test. Also, the `Expected` and `Received` values provide useful information, with these, we can see which value is expected and which value is being received.

There's more...

Now if you want to see the coverage percentage of all your unit tests, you can use the following command:

```
npm run coverage
```

Right now we only have 1 unit test for our `Home` component as you can see is in color green and at 100%, all the other files are in red with 0% because those have not been tested yet:

```
➜ testing git:(master) ✗ npm run coverage

> react-pro@1.0.0 coverage /Users/czantany/projects/React16Cookbook/Chapter11/Recipe1/testing
> node scripts/test.js src --coverage --env=jsdom

 PASS  src/client/home/index.test.jsx
  Home
    ✓ should render Home component (3ms)
    ✓ should render by default Hello World (1ms)
    ✓ should render the name prop
    ✓ should has .Home class (3ms)

----------------------------|----------|----------|----------|----------|-------------------|
File                        |  % Stmts | % Branch |  % Funcs |  % Lines | Uncovered Line #s |
----------------------------|----------|----------|----------|----------|-------------------|
All files                   |     0.88 |     3.85 |     2.27 |     0.94 |                   |
 client                     |        0 |        0 |        0 |        0 |                   |
  App.jsx                   |        0 |        0 |      100 |        0 |... ,8,11,17,18,25 |
  index.jsx                 |        0 |        0 |        0 |        0 |... 21,32,35,36,37 |
 client/about               |        0 |        0 |        0 |        0 |                   |
  index.jsx                 |        0 |        0 |        0 |        0 |  1,2,3,4,6,10,14  |
 client/home                |      100 |      100 |      100 |      100 |                   |
  index.jsx                 |      100 |      100 |      100 |      100 |                   |
 client/todo                |        0 |      100 |        0 |        0 |                   |
  index.jsx                 |        0 |      100 |        0 |        0 |      2,5,8,11,14  |
 client/todo/actions        |        0 |      100 |        0 |        0 |                   |
  actionTypes.js            |        0 |      100 |        0 |        0 |             2,3,4 |
  index.js                  |        0 |      100 |        0 |        0 |... 11,12,14,16,17 |
 client/todo/api            |        0 |        0 |      100 |        0 |                   |
  constants.js              |        0 |      100 |      100 |        0 |                 1 |
  index.js                  |        0 |        0 |      100 |        0 |   2,5,8,11,17,21  |
 client/todo/components     |        0 |        0 |        0 |        0 |                   |
  Layout.jsx                |        0 |      100 |        0 |        0 |    2,5,6,7,10,12  |
  Todo.jsx                  |        0 |        0 |        0 |        0 |... 20,22,23,26,30 |
 client/todo/container      |        0 |      100 |        0 |        0 |                   |
  index.js                  |        0 |      100 |        0 |        0 |    2,3,6,9,11,13  |
 client/todo/reducer        |        0 |        0 |        0 |        0 |                   |
  index.js                  |        0 |        0 |        0 |        0 |... 13,14,15,17,23 |
 server                     |        0 |        0 |        0 |        0 |                   |
  index.js                  |        0 |        0 |        0 |        0 |... 65,67,72,75,78 |
 server/controllers         |        0 |      100 |        0 |        0 |                   |
  api.js                    |        0 |      100 |        0 |        0 |      1,3,6,21,22  |
 server/render              |        0 |        0 |        0 |        0 |                   |
  clientRender.js           |        0 |        0 |        0 |        0 |    2,5,8,9,10,13  |
  html.js                   |        0 |        0 |        0 |        0 |... 14,16,17,18,21 |
  initialState.js           |        0 |      100 |      100 |        0 |                 1 |
  serverRender.js           |        0 |        0 |        0 |        0 |... 37,40,43,53,60 |
 shared/components/layout   |        0 |        0 |        0 |        0 |                   |
  Content.jsx               |        0 |      100 |        0 |        0 |     1,2,4,5,7,14  |
  Footer.jsx                |        0 |      100 |        0 |        0 |             1,2,4 |
  Header.jsx                |        0 |        0 |        0 |        0 |1,2,3,5,8,11,13,23 |
 shared/reducers            |        0 |        0 |        0 |        0 |                   |
  deviceReducer.js          |        0 |        0 |        0 |        0 |               1,2 |
  index.js                  |        0 |      100 |      100 |        0 |          2,5,8,10 |
 shared/redux               |        0 |      100 |        0 |        0 |                   |
  baseActions.js            |        0 |      100 |        0 |        0 |               2,6 |
  configureStore.js         |        0 |      100 |        0 |        0 |  2,3,4,7,9,10,14  |
 shared/routes              |        0 |      100 |      100 |        0 |                   |
  index.js                  |        0 |      100 |      100 |        0 |   1,2,5,6,7,9,28  |
 shared/utils               |        0 |        0 |        0 |        0 |                   |
  device.js                 |        0 |        0 |        0 |        0 |     2,6,10,14,15  |
  frontend.jsx              |        0 |        0 |        0 |        0 |      2,5,6,17,27  |
----------------------------|----------|----------|----------|----------|-------------------|
Test Suites: 1 passed, 1 total
Tests:       4 passed, 4 total
Snapshots:   0 total
Time:        3.012s
Ran all test suites matching /src/i.
```

Also, the coverage command generates an HTML version of the result. There is a directory called `"coverage"` and inside other called `"Icov-report"`. If you open `index.html` in your browser, you will see something like this:

All files

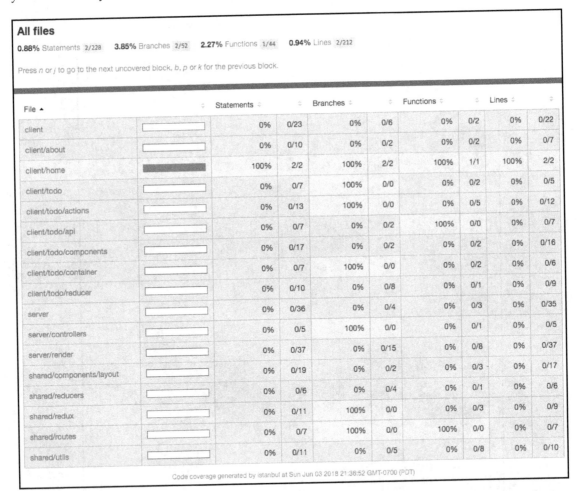

0.88% Statements 2/228 **3.85%** Branches 2/52 **2.27%** Functions 1/44 **0.94%** Lines 2/212

Press *n* or *j* to go to the next uncovered block, *b*, *p* or *k* for the previous block.

File ▲		Statements		Branches		Functions		Lines	
client		0%	0/23	0%	0/6	0%	0/2	0%	0/22
client/about		0%	0/10	0%	0/2	0%	0/2	0%	0/7
client/home		100%	2/2	100%	2/2	100%	1/1	100%	2/2
client/todo		0%	0/7	100%	0/0	0%	0/2	0%	0/5
client/todo/actions		0%	0/13	100%	0/0	0%	0/5	0%	0/12
client/todo/api		0%	0/7	0%	0/2	100%	0/0	0%	0/7
client/todo/components		0%	0/17	0%	0/2	0%	0/2	0%	0/16
client/todo/container		0%	0/7	100%	0/0	0%	0/2	0%	0/6
client/todo/reducer		0%	0/10	0%	0/8	0%	0/1	0%	0/9
server		0%	0/36	0%	0/4	0%	0/3	0%	0/35
server/controllers		0%	0/5	100%	0/0	0%	0/1	0%	0/5
server/render		0%	0/37	0%	0/15	0%	0/8	0%	0/37
shared/components/layout		0%	0/19	0%	0/2	0%	0/3	0%	0/17
shared/reducers		0%	0/6	0%	0/4	0%	0/1	0%	0/6
shared/redux		0%	0/11	100%	0/0	0%	0/3	0%	0/9
shared/routes		0%	0/7	100%	0/0	100%	0/0	0%	0/7
shared/utils		0%	0/11	0%	0/5	0%	0/8	0%	0/10

Code coverage generated by istanbul at Sun Jun 03 2018 21:36:52 GMT-0700 (PDT)

Testing a Redux Container, Actions, and Reducers

In this recipe, we are going to test a Redux Container, Actions, and Reducers. For this example, we will test the Todo list that we created in `Chapter 11`, *Implementing Server-Side Rendering*.

TIP: Remember always that we use an existing recipe you must run npm install command first to restore all the project dependencies otherwise, you will get dependency errors.

Getting Ready

We need to install the `redux-mock-store`, `moxios`, and `redux-thunk` packages to test our Redux containers. You will need to run `npm install` first to install all the dependencies:

```
npm install // This is to install the previous packages
npm install redux-mock-store moxios redux-thunk
```

How to do it...

Let's test our Redux containers:

1. Redux containers should not have any JSX code; the best practice is to have `mapStateToProps` and `mapDispatchToProps` in our `connect` method passing another component (such as a `Layout` component) in the export, for example, let's see our Todo List Container:

```
// Dependencies
import { connect } from 'react-redux';
import { bindActionCreators } from 'redux';

// Components
import Layout from '../components/Layout';

// Actions
import { fetchTodo } from '../actions';

export default connect(({ todo }) => ({
  todo: todo.list
}), dispatch => bindActionCreators(
  {
    fetchTodo
  },
  dispatch
))(Layout);
```

File: src/client/todo/container/index.js

2. You might be wondering what exactly we need to test in here. Well, the most important things we need to test in a container are the action dispatch (the `fetchTodo` action) and get our `todo` state from Redux with data. That being said, this is our container unit test file:

```
// Dependencies
import React from 'react';
import { shallow } from 'enzyme';
import configureStore from 'redux-mock-store';

// Actions
import { fetchTodo } from '../actions';

// Testable Container
import Container from './index';

// Mocking Initial State
const mockInitialState = {
  todo: {
    list: [
      {
        id: 1,
        title: 'Go to the Gym'
      },
      {
        id: 2,
        title: 'Dentist Appointment'
      },
      {
        id: 3,
        title: 'Finish homework'
      }
    ]
  }
};

// Configuring Mock Store
const mockStore = configureStore()(mockInitialState);

// Mocking the Actions
jest.mock('../actions', () => ({
  fetchTodo: jest.fn().mockReturnValue({ type: 'mock-
FETCH_TODO_SUCCESS' })
}));

describe('Todo Container', () => {
  let mockParams;
```

```
    let container;

    beforeEach(() => {
      fetchTodo.mockClear();
      mockParams = {};
      mockStore.clearActions();
      container = shallow(<Container {...mockParams}
store={mockStore} />);
    });

    it('should dispatch fetchTodo', () => {
      const { fetchTodo } = container.props();

      fetchTodo();

      const actions = mockStore.getActions();

      expect(actions).toEqual([{ type: 'mock-FETCH_TODO_SUCCESS'
}]);
    });

    it('should map todo and get the todo list from Initial State',
() => {
      const { todo } = container.props();
      const { todo: { list }} = mockInitialState;

      expect(todo).toEqual(list);
    });
  });
```

File: src/client/todo/container/index.test.js

3. Test the `fetchTodo` action. This is the code for our action file:

```
// Base Actions
import { request, received } from '@baseActions';

// Api
import api from '../api';

// Action Types
import { FETCH_TODO } from './actionTypes';

export const fetchTodo = () => dispatch => {
  const action = FETCH_TODO;
  const { fetchTodo } = api;

  dispatch(request(action));
```

```
    return fetchTodo()
      .then(response => dispatch(received(action, response.data)));
  };
```

File: src/client/todo/actions/index.js

4. This is our `actionTypes.js` file:

```
// Actions
export const FETCH_TODO = {
  request: () => 'FETCH_TODO_REQUEST',
  success: () => 'FETCH_TODO_SUCCESS'
};
```

File: src/client/todo/actions/actionTypes.js

5. To test an async Redux Action, we need to use `redux-thunk` and `moxios` to test an action that is using `axios` to retrieve data from the server. Our test file should look like this:

```
// Dependencies
import configureMockStore from 'redux-mock-store';
import thunk from 'redux-thunk';
import moxios from 'moxios';

// Action
import { fetchTodo } from './index';

// Action Types
import { FETCH_TODO } from './actionTypes';

// Configuring Store with Thunk middleware
const mockStore = configureMockStore([thunk]);

// Response Mock
const todoResponseMock = [
  {
    id: 1,
    title: 'Go to the Gym'
  },
  {
    id: 2,
    title: 'Dentist Appointment'
  },
  {
    id: 3,
    title: 'Finish homework'
```

```
  }
];

describe('fetchTodo action', () => {
  beforeEach(() => {
    moxios.install();
  });

  afterEach(() => {
    moxios.uninstall();
  });

  it('should fetch the Todo List', () => {
    moxios.wait(() => {
      const req = moxios.requests.mostRecent();

      req.respondWith({
        status: 200,
        response: todoResponseMock
      });
    });

    const expectedActions = [
      {
        type: FETCH_TODO.request()
      },
      {
        type: FETCH_TODO.success(),
        payload: todoResponseMock
      }
    ];

    const store = mockStore({ todo: [] })

    return store.dispatch(fetchTodo()).then(() => {
      expect(store.getActions()).toEqual(expectedActions);
    });
  });
});
```

File: src/client/todo/actions/index.test.js

6. Let's test our reducer. This is the Todo reducer file:

```
// Utils
import { getNewState } from '@utils/frontend';

// Action Types
import { FETCH_TODO } from '../actions/actionTypes';

// Initial State
const initialState = {
  list: []
};

export default function todoReducer(state = initialState, action)
{
  switch (action.type) {
    case FETCH_TODO.success(): {
      const { payload: { response = [] } } = action;

      return getNewState(state, {
        list: response
      });
    }

    default:
      return state;
  }
}
```

File: src/client/todo/reducer/index.js

7. We need to test two things in our reducer: the initial state and the state when the `FETCH_TODO` action is a success:

```
// Reducer
import todo from './index';

// Action Types
import { FETCH_TODO } from '../actions/actionTypes';

// Initial State
const initialState = {
  list: []
};

describe('Todo List Reducer', () => {
  it('should return the initial state', () => {
    const expectedInitialState = todo(undefined, {});
```

```
    expect(expectedInitialState).toEqual(initialState);
  });

  it('should handle FETCH_TODO when is success', () => {
    const action = {
      type: FETCH_TODO.success(),
      payload: {
        response: [
          {
            id: 1,
            title: 'Go to the Gym'
          },
          {
            id: 2,
            title: 'Dentist Appointment'
          },
          {
            id: 3,
            title: 'Finish homework'
          }
        ]
      }
    };

    const expectedState = {
      list: action.payload.response
    };

    const state = todo(initialState, action);

    expect(state).toEqual(expectedState);
  });
});
```

File: src/client/todo/reducer/index.test.js

Debugging a React application using React and Redux Dev Tools

Debugging is essential for any application, it helps us to identify and fix bugs. Chrome has two powerful tools to debug React/Redux applications integrating those to its Developer Tools. React Dev Tool and Redux Dev Tool.

Getting Ready

Using Google Chrome, you have to install both extensions:

- **React Developer Tools**: `https://chrome.google.com/webstore/detail/react-developer-tools/fmkadmapgofadopljbjfkapdkoienihi`
- **Redux DevTools**: `https://chrome.google.com/webstore/detail/redux-devtools/lmhkpmbekcpmknklioeibfkpmmfibljd?hl=es`

Also, you need to install the `redux-devtools-extension` package:

```
npm install --save-dev redux-devtools-extension
```

Once you've installed React Developer Tools and Redux DevTools, you need to configure them.

If you try to use Redux DevTools directly, it won't work; this is because we need to pass the `composeWithDevTools` method into our Redux store, this should be our `configureStore.js` file:

```
// Dependencies
import { createStore, applyMiddleware } from 'redux';
import thunk from 'redux-thunk';
import { composeWithDevTools } from 'redux-devtools-extension';

// Root Reducer
import rootReducer from '@reducers';

export default function configureStore({ initialState, appName,
reducer }) {
  const middleware = [
    thunk
  ];

  return createStore(
    rootReducer,
    initialState,
    composeWithDevTools(applyMiddleware(...middleware))
  );
}
```

File: src/shared/redux/configureStore.js

How to do it...

Let's debug our application:

1. If you want to debug your React application, open your application with Google Chrome (`http://localhost:3000/todo`), open your Google Dev Tools (Right click > Inspect), select the React tab, and you will see your React components:

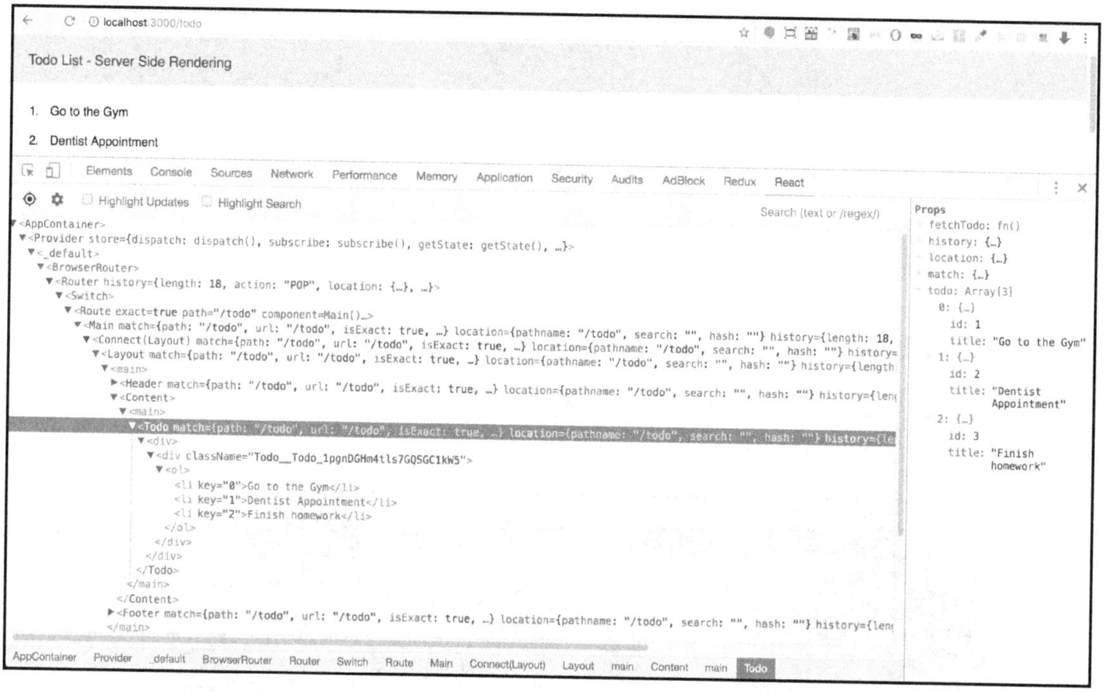

2. You can select the component you want to debug, and one of the coolest things is that you can see the props of your component in the right side:

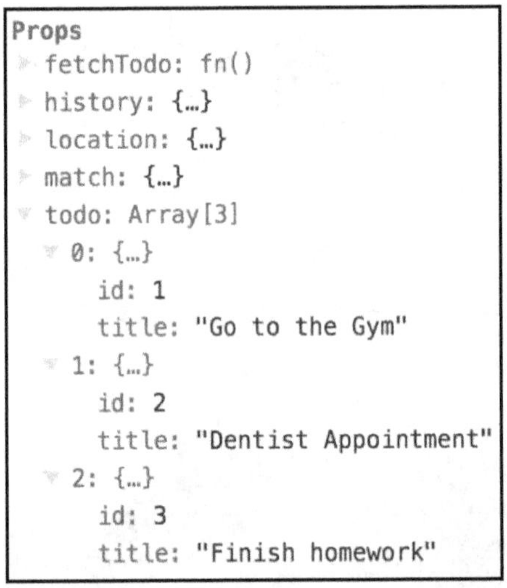

3. If you want to debug Redux in your application and see which actions are being dispatched, you need to select the Redux tab in your Chrome Dev Tools:

4. We are dispatching two actions in our Todo application: `FETCH_TODO_REQUEST` and `FETCH_TODO_SUCCESS`. The `@@INIT` action is being dispatched by default in Redux, and this happens in any application.
5. If you select the `FETCH_TODO_REQUEST` action, you will see that on the Diff tab it says, "(states are equal)". That means there were no changes within that action, but you have four tabs: **Action**, **State**, **Diff**, and **Test**.

6. If you select the **Action** tab, you can see that specific action:

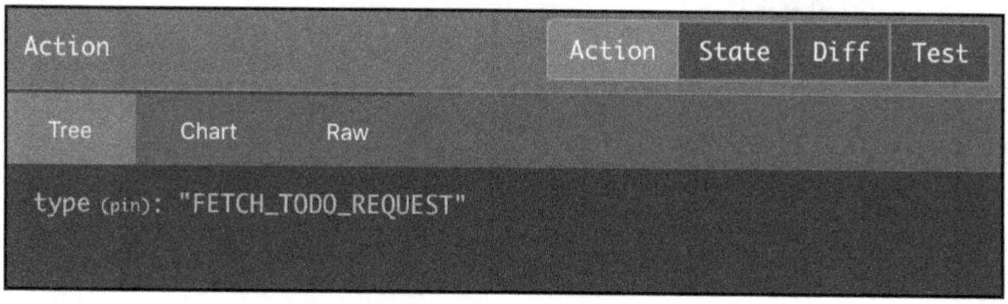

7. If you select `FETCH_TODO_SUCCESS`, you will see the data for the todo reducer:

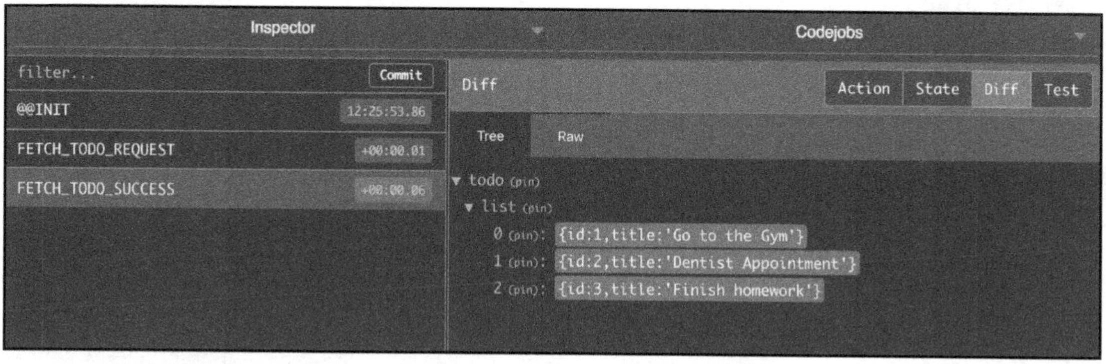

Simulating Events

In this recipe, we are going to learn how to simulate the `onClick` and `onChange` events on a simple Calculator component.

How to do it...

We will re-use the code of the last recipe (`Repository: Chapter12/Recipe3/debugging`):

1. We will create a simple `Calculator` component to sum two values (input) and then we will get the result when the user clicks on the equals (=) button:

```
import React, { Component } from 'react';
import styles from './Calculator.scss';
```

```
class Calculator extends Component {
  state = {
    number1: 0,
    number2: 0,
    result: 0
  };

  handleOnChange = e => {
    const { target: { value, name } } = e;

    this.setState({
      [name]: value
    });
  }

  handleResult = () => {
    this.setState({
      result: Number(this.state.number1) +
Number(this.state.number2)
    });
  }

  render() {
    return (
      <div className={styles.Calculator}>
        <h1>Calculator</h1>

        <input
          name="number1"
          value={this.state.number1}
          onChange={this.handleOnChange}
        />

        {' + '}

        <input
          name="number2"
          value={this.state.number2}
          onChange={this.handleOnChange}
        />

        <button onClick={this.handleResult}>
          =
        </button>

        <input
          name="result"
          value={this.state.result}
```

```
            />
          </div>
        );
      }
    }

    export default Calculator;
```

File: src/client/calculator/index.jsx

2. If you want to see this component in your browser (it was created for testing purpose), you need to include it in your routes file:

```
    import React from 'react';
    import { Switch, Route } from 'react-router-dom';

    // Components
    import Calculator from '../../client/calculator';

    const paths = [
      {
        component: Calculator,
        exact: true,
        path: '/'
      }
    ];

    const all = (
      <Switch>
        <Route exact path={paths[0].path}
  component={paths[0].component} />
      </Switch>
    );

    export default {
      paths,
      all
    };
```

File: src/shared/routes/index.jsx

3. If you want to see some basic styles, we can use these:

```
    .Calculator {
      padding: 100px;

      input {
          width: 50px;
```

```
        height: 50px;
        padding: 40px;
        font-size: 24px;
    }

    button {
        padding: 10px;
        margin: 10px;
    }
}
```

File: src/client/calculator/Calculator.scss

4. In our test file, we need to simulate the `onChange` event to change the values of our input and then simulate the click on the equals (=) button:

```
// Dependencies
import React from 'react';
import { shallow } from 'enzyme';

// Component to test...
import Calculator from './index';

describe('Calculator', () => {
  const subject = shallow(<Calculator />);

  it('should render Calculator component', () => {
    expect(subject.length).toBe(1);
  });

  it('should modify the state onChange', () => {
    subject.find('input[name="number1"]').simulate('change', {
      target: {
        name: 'number1',
        value: 5
      }
    });

    subject.find('input[name="number2"]').simulate('change', {
      target: {
        name: 'number2',
        value: 15
      }
    });

    // Getting the values of the number1 and number2 states
    expect(subject.state('number1')).toBe(5);
    expect(subject.state('number2')).toBe(15);
```

```
  });

  it('should perform the sum when the user clicks the = button',
  () => {
    // Simulating the click event
    subject.find('button').simulate('click');

    // Getting the result value
    expect(subject.state('result')).toBe(20);
  });
});
```

How it works...

If you want to see the component in your browser, run the application using `npm start`, and you will see something like this:

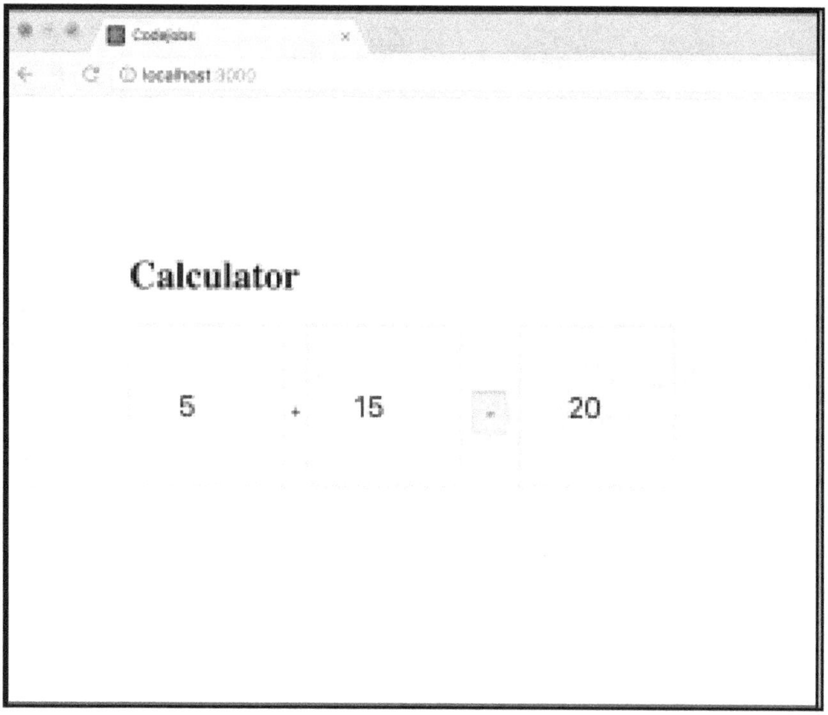

Now let's test our calculator by using the `npm test` command:

```
→ simulating-events git:(master) × npm test

> react-pro@1.0.0 test /Users/carlos.santana/projects/React16Book/Chapter12/Recipe4/simulating-events
> node scripts/test.js src --env=jsdom

 PASS  src/client/calculator/index.test.jsx
  Calculator
    ✓ should render Calculator component (4ms)
    ✓ should modify the state onChange (8ms)
    ✓ should perform the sum when the user clicks the = button (1ms)

Test Suites: 1 passed, 1 total
Tests:       3 passed, 3 total
Snapshots:   0 total
Time:        1.393s, estimated 2s
Ran all test suites matching /src/i.
```

13
Deploying to Production

In this chapter, the following recipes will be covered:

- Deploying to production on Digital Ocean
- Configuring Nginx, PM2, and a domain in our Droplet
- Implementing Jenkins (continuous integration)

Introduction

If you are reading this chapter, it's probably because you have completed your React Application (congratulations!). Now it's time to deploy it to production and show it to the world. In this chapter, we will learn how to deploy our React Application using one of the best cloud services: Digital Ocean.

> At this point, you will need to invest some money in renting the servers you will need. I will show you the cheapest way to do this, and then, if you want to increase the power of your servers, you will be able to do it without re-doing the configurations.

Deploying to production on Digital Ocean

Digital Ocean is my favorite cloud-computing platform for using virtual servers (droplets) because it is effortless to create, configure, and delete droplets, and the price is low (you can get a droplet for $5 per month—that means $0.007 per hour). Another reason why I think Digital Ocean is fantastic is that they have all the documentation up to date and customer service is quick to solve any problem you may have.

For this recipe, we are going to use Ubuntu 18.04, so you will need to know some basic Linux commands to be able to configure your droplet. If you are entirely new to Linux, don't worry, I'll try to explain each step in a straightforward way.

Getting ready

First, you need to create your Digital Ocean account, go to `https://www.digitalocean.com`. You can sign up with your Google account; this is the recommended way. Once you click on the **register** link with Google, you will see the Billing Info view:

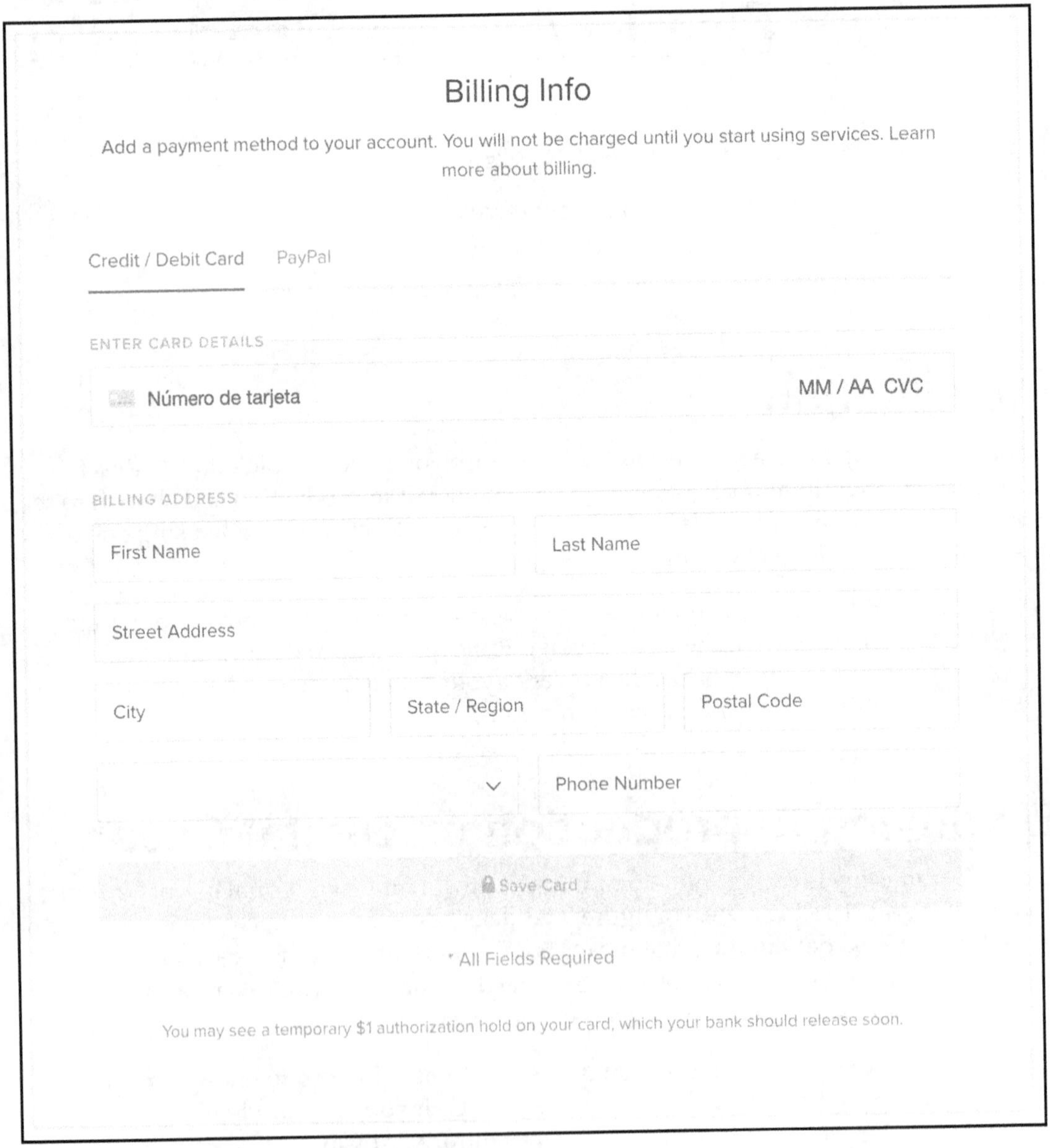

Billing Info
Add a payment method to your account. You will not be charged until you start using services. Learn more about billing.
Credit / Debit Card
PayPal
ENTER CARD DETAILS
Número de tarjeta
MM / AA CVC
BILLING ADDRESS
First Name
Last Name
Street Address
City
State / Region
Postal Code
Phone Number
Save Card
* All Fields Required
You may see a temporary $1 authorization hold on your card, which your bank should release soon.

You can register your Credit/Debit Card, or you can pay with PayPal. Once you've configured your payment information, you are ready to create your first Droplet:

How to do it...

Let's create our first Droplet:

1. Choose your Linux distribution; as I mentioned before, we are going to use Ubuntu 18.04:

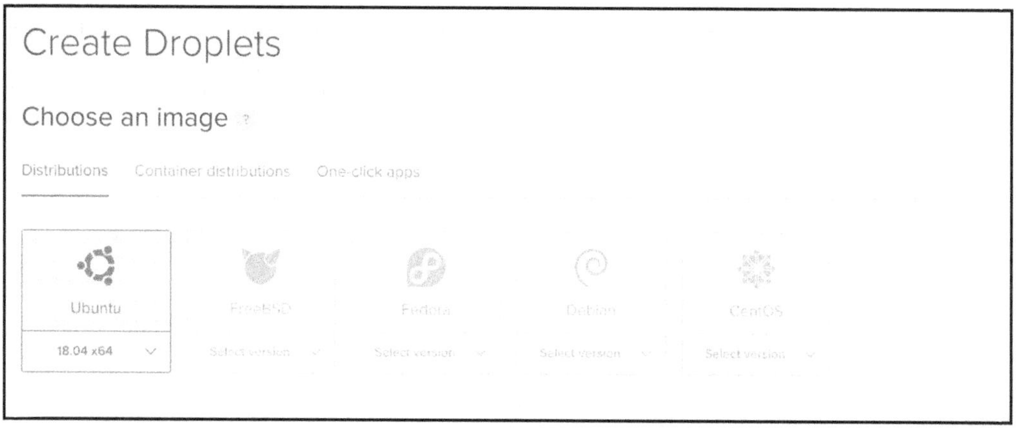

2. One-click apps are preconfigured Droplets, but I prefer to set my Droplet from scratch to have the control and be able to optimize my configuration. After this recipe, if you want to take a look at these options if you need to configure something quickly, that's fine:

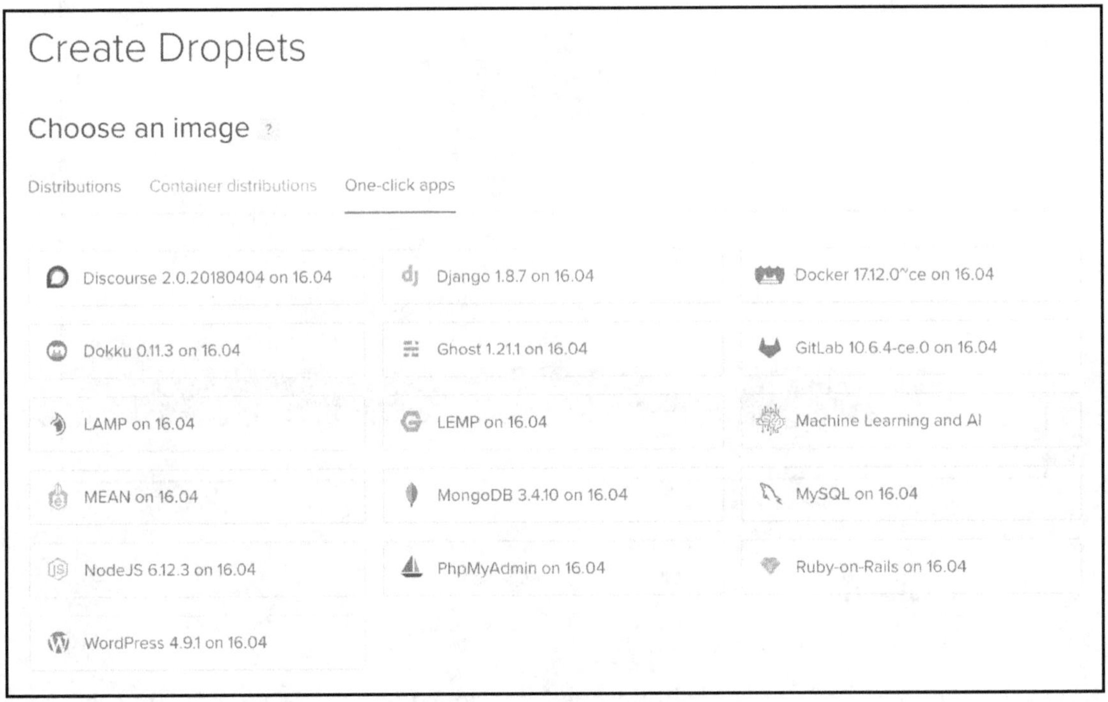

3. Choose the size of your Droplet. I prefer to use the 2 GB RAM Memory Droplet, which costs *$10 per month*. You might be wondering why I don't choose the cheapest version of 1 GB *RAM*; this is because I've tried to use this version, but I noticed that *1GB RAM* is not enough to handle NPM when you install the packages. Most of the time, this will hang up your Droplet—I know sounds ridiculous, but NPM consumes a lot of RAM.

4. If you choose the $10 Droplet, you don't have to pay that money right away. One of the best things about Digital Ocean is that they only charge you for the time you used your Droplet. That means that if after your complete this recipe (let's say you take 2 hours to complete it), you shut down (power off) your Droplet, you will only be charged for the 2 hours, which is *$0.030*. If you keep your Droplet on for the full month (30 days), you will be charged $10, so don't worry:

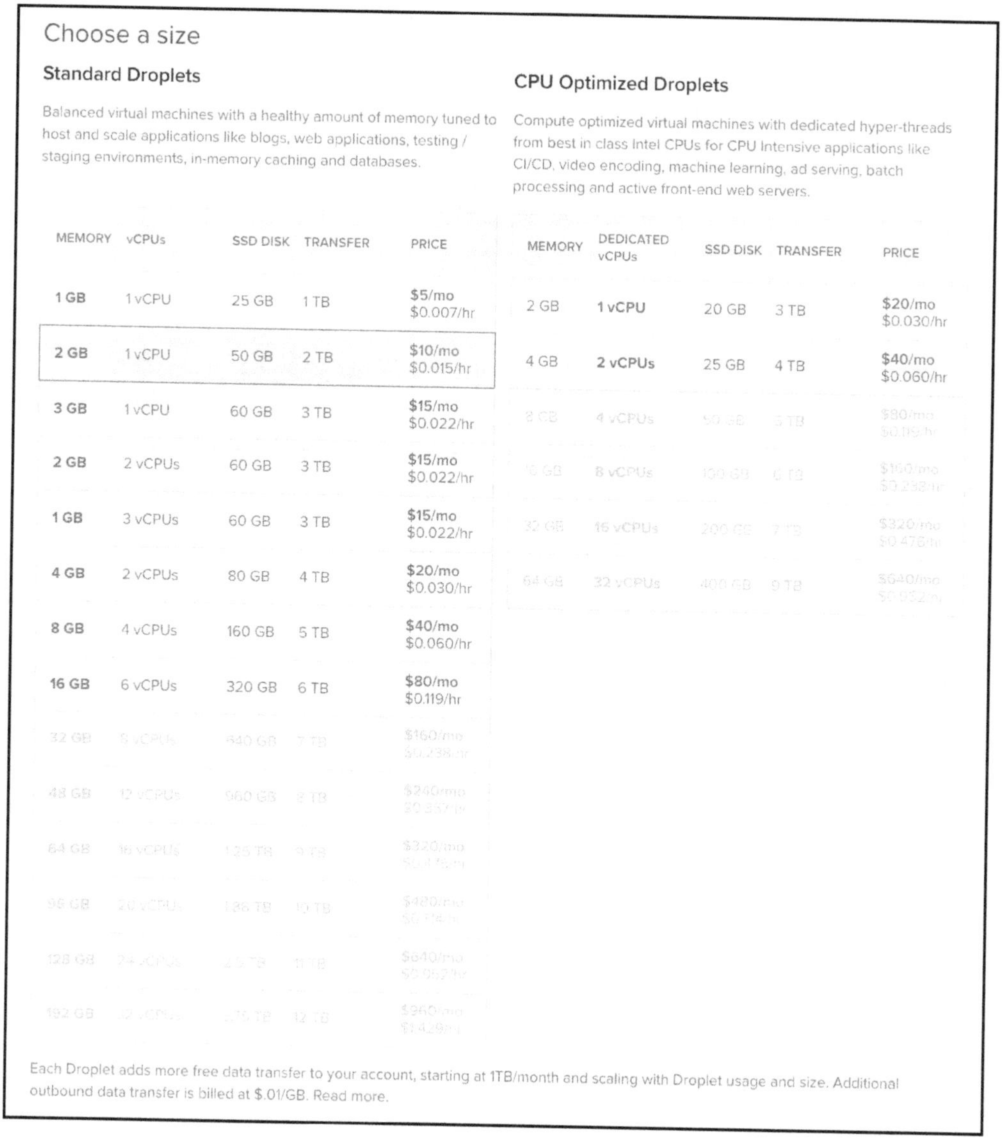

Choose a size

Standard Droplets

Balanced virtual machines with a healthy amount of memory tuned to host and scale applications like blogs, web applications, testing / staging environments, in-memory caching and databases.

MEMORY	vCPUs	SSD DISK	TRANSFER	PRICE
1 GB	1 vCPU	25 GB	1 TB	$5/mo $0.007/hr
2 GB	1 vCPU	50 GB	2 TB	$10/mo $0.015/hr
3 GB	1 vCPU	60 GB	3 TB	$15/mo $0.022/hr
2 GB	2 vCPUs	60 GB	3 TB	$15/mo $0.022/hr
1 GB	3 vCPUs	60 GB	3 TB	$15/mo $0.022/hr
4 GB	2 vCPUs	80 GB	4 TB	$20/mo $0.030/hr
8 GB	4 vCPUs	160 GB	5 TB	$40/mo $0.060/hr
16 GB	6 vCPUs	320 GB	6 TB	$80/mo $0.119/hr
32 GB	8 vCPUs	640 GB	7 TB	$160/mo $0.238/hr
48 GB	12 vCPUs	960 GB	8 TB	$240/mo [illegible]
64 GB	16 vCPUs	1.25 TB	9 TB	$320/mo [illegible]
96 GB	20 vCPUs	1.88 TB	10 TB	$480/mo [illegible]
128 GB	24 vCPUs	2.5 TB	11 TB	$640/mo [illegible]
192 GB	32 vCPUs	3.75 TB	12 TB	$960/mo [illegible]

CPU Optimized Droplets

Compute optimized virtual machines with dedicated hyper-threads from best in class Intel CPUs for CPU Intensive applications like CI/CD, video encoding, machine learning, ad serving, batch processing and active front-end web servers.

MEMORY	DEDICATED vCPUs	SSD DISK	TRANSFER	PRICE
2 GB	1 vCPU	20 GB	3 TB	$20/mo $0.030/hr
4 GB	2 vCPUs	25 GB	4 TB	$40/mo $0.060/hr
8 GB	4 vCPUs	50 GB	5 TB	$80/mo $0.119/hr
16 GB	8 vCPUs	100 GB	6 TB	$160/mo $0.238/hr
32 GB	16 vCPUs	200 GB	7 TB	$320/mo $0.476/hr
64 GB	32 vCPUs	400 GB	9 TB	$640/mo $0.952/hr

Each Droplet adds more free data transfer to your account, starting at 1TB/month and scaling with Droplet usage and size. Additional outbound data transfer is billed at $.01/GB. Read more.

5. Choose the datacenter region; this will depend on your location. If you're in the US, you will need to pick **New York** or **San Francisco**. You need to choose the datacenter closest to your location:

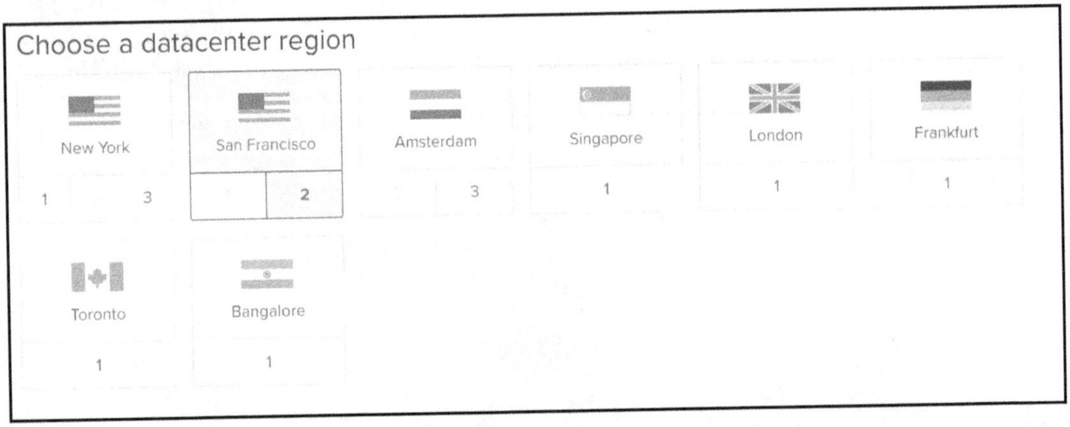

6. Name your Droplet. If you need more than one Droplet, you can select the amount here:

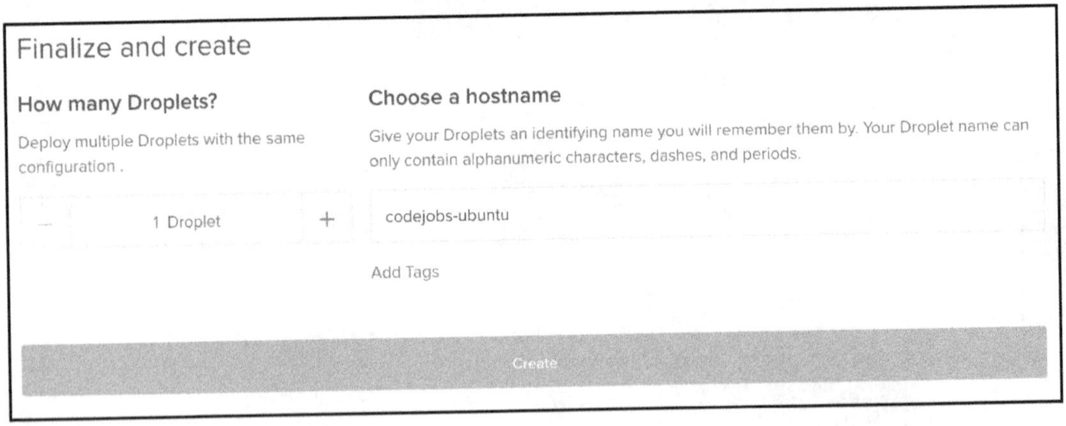

7. Once you click on the **Create** button, it will take 30-45 seconds to create your Droplet. Once it's completed, you will see your Droplet:

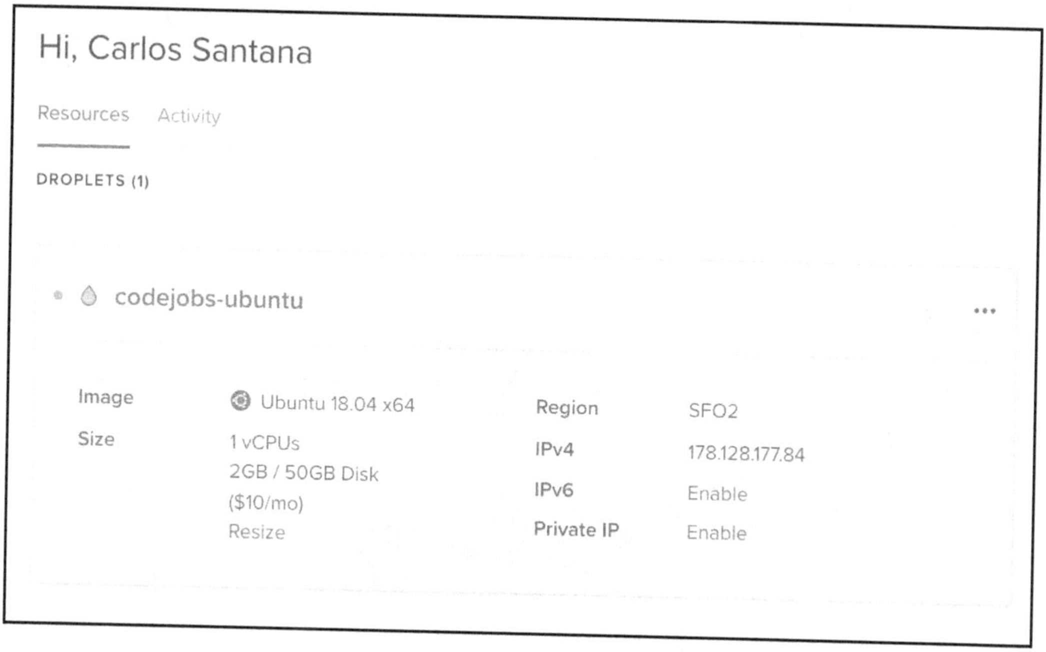

8. At this point, you should get an email with your server credentials:

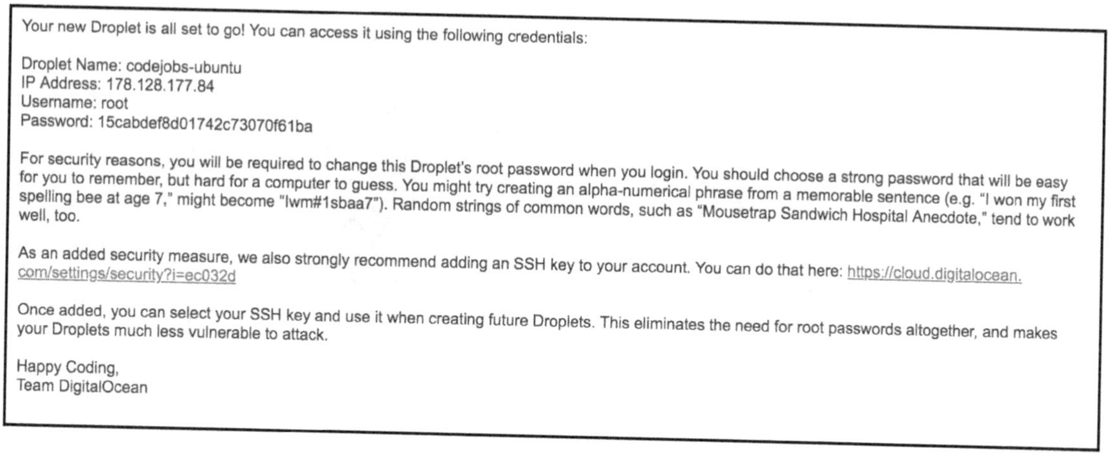

Your new Droplet is all set to go! You can access it using the following credentials:

Droplet Name: codejobs-ubuntu
IP Address: 178.128.177.84
Username: root
Password: 15cabdef8d01742c73070f61ba

For security reasons, you will be required to change this Droplet's root password when you login. You should choose a strong password that will be easy for you to remember, but hard for a computer to guess. You might try creating an alpha-numerical phrase from a memorable sentence (e.g. "I won my first spelling bee at age 7," might become "Iwm#1sbaa7"). Random strings of common words, such as "Mousetrap Sandwich Hospital Anecdote," tend to work well, too.

As an added security measure, we also strongly recommend adding an SSH key to your account. You can do that here: https://cloud.digitalocean.com/settings/security?i=ec032d

Once added, you can select your SSH key and use it when creating future Droplets. This eliminates the need for root passwords altogether, and makes your Droplets much less vulnerable to attack.

Happy Coding,
Team DigitalOcean

9. In your Terminal, you can access your Droplet with the `ssh root@YOUR_DROPLET_IP` command. When you access it for the first time, you will get a message to add this IP to your known hosts after you have to put in the Droplet password:

```
Last login: Sun Jun 17 17:08:20 on console
➜  ~ ssh root@178.128.177.84
The authenticity of host '178.128.177.84 (178.128.177.84)' can't be established.
ECDSA key fingerprint is SHA256:6YnKT4/Y1zOdtrgvFK509dKjAdLvuq0qjurs3YO1hdU.
Are you sure you want to continue connecting (yes/no)? yes
Warning: Permanently added '178.128.177.84' (ECDSA) to the list of known hosts.
root@178.128.177.84's password:
```

10. If everything works fine, you will be asked to change your UNIX password. You need to paste the current password and after you have to write the new password you want and retype it after you will be connected to the Droplet:

```
➜  ~ ssh root@178.128.177.84
root@178.128.177.84's password:
You are required to change your password immediately (root enforced)
Welcome to Ubuntu 18.04 LTS (GNU/Linux 4.15.0-22-generic x86_64)

 * Documentation:  https://help.ubuntu.com
 * Management:     https://landscape.canonical.com
 * Support:        https://ubuntu.com/advantage

  System information as of Mon Jun 18 02:33:08 UTC 2018

  System load:  0.0                Processes:           81
  Usage of /:   1.9% of 48.29GB    Users logged in:     0
  Memory usage: 5%                 IP address for eth0: 178.128.177.84
  Swap usage:   0%

  Get cloud support with Ubuntu Advantage Cloud Guest:
    http://www.ubuntu.com/business/services/cloud

0 packages can be updated.
0 updates are security updates.


The programs included with the Ubuntu system are free software;
the exact distribution terms for each program are described in the
individual files in /usr/share/doc/*/copyright.

Ubuntu comes with ABSOLUTELY NO WARRANTY, to the extent permitted by
applicable law.

Changing password for root.
(current) UNIX password:
Enter new UNIX password:
Retype new UNIX password:
root@codejobs-ubuntu:~#
```

11. Let's start configuring our Droplet. Install Node.js. For this, we will install the latest version of Node using a PPA. Right now, the current release of Node is 10.x. If when you are reading this recipe, Node has a new version, change the version in the command (setup_**10.x**):

```
cd ~
curl -sL https://deb.nodesource.com/setup_10.x -o nodesource_setup.sh
```

12. Once we get the `nodesource_setup.sh` file, run the following command:

```
sudo bash nodesource_setup.sh
```

13. To install Node, run the following:

```
sudo apt install nodejs -y
```

14. If you want to verify the version of Node and NPM you just installed, run:

```
node -v
v10.8.0
npm -v
6.2.0
```

How it works...

Using some of the recipes we performed in `Chapter 11`, *Implementing Server-Side Rendering*, I created a new GitHub repository with that code to push it to production. You can see this repository at `https://github.com/csantany/production`.

In our Droplet, we will clone this git repo (if you already have your application ready, use your repository). The production repository is public, but if you use a private repository, you need to add the SSH Key of your Droplet in your GitHub account. For this, you need to run the `ssh-keygen` command in your Droplet, and then press *Enter* three times without writing any passphrase:

```
root@codejobs-ubuntu:~# ssh-keygen
Generating public/private rsa key pair.
Enter file in which to save the key (/root/.ssh/id_rsa):
Enter passphrase (empty for no passphrase):
Enter same passphrase again:
Your identification has been saved in /root/.ssh/id_rsa.
Your public key has been saved in /root/.ssh/id_rsa.pub.
The key fingerprint is:
SHA256:fNq5k8FtDzo7IQJSkx2yu5wDH6ZYRyqUDXk8h7Inp2Y root@codejobs-ubuntu
The key's randomart image is:
+---[RSA 2048]----+
| .o oo..         |
| o+=++.          |
| o+o=.           |
|.o.=.. .         |
|. O.=.  S...     |
| E B +. .++.+    |
|+ . *  ...o* o   |
|     .    *.  .  |
|          o=     |
+----[SHA256]-----+
```

If your terminal was inactive for more than five minutes, it's possible your connection will be closed, and you will have to connect again.

After you create your SSH Key, you can see it by doing: `vi /root/.ssh/id_rsa.pub`. You need to copy the SSH Key and go to your **GitHub Account** | **Settings** | **SSH** and **GPG** Keys (`https://github.com/settings/ssh/new`). And then paste your key in the textarea and put some title to the key. When you click the Add SSH Key button, GitHub will ask for your password to confirm:

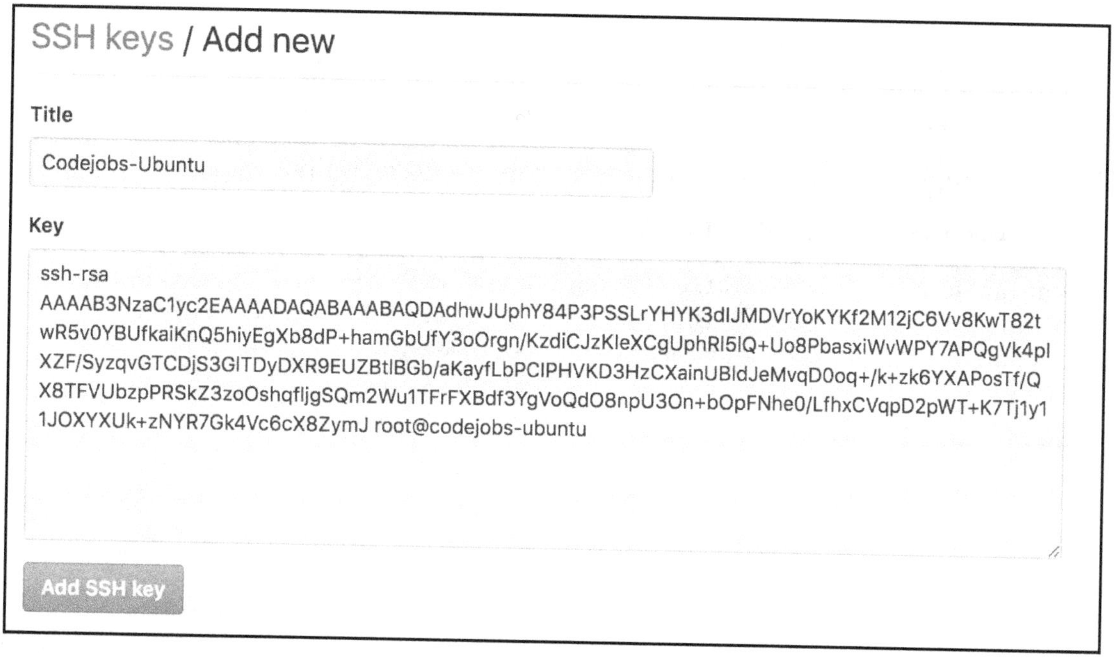

Now we can clone our repository using `git clone git@github.com:csantany/production.git`, or your repository:

```
root@codejobs-ubuntu:~# git clone git@github.com:csantany/production.git
Cloning into 'production'...
The authenticity of host 'github.com (192.30.255.112)' can't be established.
RSA key fingerprint is SHA256:nThbg6kXUpJWGl7E1IGOCspRomTxdCARLviKw6E5SY8.
Are you sure you want to continue connecting (yes/no)? yes
Warning: Permanently added 'github.com,192.30.255.112' (RSA) to the list of known hosts.
remote: Counting objects: 93, done.
remote: Compressing objects: 100% (82/82), done.
Receiving objects: 100% (93/93), 19.07 KiB | 3.18 MiB/s, done.
Resolving deltas: 100% (1/1), done.
remote: Total 93 (delta 1), reused 90 (delta 1), pack-reused 0
root@codejobs-ubuntu:~#
```

Then go to the production folder and install the NPM packages:

```
cd production
npm install
```

To test our application, let's run our npm run start-production script:

```
npm run start-production
```

If you want to verify that it works, go to your browser and open the IP of your droplet, and then add port 3000—in my case will be `http://178.128.177.84:3000` if everything works fine, you should see your application (in our case we are going to open our /todo section):

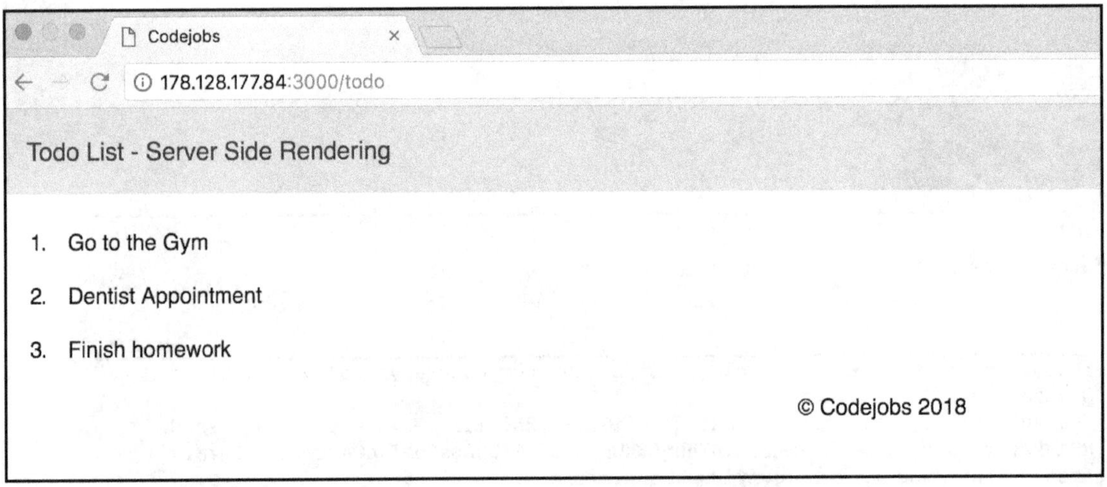

There's more...

If you want to turn off your Droplet, you can go to the Power section, or you can use the **ON/OFF** switch:

When you click it, you will get this modal:

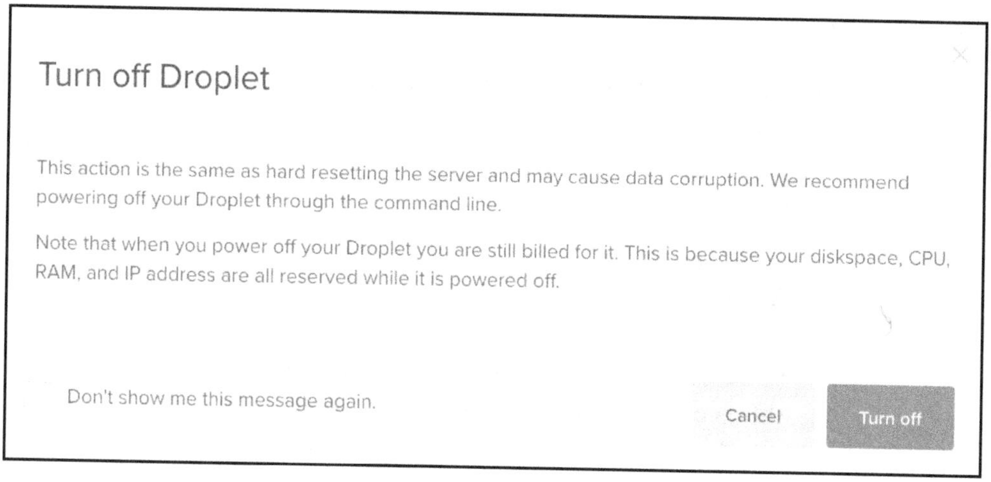

Configuring Nginx, PM2, and a domain in our Droplet

At this point, our first Droplet is ready to use, but we can see our React Application using port 3000. In this recipe, we are going to learn how to configure Nginx in our server and how to implement a proxy to redirect the traffic from port 80 to 3000. This means that we won't need to specify our port directly anymore. PM2 (Node Production Process Manager) will help us to run our Node server in production securely. Generally, if we run Node directly with the `node` or `babel-node` command and there is an error in our app, this will crash and will stop working; PM2 restarts the Node server if an error occurs.

Getting Ready

For this recipe, we need to install PM2 globally:

```
npm install -g pm2
```

Also, we need to install Nginx:

```
sudo apt-get update
sudo apt-get install nginx
```

How to do it...

Let's begin with the configuration:

1. Adjust the firewall to allow the traffic just in port 80. To list the available application configurations, we run the following command:

```
sudo ufw app list
Available applications:
   Nginx Full
   Nginx HTTP
   Nginx HTTPS
   OpenSSH
```

2. `Nginx Full` means that we will allow the traffic from ports 80 (HTTP) and 443 (HTTPS). At this point, we haven't configured any domain with SSL, so we should restrict the traffic to pass just through port 80 (HTTP):

```
sudo ufw allow 'Nginx HTTP'
```

3. If we try to access our IP, we should see our Nginx working:

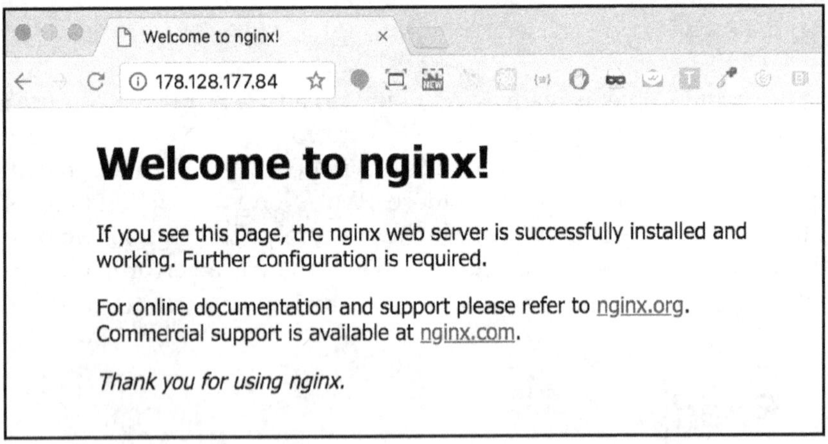

4. If you want to administrate the process of Nginx, you can use these commands:
   - **Start server**: `sudo systemctl start nginx`
   - **Stop server**: `sudo systemctl stop nginx`
   - **Restart server**: `sudo systemctl restart nginx`
   - **Reload server**: `sudo systemctl reload nginx`
   - **Disable server**: `sudo systemctl disable nginx`

5. Set up Nginx as a Reverse Proxy Server, for this we need to open our Nginx config file:

```
sudo vi /etc/nginx/sites-available/default
```

6. In the `location /` block, we need to replace it with:

```
location / {
  proxy_pass http://localhost:3000;
  proxy_http_version 1.1;
  proxy_set_header Upgrade $http_upgrade;
  proxy_set_header Connection 'upgrade';
  proxy_set_header Host $host;
  proxy_cache_bypass $http_upgrade;
}
```

How it works...

Once you've saved and closed the file, we need to verify whether we have any syntax errors. Use the following command:

```
sudo nginx -t
```

If everything is OK, you should see:

```
root@codejobs-ubuntu:~# sudo nginx -t
nginx: the configuration file /etc/nginx/nginx.conf syntax is ok
nginx: configuration file /etc/nginx/nginx.conf test is successful
root@codejobs-ubuntu:~#
```

Finally, we restart our Nginx server:

```
sudo systemctl restart nginx
```

Now we can access our IP without the port, and the React application will work fine:

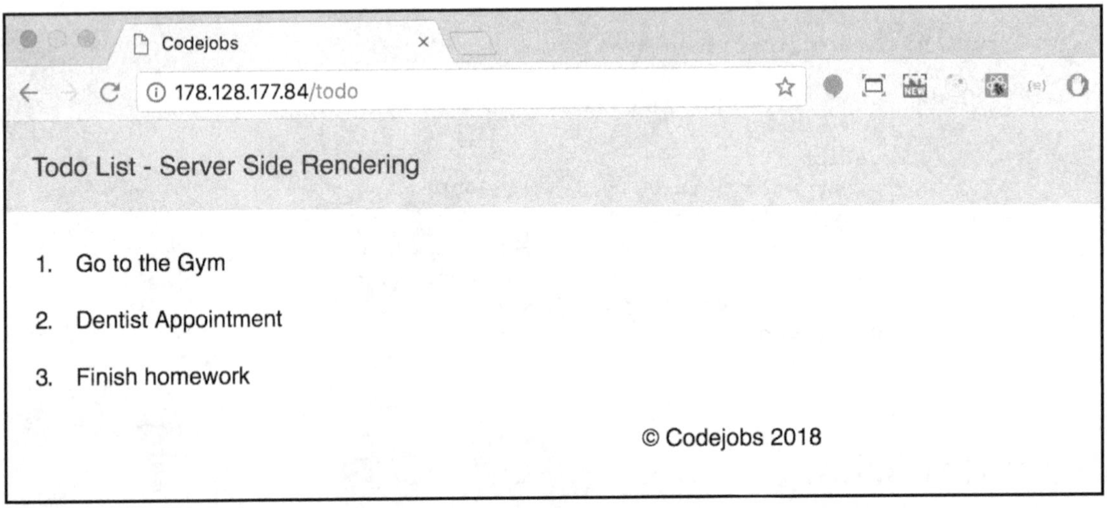

There's more...

If you want to use a domain with your Droplet, it's really easy; you need to change the Nameservers of your domain to point to Digital Ocean ones. For example, I have a domain, called educnow.com, which I'm going to use for my Droplet. I registered this domain with Godaddy, so I have to go to the domain management and select it. You can go directly to the `https://dcc.godaddy.com/manage/YOURDOMAIN.COM/dns` URL. Then go to Nameservers:

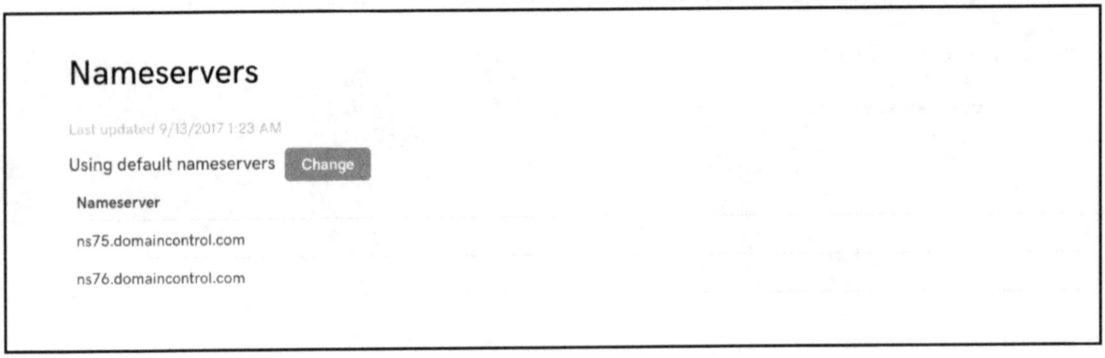

We have to click on the **Change** button, select **Custom**, specify the Digital Ocean Nameservers, and click on **Save**:

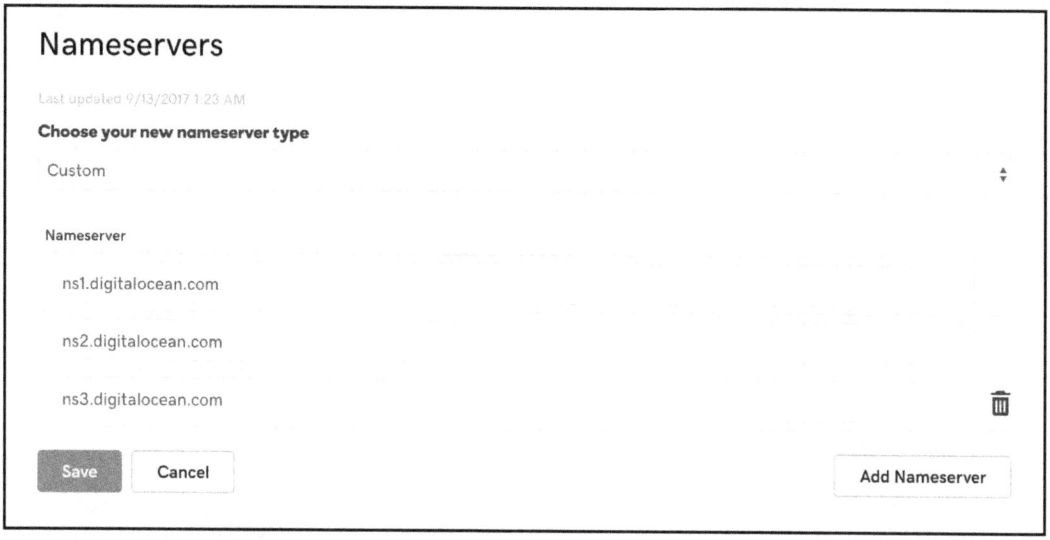

Once you've modified your Nameservers, you need to go to your Droplet dashboard and choose the **Add a domain** option:

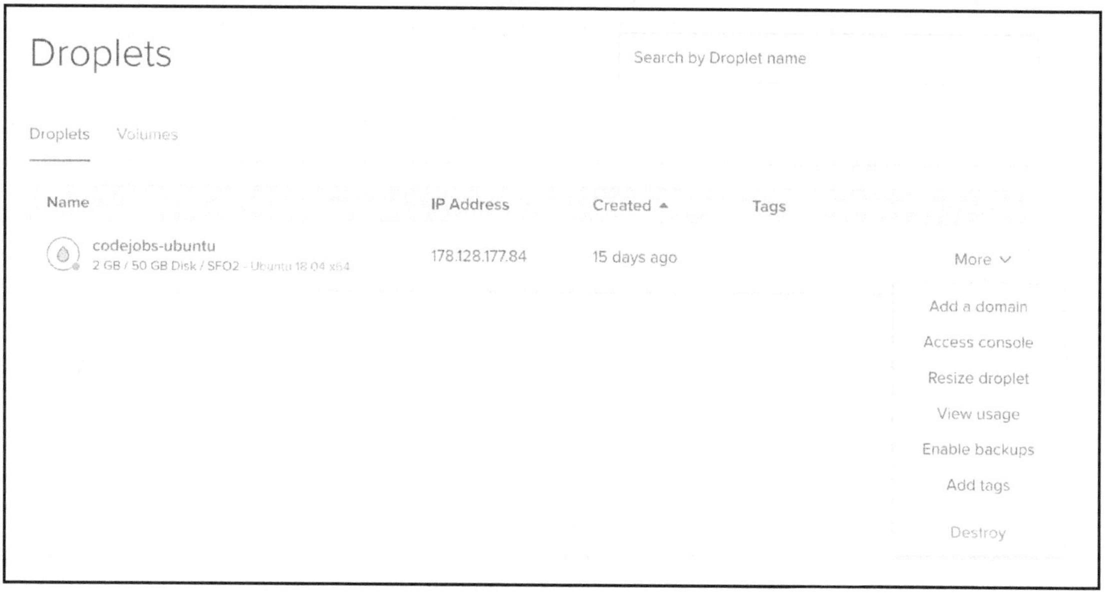

Then introduce the domain you want to link to your Droplet and click on **Add Domain**:

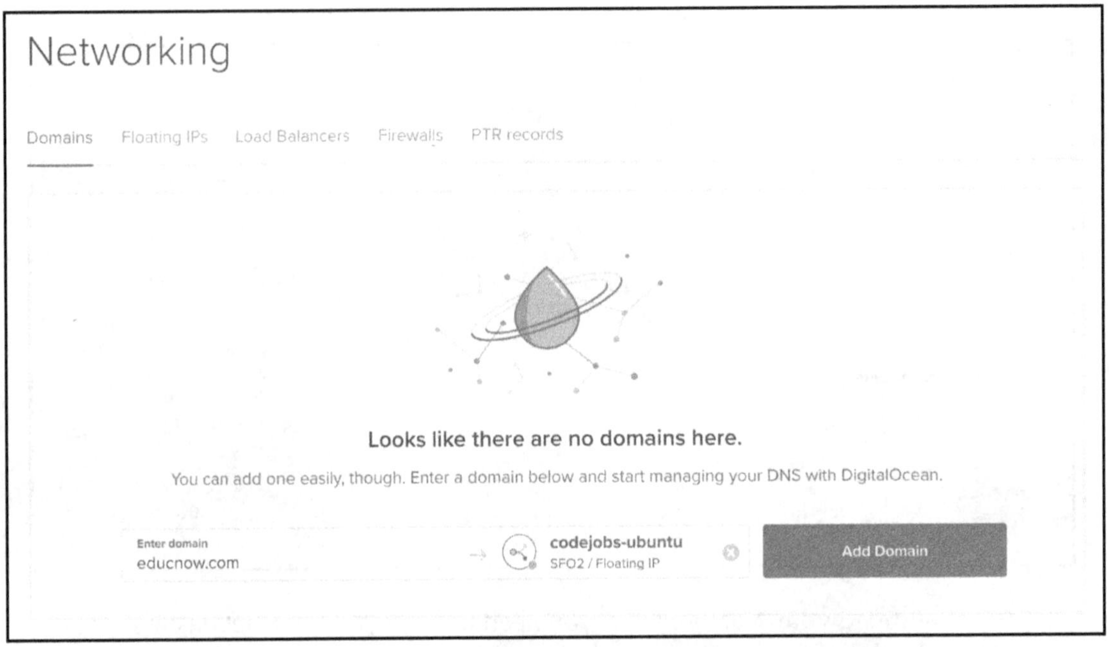

Now you need to create a new record for CNAME. Select the **CNAME** tab, in the hostname write `www`, in the alias field write `@`, and by default the TTL is `43200`—this is to be able to access your domain using the `www.yourdomain.com` prefix:

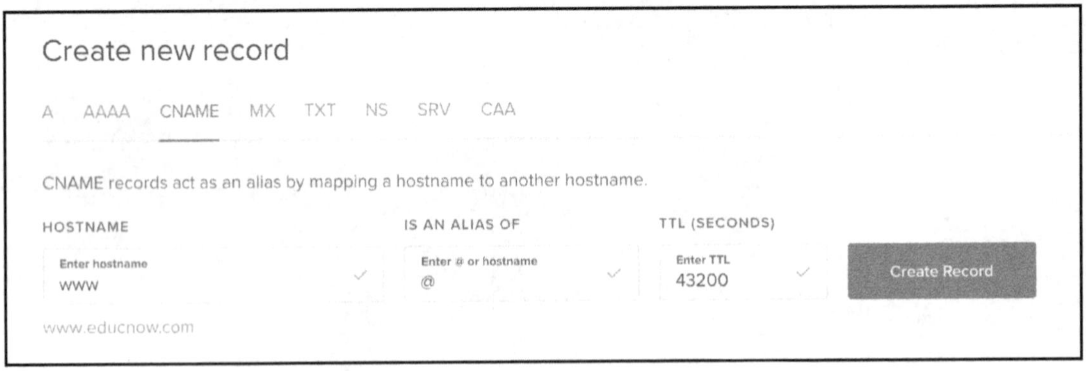

If you did everything correctly, you should be able to access your domain and see your React Application working; this process can take from 30 minutes to 24 hours depending on the DNS propagation speed.

Implementing Jenkins (continuous integration)

Jenkins is one of the most popular software for continuous integration, it's based on Java and is open source.

Getting Ready

There are some prerequisites to run Jenkins:

- You need a droplet (server) with Ubuntu 18.
- You need to install Java 8.

> TIP
>
> If you don't have Java 8 installed, you can install it with this command:
>
> **sudo apt install openjdk-8-jre-headless**

If you want to check which version of Java you have installed, you can use the `java -version` command:

```
root@codejobs-book:/home/production# java -version
openjdk version "1.8.0_171"
OpenJDK Runtime Environment (build 1.8.0_171-8u171-b11-0ubuntu0.18.04.1-b11)
OpenJDK 64-Bit Server VM (build 25.171-b11, mixed mode)
```

How to do it...

Now let's install and configure Jenkins:

1. Add the repository key to the system:

```
wget -q -O - https://pkg.jenkins.io/debian/jenkins.io.key | sudo apt-key
add -
```

2. Append the Debian package address to `sources.list`:

```
sudo sh -c 'echo deb http://pkg.jenkins.io/debian-stable binary/ >
/etc/apt/sources.list.d/jenkins.list'
```

3. Update the apt packages:

```
sudo apt update
```

4. Install Jenkins:

```
sudo apt install jenkins
```

> TIP
>
> If you get an error when you install Jenkins, you can uninstall it with:
>
> **sudo apt-get remove --purge** jenkins

5. Start the Jenkins service:

```
sudo systemctl start jenkins
```

6. If you want to see the Jenkins status, use this command:

```
sudo systemctl status jenkins
```

```
root@codejobs-book:/home/production# sudo systemctl status jenkins
● jenkins.service - LSB: Start Jenkins at boot time
   Loaded: loaded (/etc/init.d/jenkins; generated)
   Active: active (exited) since Sun 2018-08-12 07:50:22 UTC; 10min ago
     Docs: man:systemd-sysv-generator(8)
    Tasks: 0 (limit: 2362)
   CGroup: /system.slice/jenkins.service

Aug 12 07:50:21 codejobs-book systemd[1]: Starting LSB: Start Jenkins at boot time...
Aug 12 07:50:21 codejobs-book jenkins[11733]: Correct java version found
Aug 12 07:50:21 codejobs-book jenkins[11733]:  * Starting Jenkins Automation Server jenkins
Aug 12 07:50:21 codejobs-book su[11778]: Successful su for jenkins by root
Aug 12 07:50:21 codejobs-book su[11778]: + ??? root:jenkins
Aug 12 07:50:21 codejobs-book su[11778]: pam_unix(su:session): session opened for user jenkins by (uid=0)
Aug 12 07:50:21 codejobs-book su[11778]: pam_unix(su:session): session closed for user jenkins
Aug 12 07:50:22 codejobs-book jenkins[11733]:    ...done.
Aug 12 07:50:22 codejobs-book systemd[1]: Started LSB: Start Jenkins at boot time.
```

7. Jenkins runs on port 8080 by default, and we need to open the Firewall to allow the traffic to that port:

```
sudo ufw allow 8080
```

8. If you want to verify the firewall status, do the following:

```
sudo ufw status
```

If you see Status: inactive, you will need to run these commands to enable the firewall:

sudo ufw allow OpenSSH
sudo ufw enable

```
root@codejobs-book:~# sudo ufw status
Status: active

To                         Action      From
--                         ------      ----
Nginx HTTP                 ALLOW       Anywhere
8080                       ALLOW       Anywhere
OpenSSH                    ALLOW       Anywhere
Nginx HTTP (v6)            ALLOW       Anywhere (v6)
8080 (v6)                  ALLOW       Anywhere (v6)
OpenSSH (v6)               ALLOW       Anywhere (v6)
```

9. It's time to run our Jenkins for the first time and configure it. For this, you need to visit `http://<the_ip_or_domain_of_your_droplet>:8080`. In my case, it's `http://142.93.28.244:8080`:

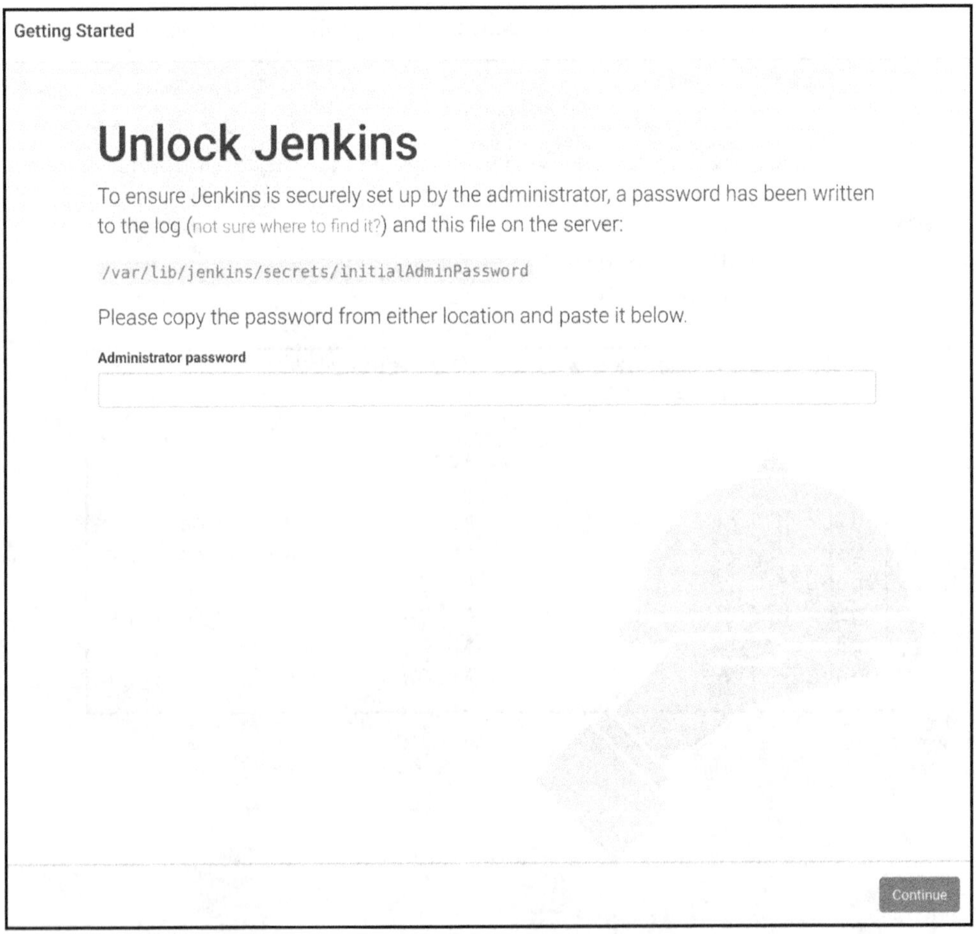

10. To see the first password, you need to run:

```
sudo cat /var/lib/jenkins/secrets/initialAdminPassword
```

```
root@codejobs-book:~# sudo cat /var/lib/jenkins/secrets/initialAdminPassword
182c45bf4ab442aa953f56bec8ac0d34
```

11. You will see the Welcome to Jenkins page. You have to select the "Install suggested plugins" option:

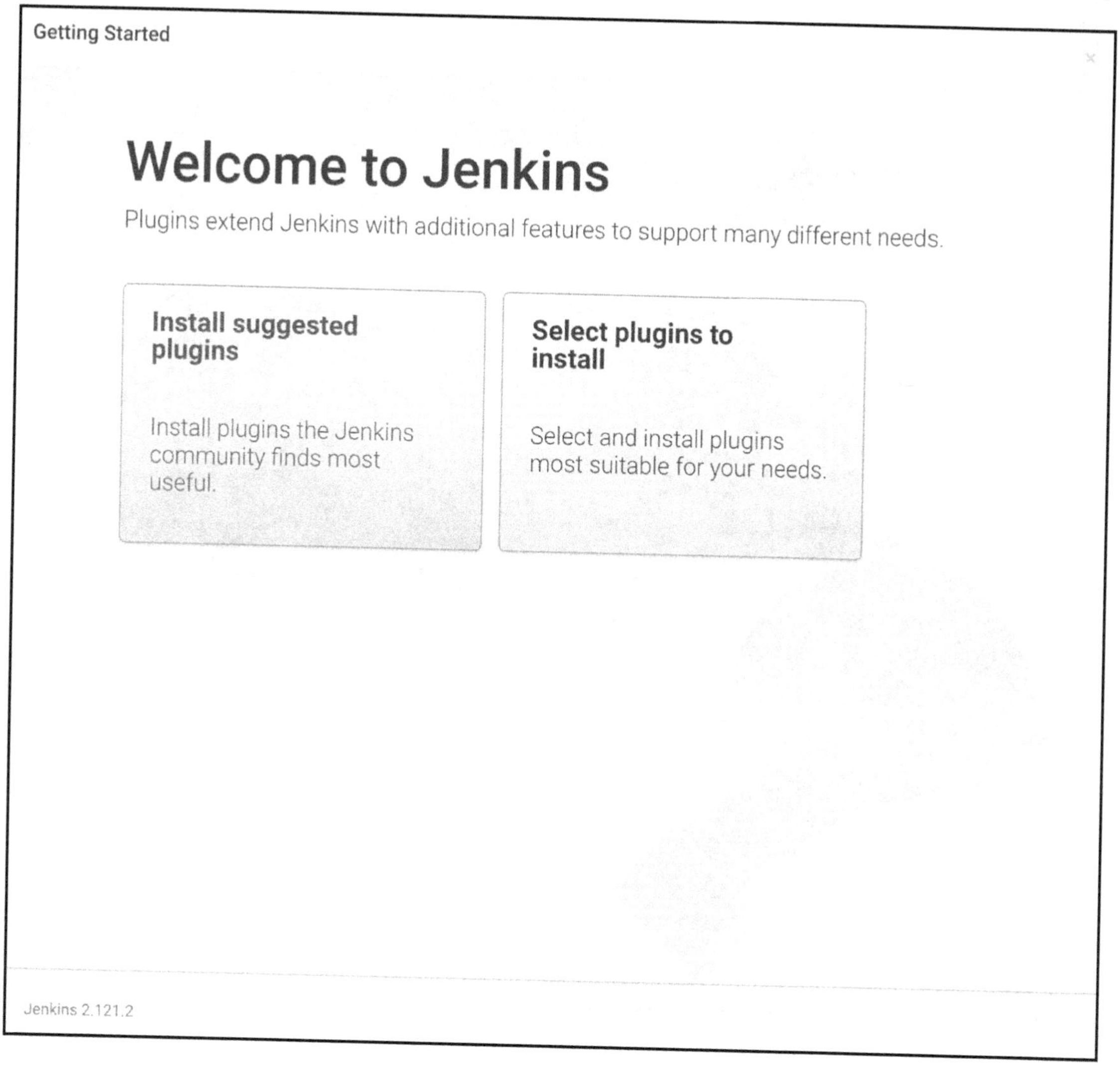

Getting Started
Welcome to Jenkins
Plugins extend Jenkins with additional features to support many different needs.
Install suggested plugins
Install plugins the Jenkins community finds most useful.
Select plugins to install
Select and install plugins most suitable for your needs.
Jenkins 2.121.2

12. You will see the installation process:

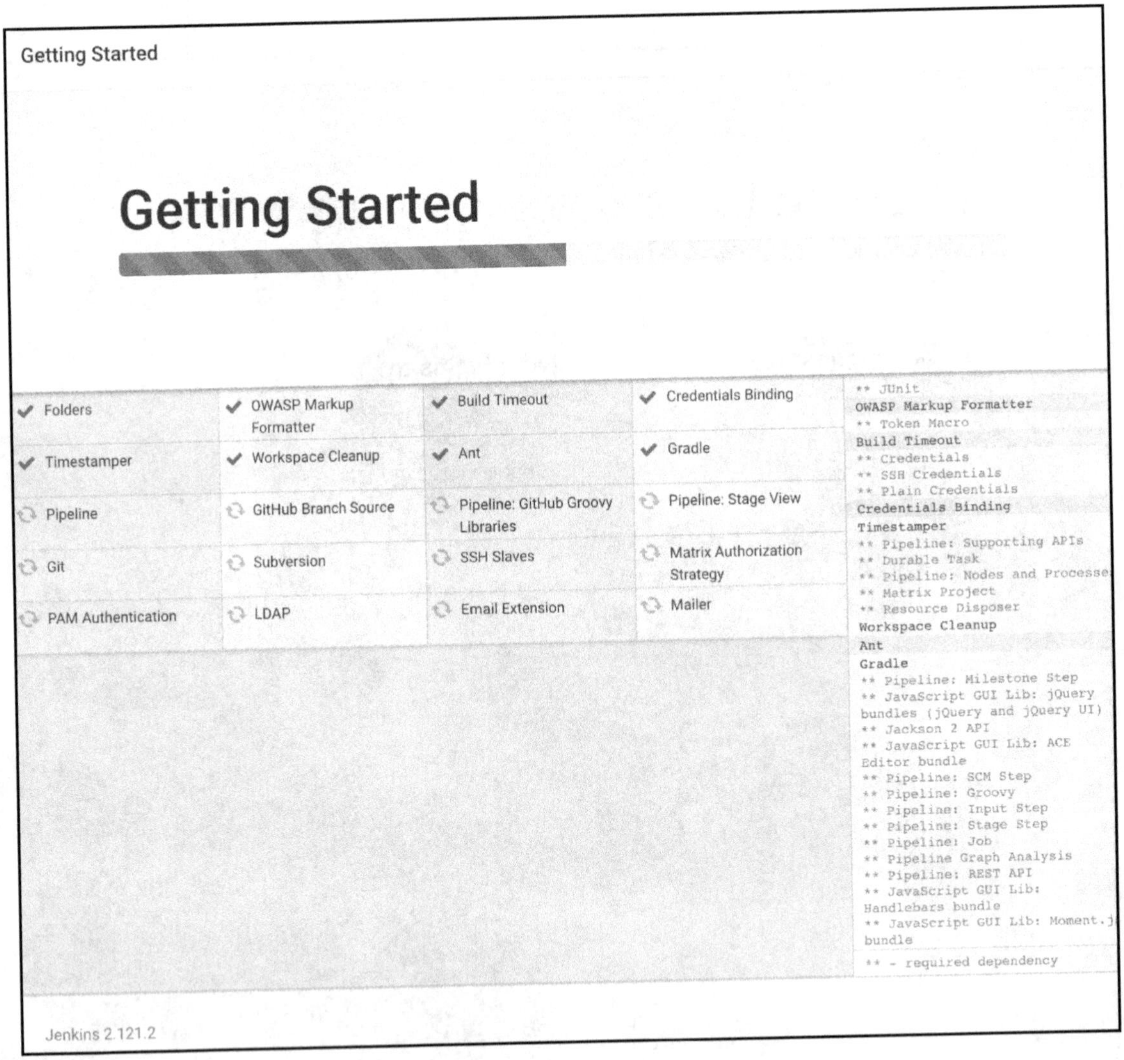

13. Once the installation is complete, you need to create your first admin user:

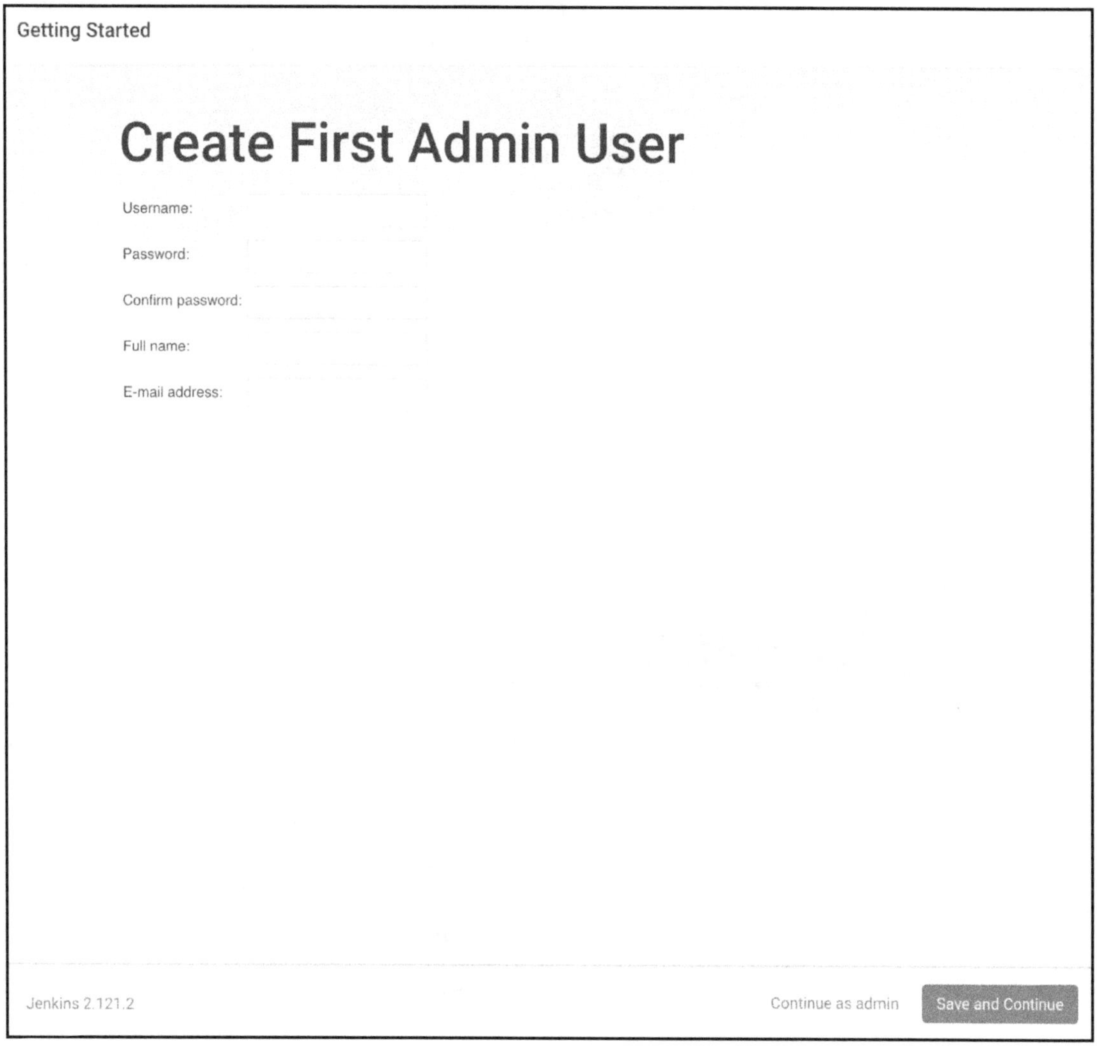

14. Confirm the Jenkins URL if you don't want to change it. Click Save and Finish:

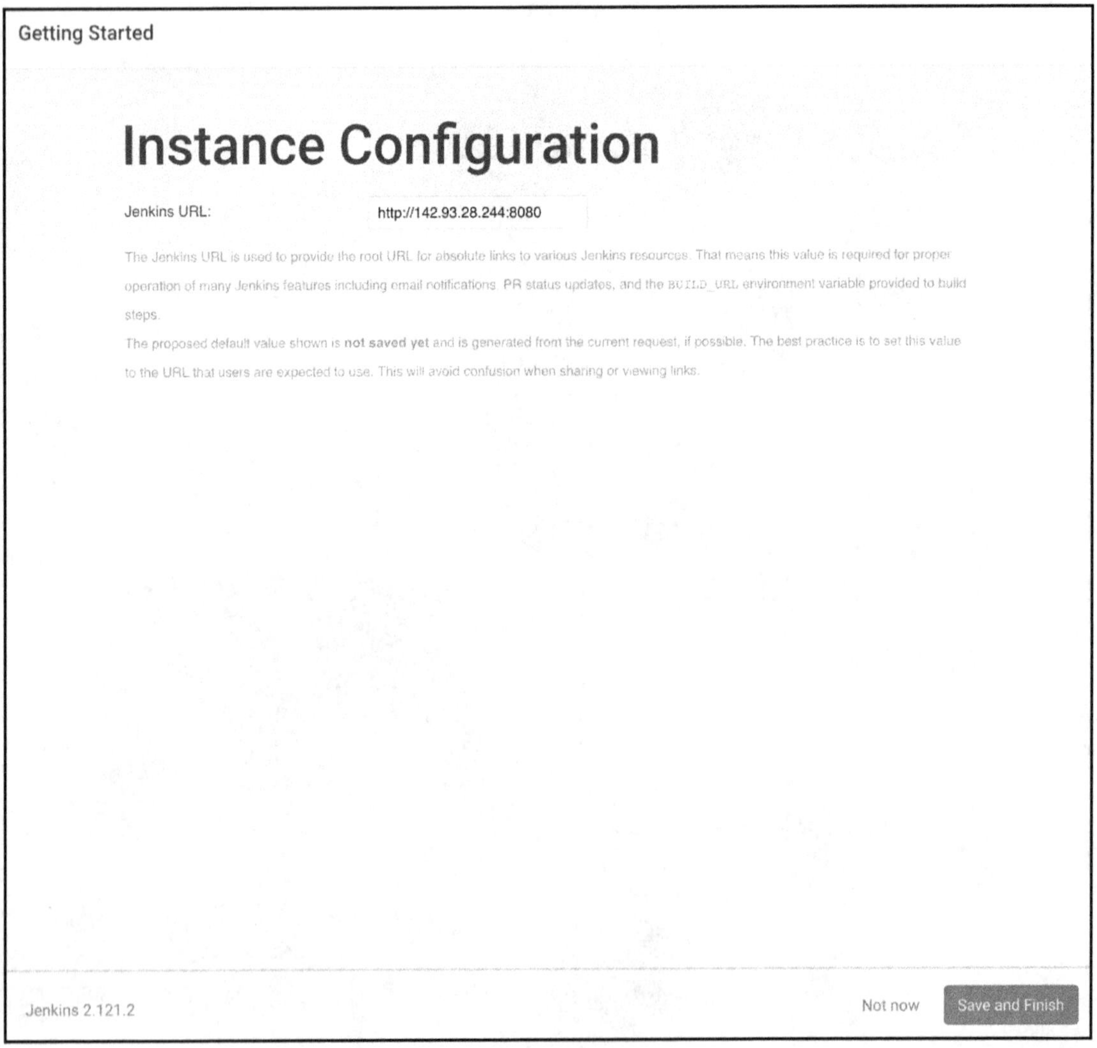
Getting Started
Instance Configuration
Jenkins URL:
http://142.93.28.244:8080
The Jenkins URL is used to provide the root URL for absolute links to various Jenkins resources. That means this value is required for proper operation of many Jenkins features including email notifications, PR status updates, and the BUILD_URL environment variable provided to build steps.
The proposed default value shown is not saved yet and is generated from the current request, if possible. The best practice is to set this value to the URL that users are expected to use. This will avoid confusion when sharing or viewing links.
Jenkins 2.121.2
Not now
Save and Finish

15. Jenkins is ready:

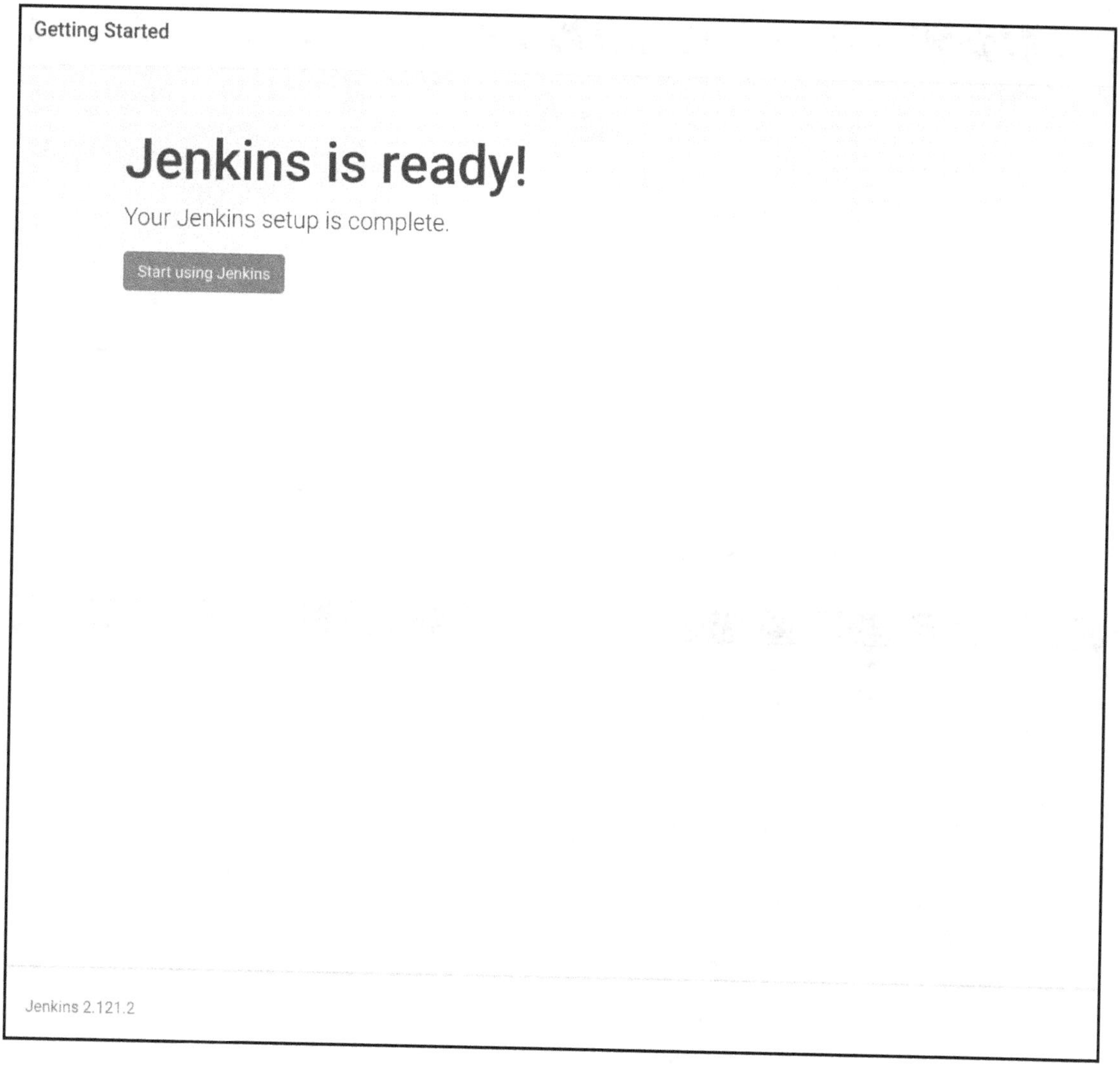

16. The first view you will see in Jenkins is this one:

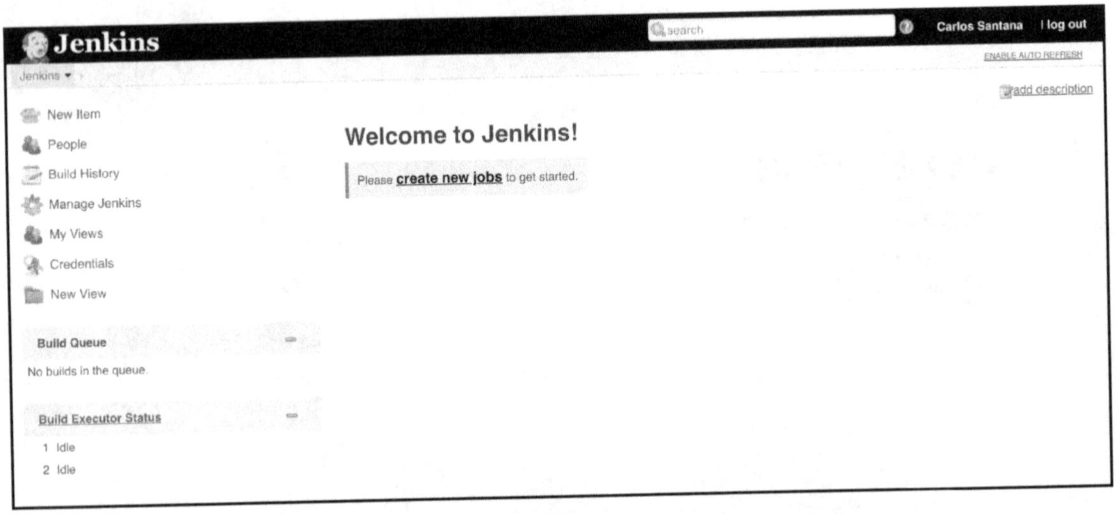

17. Go to Manage Jenkins > Manage Plugins to install the GitHub plugin:

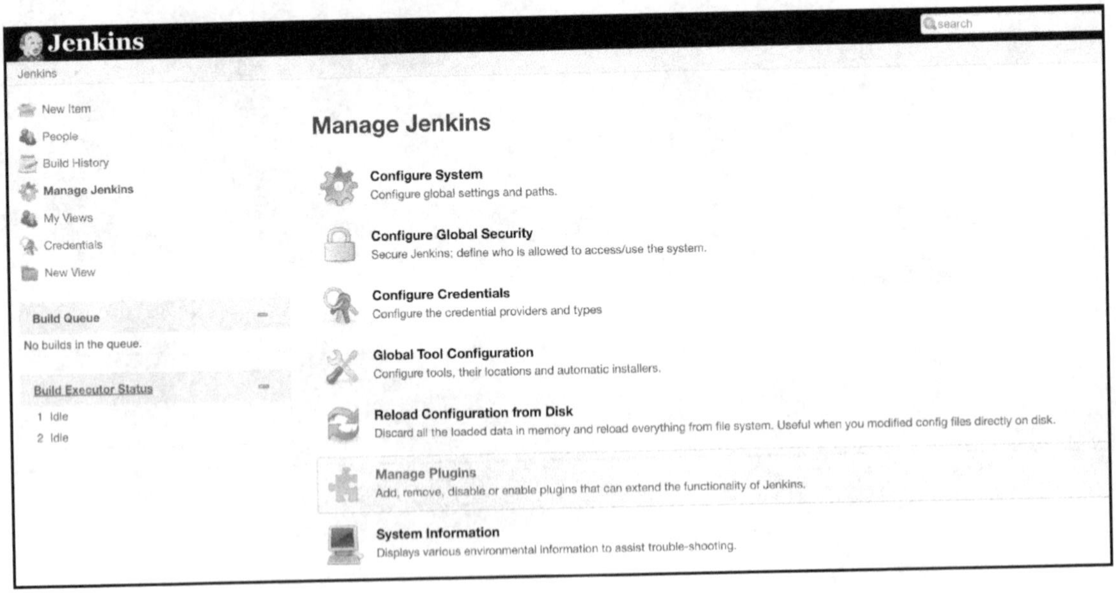

18. Select the **Available** tab and then search for **GitHub Integration**. Now select the checkbox option and click on the **Download now and install after restart** button:

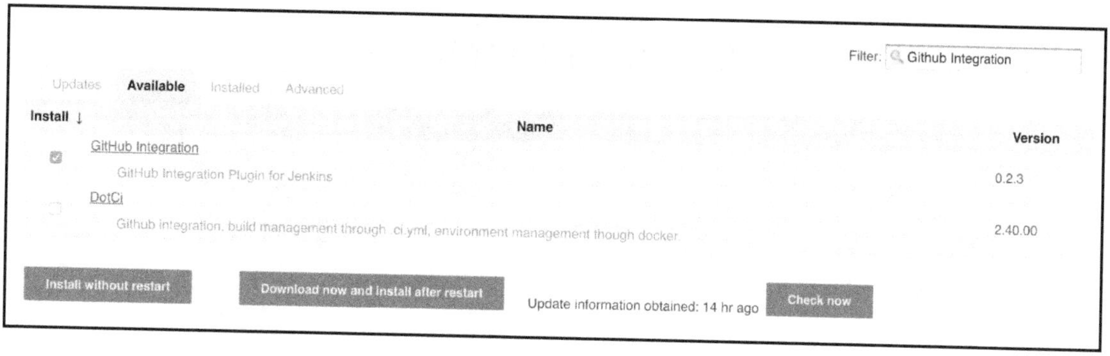

19. Select the **Restart Jenkins when installation is complete, and no jobs are running** option:

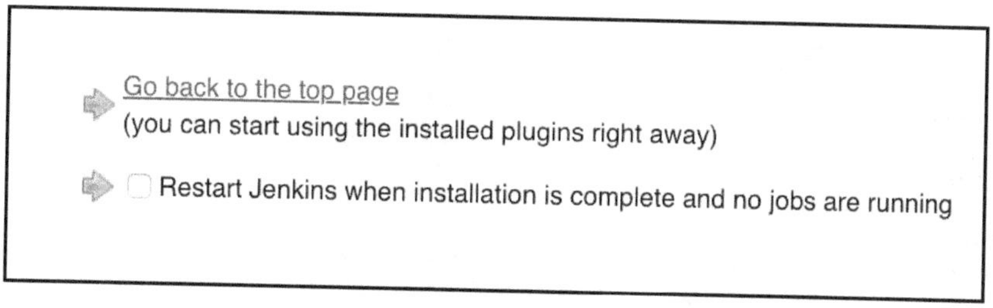

20. You will see this message:

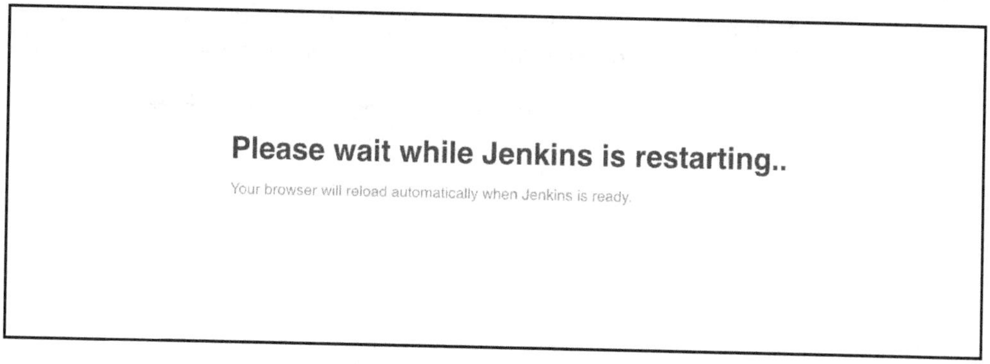

21. Wait one minute and then refresh the page. You may need to log in again.
22. Go back to **Manage Plugins**; now you need to install the **Post build task plugin**.

23. We can create our first Job by clicking on **create new jobs** on the homepage:

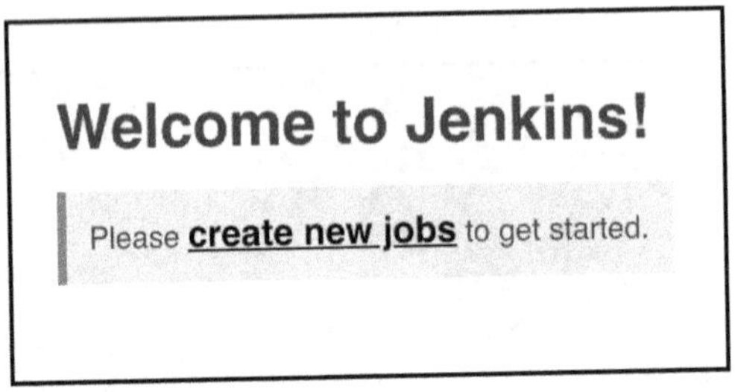

24. Write the name of your job, select the **Freestyle project** option, and click on the **OK** button:

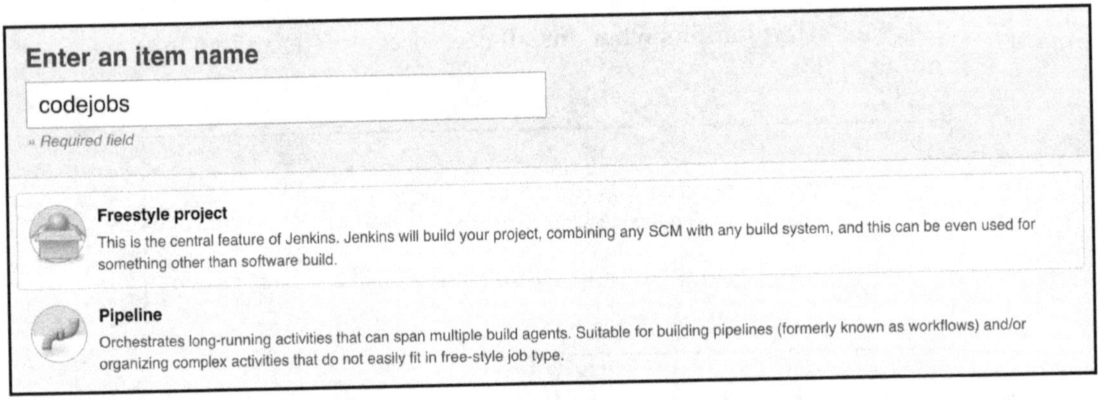

25. In the General configuration, go to the **Source Code Management** section, select the **Git** option, and then write your GitHub project HTTPS URL (if you select your SSH URL, you will need to add new SSH keys for Jenkins in your GitHub):

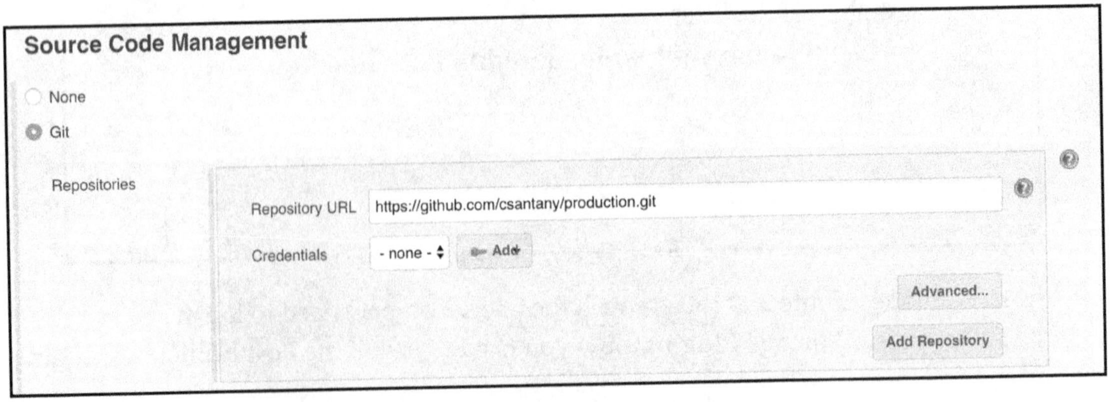

26. If your repository is private, you need to click on the **Add** button to specify your GitHub credentials (username and password):

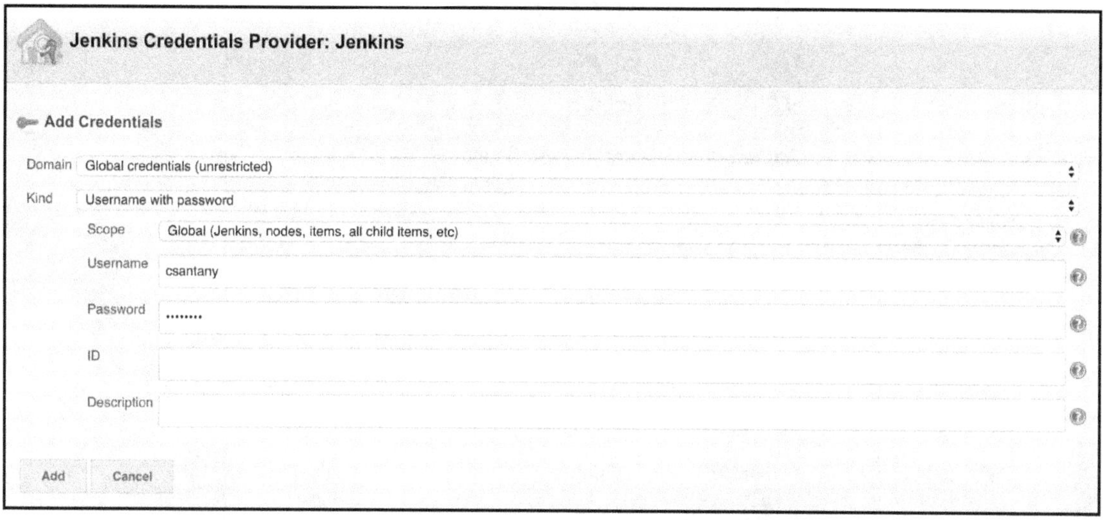

27. Select your credentials and make sure the `master` branch is selected as your main branch (it's recommended to use the master instead of others branches):

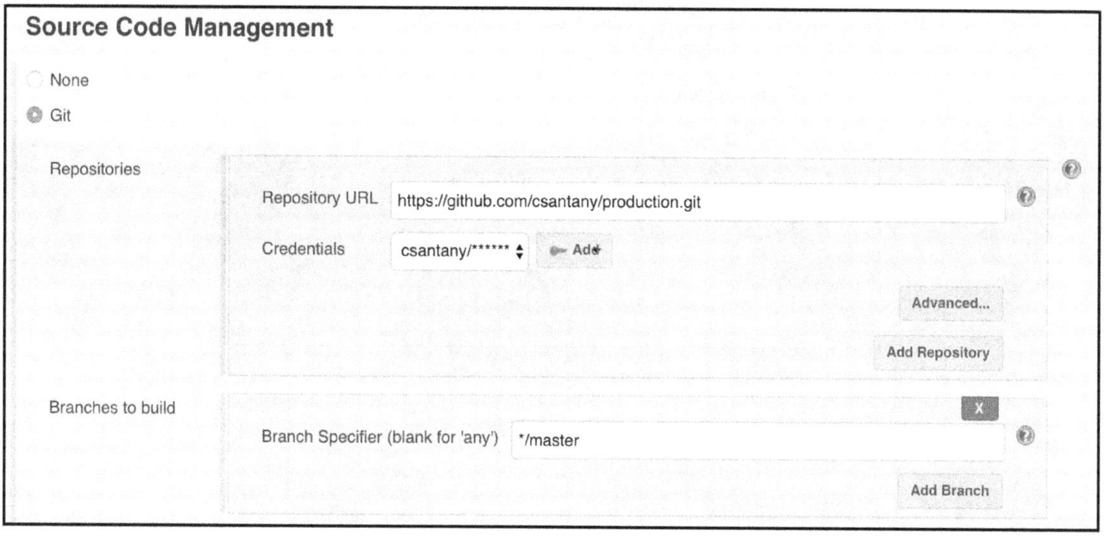

28. Select the **Post build task** option on the **Post-build Actions**:

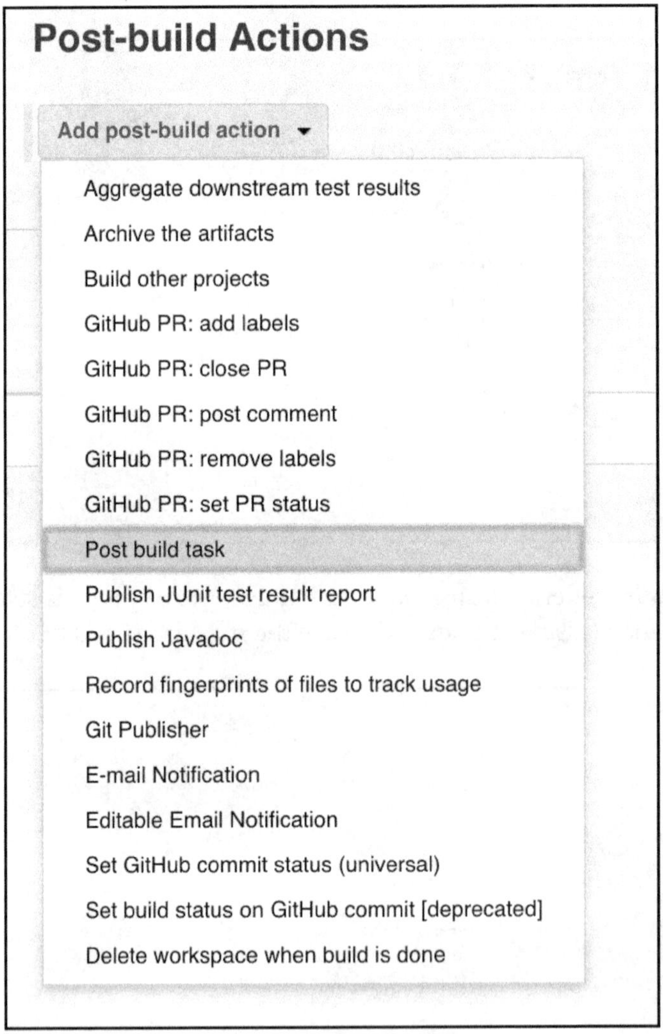

29. In the textarea script, add `npm install && npm run start-production`. Click on **Apply** and then on the **Save** button:

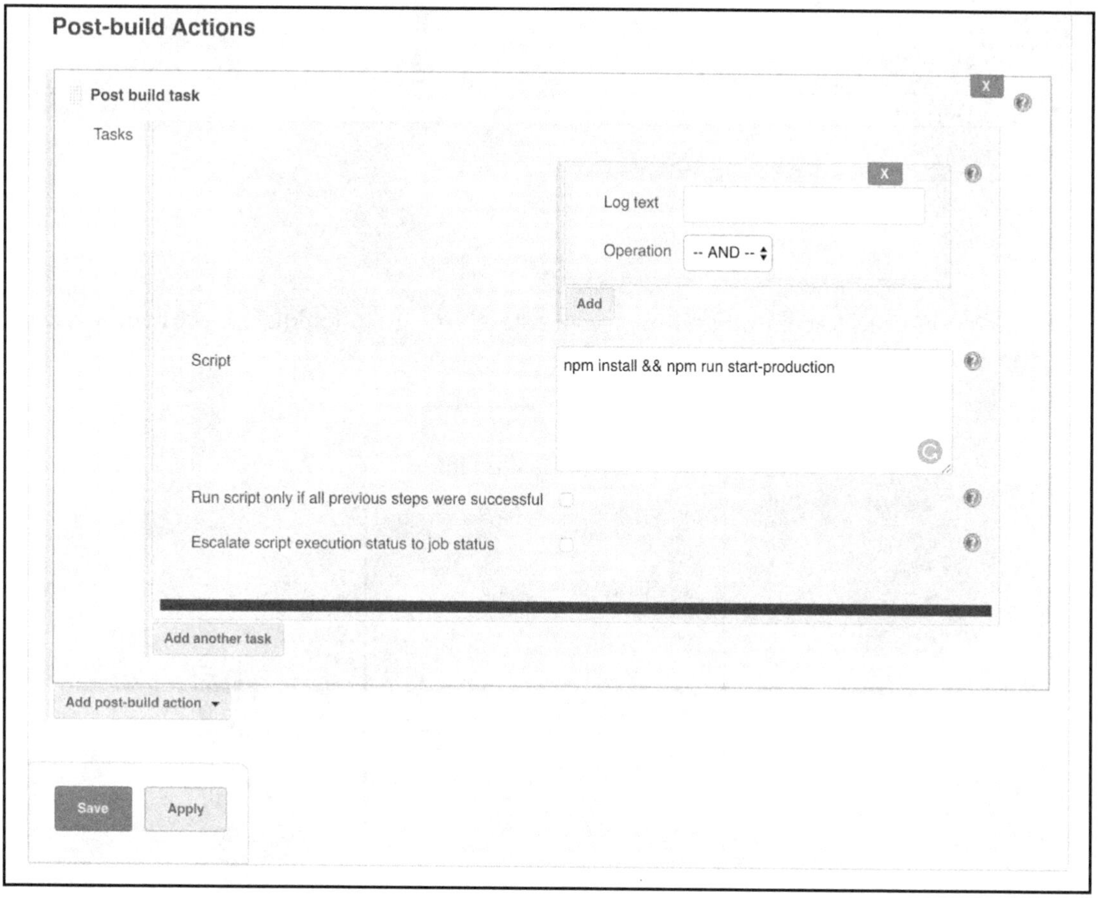

How it works...

We've configured our Jenkins job, now let's test it. I'm going to modify a simple file to be sure the Jenkins works properly.

> TIP: At this point (if you followed the first recipe), you must stop the PM2 server with the command "**npm run stop**" and then remove the production directory that we cloned before, to avoid problems with the Jenkins job.

Let's modify our Home component; I'll add an extra text **(Jenkins)**:

```
import React from 'react';
import styles from './Home.scss';

const Home = props => (
  <h1 className={styles.Home}>Hello {props.name || 'World'}
(Jenkins)</h1>
);

export default Home;
```

File: src/client/home/index.jsx

After that, you need to commit and push to master. Now go to Jenkins, select your job, and click on `Build Now`:

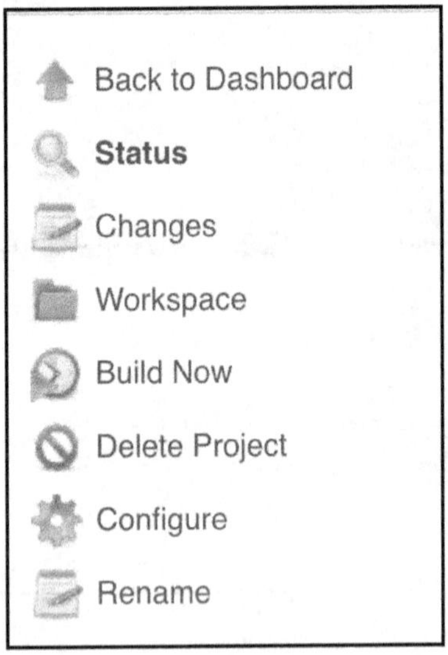

After that, click on the latest build (in my case it's #5 because I did some tests before, but for you, it will be #1):

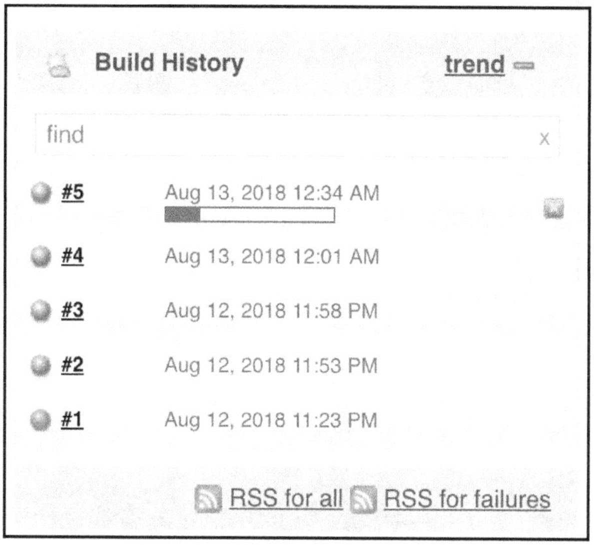

In the build, you will see who (user) started the build and which is the revision (last commit of master) that is building. If you want to see the Console Output, you can click on that option on the left menu:

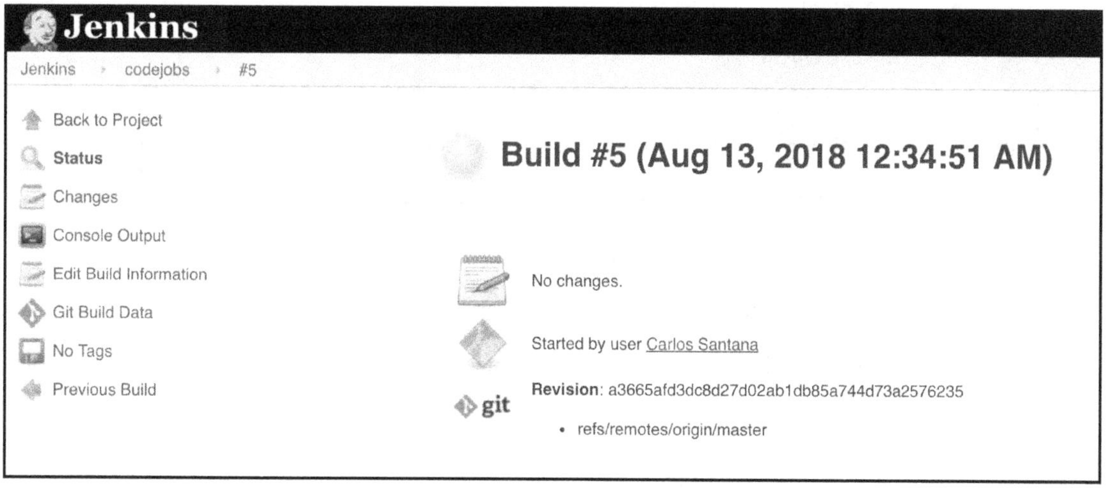

If you look at the **Console Output**, you will see tons of commands:

Console Output

```
Started by user Carlos Santana
Building in workspace /var/lib/jenkins/workspace/codejobs
 > git rev-parse --is-inside-work-tree # timeout=10
Fetching changes from the remote Git repository
 > git config remote.origin.url https://github.com/csantany/production.git # timeout=10
Fetching upstream changes from https://github.com/csantany/production.git
 > git --version # timeout=10
using GIT_ASKPASS to set credentials
 > git fetch --tags --progress https://github.com/csantany/production.git +refs/heads/*:refs/remotes/origin/*
 > git rev-parse refs/remotes/origin/master^{commit} # timeout=10
 > git rev-parse refs/remotes/origin/origin/master^{commit} # timeout=10
Checking out Revision a3665afd3dc8d27d02ab1db85a744d73a2576235 (refs/remotes/origin/master)
 > git config core.sparsecheckout # timeout=10
 > git checkout -f a3665afd3dc8d27d02ab1db85a744d73a2576235
Commit message: "Updating home"
 > git rev-list --no-walk a3665afd3dc8d27d02ab1db85a744d73a2576235 # timeout=10
Performing Post build task...
Match found for : : True
Logical operation result is TRUE
Running script  : npm install && npm run start-production
[codejobs] $ /bin/sh -xe /tmp/jenkins166381717114813458.sh
+ npm install
npm WARN react-pro@1.0.0 No description
npm WARN react-pro@1.0.0 No repository field.
npm WARN optional SKIPPING OPTIONAL DEPENDENCY: fsevents@1.2.4 (node_modules/fsevents):
npm WARN notsup SKIPPING OPTIONAL DEPENDENCY: Unsupported platform for fsevents@1.2.4: wanted {"os":"darwin","arch":"any"} (current:
{"os":"linux","arch":"x64"})

audited 36937 packages in 15.991s
found 0 vulnerabilities

+ npm run start-production

> react-pro@1.0.0 start-production /var/lib/jenkins/workspace/codejobs
> npm run stop & npm run build-production && NODE_ENV=production BABEL_ENV=production pm2 start --interpreter babel-node src/server


> react-pro@1.0.0 build-production /var/lib/jenkins/workspace/codejobs
> npm run clean && npm run build-client-production && npm run build-server-production
```

Every time we run a new build, Jenkins will fetch the latest changes of the repository:

```
git config remote.origin.url https://github.com/csantany/production.git
```

Then will get the last commit of the master:

```
git rev-parse refs/remotes/origin/master^{commit}
```

And finally, it will execute the commands we specified on the Post build task:

```
npm install && npm run start-production
```

If everything works fine, you should see **Finished: SUCCESS** at the end of the output:

```
[PM2] Spawning PM2 daemon with pm2_home=/var/lib/jenkins/.pm2
[PM2] PM2 Successfully daemonized
[PM2] Starting /var/lib/jenkins/workspace/codejobs/src/server in fork_mode (1 instance)
[PM2] Done.
┌──────────┬────┬──────┬───────┬────────┬─────────┬────────┬──────┬─────────┬─────────┬──────────┐
│ App name │ id │ mode │ pid   │ status │ restart │ uptime │ cpu  │ mem     │ user    │ watching │
├──────────┼────┼──────┼───────┼────────┼─────────┼────────┼──────┼─────────┼─────────┼──────────┤
│ server   │ 0  │ fork │ 20453 │ online │ 0       │ 0s     │ 100% │ 24.7 MB │ jenkins │ disabled │
└──────────┴────┴──────┴───────┴────────┴─────────┴────────┴──────┴─────────┴─────────┴──────────┘
 Use `pm2 show <id|name>` to get more details about an app
POST BUILD TASK : SUCCESS
END OF POST BUILD TASK : 0
Finished: SUCCESS
```

Now wait 30 seconds or 1 minute and then visit your production site (in my case `http://142.93.28.244/`) – you will see the new changes:

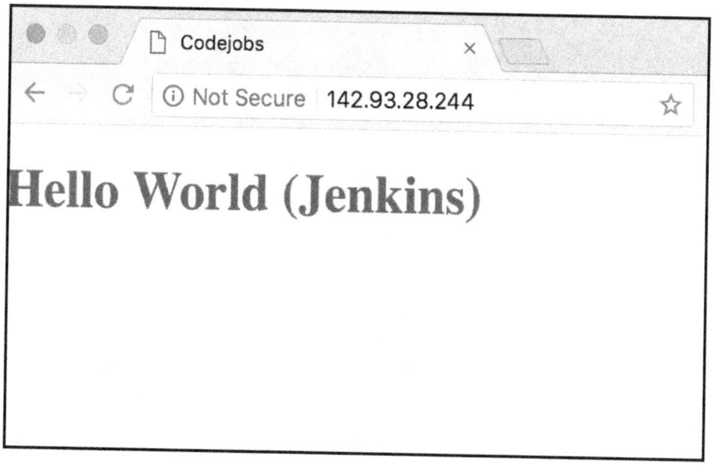

If you're wondering where the files are stored, you can see them at `/var/lib/jenkins/workspace/<your_jenkins_job_name>`.

14
Working with React Native

In this chapter, the following recipes will be covered:

- Creating our first React Native application
- Creating a Todo List with React Native
- Implementing React Navigation V2

Introduction

React Native is a framework for building mobile apps using JavaScript and React. Many people think that with React Native you make some "mobile web app" or a "hybrid app" (such as Ionic, PhoneGap or Sencha), but you build a native app because React Native converts your React code to Java for Android or Objective-C for iOS apps. React Native uses most of the React concepts, such as components, props, state and lifecycle methods.

Advantages of React Native:

- You code once, and you get two native apps (Android and iOS)
- You don't need to have experience with Java, Objective-C, or Swift
- Faster development
- MIT license (open source)

Requirements for Windows:

- Android Studio
- Android SDK (>= 7.0 Nougat)
- Android AVD

Requirements for Mac:

- XCode (>= 9)
- Simulator

Creating our first React Native Application

In this recipe, we are going to build a React Native application and understand the main differences between React and React Native.

Getting Ready

To create our new React Native application, we need to install the `react-native-cli` package:

```
npm install -g react-native-cli
```

How to do it...

Now, to create our first app:

1. Let's do it with this command:

```
react-native init MyFirstReactNativeApp
```

2. After we built our React Native app, we need to install Watchman, which is a file-watching service required by React Native. To install it, go to `https://facebook.github.io/watchman/docs/install.html` and download the latest version for your OS (Windows, Mac, or Linux).
3. In this case, we are going to use Homebrew to install it for Mac. If you don't have Homebrew, you can install it with this command:

```
/usr/bin/ruby -e "$(curl -fsSL
https://raw.githubusercontent.com/Homebrew/install/master/install)"
```

4. To install Watchman, you need to run:

```
brew update
brew install watchman
```

5. To start the React Native project, we need to use:

```
react-native start
```

6. If everything works fine, you should see this:

```
→ MyFirstReactNativeApp react-native start
Scanning folders for symlinks in /Users/czantany/projects/MyFirstReactNativeApp/node_modules (14ms)

  Running Metro Bundler on port 8081.

  Keep Metro running while developing on any JS projects. Feel free to
  close this tab and run your own Metro instance if you prefer.

  https://github.com/facebook/react-native


Looking for JS files in
   /Users/czantany/projects/MyFirstReactNativeApp


Metro Bundler ready.

Loading dependency graph, done.
```

Sometimes you can get errors from Watchman, for example, Watchman error: too many pending cache jobs. Make sure watchman is running for this project.

TIP

If you get that error or another, you have to uninstall Watchman by doing: `brew unlink watchman`

And then reinstall it using:

```
brew update && brew upgrade

brew install watchman
```

7. Open a new terminal (*Cmd* + *T*) and run this command (depending on the device you want to use):

```
react-native run-ios
or
react-native run-android
```

8. If there are no errors, you should see the simulator running the default application:

Now that we have our application running, let's open our code and modify it a bit:

1. Change the `App.js` file:

```
...
export default class App extends Component<Props> {
  render() {
    return (
      <View style={styles.container}>
        <Text style={styles.welcome}>
          This is my first React Native App!
        </Text>
```

```
            <Text style={styles.instructions}>
              To get started, edit App.js
            </Text>
            <Text style={styles.instructions}>{instructions}</Text>
          </View>
        );
      }
    }
    ...
```

File: App.js

2. If you go to the simulator again, you will need to press *Cmd* + *R* to reload the app to see the new changes reflected:

3. You're probably wondering if there is a way to do automatic reload instead of doing this process manually, and of course, there is a way to enable the **Live Reload** option; you need to press *Cmd* + *D* to open the development menu and then select the **Enable Live Reload** option:

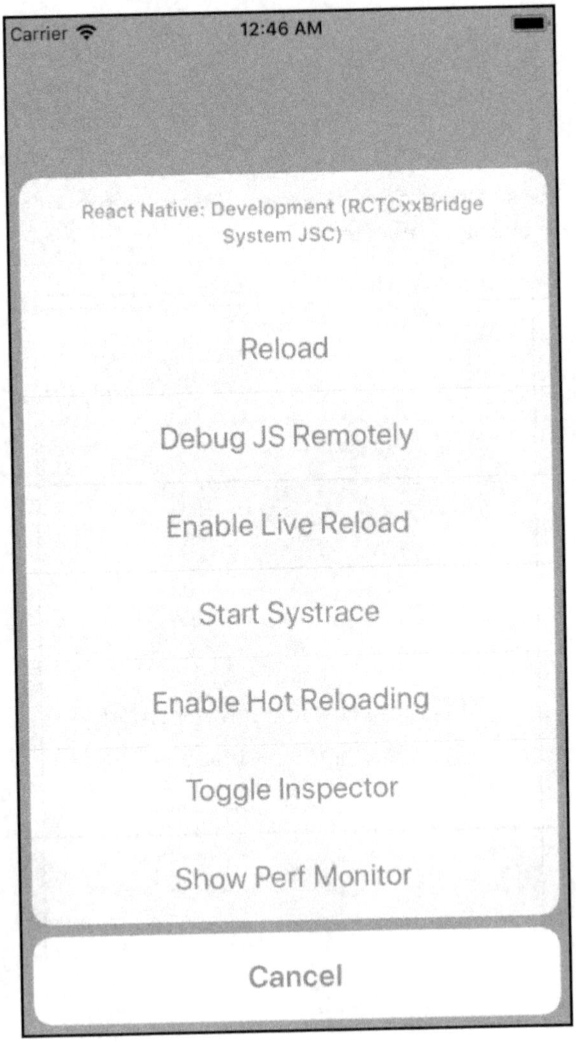

4. Another exciting option is Debug JS Remotely. If you click on that one, it will automatically open a Chrome tab where we can see the logs we added to our application using `console.log`. For example, if I add `console.log('==== Debugging my First React Native App! ====');` in my render method, I should see it like this:

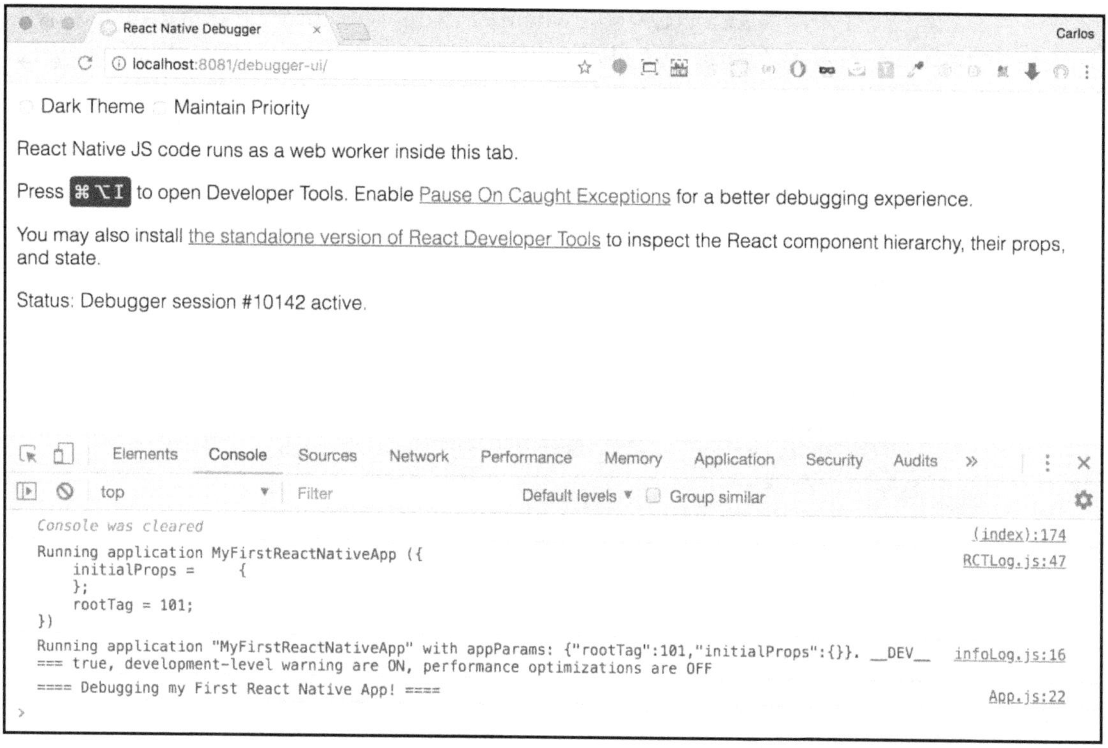

5. Let's go back to the code. Maybe you are a little bit confused about the code you saw in `App.js` because you didn't see a `<div>` tag or even worse the way the styles are being created like an object instead of using a CSS file as we do in React. I've got some good news and some bad news; the bad news is that React Native does not support CSS and JSX/HTML code as React does. The good news is that once you understand that the `<View>` component is the equivalent of using a `<div>`, `<Text>` is the equivalent of using `<p>`, and the styles are like CSS modules (object), everything else works the same as React (props, state, lifecycle methods).
6. Create a new component (`Home`). For this purpose, we have to create a directory called components, and then we save this file as `Home.js`:

```
// Dependencies
import React, { Component } from 'react';
import { StyleSheet, Text, View } from 'react-native';

class Home extends Component {
  render() {
    return (
      <View style={styles.container}>
        <Text style={styles.home}>Home Component</Text>
      </View>
    );
  }
}

const styles = StyleSheet.create({
  container: {
    flex: 1,
    justifyContent: 'center',
    alignItems: 'center',
    backgroundColor: '#F5FCFF',
  },
  home: {
    fontSize: 20,
    textAlign: 'center',
    margin: 10,
  }
});

export default Home;
```

File: components/Home.js

7. In `App.js`, we import the `Home` component, and we render it:

```
// Dependencies
import React, { Component } from 'react';
import { StyleSheet, Text, View } from 'react-native';

// Components
import Home from './components/Home';

class App extends Component {
  render() {
    return (
      <Home />
    );
  }
}

export default App;
```

File: App.js

How it works...

As you can see, creating a new React Native application is very easy but there are some key differences between React (using JSX) and React Native using a special markup with object styles even there are some limitations on the styles as well, for example, let's create a flex layout:

```
// Dependencies
import React, { Component } from 'react';
import { StyleSheet, Text, View } from 'react-native';

class Home extends Component {
  render() {
    return (
      <View style={styles.container}>
        <View style={styles.header}>
          <Text style={styles.headerText}>Header</Text>
        </View>

        <View style={styles.columns}>
          <View style={styles.column1}>
            <Text style={styles.column1Text}>Column 1</Text>
          </View>

          <View style={styles.column2}>
```

```
          <Text style={styles.column2Text}>Column 2</Text>
        </View>

        <View style={styles.column3}>
          <Text style={styles.column3Text}>Column 3</Text>
        </View>
      </View>
    </View>
  );
 }
}

const styles = StyleSheet.create({
  container: {
    flex: 1,
    height: 100
  },
  header: {
    flex: 1,
    backgroundColor: 'green',
    justifyContent: 'center',
    alignItems: 'center'
  },
  headerText: {
    color: 'white'
  },
  columns: {
    flex: 1
  },
  column1: {
    flex: 1,
    alignItems: 'center',
    justifyContent: 'center',
    backgroundColor: 'red'
  },
  column1Text: {
    color: 'white'
  },
  column2: {
    flex: 1,
    alignItems: 'center',
    justifyContent: 'center',
    backgroundColor: 'blue'
  },
  column2Text: {
    color: 'white'
  },
  column3: {
```

```
    flex: 1,
    alignItems: 'center',
    justifyContent: 'center',
    backgroundColor: 'orange'
  },
  column3Text: {
    color: 'white'
  },
});

export default Home;
```

File: components/Home.js

You probably don't like looking at a huge file (me neither), so let's separate our component and our styles:

```
import { StyleSheet } from 'react-native';

export default StyleSheet.create({
  container: {
    flex: 1,
    height: 100
  },
  header: {
    flex: 1,
    backgroundColor: 'green',
    justifyContent: 'center',
    alignItems: 'center'
  },
  headerText: {
    color: 'white'
  },
  columns: {
    flex: 1
  },
  column1: {
    flex: 1,
    alignItems: 'center',
   justifyContent: 'center',
    backgroundColor: 'red'
  },
  column1Text: {
    color: 'white'
  },
  column2: {
    flex: 1,
    alignItems: 'center',
```

```
    justifyContent: 'center',
    backgroundColor: 'blue'
  },
  column2Text: {
    color: 'white'
  },
  column3: {
    flex: 1,
    alignItems: 'center',
    justifyContent: 'center',
    backgroundColor: 'orange'
  },
  column3Text: {
    color: 'white'
  },
});
```

File: components/HomeStyles.js

Then in our `Home` component, we can import the styles and use them in the same way as before:

```
// Dependencies
import React, { Component } from 'react';
import { StyleSheet, Text, View } from 'react-native';

// Styles
import styles from './HomeStyles';
...
```

File: components/Home.js

Here is the result of the code:

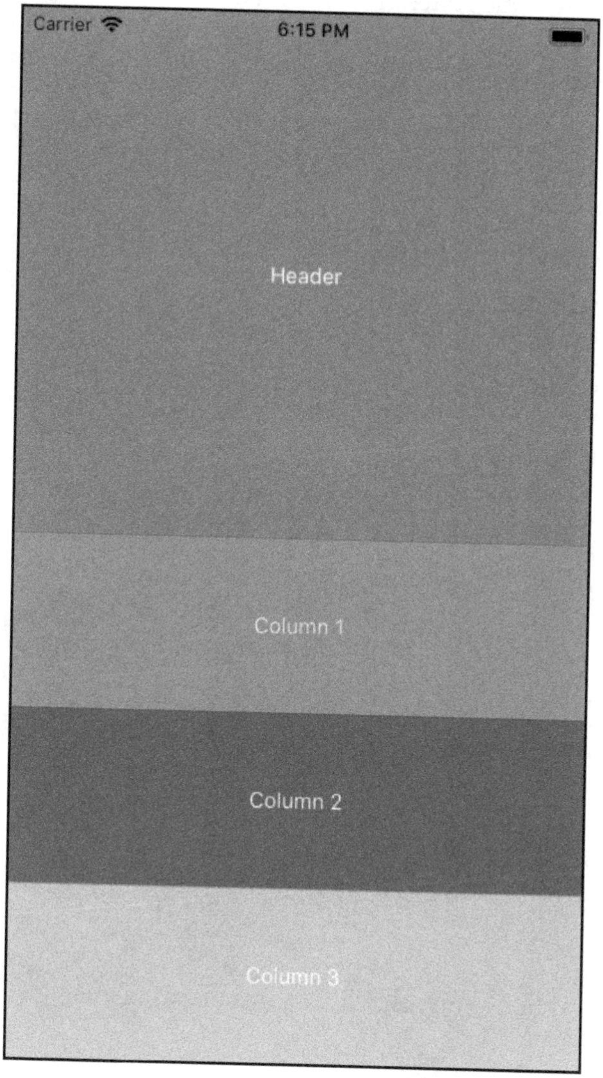

But there is something unusual.

As you can see, I created styles for the `<Text>` components (headerText, column1Text, and so on), and this is because some styles are not allowed in the View component. For example, if you try to add the `color: 'white'` property to the `<View>` component, you will see that the property won't work and Header will have the black text:

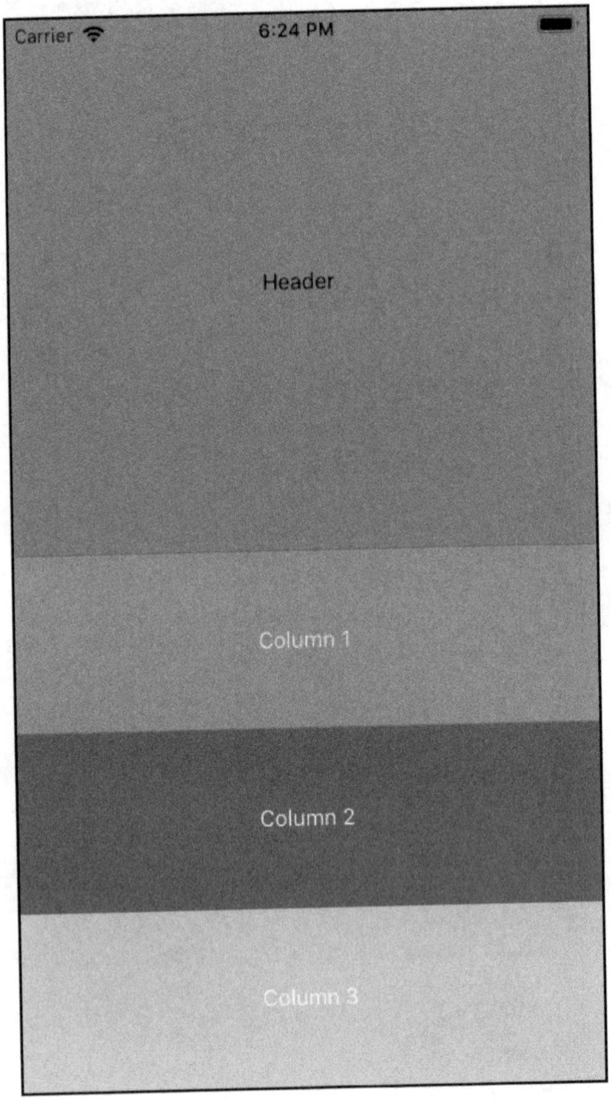

Creating a Todo List with React Native

In this recipe, we are going to learn how to handle events in React Native and how to handle the state by creating a simple Todo list.

How to do it...

For this recipe, I created a new React Application called "MySecondReactNativeApp":

1. Create an `src` folder and move the `App.js` file inside. Also, modify this file to include our Todo list:

```
import React, { Component } from 'react';

import Todo from './components/Todo';

export default class App extends Component {
  render() {
    return (
      <Todo />
    );
  }
}
```

File: src/App.js

2. Our `Todo` component will be:

```
import React, { Component } from 'react';
import {
  Text,
  View,
  TextInput,
  TouchableOpacity,
  ScrollView
} from 'react-native';

import styles from './TodoStyles';

class Todo extends Component {
  state = {
    task: '',
    list: []
  };
```

```
onPressAddTask = () => {
  if (this.state.task) {
    const newTask = this.state.task;
    const lastTask = this.state.list[0] || { id: 0 };
    const newId = Number(lastTask.id + 1);

    this.setState({
      list: [{ id: newId, task: newTask }, ...this.state.list],
      task: ''
    });
  }
}

onPressDeleteTask = id => {
  this.setState({
    list: this.state.list.filter(task => task.id !== id)
  });
}

render() {
  const { list } = this.state;
  let zebraIndex = 1;

  return (
    <View style={styles.container}>
      <ScrollView
        contentContainerStyle={{
          flexGrow: 1,
        }}
      >
        <View style={styles.list}>
          <View style={styles.header}>
            <Text style={styles.headerText}>Todo List</Text>
          </View>

          <View style={styles.add}>
            <TextInput
              style={styles.inputText}
              placeholder="Add a new task"
              onChangeText={(value) => this.setState({ task:
               value })}
              value={this.state.task}
            />

            <TouchableOpacity
              style={styles.button}
              onPress={this.onPressAddTask}
            >
```

```
            <Text style={styles.submitText}>+ Add Task</Text>
          </TouchableOpacity>
        </View>

        {list.length === 0 && (
          <View style={styles.noTasks}>
            <Text style={styles.noTasksText}>
              There are no tasks yet, create a new one!
            </Text>
          </View>
        )}

        {list.map((item, i) => {
          zebraIndex = zebraIndex === 2 ? 1 : 2;

          return (
            <View key={`task${i}`} style=
             {styles[`task${zebraIndex}`]}>
              <Text>{item.task}</Text>
              <TouchableOpacity onPress={() => {
               this.onPressDeleteTask(item.id) }}>
                <Text style={styles.delete}>
                  X
                </Text>
              </TouchableOpacity>
            </View>
          );
        })}
      </View>
    </ScrollView>
  </View>
 );
 }
}

export default Todo;
```

File: src/components/Todo.js

3. Here are the styles:

```
import { StyleSheet } from 'react-native';

export default StyleSheet.create({
  container: {
    flex: 1,
    backgroundColor: '#F5FCFF',
    height: 50
```

```
},
list: {
  flex: 1
},
header: {
  backgroundColor: '#333',
  alignItems: 'center',
  justifyContent: 'center',
  height: 60
},
headerText: {
  color: 'white'
},
inputText: {
  color: '#666',
  height: 40,
  borderColor: 'gray',
  borderWidth: 1
},
button: {
  paddingTop: 10,
  paddingBottom: 10,
  backgroundColor: '#1480D6'
},
submitText: {
  color:'#fff',
  textAlign:'center',
  paddingLeft : 10,
  paddingRight : 10
},
task1: {
  flexDirection: 'row',
  height: 50,
  backgroundColor: '#ccc',
  alignItems: 'center',
  justifyContent: 'space-between',
  paddingLeft: 5
},
task2: {
  flexDirection: 'row',
  height: 50,
  backgroundColor: '#eee',
  alignItems: 'center',
  justifyContent: 'space-between',
  paddingLeft: 5
},
delete: {
  margin: 10,
```

```
    fontSize: 15
  },
  noTasks: {
    flex: 1,
    alignItems: 'center',
    justifyContent: 'center'
  },
  noTasksText: {
    color: '#888'
  }
});
```

File: src/components/TodoStyles.js

How it works...

The first thing we did in our component was set our state. The `task` state is for the input to create new items, and the `list` state is to save all the tasks items:

```
state = {
  task: '',
  list: []
};
```

The `TextInput` component creates an input element, the main difference from the input in React is that instead of using the `onChange` method, it is using `onChangeText` and by default gets the value, and we can update our state directly:

```
<TextInput
  style={styles.inputText}
  placeholder="Add a new task"
  onChangeText={(value) => this.setState({ task: value })}
  value={this.state.task}
/>
```

The `TouchableOpacity` component is to handle click events (`onPress` in React Native) and can be used as a button. Maybe you're wondering why I didn't use the component `Button` directly; this is because on iOS it's not possible to add a background color to the button, it only works with backgrounds on Android. Using `TouchableOpacity` (or `TouchableHighlight`), you can personalize the styles, and it works perfectly as a button:

```
<TouchableOpacity
  style={styles.button}
  onPress={this.onPressAddTask}
>
  <Text style={styles.submitText}>+ Add Task</Text>
</TouchableOpacity>
```

In the render of the tasks, I implemented a Zebra style (mixed colors) for the tasks. Also, we are handling `onPressDeleteTask` to remove each item by clicking the **X** button:

```
{list.map((item, i) => {
  zebraIndex = zebraIndex === 2 ? 1 : 2;

  return (
    <View key={`task${i}`} style={styles[`task${zebraIndex}`]}>
      <Text>{item.task}</Text>
      <TouchableOpacity onPress={() => {
       this.onPressDeleteTask(item.id) }}>
        <Text style={styles.delete}>
          X
        </Text>
      </TouchableOpacity>
    </View>
  );
})}
```

If we run the application, the first thing we are going to see is this view:

If we don't have any tasks, we will see the "**There are no tasks yet, create a new one!**" message.

As you can see, there is an input on the top that has the "**Add a new task**" placeholder. Let's add some tasks:

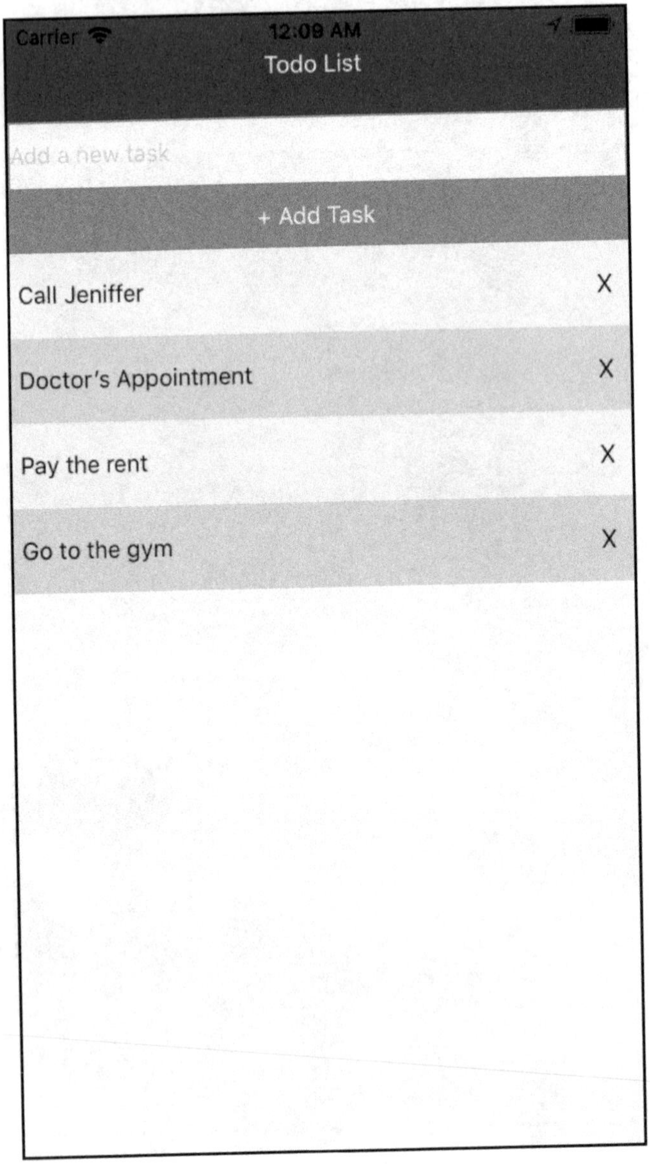

Finally, we can delete the tasks by clicking on the **X**; I'll remove the **Pay the rent** task:

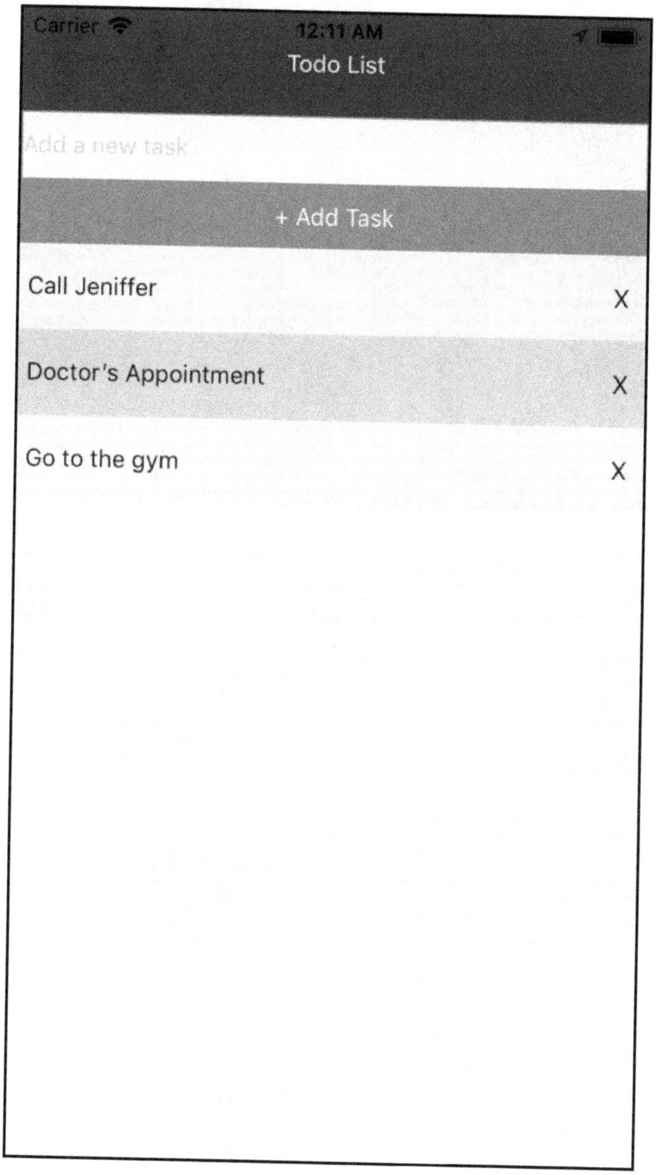

As you can see with this basic Todo list, we learned how to use the local state and how to handle click and change events in React Native.

There's more...

If you want to prevent the user from deleting a task by accident, you can add an Alert that will ask the user whether they are sure they want to remove the selected task. For this, we need to import the Alert component from react-native and modify our onPressDeleteTask method:

```
import {
  Text,
  View,
  TextInput,
  TouchableOpacity,
  ScrollView,
  Alert
} from 'react-native';
...

onPressDeleteTask = id => {
  Alert.alert('Delete', 'Do you really want to delete this task?', [
    {
      text: 'Yes, delete it.',
      onPress: () => {
        this.setState({
          list: this.state.list.filter(task => task.id !== id)
        });
      }
    }, {
      text: 'No, keep it.'
    }
  ]);
}

...
```

If you run the application and you try to delete a task now, you will see this native alert:

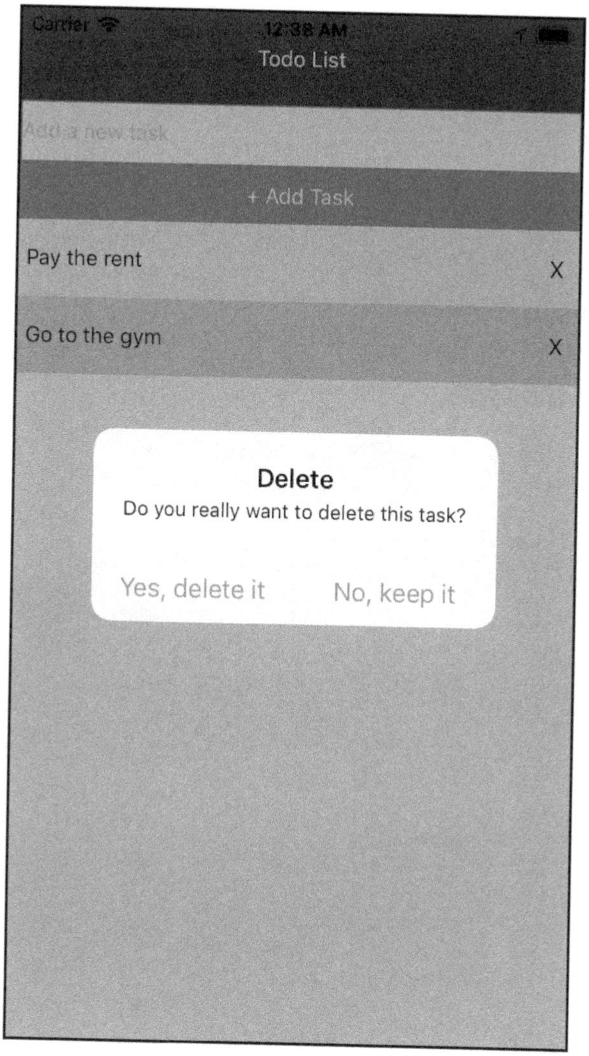

Implementing React Navigation V2

In this recipe, we are going to learn how to implement React Navigation V2 in our React Native application. We will create a simple navigation between sections.

Getting Ready

We need to install the `react-navigation` dependency:

```
npm install react-navigation
```

How to do it...

Let's implement React Navigation v2:

1. Include `createDrawerNavigation` and `DrawerItems` from react-navigation and the components we want to render as sections (Home and Configuration):

```
// Dependencies
import React, { Component } from 'react';
import { StyleSheet, View, ScrollView, Image } from 'react-
native';

// React Navigation
import { createDrawerNavigator, DrawerItems } from 'react-
navigation';

// Components
import Home from './sections/Home';
import Configuration from './sections/Configuration';
```

File: App.js

2. In CustomDrawerComponent, we will render the Codejobs logo and the menu (you can modify this as you need it):

```
// Custom Drawer Component
// Here we are displaying the menu options
// and customizing our drawer
const CustomDrawerComponent = props => (
  <View style={styles.area}>
    <View style={styles.drawer}>
      <Image
        source={require('./assets/codejobs.jpeg')}
        style={styles.logo}>
      </Image>
    </View>

    <ScrollView>
      <DrawerItems {...props} />
    </ScrollView>
```

```
    </View>
  );
```

File: App.js

3. Create `AppDrawerNavigator`, specifying the components we want to display in the menu as sections (Home and Configuration). Also, we need to pass `contentComponent` with the `CustomDrawerComponent` we created before:

```
// The left Drawer navigation
// The first object are the components that we want to display
// in the Drawer Navigation.
const AppDrawerNavigator = createDrawerNavigator({
  Home,
  Configuration
},
{
  contentComponent: CustomDrawerComponent
});
```

File: App.js

4. Create the App class and render the `AppDrawerNavigator` component:

```
class App extends Component {
  render() {
    return (
      <AppDrawerNavigator />
    );
  }
}

// Styles for left Drawer
const styles = StyleSheet.create({
  area: {
    flex: 1
  },
  drawer: {
    height: 150,
    backgroundColor: 'white',
    alignItems: 'center',
    justifyContent:'center'
  },
  logo: {
    height: 120,
    width: 120,
    borderRadius: 60
```

```
    }
  });

  export default App;
```

File: App.js

5. Create the section components; the first one is the Home component:

```
// Dependencies
import React, { Component } from 'react';
import { View, Text, Image, TouchableOpacity } from 'react-native';
// Styles
import styles from './SectionStyles';
class Home extends Component {
  // Here we specify the icon we want to render
  // in the menu for this option
  static navigationOptions = {
    drawerIcon: () => (
      <Image
        style={styles.iconsItem}
        source={require('../assets/home.png')}
      />
    )
  }
  render() {
    return(
      <View style={styles.container}>
        {/* Hamburger menu */}
        <TouchableOpacity
          onPress={() => this.props.navigation.openDrawer()}
          style={styles.iconMenu}
        >
          <Image
            style={styles.menu}
            source={require('../assets/menu.png')}
          />
        </TouchableOpacity>

        {/* Here is the content of the component */}
        <Text style={styles.titleText}>I'm the home section</Text>
      </View>
    );
  }
}
export default Home;
```

File: sections/Home.js

6. Here is the Configuration section component:

```
// Dependencies
import React, { Component } from 'react';
import { View, Text, Image, TouchableOpacity } from 'react-native';

// Styles
import styles from './SectionStyles';

class Configuration extends Component {
  // Here we specify the icon we want to render
  // in the menu for this option
  static navigationOptions = {
    drawerIcon: () => (
      <Image
        style={styles.iconsItem}
        source={require('../assets/config.png')}
      />
    )
  };

  render() {
    return (
      <View style={styles.container}>
        {/* Hamburger menu */}
        <TouchableOpacity
          onPress={() => this.props.navigation.openDrawer()}
          style={styles.iconMenu}
        >
          <Image
            style={styles.menu}
            source={require('../assets/menu.png')}
          />
        </TouchableOpacity>

        {/* Here is the content of the component */}
        <Text style={styles.titleText}>I'm the configuration
        section</Text>
      </View>
    );
  }
}

export default Configuration;
```

File: sections/Configuration.js

7. You may have noticed we are using the same styles on both components, that's why I created a separate file for the styles:

```
import { StyleSheet } from 'react-native';

export default StyleSheet.create({
  container: {
    flex: 1,
    backgroundColor: '#fff',
    alignItems: 'center',
    justifyContent: 'center',
  },
  iconMenu: {
    position: 'absolute',
    left: 0,
    top: 5
  },
  titleText: {
    fontSize: 26,
    fontWeight: 'bold',
  },
  menu: {
    width: 80,
    height: 80,
  },
  iconsItem: {
    width: 25,
    height: 25
  }
});
```

File: sections/sectionStyles.js

8. You can find the assets we are using in the repository (`Chapter14/Recipe3/ReactNavigation/assets`).

How it works...

If you did everything correctly, you should see this:

The first component that is being rendered is the `Home` component. If you click on the Hamburger menu, you will see the drawer with the two sections (`Home` and `Configuration`) with their respective icons and the Codejobs logo at the top:

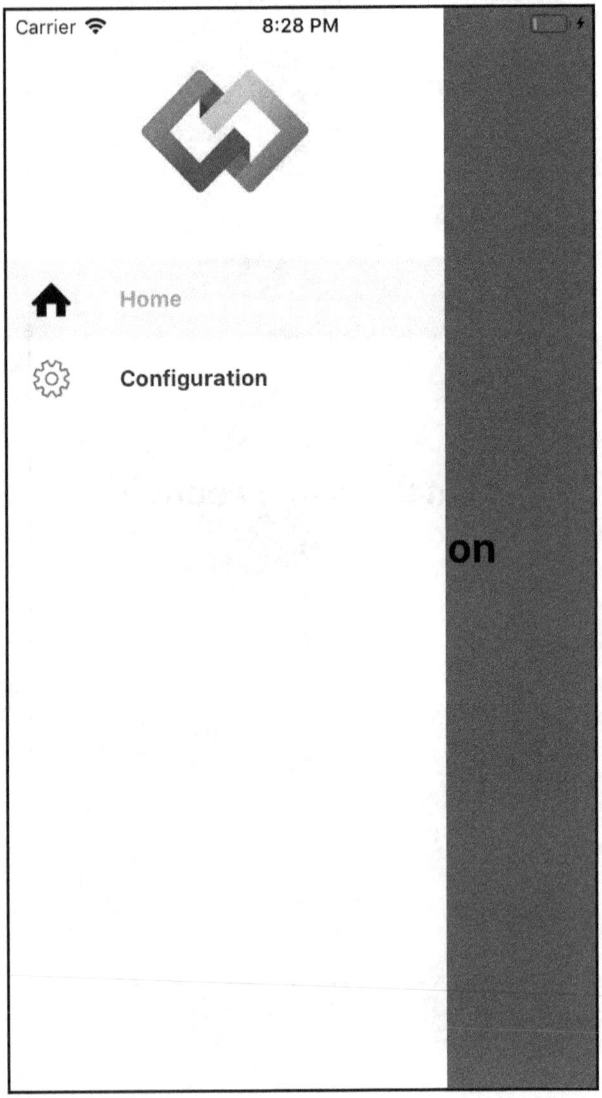

Finally, if you click on **Configuration**, you will see that component as well:

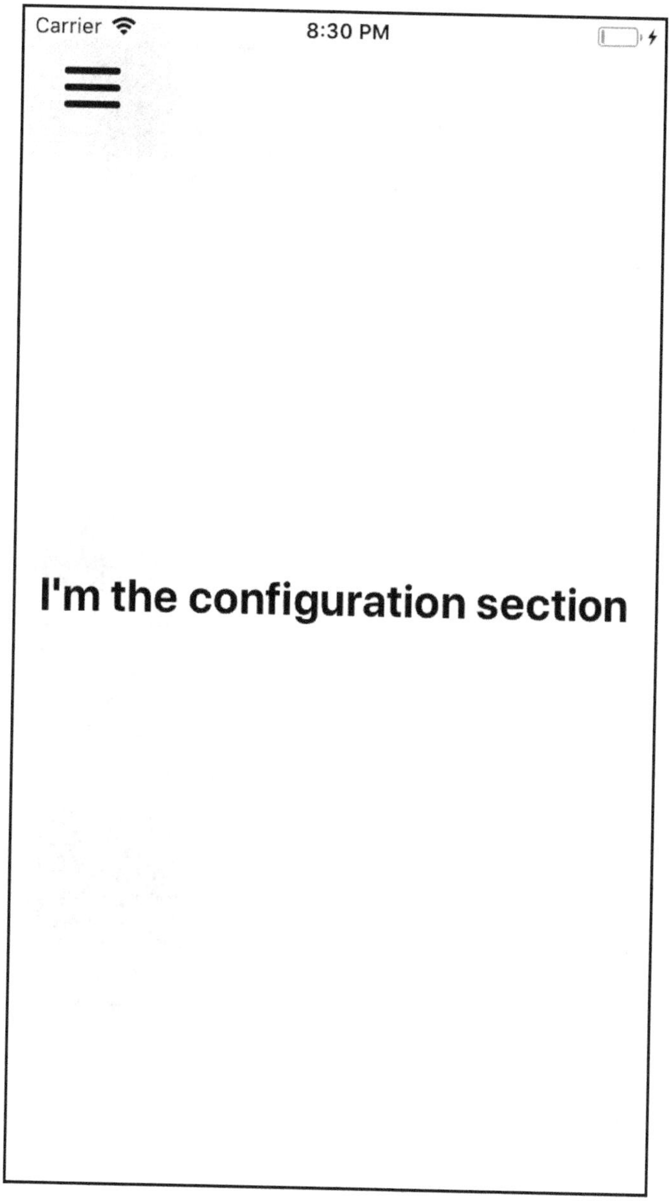

If you see the drawer again, you will notice that the current section that is open is also active in the menu (in this case, Configuration).

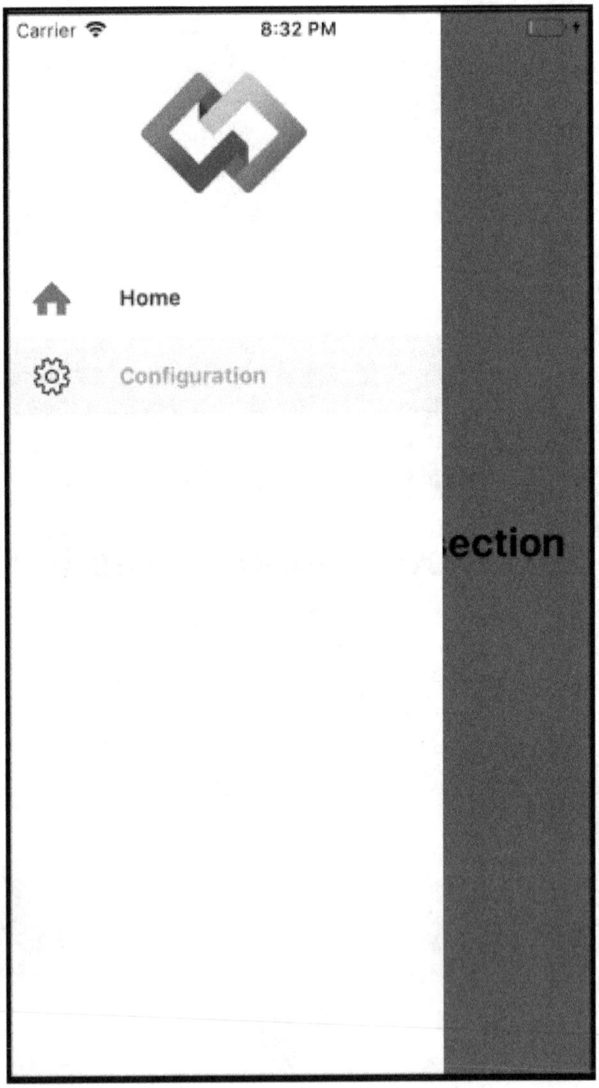

Most Common React Interview Questions

I would like to end this book by giving you some of the most common questions of React and JavaScript in job interviews:

- React questions:
    - What is React? How is it different from other JS libraries/frameworks?
    - What happens during the lifecycle of a React component?
    - What can you tell me about JSX?
    - What's the difference between Real DOM and Virtual DOM?
    - What are the limitations of React?
    - Explain the purpose of `render()` in React
    - What is a state in React and how is it used?
    - What's the difference between states and props?
    - What's an arrow function in React? How is it used?
    - What's the difference between a Class component and a Functional Component?
    - What's the difference between a stateless component and a pure component?
    - Explain the lifecycle methods of React components in detail.
    - What are Higher Order Components (HOC)?
    - What is Redux?
    - How is Flux different from Redux?
    - What are refs used for in React?
    - What is the difference between action and reducer in Redux?
    - How can you improve the performance of a React Application?

- JavaScript questions:
    - What is the difference between a callback and a promise?
    - What is hoisting?
    - What is the difference between apply and call?
    - What is a closure and how/why would you use it?
    - How does event delegation work?
    - What's the difference between bubbling and capturing?
    - What does `bind()` do?
    - What's the difference between a variable that is null, undefined, or undeclared?
    - What's the difference between == and ===?
    - What is "lexical" scoping?
    - What is functional programming?
    - What is the difference between classical inheritance and prototypal inheritance?

Other Books You May Enjoy

If you enjoyed this book, you may be interested in these other books by Packt:

Full-Stack React Projects
Shama Hoque

ISBN: 9781788835534

- Set up your development environment and develop a MERN application
- Implement user authentication and authorization using JSON Web Tokens
- Build a social media application by extending the basic MERN application
- Create an online marketplace application with shopping cart and Stripe payments
- Develop a media streaming application using MongoDB GridFS
- Implement server-side rendering with data to improve SEO
- Set up and use React 360 to develop user interfaces with VR capabilities
- Learn industry best practices to make MERN stack applications reliable and scalable

React Native Blueprints
Emilio Rodriguez Martinez

ISBN: 9781787288096

- Structure React Native projects to ease maintenance and extensibility
- Optimize a project to speed up development
- Make a React Native project production-ready
- Use external modules to speed up the development and maintenance of your projects
- Explore the different UI and code patterns to be used for iOS and Android
- Get to know the best practices when building apps in React Native

Leave a review - let other readers know what you think

Please share your thoughts on this book with others by leaving a review on the site that you bought it from. If you purchased the book from Amazon, please leave us an honest review on this book's Amazon page. This is vital so that other potential readers can see and use your unbiased opinion to make purchasing decisions, we can understand what our customers think about our products, and our authors can see your feedback on the title that they have worked with Packt to create. It will only take a few minutes of your time, but is valuable to other potential customers, our authors, and Packt. Thank you!

Index

S

T

W

X

CPSIA information can be obtained
at www.ICGtesting.com
Printed in the USA
BVHW010203181119
564139BV00008B/227/P

9 781783 980727